FOURTH REPORT

OF THE

RECORD COMMISSIONERS

OF THE

CITY OF BOSTON.

1880.

DORCHESTER TOWN RECORDS.

SECOND EDITION, 1883.

CLEARFIELD

Originally published
Boston, 1883

Reprinted for
Clearfield Company, Inc. by
Genealogical Publishing Co., Inc.
Baltimore, Maryland
2002

International Standard Book Number: 0-8063-5165-9

Made in the United States of America

[DOCUMENT 9 — 1880.]

CITY OF  BOSTON.

FOURTH REPORT

OF THE

RECORD COMMISSIONERS.

BOSTON, Sept. 1, 1880.

The following report of the Committee on Printing explains not only the form of this volume, but the length of time which has been needed for its preparation: —

CITY OF BOSTON,
IN BOARD OF ALDERMEN, Nov. 2, 1879.

The Committee on Printing respectfully offer the following report upon printing the Town Records of Dorchester : —

In February last the following order was passed by the City Council : —

"*Ordered*, That the Record Commissioners be authorized to have transcribed and indexed the land records of the town of Dorchester, and to have the same printed and distributed in the same manner as their previous reports, at an expense not exceeding $1,000; to be charged to the appropriation for Printing."

Under this order the Record Commissioners have supplied about a hundred pages of copy, which have been put in type; but the work is now suspended, to await the further action of the City Council

On the 25th of September the following petition was presented in the Common Council : —

"*To the Honorable the City Council of the City of Boston:* —

"The undersigned, citizens of Boston and others, respectfully represent that, by an order passed Feb. 18, 1879, the Record Commissioners were authorized to print certain extracts from the Town Records of Dorchester.

"They further represent that, in their opinion, it would be unwise and inexpedient to neglect any portion of said records, and that the appearance in print of an incomplete and mutilated transcript thereof would be greatly to be deplored.

"They therefore pray that said order may be so amended as to authorize said commissioners to include, in their forthcoming report all the records contained in the first volume of the Records of the Town of Dorchester, or so many consecutive pages thereof as said commissioners may be able to print with the appropriation already made therefor.

MARSHALL P. WILDER.   EDMUND J. BAKER.
JAMES H. MEANS.   S. J. BARROWS.
OLIVER HALL.   E. J. BISPHAM.
EBENEZER CLAPP.   EDWARD JARVIS.
JOHN H. ROBINSON.   BENJAMIN CUSHING.
ROSWELL GLEASON.   ROBERT VOSE.
F. W. LINCOLN.   ERASMUS D. MILLER.
HENRY HUMPHREYS.   JAMES H. UPHAM.
M. D. SPAULDING.   THOMAS GROOM.
SAMUEL ATHERTON.   THOMAS F. TEMPLE.
WILLIAM E. COFFIN.   WILLIAM B. TRASK."

This petition was referred to the Committee on Printing, with directions to hear the petitioners. The following order was also referred to the committee: —

"IN COMMON COUNCIL, Sept. 25, 1879.

"*Ordered,* That, under the order authorizing the transcribing and indexing of the land records of Dorchester, the Record Commissioners be authorized to have transcribed and indexed so much of the first volume of the Town Records of the town of Dorchester as the appropriation made in said order will defray the expense of preparing and publishing."

At a hearing of the petitioners and others interested, several gentlemen of the Dorchester Antiquarian Society and others appeared, and earnestly advocated the objects of the petition. Mr. Whitmore, the Record Commissioner, also appeared, and fully stated his views, in opposition to the petitioners.

The difference of opinion between the Record Commissioners and the petitioners relates mainly to the essential change involved in the plan of the commissioners, by adopting the views of the petitioners. The plan of the Record Commissioners, for Dorchester and other sections of the city, is substantially to print a collation from the ancient records, and especially relating to lands; while the petitioners desire the complete reproduction in print of the ancient records, so far as the same limited expenditure will permit. The most ancient records are the most dilapidated; and it is considered more important to save the most ancient from destruction, than it is to present a collation of them down to a later time.

The statutes of the Commonwealth make very careful provisions for the proper production, care, and preservation of public records. It is further provided, that "when the records of a county, city, or town are becoming worn, mutilated, or illegible, the County Commissioners, City Government, or Selectmen, shall have fair, legible copies seasonably made." This requirement is imperative, and the committee have sought, in view of it, to give the whole subject before them the careful consideration its magnitude and importance require.

It being essential to preserve and renew the ancient records, according to law, the only question to consider is, what is the best method of accomplishing this object? The requirement of the law is met by transcribing the original, and substantially binding the copy. But this method, at considerable expense, produces but a single copy, to be preserved in one place only, for reference in all future time. This isolates the book from the public inspection, and renders it only a book of ref-

REPORT OF RECORD COMMISSIONERS. III

erence to painstaking inquirers only. The volumes printed by the Record Commissioners are in editions of 1,500 copies, and are placed in the bound volumes of the City Documents for perpetual preservation, and in various libraries of the city, accessible to all the people, as well as in many private hands and libraries of those more especially interested in their contents.

The committee consider the Record Commission entitled to public thanks for their valuable services to the city, gratuitously rendered, and the commendable economy of expenditure they seek to maintain. But the committee are convinced that the basis of operations planned by the commission does not sufficiently cover the legitimate work to be done on the ground they occupy. And the committee feel assured, from the expressed opinions of Commissioner Whitmore, that there is no difference of opinion as to the desirability of reproducing the ancient records in print, with the exception of the cost involved in the change of plan now pursued by the Record Commission.

The ordinance creating the office of the Record Commissioners defines their duties as follows: " To complete, as far as practicable, the record of births, deaths, and marriages in the town and city of Boston, prior to A.D. 1849."

The commissioners, in their first report (City Document No. 92, 1876), say, "A reasonable construction of the duties of the commissioners seems to include therein all such investigations as will directly assist in perfecting the record of the vital statistics of Boston."

The second report of the commissioners (City Document No. 46, 1877) takes a new departure from the preceding limited sphere of operation, by special order of the City Council to print "a transcript of the first volume of the Town Records and of the Book of Possessions." This report of the commissioners presents in print "faithful transcripts of the two earliest volumes of the records of the town of Boston." The report further says, "The records of the town of Boston, now in the custody of the City Clerk, may be described as follows:—

"Ten volumes, of which the first is here printed, containing the acts of the town from 1634 to 1822. The first volume (1634–1660) contains also the acts of the Selectmen; the second volume (1660–1728) contains the acts of the Selectmen from 1660 to 1701, and thenceforward it records only the proceedings of the town. In 1701 the system was established of recording the doings of the Selectmen separately, and twenty-three volumes contain their records until 1822."

These books, with a few miscellaneous volumes, comprise the old records of the city proper. By annexations are added Charlestown, Dorchester, Roxbury, West Roxbury, and Brighton.

The commissioners say, in their second report, "It is hoped that the City Government will authorize the Record Commissioners to continue the work of publishing the records; of course, not in full, but by means of such judicious selections as will afford valuable information about our predecessors."

The third report of the commissioners (City Document No. 39, 1878) is devoted to the Charlestown land records. This report says, "The commissioners may perhaps anticipate that other portions of the city, as Roxbury and Dorchester, may call for a similar publication of their records of early grants and possessions of land. There has also been a feeling manifested in favor of printing the first volume of deeds for Suffolk County, inasmuch as the expense would be but little greater than that of a manuscript copy. Certainly the old town of Boston requires a second volume of extracts from its records, to complete the grants of lots and the laying out of streets. Whilst the commissioners will cheerfully discharge any duties of the above-named nature which may be assigned to them, they beg leave to repeat their previous notice that their main duty is still unfulfilled. The transcripts of the church records, to supplement and complete the records preserved by the City Registrar, are still to be made. They hope, therefore, to receive instructions during the next year, to make a beginning upon their most necessary and long-delayed work."

The next report of the Record Commissioners will be the Dorchester records, provided for by the order at the beginning of this report. This order authorizes a collation of the land records only; and the initiation of the work produces the remonstrance of the gentlemen interested in the records of Dorchester, who desire that the work shall be a reproduction of the ancient records as far as the work progresses, on the same appropriation. It is evident to the committee that the petitioners are right in their position, and their views ought to be sustained. The records should be published complete. The cost at most will be small compared to the value of their preservation. It is also evident to the committee that the extensive work laid out by the Record Commissioners is proceeding on a plan far too contracted properly to accomplish the objects intended and desirable to be attained.

The reports of the commissioners are based upon specific appropriations not exceeding one thousand dollars, respectively, and usually result in expenditures considerably less than the sum named. The committee are of opinion that five thousand dollars ought to be annually appropriated, as an element of the appropriation for printing, for expenditure under requisitions by the Record Commissioners, in accordance with special orders by the City Council. This would enable the commissioners to carry out a judicious system of annual work, and meet the legal requirements for reproducing the ancient records complete. The result of the expenditure would probably be the best economy in the end, as well as largely aid the citizens in the knowledge of the ancient times and memorable historical events. It must be considered that we are now living in the third century of the city's existence; and that our preservation of the ancient records is not for ourselves alone, but for the unknown centuries to come.

The committee recommend the passage of the following orders.

HUGH O'BRIEN,
Chairman.

Ordered, That the order of February last, authorizing the Record Commissioners to have transcribed and indexed the land records of the town of Dorchester, be, and the same is, hereby rescinded.

Ordered, That the Record Commissioners be authorized to have transcribed and indexed the first volume of the records of the town of Dorchester; and to have the same printed and distributed in the same manner as their previous reports, or so many consecutive pages of the same as can be done at a cost not exceeding one thousand dollars; to be charged to the appropriation for Printing.

This report was accepted, and the orders were duly passed. The commissioners, being thus relieved from the responsibility of using any discretion in the matter, have attempted only to print the requisite number of pages of the Dorchester Records as they stood in the original. The copying was entrusted to Miss Susan B. Kidder, whose skill in such matters is well known; and Mr. William B. Trask very kindly volunteered to compare her copy with the original. It is believed, therefore, that an accurate transcript has been obtained.

In printing, the *forms* of the letters have been preserved, not their true meaning. Thus *u* is used for *v*, because the written *v* was of the shape of the printed *u;* but, of course, our ancestors did not transpose the sounds of the letters. The initial *F* has been employed, although the written form was more nearly *ff;* but the use of this form would have made the page more uncouth than it is. It was intended also to follow the abbreviations where possible, without having special types cut, but the forms y^e, y^t, etc., have been printed *the, that,* etc.

It is a mistaken idea to suppose that those words had the *y* sound; they were pronounced with the *th*, as at present.

Of the value of these records much may be said. The successive clerks of the town unfortunately kept all their records in one book, and a continuous transcript obliges us to print many matters of little value then, and of even less now. Still, as so little is known of the rise of our town system, it would be, perhaps, difficult to say of any part of this book, that it does not have some value to some student. Thus, on p. 289 of our pagination, will be found a document often referred to as "The Directory," which is a curious statement of the powers of the selectmen, and of the rise and progress of town government.

Great pains have been taken to obtain a good index; but a thorough index of subjects, as well as names, would have been an additional expense, which the commissioners did not feel warranted in incurring.

In accordance with the suggestion of the Committee on Printing, the City Council this year has appropriated the sum of five thousand dollars for the publication of historical documents.

The following four volumes have been decided upon, and progress has been made on all of them, so that they may be completed during the present financial year: Fifth Report, the "Gleaner" articles on Boston land-titles, by the late N. I. Bowditch. Sixth Report, Roxbury Land Records. Seventh Report, Continuation of the Boston Town Records. Eighth Report, Boston Births, Baptisms, Marriages, and Deaths, chronologically arranged.

The commissioners hope to issue their fifth and sixth reports before December 31, 1880.

Respectfully submitted,
WILLIAM H. WHITMORE,
WILLIAM S. APPLETON,
Record Commissioners.

PREFACE TO THE SECOND EDITION.

The local demand for this volume, as has also been the case with the third and sixth reports, having very rapidly exhausted the first edition, the City Council instructed the Commissioners to reprint this report, and to have it stereotyped, as the later volumes are.

In complying with this order the opportunity was availed of to have a thorough revision, by the renewed kindness of Mr. William B. Trask. Numerous small corrections have been made, but none calling for special mention.

WILLIAM H. WHITMORE,
WILLIAM S. APPLETON,
Record Commissioners.

BOSTON, Sept. 6, 1883.

DORCHESTER TOWN RECORDS.

[**5.**] Also Edward Ray[nsford] and John Grenway and John Goyte shall ha[ve each] of them a p'portionable quantity of Marish adjoyneing to their necke of L[and].

Jan: 21. All other the Planters in Dorchester not before named, shall have their p'portion of Marish ground by the river of Naponsett, according to the quan[tity] of their home lotts.

Also it is generally agreed that whosoever doth not mowe his owne lott shall not sell it to any for above Two pence an acre
signed
     JOHN: MAVERICKE [whosoever[1]]
     JOHN: WARHAM.
     WILL: GAYLARD.
     WILL: ROCKEWELL.

16 Jan: 1632. It is ordered that Edmond Hart, Roger. Clap, George. Phillips, John Hulls, Bray Wilkeins, William Hulbeard, Stephen ffrench, John Benham, and John Haydon, are to have their great lotts of 16 acres a peece, next the great lotts, that are all redy layde out towardes Naponsett. signed
     JOHN. MAVERICKE.
     JOHN. WARHAM.
     WILLIAM. GAYLARD.
     WILL. ROCKEWELL.

Anno. April. 3. 1633. It is agreed that a doble rayle with mortesses in the posts, of 10 foote distance one from the other, shall be set up in the Marish, from the corner of Richard Phelps, his pale Eastward to the Creeke, by the owners of the Cowes vnder named, p'portionally, 20 foote to every cowe.

	Cowes	foote
m[r] Ludlowe.	2	40
m[r] Johnson.	1	20
Henry Woolcott,	3	60
m[r] Rosseter.	4	80
m[r] Terry.	2	40
m[r] Smith.	2	40
m[r] Gallope.	1	20
Thom ffoard.	2	40
m[r] Warham.	3	60
m[r] Mavericke.	2	40
m[r] Hull.	3	60
Mathew. Graunt.	2	40

---

[1] This unconnected word is probably part of an unfinished entry. — W. H. W.

	Cowes	foote
Will. Rockewell.	2	40
John. Hoskeins.	3	60
Nicho: Denslowe.		
Giles Gibbes.	1	20
William Phellps.	2	40
Symon. Hoite.	2	40
m^r Stoughton.	4	80
¹Eltwid Pumery.	2	40
William Gaylard.		20
George Dyer	2	40

And this to be done by the 7th of May next ensuing, upon the payne of forfiture of 5 Shillings for every Cowe in cause it be not done by the tyme appoynted and for the tyme to come every other owner that shall have milch Cowes they shall pay 12 pence a peice for every cowe. towarde the maynetayneing of these rayles.

signed

JOHN: MAVERICKE.
JOHN: WARHAM.

[**6.**] *5 Aug: 1633.* It is consented vnto, that John Witchfeild, and John Newton. shall have all that plott of Marish ground, that lyeth betweene Nicholas Denslowe and the brooke next to Rockesbury equally to be devided betweene them.

In the necke Southward of the plantation these lotts following are agreed to be set downe m^r. John. Cogan. m^r. Hill. m^r. Duncan, m^r. Ludlowe, m^r Russell, m^r Pinney, m^r. Richards, m^r Way 4 acres a peece adjoyning on to the other. And m^r Williams 8 acres in the same at the poynt next m^r Stoughtons lott.

In Naponset necke captin Lovell, m^r Tilly, Elias Parkeman, John Rocket, Captin Lovell and his sonne 6 acres, the rest 4 a peece; Item. m^r. Egelstone to have a lott on this side of the way going to Rockesbury.

In the end of the lotts next the great marish they are to set downe these following.

nicho: Vpsall, Bernard Capen, Phillip Randall, James Parker, 4 acres a peece. John Hoskeins, & the Widdow Purchase, betweene the 26 rackes John Hoskeins 3 acres, the Widdow Purchase 4

signed

JOHN MAVERICKE.
WILL. GAYLARD.

It is agreed betweene captin. William Lovells. m^r. John Tilly. that the landing place in their lotts towardes Naponset, & the way to that and the well shall be common to them both, in whose of their lotts they fall.   signed

JOHN MAVERICKE.
WILLIAM GAYLARD.
WILL. ROCKEWELL.

---

¹ See Savage's Dictionary for this name under Pomeroy. — W. H. W.

An agreement made by the whole consent and vote of the Plantation made Mooneday 8th of October, *1633*.

Inprimus it is ordered that for the generall good and well ordering of the affayres of the Plantation their shall be every Mooneday before the Court by eight of the Clocke in the morning, and p'sently upon the beating of the drum, a generall meeting of the inhabitants of the Plantation att the meeteing house, there to settle (and sett downe) such orders as may tend to the generall good as aforesayd; and every man to be bound thereby without gaynesaying or resistance. It is also agreed that there shall be twelve men selected out of the Company that may or the greatest p't of them meete as aforesayd to determine as aforesayd, yet so as it is desired that the most of the Plantation will keepe the meeteing constantly and all that are there although none of the Twelve shall have a free voyce as any of the 12 and that the greate[r] vote both of the 12 and the other shall be of force and efficasy as aforesayd. And it is likewise ordered that all things concluded as aforesayd shall stand in force and be obeyed vntill the next monethly meeteing and afterwardes if it be not contradicted and other wise ordered upon the sayd monethly meete[ing] by the greatest p'te of those that are p'sent as aforesayd. Moreover, because the Court in Winter in the vacansy of the sayd . . . . . . this said meeting to continue till the first Mooneday in the moneth [7.] m^r Johnson, m^r Eltwid Pummery [m^r. Richards], John Pearce, George Hull, William Phelps, Thom. ffoard.

It is ordered that all the pale of the feilds now inclosed shall be still kept in severall, well and sufficiently fenced, and if that upon warning every man doth not keepe his ground fenced, then such as are appoynted for that purpose to see the Pale sufficient and find not sufficient shall fence the same, and such as are delinquent shall pay 3 shillings a goad and the same p'sently to be levied out of their goods by sale or otherwise according to the order in this booke formerly entered, and this to be done a fourteene nights or Three weekes at most.

The names to see to the fences aforesayde are these; for the South feild next Mr Waram, Mr Smith & Goodman Grenway, for the *Westfeild*, Goodman Thorneton, Phillips, for the east feild Goodman. Hoskeins, Symon Hoyte, for the north feild Goodman Hosseford & David Wilton. |

Whereas there hath beene divers chardges and expences in former tymes layde out by the first planters for securing the necke of land and keepeing the Cowes & Goates in some campes:

It is ordered that every man for future tyme that put any Cattle in the necke be of what condition soever shall p'sently pay Two shillings an head towardes the sayd chardges as also every cowe into the heard p'vided this doth not extend to any that hath formerly payde neither to any that shall pay after the first tyme.

signed.

JOHN MAVERICKE. |
JOHN WARHAM. |
WILL. GAYLARD. |

Mooneday. 3. November 1633 It is now ordered that if the overseers aforesayde do upon vewe find any pales of the feilds aforesayde defective and give noticeto the p'tye that is to amend it and he doth not do it within Two days after he is to pay 5ˢ for every 2 dayes vntill the next meeteing and then p'sently to be levied. |

It is ordered likewise that if any doe pull downe any pale or throwe downe he is p'sently to amend or elce to pay 5. shillings for so doing.

It is ordered that there shall be a generall Rate thorow out the Plantation to the making and maynetayneing gate & fences of the Plantation and bridges; and that the Raters shall be mʳ Woolcott, mʳ Johnson, Geo. Hull Will. Phelps, Eltwid Pumry, and Giles Gibbes.

It is generally agreed that mʳ. Israel Stoughton shall build a water mill, if he see cause.

It is agreed that their shall be a decent burying place bounden in upon the knapp by Goodman Grenwayes. and that shall be done by the Raters aforesayde, and also a bare to carry the dead on.

[8.] — It is order[ed that a pound shall be] also made & set up upon the knapp of ground on [the right hand] of Walter Filers and Goodman Hoskeines out of the publique rate.

It is ordered that such as desire to have lotts shall upon the monethly meeteings manifest the same, and then the company p'sent are to approve of the same, and in what quarter, and then they are to repayre to William Phelps & Ancient Stoughton, and they to set out the same and such as desire lotts are to allow in p'sent worke for their paynes.   signed

       JOHN MAVERICKE.
       JOHN WARHAM.
       WILLIAM GAYLARD.

2ᵈ December 1633. It is ordered that for such as have great lotts they shall joyne this yeere in paling and if they will not then such as are beyond if they will pale are to remoove to the last that will pale and he that will not to go without, every one that will pale to give in his name by to morrowe sevennight: and they that p'mise to pale it is agreed that there pales posts and Rayles are to be in place by the last of ffebruary next, or elce forfeited their lots to any one that the Plantation shall thinke fit to pale & enjoy it;

Item, ordered that Rich: Rocket is to have an acre addition to his home lott in consideration of removing his pale in regard a publicke way is to be through his lott;

Item. It is ordered that William Hosford shall have one of the Two great lotts that were captin Southcotts.

Item it is ordered that after the decease of Every p'son that have seates in the meeteing house the officers of the church in their discretion to order who shall succeed in those seates and to be sould, and the mony expended for the reparations of the sayde meeteing house.   signed

       JOHN MAVERICKE
       JOHN WARHAM.
       WILLIAM GAYLARD

The 6ᵗʰ January, Mooneday, 1633. It is ordered that their shall be a fort made upon the Rocke, above mʳ Johnsons, and that the chardge thereof shall arise out of p'te of the publicke rate now made in the Plantation and to that end the sayde rate is to be dobled which is to be payd to Thommas fford, and Roger Clapp, who are appoynted to receave the same and payment to be made before the first day of ffebruary next, at the house of the said Thommas Ford:

It is agreed that the great lotts from mʳ Rosciters to John Hills lott tow[ards] Naponset in bredth and eight score in length shall be forthwith enclosed by good sufficient Pale and that the pale shall be set up and finished by the 20 of March next, and whosoever fayles shall forfeit his sayd lot: And [these] pales to be sixe foote long and the rayles to be not above 10 foote between [9.] the Postes.

Item. It is ordered that the marsh and swamp before Goodman Hosford and Davy Wil[ton] shall be devided among themselves and Symon Hoyte.

Item it is ordered that all trees that are now felled out of the lotts or shall be hereafter and not vsed within three moneths all men who have occasion to vse them may take them Provided Mr. Israel Stoughton for the p'sent is given 12 moneths tyme for such trees as he hath now felled for his house, and the mill which he is to build at Naponset.

Item, it is ordered that Mʳ Israell Stoughton shall have the privaladge of a weare at Naponset adjoyning to his mill and shall injoy it from the sayd weare to the bridge where now it is over the sayde Naponset without interruption as also betweene the sayde weare and the salt water, that none shall crosse the river with a nett or other weare to the p'judice of the syde weare, And the said Mʳ Stoughton is to sell the alewives there taken to the plantation at 5ˢ per thousand And that all fish besides that is taken there the Plantation to have at reasonable rates before any other plantation And the sayd Mʳ Stoughton is to afford the sayd allwives at a lower rate than 5ˢ per Thousand if he cann.

Item. the sayd Mʳ Stoughton doth p'mise not to sell away the said mill to any without the consent of the plantation first had obtayned.

Item. It is ordered that moses Mavericke shall have the lott that was allotted for Edward Ransford.

Item. It is ordered that Mʳ Hill shall have that p'cell of ground adjoyneing to his former lott betweene it and John Iles.

signed
JOHN MAVERICKE.
JOHN WARHAM.

Mooneday the 5ᵗʰ 1634. It is ordered that for all the pale above the Plantation if any trespasses be done by swine that are not deemed to be vnlawfull he that ownes the pale shall pay the trespas whose corne soever it be.   signed

Saturday 17ᵗʰ 1634. It is ordered that such as are to make the fences of pale in the new feild toward Naponsett, and they do not do it by Tuseday night next whosoever doth the same shall have fower shillings a goad for his labour. signed

JOHN MAVERICKE.
JOHN WARHAM.
WILL: GAYLARD.

The 20th of May 1634. It is ordered that after Two nights for any pale that is not done, there shall be 20^s for every goad vndone.

It is ordered that within these Two days all pig sties shall be removed [from] all the pales of the feilde upon payne of 20^s a day for every day that [. .] piggs sties so stand not demolished.

[10.] It is ordered that Mr. Woolcott Mr Johnson & Walther ffiler shall veiwe the pales of the great lotts and if they find any pale insufficient they shall forthwith give notice to him that is to impall who if he doth not amend within one day after he shall pay 10^s a day for the tyme it standes insufficient and the sayd p'tyes shall report or deeme the pale sufficient. Afterward he whose swine are taken trespassing in the sayd lotts shall make good any trespas shall be by them committed and the sayd p'tyes or any other shall amend any pale after the sayd notice, they shall have 5^s p' goad for amending them.

JOHN MAVERICKE.
JOHN WARHAM.
WILLIAM GAYLARD.

24 May 1634. It is ordered that Thomas fford and John Phillips shall veiwe the pales of the East feild toward the South and if they find any defect in the pale to give notice to the delinquent, and the same penalty and conditions of the order of the 20th of May to stand in force to all intents and purposes.

*Westfeild. It is ordered that Mathew Graunt, George Phillips and John Moore shall do in like manner and the like conditions as aforesayd.

Northfeild. John Hoskines and Symon Hoyte to do the like in that feild and the same conditions in that feild also to stand.
signed
JOHN MAVERICKE.
JOHN WARHAM.
WILLIAM ROCKEWELL.

Second June 1634. It is ordered that Goodman Witchfeild and Goodman Hoyte shall have to be divided betweene them the marsh that lies in the north side of the necke towardes Boston over agaynst Mr Rainsfords house in Boston, being for 8 acres by estimation.

Item   John Hoskeines seinor to have 4 acres of medow in the necke where the dogg was killed.

Item   Thomas Geofry to have the lott was Mr Egelstones by Mr Hathorne.

It is ordered that the captin shall have 30 1 p' annum to begin at the begining of January last and that Mr Rosciter and George

Hull, Ancient Stoughton, Richard Collicott, Mr Williams, John Pearce, John Bursly shall make a rate to levy the same.

Mr Hathorne 2 acres is to have in the dead Swamp.

It is ordered that Richard Collecott may have a roome to build an house in the place called the church yeard

WILLIAM GAYLARD.
WILLIAM ROCKEWELL.

[11.] *The first of September, 1634.* There is graunted to Alexander Miller servant to Mr Stoughton 3 acres of ground lyeing without John Phillips lott toward naponsett.

John Grenway is to have 2 acres and halfe of medow to make up his medow at home adjoyning to the necke where his 8 acres was formerly graunted.

It is ordered that the lott which was graunted formerly to John Rocket shall be transferred to Robert Elway.

It is ordered that Mr Nathaniell Hall, shall have 3 acres which was formerly graunted to Mr Captin Lovell.

It is ordered that Mr Johnson shall have Twelve acres neere his medowe upp Naponset.

Item It is ordered that Bray Clarke and John Allen shall build an house upon the Rocke by John Holman.

Item It is ordered that within o^r Plantation none shall take upp a lott before his tyme be determined with his M^r within a moneth or Two.

Item John Nile. ffran Tuchill. John Levit. Thom. Rawelines John Knite, Bray Clarke, John Allen, Thom Tilestone, Aron Cooke shall have 3 acres a peece upp Naponset. Andrew Pitcher.

Item It is ordered that Mr Newbery shall have 30 acres for his accommodation in the Plantation.

Item It is ordered that Mr Newbery is to have for his purchase that he bought of Mr Pincheon the house Mr Pincheon. built 40 acres of upland ground to the house 40 of marsh 20 acres in Quantq necke.

Item It is ordered that Rich: Callecott shall set up an house without the pale halfe an acre for a garden whereas William Hosseford desiring to have some medowe next Mr Williams which could not be graunted nowe therefore it was graunted that none should have a lott their vntill he be heard therein.

October. 28, 1634. It is agreed that their shall be Tenn men chosen to order all the affayres of the Plantation, to continue for one yeere, & to meete monethly according to the order Oct: 8. 1633, in the page 15 and no order to be established without seven of them at the least and concluded by the major p'te of these seven of them and all the inhabitants to stand bound by the orders so made as aforesayd according to the scope of a former order in May 11th 1631.

At this meeteing Tenn men were chosen whose names are inserted in the margint.[1]

---

[1] Mr Newbery, Mr Stoughton, Mr Woolcot, Mr Duncan, Go. Phelps, Mr Hathorne, Mr Williams, Go. Minot, Go. Gibbes, Mr Smith. [Side note in orig. — W. H. W.]

It is agreed that whosoever is chosen in to any office for the good of the Plantation, he shall abide by it, or submit to a fine as the company shall thinke meete to impose.

Nicholas Vpsall is chosen vnto the office of Baylife in this Plantation for the yeer ensuing, and is by vertue of this office to Levie fincs amer[ced] & rates by way of destrayneing goods or impounding cattle for the [satis.]fieing of them.

[12.] *November 3^d 1634.* It is ordered that no man within the Plantation shall sell his house or lott to any man without the Plantation whom they shall dislike off.

It is also ordered by the p'sons above elected that every of them shall meete the first Monday in every moneth at 8 of the clocke in the morneing and in case of defect to pay 6^d (if he come not before 9 of the clocke to forfeite 12^d) if they come not at all to forfeite 2^s according to the former order October 28 : *1634.*

It is also ordered their shall be a sufficient cartway. be made to the mill at Naponset at the common chardge if the chardge exceed not above five pounds.

It is also ordered that the New buring place last agreed on shall be forthwith impalled with doble rayle and Clere bord pale ffive rod square.

Its also ordered that their shall be a post stayres made to the meeteing house in the outside.| And the loft to be layd and a windowe in the loft.

Its also ordered that the common gates shall be forthwith made and set up sufficiently with the pales belonging to the same one at Mr Woolcotts, one at Walther Filers. one at Goodman Poapes, one at Goodman Grenwayes. and to be palled betwixt William Horsefords lott and the Creeke.

Also a pound to be made with sawne bars and Posts to be set all the newe way next Mr Maverickes.

Its ordered that no man shall fall the trees that stand at the Corner of Mr Newberyes Lott on the Rocke |. also the trees neere William. Horsefords house are to remayne to his use.

November 22th. 1634. It is ordered that Thommas Thorneton, Thomas Sandford, Henry Wright shall have 4 acres of ground on the west side of the way by M^r. Hathornes by the brooke on Roxbury boundes. Thommas Thorneton is to take [his] 4 acres first and the other if it be their to be had.

It is ordered that John Poape and Thom : Swift shall have each of them 5 acres of ground adjoyning to the lotts of Witchfeild, John Newton etc : also adjoyning to them Thom : Baskecomb, Aron Cooke, John Gapin are [to] have each of them 4 acres.

It is ordered that Thom : Andrewes shall have 2 acres of ground betwixt M^r. Hathornes house and the high way from Roxbury, also John Witchfeild to have one acre and the rest of the ground M^r. Hathorne is to have appropriated vnto his lott

It is ordered that John Nile, Francis Tuchine, John Levit, Thom : R[awlines], John Knite, John Alline, Thom : Tilestone, Aron Cooke, Andrew [Pitcher] Richard Fry, George Strang [13.]

Joseph Holly, Joseph Clarke, shall have six acres of land graunted them [for] their small and great lotts at Naponset betwixt the Indian feild and the mill. Also Giles Gibbes, is to have 3 acres at the same place.

Its also graunted to Mr Richards to have 6 acres of land adjoyning to those formerly named.

December. first. 1634. It is ordered that Rodger Clapp, John Hulls, Geo: Phillips, William Hulbard, Stephen French, John Haydon shall have 8 acres a pcice on Roxbury boundes betwixt the Two markt trees to begin at either end which they shall agree off. to go in 40 rod from the boundes of the fresh marshes are to be excepted from these lotts. Mr Hathorne to have 12 acres on this side of the markt tree. Thom: Holcomb to have 8 acres Nicholas Upsall to. Thomas Duee to have 8 acres with them Richard Callecott to have 10 acres.

M^r. Richards, Richard Collecott, Thom. Holcomb Thom. Duee, are to cast their lotts together next to those above named.

Its ordered that all these shall fence in the lotts agaynst the next spring or to leave them to such as will so doe.

It is granted that Mr Newbery shall have the hedgey ground that lies in the bottom betwixt his house and the water next Mr Cottingtons farme in p'te of the medow that he is to have.—

December. 29th 1634. It is ordered that the rate that is to be payed to captin Mason for his mayntayneance shall be forthwith gathered by Nicholas Upsall.

It is ordered that a gate shall be set up in the common path in the great lotts by Richard Collecotts house to be made and mayntayned at the chardge of such as have ground their.

It is ordered that the ends of the great lotts that are not impalled shall be inclosed by the first of Aprill next from Mr Warhams lott to Henry Smithes lot and in defect to pay for every goad 5^s

It is also ordered that if any hoggs commit any trespasse in any of the corne feilds within the Plantation that the owner of the Pall where they breake in shall pay the on halfe of the trespasse, and the swine shall pay the other halfe of the trespasse. Provided that all piggs vnder the age of 3 quarters shall not be lyable to pay any trespasse. And therefore every man is ordered to make his Pale sufficient by the first of Aprill as shall be approved of by such as are appoynted to vew it upon payne of 5^s for every goad that is found defective and so at all tymes to maynteyne it sufficient.

Febr. 10 1634. It is granted that Thomas Marshall have 8 goad in bredth next unto Thomas Gu[nne] in the late buriall place for building.

It is graunted that the plat of ground betwixt Mr Parkers and the bridge conteyning 7 acres and halfe to be devided 2 acres to captayne Mason. 2 acres to Jno Hollard and 3 acres and halfe to [^{1}Roger Mathewes] George Procter.

---

^{1} Erased in original.

It is ordered that fower bulls, shall constantly goe with the drift of milch Cowes and for the yeere ensuing Mr Israel Stoughton is to keep on[e] bull. William [**14.**] Rockewell on[e]. and Thomas fford 2 bulls and for their pay they are to have 12^d for every milch Cow.

Also for the necke of land with the heyfers. Mr Holman is to keepe one bull and Symon Hoyte one. Thomas fford one. and to have the like pay as the cowes.

It is also ordered that there shall be a sufficient cart way made betwixt the rocke and Mr Richards house or elce to goe thorow his lott according to a former order.

Giles Gibbes was defective in comming to the meeteing Febr: First.

For the p^{r}vension of publique complaynts for defect of payments in the Plantation, it is ordered that such as are defective at the appoynted tyme of payment in any Rates taxations or payments the names shall be brought in to the p'sons appoynted by the Plantation for publique busenesses, before they make any publique complaynts of it, and by them some course to be taken for the speedy satisfying of such defects.

It is graunted vnto Hugh Rosciter and Richard Rocket to have each of them 8 acres of land on the west side of the brooke adjoyning to Mr Rosciters ground as farr forth as the Plantation hath any right to dispose of it|.

It is graunted to Mr Israel Stoughton to have sixe rod square at Mr Rossiters fishouse for the building of a house to put corne baggs in for the mill, for which he hath p'mised to leave so much on the knapp before his shopp formerly graunted him.

It is graunted to Mr Egelstone to have 3 acres of ground in the necke behind his lott.

The persons appoynted to veiwe the pales are for the great lotts Mr Woolcott and Mr Terry. for the West field. Thom: Moore and Walther Filer. ffor the Southfeild, Thomas Ford, and Cristopher Gibson. for the East feild. Will Phelps and Mr Thomas Stoughton, for the Northfeilde, Will. Horsford, Rodger Clapp.

Aprill 17th 1635. It is ordered that Nicholas Vpsall, and Mathew Graunt shall p'ceed in the measureing of the great lotts as they have begun, for which they are to be payed 2^d an acre by the owners of the land and this measuring to stand for continueance.

It is ordered that M^r. Newbery and M^r. Wollcott shall have power to lay out a yard for Tho: Geofery where they shall thinke fit neere Goodman Randel if so be he vse the same for a yard.

It is ordered that there shall be a way palled out from the buring place to M^r. Brankers by the 16 day of May next to be palled by the severall men that owne the lotts and whosoever shall be defective to pay for every rod not palled 5^s this order to stand the 25 march.

It is ordered that John Phillips and Thomas Hatch shall have each of them 2 acres of land that lyes betwixt the ends of the great lotts and 3 acres that is graunted to Alexander Miller [**15.**]

if so much be there p'vided they leave a sufficient highway at there great lotts . . .

It is graunted to John Grenway and John Benham to have devided betwixt them [ ] acres of land on the pine necke formerly graunted to John Goite on condition that he come not over to possesse it the next Somer, which ground is graunted them to make good the ground which they left out in their home lotts.

It is graunted to Giles Gibbes to have 2 acres of medow ground betwixt M^r. Thomas Stoughtons lott, and the sandy poynt at the necke.

It is also ordered that the lott of medow that was Symon Hoytes next to boston side Joyning to John Witchfeild shall be devided betwixt M^r. Rodger Williams and Gyles Gibbes.

It is graunted to William Horseford to have 4 acres of medowe ground next to Goodman Denslowes medow ground.

It is also graunted to M^r. Williams to take 2 acres of medow ground after William Horseford.

It is graunted to M^r. Tilly to take up 4 acres of medow at the necke if so much be there after M^r. Williams. and William Horseford.

It is graunted to Jonathan Gellet: to fence in halfe an acre of ground about his house leaving a sufficient highway.

It is graunted to John Haydon, to have an acre and halfe of swamp betwixt the Wolfe Trapp and the dead swamp.

It is agreed with Thomas Thorneton and Thomas Sanford to vnder take the keepeing of the Cowes for the space of 7 moneths, to begin the 15th of Aprill for which they are to have 5^s 3^d the Cowes if there be six score, if not so many the owners of the Cowes are to make up their pay 31^{li}. 10^s. if there be more they are to take their advantidge and this to be payed the one halfe in May, and the other halfe at the 7 moneths end.

In consideration whereof the fore sayd p'tyes do p'mise to fetch all the Cowes from Jonathan Gillets house to M^r. Woolcotts, and from John Greenwayes to Walther Filers and to drive them forth in the morneing an hower after sun rising ; and at comming in to drive them thorow and turn over the bridge those that are beyond that way : also one of them doth p'mise to Keepe them every lords day. and the Plantation to find an other according as shall be agreed in an equall p'portion :

It is graunted to George Minot to have six acres of Marsh over agaynst fox poynt. also to Jonathan Gillet 4 acres next to him at the same place. and to the widow Purchase 4 acres more in the same marish :

It is graunted that Thomas Ford shall enjoy a p'cell of ground to the valew of 2 acres which he hath impalled in M^r. Ludlowes necke which was graunted to Peeter Peecke. Provided that he leave a sufficient highway if it be thought fit by the Plantation.

July 5th 1635. It is graunted that Thomas Duee shall have 2 acres of moweing ground neere the fresh Marsh which he hath formerly mowen in satisfaction for on acre of ground which he left in common at his house.

[16.] If there be no exception agaynst by the next meeting.

It is graunted to William Phellps to fence in 2 acres and halfe of dry ground adjoyneing to his medowe ground in the little necke, in satisfaction for what he wants in his home lott.

Whereas there is a former order for all swine that shall trespasse in any of the Corne feilds, the pale where the swine come in to pay one halfe and the swine the other : It is now further ordered that such swine as trespass shall be impounded and there to be kept till the owner shall pay the trespasse, as shall be Judged by Two of the members : and if the owner in 3 dayes after notice take not of the swine and satisfie the trespasse then it may be lawful for the Baylife to sell the swine as he can and pay the trespasse and retourne the overpluss to the owner.

also ownour of the pales where swine come in it shall be lawfull for the Baylife to attach his goods and satisfy halfe the trespasse according to the former order.

And further it is ordered that the same Course shall be taken for the levying of any trespasse that shall be committed by goates or other cattle.

It is ordered that if any breake Oop the pound or take out cattell violently shall forfeit 5 pound sterling to be imployed for generall works in the Plantation. and if it cannot be proved who brake the pound then the p'ty that is the owner of the Cattell shall fill the pound agayne, or elce he shall be taken to be the trespasser —

The 12th of August 1635. These are to testify to all whome it may concern that I Thomas Holcombe have sould and give full possession vnto Richard Joanes both of Dorchester 4 acres of ground with my houses and all things thereto p'tayning and 8 acres of ground of my great lott on Roxbury bounds and 6 acres of medow ground on the side Naponset river and 3 acres on the other side the river : —

I, Thomas Duee of Dorch : do likewise fully confirme vnto Richard Joanes of Dorch : and give him full possession of 4 acres of ground with my house and all thereto belonging, also 8 acres of ground of my great lott, also tenn acres of medowe on the side Naponset, and 4 acres of medowe on the other side, and 2 acres of medowe in the fresh marsh.

TD
The marke of Thomas Duee.

The ijth day of November, 1635 — It is ordered that M^r. Nathaniell Duncan, M^r. Demicke, Thomas Ford and Mathew Graunt, or any two of them shall have power to lay out an hundred and fifty acres of medow to M^r. Israel Stoughton, in a medow lying six miles above his mill at Naponset river **[17.]** and was graunted him by order of Court. And likewise next there vnto t . . . out an hundred acres of medow vnto M^r. Thomas Newbery as that was likewise graunted him by order of Court togeather with an hundred acres of Upland gr[ound] and likewise it is ordered and agreed upon whereas M^r. Newbery hath relinquished a former graunt from the Plantation of 40 acres of Marish and 20 acres of Upland in squantum Necke he is now to take all the ground from his house to M^r. Willsons farme, in consideration thereof.

It is ordered that John Levite shall have 8 acres of Upland ground and 4 acres of Marsh ground, to lye on the West side of M^r. Ludlowes Necke next Naponset river.

It is graunted to John Hulls to have 2 acres of medowe that lyes in a small gurt on the side the fresh marish.

It is graunted to Joshua Charter to have 3 acres of medow ground in the fresh Marish next M^r. Rodger Williams.

It is graunted to M^r. William Hill, to have 9 acres of Upland ground in the little necke at Squantum, in Lue of 12 acres he was to have there in lott.

It is graunted to William Hannum to have one acre of Medow ground in the fresh marish.

The names of such as are chosen for ordering the affayres of the Plantation, November 1635, to continue for halfe a yeere.

> William Philps.
> Nathaniell Duncan.
> M^r. George Hull.
> M^r. Democke.
> William Gaylar.
> M^r. Roger Williams.
> George Minot.
> John Phillips.
> M^r. Newbery.

Walter Filer is chosen Baylife for this halfe yeere and it is ordered that he shall levie all rates fines or amercements for the Plantation, by impounding the offenders goods, and there to detayne them till satisfaction be made, and if the owner of the goods doe not make satisfaction within fower days it shall be lawfull for him to sell the goods and returne the overplus to the p'tie offending, and be allowed twelve pence for every distress and ij^d. for every impounding and if the sayd Baylife shall [be] negligent in dischardgeing his office and delay the taking distresse he shall be liable to a fine as shall be thought fitt p' the Tenn men.

The 17th day of December 1635. It is ordered that Robert Deeble shall have inlardgment of Two goad in length from his house vpward, and that, and that his sonne T[hommas] Deeble [18.] shall have six goad next him, to goe with a right lyne vp from the pale before his house on condition for Thommas Deeble to build a house there within one yeere or elce to loose that goad graunted him.

It is ordered that Thomas Andrews shall have Three acres of ground next his house neere Mr Hathornes in leive of a great lott and that he pale it in to leave a sufficient highway of Three goads at least.

It is ordered that George Minot shall have halfe an acre of ground neere Mr Newberys pale for building a house.

It is ordered that William Rockewell shall have halfe an acre of ground next Mr Stoughtons neere the fish house to build him an house with condition that if he goe away, and leave the Plantation he leave the sayd house and ground to the Plantation in paying him the chardge.

It is ordered that no man shall fell any trees within 20 goads of the meeting house upon pennalty of Tenn shillings for every tree that is felled to be levyed by distresse vpon his goods.

It is ordered that Thomas Ford shall have six acres of the fresh marsh neerest the towne in liev of 2 acres he was to have from M^r. Newbery over the Watter and more that he was to have there.

It is ordered that M^r. Stoughton according to a veiu made by men appoynted for setting out his 150 acres of fresh marsh that from above a stake set up by him about the vpper end of the Marsh, he is to take that p'te above to the Cedar swamp, except on[e] acre all above for Thirty acres and so to measure out the Rest of his hundred and fifty acres downe wards of both sides the water the 30 acres also be taken of both sides the River : —

It is ordered that M^r. Newbery shall measure out his hundred acres of the same marsh following on this side of the river, if so much their or elce to take it over the Water. —

The 4th of January. 1635. It is ordered that the p'tyes here vnder written shall have great lotts at the bounds betwixt Roxbury and Dorchester at the great hill betwixt the sayd bounds and above the marsh as foll. not to inclose medowe.

Henry Fookes	20 acres
Widdow Purchase	16 "
Mathias Sension	20 "
Thomas Thornton	16 "
Thomas Samfford	16 "
Henery Wright	20 "
William Hannam	16 "
Barnard Gapin and his sonne	30 "
Thomas Swift	20 "
Robert Deeble and his sonne	30 "
[19.] William Sommer	20 "
Roger Clap	16 "
Aron Cooke	16 "
John Pope	20 "
m^r. Pinny	20 "
M^r. Demicke	20 "
John Eales	20 "
George Proctor	20 "
Richard Wade	20 "
Robert Winchill	16 "

The 18th January 1635. It is ordered that all the hoame lots within Dorchester Plantation which have bene granted before this p'sent day shall have right to the Commons and no other lotts that are graunted hereafter to be commoners : Also that Two men shall not Common for one hoame lott.

It is ordered that Thomas Marshfeild shall have 12 acres of

Planting ground on Squantum Necke which was formerly graunted him for his great lott.

It is ordered that John Moore shall have Tenn acres for his great lott in the same place: —

It is ordered that Edmond Munnings, Joseph Flood, Thomas Joanes, shall have each of them 8 acres on Squantum Necke as an addition to their great lotts on Roxbury bounds bought of William Hulbert, John Haydon and George Phillips.

It is ordered that Elias Parkeman shall have a great lott of Tenn acres at Sqantum necke.

It is ordered that Mr Gilbert M^r makepeace. Mr Joanes, Richard Collicott, George Dyar, and Walther Filler shall make a rate for fifteene pounds for Captine.

The 1st of February 1635. . . . . . . William Gaylar shall have about 2 acres of medowe next
[Here a half leaf is gone.]

[**20.**] — It is ordered that Will: Sumner is to have 3 acres of the fresh marsh next Goodman Ford.

It is ordered that John Phillips shall have for Edward Hart Three quarters of an acre medowe at Squantum necke. —

It is ordered that whereas their was graunted to M^r. Williams 8 acres next to John Moores lott for his great lott that now the Rest that is there shall be added to the value of 6 acres more.

The names of those which have medow graunted them the 18th ffebru: 1635. In the fresh marsh neerest the Towne. —

First Marsh		Second Marsh	
Oliuer Purchase	2 acres	M^r. Joanes	5 acres
Thom: Thorneton	2 acres	Jos: Flood	3 acres
Goodman Sampford	2 "	Will. Preston	3 "
Henry Wright	2 "	Roger Clap	2 "
Christopher Gibson	2 "	Good: Hill	2 "
Saunder Miller	2 "	M^r. Makepeace	2 "
Austin Clement	2 "	M^r. Bates	2 "
John Binham	½ acre	William Hannam	1 acre
Thom Swift	½ acres	George Proctor	2 acres
M^r. Democke	2 acres	John Miller	2 "
Richard Callecott	4 "	Barnebe Foeer & John Smith	4 "
George Minot	6 "	Thom: Stilestone	2 "
George Hull	2 "	Kemmerly	2 "
John Phillips	6 "	Joshua Tuchill	2 "
Nathaniell Duncan	2 "	David Price	2 "
John Pearce	2 "	M^r. Holman	4 "

[Here ½ page missing, being torn.]

[**21.**] Giles Gibbs 10 acres Richard Rocket 6 acres.

It is ordered that all the feilds for Corne shall be inclosed p' the fourteenth of March and whosoever is defective in so doing it shall pay five shillings to be levyed p' distresse and after that day any hoggs found in corne feilds shall be impounded and pay damadge according to order of Generall Court.

The first of March. 1635. It is ordered that the ground that was left betwixt William Gaylard and Eltwid Pommery, which was left for a high way shall now remayne to the vse of William Gaylard. till the Towne shall agayne require it.

It is ordered that whereas Walther Filler was by vert[u] of his Baylife office to levy all rates, fynes and amercements, p' pounding the offenders goods and so to sell the goods and returne the overplus as in the order made in November, 1635, he hath now further power given him not only to recover such rates and fines by pounding of cattle or piggs but also to distrayne any other goods and thereof to make sale to pay such rats or fynes and to Returne the overplus to the offenders.

The 27 June 1636. A meeteing of 12. men formerly chosen by the Plantation for ordering the affayres thereof whose names are vnder written.

Mr. Ludlow.	Richard Callicot
Mr. Stoughton	Austin Clement.
Mr. Duncan	Mr. Demicke
Mr. Hull	George Dyar.
Goo: Gaylard	John Phillips
George Minot	Mr. Williams
Thomas Ford	

It is ordered that John Gapin shall have on acre to build an house in, next to Goodman Swifts, with the Consent of Goodman Dyar in lue of an acre formerly p'mised vnto him.

It is ordered that or brother Minot, [and] Goodman Ford do vewe the ground or brother Wright desires and reports the resonableness of it the next meeteing

It is ordered that Nicholas Vpsall shall keepe an house of entertaynement for strangers.

It is ordered that Mrs. Johnson that was shall have on acre of medowe next Goodman Eales Pale confirmed vnto her.

It is ordered that Richard Callecott shall have 4 acres of medowe in the higher Marish ground at the Southerne Corner of the great marsh, relinquishing his former graunt of 4 acres in the same great Marsh.

[22.] The names of such as are to have medow in the Marsh by Goodman Grenwayes.

Mr. Mather.	2 acres	Thomas Lumbert.	2 acres
Mr. Wareham,	2 "	John Hulls.	2 acres
Will: Gaylard,	2 "		

John Grenway j acre one more if so fall out
George Minot 4 acres and six acres more in the fresh Marsh next Richard: Callicott

Mr. Duncan.	3 acres
Mr. Hill	2 acres
Walther filer	2 acres
Anc: Stoughton	2 "

Jellets. — 2 acres
Good. fford — 2 "
Good. Dyar — 3 "
John Eales   2 acres betweene that medow he hath of Mrs Johnson and the Creeke.

It is ordered that Mr. Ludlow may have strayte downe to the sea the marsh that lyes next the 4 acres to his hoame lott. —
And that all that are of Mr. Duncans side shall have the ground to themselves before their doores makeing and maynetayneing a sufficient high way so far as Mr. Stoughtons reserveing as much as may set a meeteing house betweene Good. Johns. and where Goodman Rockewell now dwells.

It is ordered that George Hull shall have the medow that lyes before his doore where he now dwells to Henry wayes downe to the sea makeing a sufficient way for passidge that way. —

It is ordered that the highway from Mr. Stoughtons to Mr. Ludlowes shall be 3 Lugg broad all along and so downe to Nicholas Vpsall, 4 Lugg.[1]

It is ordered that Elias Parkeman should have the marsh before his doore.

It is ordered that John Phillips shall have six acres next to Goodman Minot, and Richard Collicot in the fresh marsh.

It is ordered that Barnard and John Gapin shall have 2 acres in the marsh next Goodman Grenwayes.

It is ordered that Goodman Bates, shall have 2 acres in the Marish next Goodman Grenwayes.

It is ordered that Nicholas Vpsall and Will. Rockewell shall have all that marsh next the Rocky hill, and Mr. Rossiters fish house equally devided. —

It is ordered that Mr. Demicke shall have 2 acres in the marsh next to Good-man Grenwayes. . . .

[23.] It is ordered that Mr. Israel Stoughton shall have halfe an acre [near] William Rockewells house and the salt Marsh in a long slip . . .

It is ordered that Goodman Minot be next Mr. Ludlowes Lott.

July 5th 1636

Mr. Ludlow.   Thomas fford.
Mr. Stoughton.   Richard Collicot.
Mr. Hull.   Austin Clement.
Natha: Duncan.   Mr. Willigms.
Mr. Democke.   John Phillips.
George Minot
George Dyar.

It is ordered that George Minot, Mr. Duncan, John Phillips and Austin Clement relinquishin there former great lotts in the fresh marsh shall [in] lew of them have the sayd p'portions in a lesser medowe lying neerer Naponset. South and by East from the

---

[1] A lug is sixteen and a half feet square. — W. H. W.

Markt tree, George Minot 6 acres Duncan . 2 acres John Phillips 6 acres, Austin Clement 2 acres.

It is ordered that Aron. Cooke relinquishing a former graunt of 4 acres of medow in the second Marsh, hath 4 acres now graunted in the hither great marsh adjoyning to Goodman Collicot.

It is ordered that M^r. Duncan shall have 10^s payd him by the Towne for to transcribe all these orders into a new booke in a fayre legible hand.

It is ordered that Aron Cooke shall have halfe an acre of ground over agaynst his lott by the brooke neere the dead swamp to build his house upon.

It is graunted that these men whose names ensue shall have lotts at Squantum necke according to the p'portion here expressed M^r. John Tilly as the great lott to his brothers hoame lott 12 acres, and M^r. Holland 12 acres M^r. Richards 10 acres, Good: White 12 acres, John Whitcomb 12 acres to plasters lott and John Hull 8 acres.

It is graunted vnto Nicholas Vpsall, 8 acres of upland upon the Indian hill by Thomas Tilestone, also William Rockewell hath 8 acres to his former, as inlardgements to there former lotts.

It is graunted to Christopher Gibson halfe an acre of marsh lying at the end of John Moores lott by the shipp.

It is graunted to M^r. Hill that his 9 acres free graunted at Squantum necke shall have 7 more added to it, so it be sixteene acres.

It is graunted to Richard Collicott as an additon to his great lott six acres of land in Narraganset way beyond Naponset upon the bounds betw[een] us and Mount Wolleston.

It is graunted to M^r. Duncan a slip of upland lying to his marsh by John Phillips, about 2 acres.

[24.] It is graunted vnto Mr Dimocke that he shall have all the ground betweene his pale and Goodman Denslow and Bartholomew by the side of the high way, p'vided he p'judice not the way for Carts, Cattle and passengers, but maynetayne a Cart Gate, etc., both the upland and the marsh not formerly graunted.

It is ordered that the common to be devided betweene the inhabitants on that row on M^r. Duncans side graunted in a former order shalbe devided amongst them by acre according to the Auncient lotts that lye there that is to say that he that was to have 8 acres 6 or 4 shall [have] his p'portion of the common according thereto it being all first measured.

It is graunted that the ground about Rocky hill shall belong to M^r. Ludlow, M^r. Johnsons house, George Minot, M^r. Hill, John Eales and Elias Parkeman, in community amongst them, p'vided they do nothing to p'judice the common passidge of people. Carts or cattle, both to the sea or any other as there may be occasion, this graunt being not to hinder any fortification, if the Countery at any tyme see cause, the bounds being (togeather with the wayes) from Jonathan Gillets pale and so round to their severall grounds. . . . . .

It is graunted to M^r. Ludlow, M^r. Hill and the neighbours that haue lotts with them that they may run a pale downe into the sea at the Corner by Mr Ludlowes, and an other betweene Mr Hill and John Eales for the securing there Corne, and saving of much fensing, p'vided they leave stiles and gates for p'sons and cattle, when p'sons are disposed to travell or drive Cattle or swine that way to Clamming. . . .

It is granted to Nicholas Vpsall, to the quantity of 5 good square of ground adjoyning to Goodman Rockewells lott on the comon for a garden.

The former graunt of Nine goad to Good. Ford in the Common by Mr Mavericks house being yeilded up by him to the Towne, he was graunted in lew thereof nine goad in length of the sayd comon by the pound.

The 2^d of October 1636. It is ordered, that Brey Wilkeines shall have six acres of Vpland in p'te of his great lott being a little necke lying by M^r. Makepeaces and M^r. Brankers meddowe. . . . .

The names of such as were chosen for the ordering of the affares of the plantation to begin from the second of January, being the first Moone day of the month and so to continue the monethly meeteings for six monethes or till new be chosen, 8 of which number being p'sent, they may act and order any thing in the Plantation according to the scope of former orders to that effect. If any of these shall be absent without good cause, allowed by the rest, [he] shall pay for his so fayleing 5 shillings, any that shall come after the houre of 8 of the clock to pay 12 pence, and after 9 to pay 2 shillings: if any stay longer to pay the full fine of 5 shillings, when 3 of these are come together they shall Judge of the tyme this act to continue for a firme order from Time to tyme.

Mr Stoughton	John Hollman
m^r Glouer	m^r Hill
Henry Withington	Will. Gaylard
Nathaniell Duncan	Cristofer Gibson
George Minot	John Pierce
Richard Collicott	Mr Joanes

[**25.**] It is ordered that 4 Barrells of powder in the meeteing house of the Countryes store shall be disposed of and sould for the bringing in new powder in the place p' the p'tyes vnder mentioned.

By Nathaniell Duncan, one barrell
By Richard Collicot, one barrell
By Nicolas Vpsall, one barrell
By John Gapin one   barrell

Joseph Flood is chosen Baylife during the tyme of the 12 men, now Chosen and till new be Chosen to that office, and it is ordered that he shall levie all fynes, rates or amercements for the Plantation p' impounding the offenders goods; and there to detayne them till satisfaction [be] made, and if the owner of the goods shall not make satisfaction within 4 dayes it shall be lawfull for him to sell the goods and to returne the ouerplus to the p'ty offending, and to [be] alowed 12^d for euery distresse, and 2^d for euery imponding of Cow, horse or hogg and for every gote a penny, and if the sayd Baylif shall be necligent in dischardgeing his office and delay the taking distresse he shall be loyable to a fyne as shall be thought fit by the 12 men.

It shall be lawfull for the sayd Baylife to recouer any rates or amercements p' way of distresse [on] any goods.

It is ordered that whereas there was half an acre of Marsh formerly graunted to Christou [er] Gibson lying at the end of John Moores lott next the ship, the sayd halfe an acre is given ouer to the sayd JohnMoore p' the said Christo: Gibson. . . .

It is ordered that euery p'ticular inhabitant shall take a veiwe of his house and garden and hoame lotts how they lye bounded (towardes other mens, or towardes the commons) according to the poynts of the compasse, and so of their great lotts and medow ground as they lay bounded euery way, and the number of acres of all such lands.

A note of which to be brought into the 12 men to be Judged of an amongst them 4 to be chosen according to order of Court with the Advise of an Assistant to see it recorded one a booke p'te

It is ordered that William Gaylar, George Dyar, and M^r. Hathorne shall make a rate for 25^{li}. for publicke use.

January 16 1636. It is ordered that there shall be a way paled out from the Creeke joyning to M^r. Williams great lott to the Corner of Mr. Newberyes great lott and euery man to pale the end of his lott: and also from the corner of Mr Richards lott to the sayd Creeke to be paled by John Moore and Edmond Munnings, p'portionabely to their lotts.

It is ordered that there shall be one intire sufficient ffence from the Lower Corner of M^r. Newberyes great Lott and so round the great lotts towards the Comons to the pale of the six acre loots and from those lotts to the riuer of Naponsett which pale from the farther Corner of the great lotts to the six acre lotts and from the six acre lotts to the riuer to be paled and maynetayned by those which possesse the six acre lotts, and by those that haue formerly paled the farther side of the great lotts, and for those which haue paled the hither side formerly to doe that still, all this to be done very sufficiently by the 20th of March next.

It is farther ordered that George Meinot and John Philips, shall see to the farther side that their be sufficient pale, and M^r. Glover, and Mr Holmand to looke to the hither side and where they shall find any defect to p'sent it to the 12 men.

It is farther ordered that what Tresspasses shall hereafter be done the Tressepasser shall pay the one halfe of the dammadge, and he that is defective in his pale the other halfe; [**26.**] and this order to be generall thorough the whole Plantation. Provided that if any cattle be knowen to be common pale-breakers; they shall pay the whole Trespasse.

It is ordered that Henry Withington shall see the makeing of the gate to the great lotts at the chearge of those which haue their lotts according to a former order, and the sayd gate to be maynetayned p' all the sayd great lotts and also by the six acre lotts.

It is ordered That John Philips, and Christouer Gibson, shall stake out a Cart way through the great lotts.

It is ordered that Brey Wilkeines shall have one acre on the necke of the 3 acre Lott which was formerly graunted to Jo: Knell, the other two acres to remayne to Mr Holland in whose possession it is, which acre the sayd Bray is to haue upon Condition he remayne in the Plantation, elce to leaue it to the Plantation, and not to alienate it without app'bation of the Twelue men.

It is ordered that whosoeuer breaketh open any pale shall pay fiue shillings.

It is ordered that all the hoame lotts shall be sufficiently paled by the first of March.

Zachariah Whiteman, Henry Withington to vew the pale in the feild next to their houses.

Edmond Munnings and George Dyer to vew the feild next to their houses.

Mr Makepeace, John Moore to vew the feild next their houses.

Joseph ffarneworth and Goodman Read to veiw the feild where they dwell.

William Summer, Goodman Hawes to vew the feild where they dwell.

John Poape and Edward Clap to vew their feild.

All those which are appoynted to vew those feilds are to p^{e}sent any defect of bad paling or not paling at the Time appoynted to the Twelve men.

It is ordered that M^r. Israel Stoughton shall haue a hundered and fifty acres of vpland ground ouer the riuer of Naponset next the mill, of which fourty acres to be that which is in possession of the Indeans, and this in lue of so much p'mised him, and for all his deuision of any land beyound the Riuer, except the Change of the end of his great lott, and this graunted him one condition he submitt to any order that shall be here after made for not alienateing this portion or any other land from the Plantation.

It is ordered that Tenn men shall be chosen to order all the affayres of the Plantation on this manner. They shall continue a monethly meeteing dureing their tyme that they are Chosen, which shall be six months after election. At which meeteings they shall consult of and act what may be for the good of the Plantation, and after they haue made such acts and that by the major p'te of as many of them as are p^{e}sent which should be seauen at least they shall upon the next Lecture Day after Lecture read them to the Company of free men who are to be warned at p^{r}ent to stay. And then all acts and conclusions as shall not be contradicted by the major p'te of the free men p^{r}sent, shall stand for orders and bind the Plantation and euery inhabitant thereof.

It is ordered that all the land both of the great necke and about the Towne and of both sides the Riuer of Naponsett which is not allredy allotted out shall be deuided into p'priety to each hoame lott according to p'portion agreed vpon so far in the Countery one both sydes the Riuer the place called mother brooks.

[**27.**] It is ordered that Mr Glouer shall haue 30 acres of vpland . . . medow beyond Naponsett about a mile from the mill in lieu of a Twenty acre lott amongst the great lotts beyound the fresh marsh which he leaues to the Plantation.

It is ordered that M^r. Holland shall haue all that rest of ground, marsh inclosed, or vpland joyneing vnto the Two acres on M^r. Ludlowes necke graunted formerly to Thomas fford leaueing a sufficient high way also he shall haue a little plott of marsh which is without the inclosure, payeing Thomas fford the charges he hath beene at in ditching.

It is ordered that M^r. Joanes shall haue an acre and halfe of land joyneing to the end of his swamp next the Towne with a round hill in it.

It is ordered for the better payment of heardsmen that whosoeuer shall put any cattle to keepe, and neglect to bring in his mony to the say heardsman for such cattle at such tymes as shall be agreed, for after some Generall warneing one a lecture day it shall be lawfull for the Baylife to impound any cattle of such p'sons and their to deteyne them for a day in which tyme if the p'ty hauing noteice thereof doe not bring in his money the sayd Baylife with 2 freemen shall price and make sale of such Cattle and take satisfaction for what is due to the heardsmen 3 shill. for himself p'ty for levying the distresse, and then to return the ouerplus to the p'ty delinquent.

It is ordered that Mr Stoughton and M^r. Holman shall furneish 3 Bulls for the heard of cowes of that side the Towne and to be payd 12^d for each Cow and the mony to be payd into the heards men.

It is ordered that Mathias Sension and Thomas Sampford shall keepe the Cowes this yeere to begin the 17th day of April and to continue the keepeing them till the 15th of Nouember to haue for their pay in keepeing 5 shill^s the head for as many as are brought in ; The sayd five shill. p' head to be payd ⅓ in hand ⅓ at halfe the tyme the other at the end of the tyme.

It is also ordered that all that haue Cowes shall put them to the Keepers to be kept in the ordinary Cow pasture, and none to be put away at the Necke of land or keepe them otherwise about the Towne or from the heard, one payne of 10^s for [such] offending. Also that all that liue Northwards from the meeting house shall [. . .] their Cows into the open place befo^r the meeteing house within an hower of [sunne] riseing and their the Keepers to be ready to driue them away and so to blow their horne along the Towne and whosoever bring not their cowes before Mr Stoughtons house within an hower of sunnerising, the Keepers shall stay no longer [but] drive away those which are redy to the Pasture and those which through their [owne] neglect haue their Cowes behind shall not make that any Barre of payment to the Keepers.

It is ordered that Mr Holman shall haue 20 acres of vpland beyound the . . . next to Mr Hutchissons.

It is ordered that Mr. Joanes shall have 20 acres of vpland for a great Lott [which] he had p'missed him for that that was Silvisters, for which he is to haue, the lott of 20 acres which was formerly graunted to Mr. Glouer, which one some [conside]ration he left vnto the Plantation according to a former order.

It is ordered that M^r. Holman shall haue 10 acres of playne mowing ground ad[ded] to his former graunt of 20 acres next M^r. Hutchissons, in lieu of p'te of [his] devision beyound the Watter.

The 2^d of May. Whereas by a former order it was concluded the great and little necke [should be] forthwith diuided amongst the inhabitants it is thought meete and agreed [. . .] shall challeng after diuision and posession any portion there as his [&] [Portion of leaf gone.] [**28.**] giuen and graunted to him and his for euer upon these Termes videlicett That if some shall desire to plant and others to keepe Cattle The Minor p'te shall fence agaynst the Major, that is if the Minor p'te will imp've their p'priey to Corne or the like, and the Major pte to Cattle, the Minor shall then fence agaynst the Major at his own p'ill, and so the like if the Minor will keepe Cattle and the Major plant they must secure the Majors Corne and be lya[ble] to pay dammage if they doe not; Provided that the Count be according to the most voyses and not according to the greatest number of acres. For p'venting of ouer burthening the same land it is mutually agreed that after October next six score Cowes shall be Counted the full stock for the whole necke being in Count 480 acres and so each man to haue commons according to his Number of acres and no man to exceed, other Cattle being alowed as followith, fiue goates to one cow, male and female Counted alike, and goates of a yeere old all vnder that age: 10 Kids to one Cow; two yearlings to one Cow; 3 Two yeerelings 2 Cowes, one working oxe to a Cow, one Mare and a Colt to Two Cowes, 4 Calues for one Cow; a yeereling Colt for a Cow, and a Two yearling so likewise untill 3 yeere old. This order to Continue vntill it be altered by the major p'te of voyces.

The 9th of May. It is ordered that the Necke of land conteyneing by measure about 480 acres shall be from henceforth the p'p inheritance of the p^{r}sent inhabitants of the Towne of Dorchester in this manner: every hoame lott that hath a dwelling house thereon or inhabitant incumbant in the Towne; he or it shall haue one acre to the sayd lott, and other hoame lotts halfe an acre; then the remayner to belong to the same planters by this rule. Three fifts to mens estates owne p'p' as vsuall they have burden; and 2 fifts to p'sons equally thus Counted. All men with their wiues and Children in the Plantation vnder their p^{r}sent gouerment in famalyes to be Counted; Provided allowance be made where house and lotts are intire allbeit for p^{r}sent they haue no p'sons incumbant according to the p'portion of such as Lately did inhabite them.

It is ordered that any of the members or housekeep'rs which shalbe Chosen to goe for a souldier and haue a Charge of busenesse to leaue behind him, he may commend the Care of his busenesse to some freind which he shall nominate who if he cannot of himself or p'cure others to doe it at the sames wages that is giuen to the souldiers it shall be lawful for Henery Withington M^r. Brankard, M^r. Bates and Nathaniell duncan or any of them to enjoyne any who they shall thinke fitt to worke in this k[ind] for the helpe of such as shall need, and if any being so joyned shall refuse to worke he shall pay fiue shill. for such refusall to be leuied by distresse.

It is ordered also that any that haue servants or any other which goe in the servize shall haue the Benefitt of this order.

The 2ᵈ September 1637. These are to testifie to all whō that may Concerne that I John Brancher haue sould and giue full possessⁿ — vnto Ambrose Martin my dwelling howse and cow howses ioyning with my hoame lot of about 3 or 4 akers and my great lot of 16 ackers with and without paling. Also [8] ackeʳˢ of meddow 6 akers of the medow this side of neponset Riū, and 2 akers beyond the riuer Witnes my hand the day abovementioned.

JOHN BRA[NKER]

[**29.**] *Septem 10ᵗʰ 1637.* There is graunted vnto William Hannam that p'te of the swamp lying oū agaynst his howse so farre as Rich: Wades pale hee paying his p'te of the charge with the rest of his neighbours, mayntayning a bridge ou[er] the watʳ.

The howse of Willm̄ Hannam with the sayd p'te of his swamp, his hoame lott and great lot, and one aker of meddow hee hath made sales of vnto Jonas Humphries with his Interest in the Com̄ons.

The 10 men assembled whose names are vnder written. Concluded of these ord[ers] foll: upon the 8ᵗʰ of November, 1637 —

Mʳ. Glouer
Nathaniell Duncan   Edward Clap
Mʳ. Joanes   Roger Clap
Mʳ. Bates   Will. Sumner
Richard Collicot
Mʳ. Homan

It is ordered that Will. Sumner and Good: Hawes shall haue the p'te of the swamp befoʳ their dore and end of their lotts they paying their p'te [of] makeing a sufficient Cart Bridge ouer the water.

It is ordered that Nathaniell Duncan shall Audit the account for Cunstables both for the Country and Plantation.

It is agreed that Mʳ. Stoughton & Mʳ. Glouer see the mending of the highway to the mill and to be payd out of the Towne rates.

It is ordered that Mʳ. Bates and Roger Clap shall make inquiry what Marsh or medow ground is not yet alotted out.

It is ordered that Will. Sumner see the mending of p'ce of the bridge betweene Roxbury and Dorchester.

Whereas the Widow Purchase had 16 acres graunted amongst the .. acre lotts and at the laying out thereof was alowed 20 acres [the] ouerplus at the hither end is graunted in p'per to Oliuer Purchase.

It is graunted to Thom: Luis to have 6 acres Planting land neere the Mill one Condition he shall keepe Cowes or young Cattle at such Rates as the Tenn men shall agree with him which if he refuse

DORCHESTER TOWN RECORDS.   25

to do he shall yeeld vp such land or house built to the Plantation in paying him what Costs and Charges he shall be by the 10 men adjudged to [been] at.

It is graunted to Henry Maudly about a quarter of an acre of land without the gate Joyneing to the pale neere Good: Munnings [to build] an house with Condition not to sell or let it without the Consent of the 10 men.

It is agreed— By a Generall vote of all the Plantation that there shal be a meeteing house built betweene M^r. Brankers and M^r. . . . it is agreed that a 100 £ shall be levied by a rate for the building of the house.

                M^r. Stovghton   Good: Munings
                Mr Glouer   M^r. Bates
                M^r. Butler   Nath: Duncan
                [other name illegible.]

[30.] It is agreed that M^r. Mathers shall have his 100 acres layd out over the Water next M^r. Holmans and Richard Collicots.

It is ordered that M^r. Holman and M^r. Holland make the way by Mr. Glouers —— of land at the end of the 6 acre lotts before his owne and M^r. Rich: lot.

It is ordered that Andrew Pitcher shall haue the 3 acres makeing and maynetayneing a pale from the end of the sayd 6 acre lotts to Good. Whiteman's medow.

Whereas by order of Generall Court it is left to euery Plantation to make such order as in their discretion they shall think fitt for p^{r}venting trespasses by swine on pennalty of the Plantations neglect of makeing or not executeing such order to pay all such Trespasses as shall be made p' swine. It is therefore ordered that none shall keepe any swine to let them runne in the Commons without sufficient yoakes and Ryngs within one miles of any Corne feild one payne of 5^s for every hog or pigg taken and impound p' any p'son which is not so yoaked and ringed, besides the Trespasses made by any such hoggs to pay doble damage, the damage to be Judged p' any of the neighbors such penalty and damage to be leuied p' distresse and this order to take effect the first of ffebriary next.

By a meeteing of 20 men[1] Chosen to order all the affayres of the Plantation

The 2d of January 1637. It is ordered that M^r. Gilbert shall have 16 acres of upland neere his medow ouer the water to be layd out by M^r. Glover, M^r. Holman, Rich: Collicott, Goodman Greenway and this in lieue of 12 acres due vnto him at squantum necke and in lew of any right he may demaund for the Calves Pasture.

Prouided that he fell noe Timber within the sayd 16 acres vnlesse for his owne vse vntill the meeteing house be built.

It is ordered that M^r. Joanes, Jos: fflood, Barnard Gapin,

---

[1] Mr. Stoughton, Mr. Glouer, M^r. Holman, Nath: Duncan, Will, Gaylor, Mr. Parker, John Pierce, M^r. Holland, George Dyer, Rich: Colicot, m^r. meinot, m^r. withington, John Pope, Will Sumner, John Moore, M^r. Bates, John Grinway, Roger Clap. Ed: Clap.

Will: Blake Christouer Gibson, Jo: Phillips shall haue confirmed to them the ground Joyneing to there hoame lotts to the other pale alowing 3 goad for a highway. Prouided that none in this graunt come below the bridge towards Goodman Vpsalls.

It is ordered that M^r. Gilbert shall have the Court where M^r. Wolcot put his hay confirmed to his house.

It is ordered that Christouer Gibson shall have 4 akers of medow at the North East and Joyneing next to M^r. Hawkinses. —

Jo: Kinsly is limited for his Marsh in the necke next Good: Gaylo^{rs} which was sould him by Aron Cooke to haue only 4 akers.

It is ordered that no p'son whatsoeuer shall fell any Trees within the Commons of Dorchester for any vse to make sayles of without the Plantation one payne of losse of their labour and 5^s to be leuied by distresse for euery tree so felled.

It is ordered that Austin Clement is to have one aker of land joyneing to his hoame lot to be layd out in convenient place not to hinder M^r. Hawkins p'prty.

It is ordered that Nicholas Vpsall and Will Rockewell are to take what is theirs where their 8 akers was granted and none elcewhere and that equally betwixt them.

John Moore is to haue in lieu of Calves Pasture 1 acre and halfe beyond . . . . wards to . . comons for a yeere C Gibs. and Jo. Pierce take out.

[32.] It is ordered that Goodman Greenway shall possesse only 4 akers of Marsh ground adjoyneing to the pine necke one which end of the necke he will.

It is ordered Good. Greenway shall haue all the vpland one the pine necke for his great lott except 4 acres belonging to Good: Binham and six Acres bought of Moses Mauericke.

It is ordered that Edmond Munnings shall haue that p'te of land joyneing to his house in lue of Calves Pasture: alowing 4 Goad for a high way to the necke to be layd out By Good: Gaylor, M^r. Glouer, M^r. Bates, and John Poape.

It is ordered that M^r. Tilly shall have 4 akers of vpland ouer agaynst M^r. Holland and 2 akers of Marsh if so much there adjoyneing out of p'priety and this without consideration of Comons or Challenge of any Cartway through the great lotts, and not to turne out swyne or cattle out of his owne land but one his own p'll in reguard of Corne feilds that lye vnpaled.

It is ordered that M^r. Makepeace shall have 4 akers of Marsh joyneing to his land bought of John Leuit at Mr Ludlowes necke to be layd out by M^r. Bates and M^r. Holland.

It is ordered that Richard Collicot shall have 2 akers of land beyond his house joyneing to the pales of the great lotts beyound the path and M^r. Holman to have 2 akers more following him and M^r. Richards to haue 2 akers more there if so much within the highway, or elce to haue 2 akers next his house p'vided the wood be left for comons 1 yeere except some Trees for shadow. Christo: Gibson, Goo: Pierce, to lay out the 6 akers.

It is ordered that M^r. Holland and Robert Elwell shall have that

---

¹ Page 31 of the original is a map of very primitive construction of which we give a facsmile on page 322 of this volume. — W. H. W.

DORCHESTER TOWN RECORDS. 27

slip of upland and marsh lyeing from the further Corner of Mr Richards lott to their houses leauing a free passige for Carts, or any other Carriadges that way.

It is ordered that M^r. Holland haue all the rest of the marsh joyneing to the pyne necke after 4 akers graunted to Good : Greenway and one aker more to be reserued to the disposall of the Plantation. M^r. Glouer and Good : Gaylor to lay it out.

It is ordered that M^r. Joanes have 2 akers of Marsh joyneing to his other Marsh p' the Trees towards fox poynt.

It is ordered that Good. Gapin shall hauve 2 akers more thereabouts.

It is ordered that M^r. Bates shall have 6 acres of Marsh one the necke next Jo : Kinsly, in lieue of 2 akers due to him in the Calves Pasture and other akers taken from his p'dicessours.

It is agreed If George Way or his agent doe proue a legall = graunt from the inhabitants of this Towne of a great lott for him Come or not Come and the quantity and according to the euidence we shall yeeld full satisfaction according to o^r power.

It is ordered that John Whipple shall haue 8 akers of land graunted him in full of all allotments to be layd out by M^r. Stoughton and M^r. Glouer about the mill as may be least p^ejuditiall to the plantation, this graunt being in reguard of a former p'mise vpon record.

It is ordered that from hence forwards noe house within the great lotts from the higher pale to the sea and the Riuer of Naponset shall be p'mitted to keepe any swine or Cattle without their owne fence to indamage other mens corne feilds one payne of paying doble [**33.**] Dammages for any Trespasses made by such swyne or cattle, to be levyed by distresse.

It is ordered that the p'tyes vnderwritten shall haue each of them satisfaction in lieu of the calues Pasture from the Burying place towards John Phillips.

M^r. Trobrige 1 aker. M^rs. Tillie 1 aker
Good. Kimerly 1 aker.
John Phillips an aker neere his house
M^r. Blake one aker.
Good Wade one aker putting in his pale at the Corner of his lott for Bettering the highway.
Good : Tomkines 1 aker.   Goo : White 1 aker
Good : Hawes 1 aker
Good : Hunphries 1 aker.   Willia[m] Sumner 1 aker
Good : Mede to haue one aker joyneing to M^r. Bates pale to goe 3 Goad from the pale the rest aboue mentioned not limited all redy to be layd out p' M^r. Glouer, Good. Gaylor and Good : Dyer.

It is ordered that the Widow Smed shall haue 2 akers below the burying place viz : j aker in lieu of the Calues Pasture the other in lieu of meddow.

Also Oliuer Purchase to haue one aker their in reguard of some p'mise formerly made and 1 aker for M^r. Oliuer in lieu of the Calues pasture to be also layd out p. Good. Gaylo^r. and Good. Dyar, to leaue 4 Goades for the high way from the burying place to Good: Wade, and 3 goad the other way from John Hills vp to the wood.

It is ordered that the p'tyes vnderwritten shall haue their portions in satisfaction of the Calues pasture in the Marsh beyound the Trees ouer agaynst the fox poynt.

Thom: Demock 2 akers
Thom: Lumbert 2 akers } these had so much formerly graunted.
Joseph Farenworth 2 akers

Thom: Wiswall to haue 2 akers towards fox poynt.
Joseph Flood to haue 2 akers there.
M^r. Martin 3 acres
Thom: Millet 2 acres there.

It is ordered that M^r. Trobridge have 2 acres of Marsh in M^r. Ludlowes necke where its out of p'priety.

It is ordered that Robert Elwell shall haue two acres of Marsh at M^r. Ludlow[es] necke.

M^r. Blake to haue 2 akers of Marsh at M^r. Ludlowes necke
Good: Procter, 1 acre and halfe at M^r. Ludiowes necke.
John Pierce 2 akers there next Good: Gibsons.
It is ordered that John Binham shall have 2 akers there.
It is ordered that Robert Looke shall have 2 akers there.

It is ordered that M^{rs}. Biggs shall have 1 acre of Marsh in lue of Calues Pasture neere her owne at the necke.

It is ordered that M^r. Billingham shall haue one acre of Marsh in lue of Calues Pasture joyneing to his owne at the necke.

It is ordered that the Widow foster shall haue one aker of Marsh in lue of Calues Pasture next M^r. Bates at the neck.

It is ordered that George Weekes shall have one acre in lieu of Calues Pasture ioyning to the side of his meddow.

It is ordered that M^r. Butlar is to haue a knap of land ouer agaynst his house to be set out p' Roger Clap and Edw: Clap so as is not p'judicial to the neighbors or the high way.

[34.] Nicholas Clap to haue a slip of marsh lyeing by the pyne necke joyneing to his about an acre or 2 to be layd out by Will. Sum^r.

It is ordered that John Hill shall haue one acre from the little necke towards the old harbor.

It is ordered that Good: Lane shall haue one acre there.

It is ordered that Will. Somner shall haue 3 acres neere Good. Munnings by the pyne necke.

It is ordered that M^r. Hathornes house shall haue 2 acres there.
It is ordered that Thom: Swift shall haue 1 acre there.

It is ordered that Anthony Newton shall haue 3 akers of Vpland behind M^r. Bates lott if so much there; but not to build any house there to the p'judice of the great lotts.

It is ordered that Good: Oldrich shall haue one aker of upland to build a house amongst others aboue the burying place.

It is ordered that Good: Gapin shall haue about halfe an acre of land joyneing to his lotte if it be not p'juditiall on vew of John Phillips and Christo. Gibson.

It is ordered that Thom: Swift shall haue one acre in lue of Calues pasture neere the markt tree.

It is ordered that Roger Clap haue about halfe an acre joyneing to the medow at Po.[1] poynt in lew of calues pasture for M^r. Wicthfeilds house.

It is ordered that M^r. Blake, John Hull, Thom : Millett shall haue each of them 8 acres of planting ground in full of there great lotts at the side of the six acre lotts towards the mill.

It is ordered that M^r. Blake and John Hull shall leaue those or the other p'ts of their great lotts in Commons as long as the outside of the great lotts are left in commons.

It is ordered that Robert Elwell, Brey Wilkeins, Henery Way, James Priest shall haue allotments at Mannings Moone.

It is ordered that Thom. Tilestone and John Smith shall haue an acre and halfe of Upland equally devided betweene them layd out by Good : Gibson, John Pierce one the Rocky Hill betwixt Good : Meinots and Good : Procters to build houses on.

It is ordered that John Poape haue an acre of land behind Good : Sampford to one veud by Goo : Gaylor and Good : Dyer.

It is ordered that he haue more 2 akers of meddow p' Goo : Munnings.

It is ordered that Thomas Joanes shall haue ½ an acre of land added to the acre and ½ formerly graunted him.

It is ordered that all the land in common within Dorchester one both sides the Riuer Naponset shall be deuided according to the rule alredy agreed vpon for deuideing the necke all convenient watering places to be left common[2] and this diuision to be according to states and p'sons as it stands now 16 January the tyme of the making this order. The 20 men to Judge of Circumstances in setting downe mens estates.

March 18th. It is ordered that all the hoame lotts and great lotts shalbe sufficiently fenced agaynst swine and great cattle p' the 25th of this moneth. on payne of thre shillings for euy goad found defectiue, to be leuied p'distresse, besides damedg.

[**35.**] The Proportion which each man is to haue in the necke according to the rule agreed on for deuideing the same as here vnder foll . . . .

The Proportion which each man is to haue of the Cowes Pasture and other land according to the same rule of deuision for euery on this side the Riuer.

	akers.	quarters.	rodes.	akers.	quarters.	rodes.
M^r. Stoughton	26	¾	½	26	¾	20
M^r. Glover	20	½	12	20	½	12
M^r. Whitman	13	¼	..	13	1	
M^r. Bates	8	3	..	8	3	
M^r. Meinot	7	1	20	8	3	
M^{rs}. Newbery	7	1	28	7	1	28
Ed. Munnings	10	3	12	10	3	12
N. Duncan	5	¾		5	3	
J. Holman	8			8		
Tho : Richards	11	2	20	12		

---

[1] Powow probably. — W. H. W.
[2] The Comons watering places to be restored to the Cow walke. — *Marginal note.*

	akers.	quarters.	rodes.	akers.	quarters.	rodes.
M^r. Trobridge	7	1	20	7	1	20
M^r. Hill	7	3	20	8	–	10
M^{rs}. Biggs	4	2	20	4	3	2
M^{rs}. Tilly	4		30	4	–	30
M^r. Mather	12	..	"	12	–	–
M^r. Martin	4	..	..	6	2	20
M^r. Gilbert	9		20	9	1	28
M^r. Hawkins	8	2	24	11	–	20
M^{rs}. Knight	2		10	10	3	–
M^r. Butlar	6	2	10	9	–	10
M^r. Aderton	6	3	30	13	2	–
M^r.Withington	7	2	2	7	3	6
Widow Smed	3	..	8	3	–	8
M^r. Parker	3	2	30	3	3	12
Thom : Joanes	5	3	30	6	1	10
Alexander Miller	4	..	20	4	–	20
Andrew Pitcher	1	2	35	1	2	35
Austen Clement	3	1	1	3	1	1
Brey Wilkeins	2	3	32	2	3	32
Henery Way	2	2	12	2	2	12
Chr. Gibson	3	3	32	3	3	32
David Price	2	2	12	2	2	12
Ed : Clap	4	1	12	4	2	32
Ed : Bullocke	3	3	8	2	1	8
Ed : White	3	..	35	3	–	35
Geo : Dyer	4	2	32	4	3	32
Geor : Procter	4	1	5	4	1	4
Geo : Weeks	3	2	36	4	2	10
Tho : Dickerman	3	1	17	3	2	37
Ralf. Tomkins	2	3	37	2	3	37
Rich : Wright	3	1	18	3	1	18
Jonas Humfry	2	3	16	3	1	6
Henery Wright	2	3	4	2	3	26
Joseph Tuchill	3	1	32	3	1	32
John Moore	3	3	37	4	2	37
John Whetcomb	4	3	10	4	3	10
John Smith	2	0	30	2	–	30
Widd. ffoster	2	..	30	2	–	30
John Phillips	8	..	17	8	–	17
Joseph Flood	3	..	35	3	2	10
John Capen	2	..	10	2	1	30
***o Eales	5	2	20	5	2	20
**o Nile	2	1	2	2	1	2
** Heydon	4	..	12	3	1	12
** Hill	3	..	3	3	1	23
** Pope	4	..	18	4		18
o Holland	6	..	20	6		20

[**36.**] The rest of the Division of the Neck. | Rest of the Division of other land.

	akers.	quarters.	rodes.	akers.	quarters.	rodes.
John Hull	4	–	36	4	–	36
John Grinway	4	3	6	4	1	6

DORCHESTER TOWN RECORDS.

	akers.	quarters.	rodes.	akers.	quarters.	rodes
John Kinsly	3	2	10	3	2	10
John Binham	3	2	10	3	2	10
Joseph Pharneworth	5	1	32	5	1	32
Nicho: Clap	3	2	28	4	..	8
M^r. Billingam	3		30	3	..	30
Nicho: Upsall	4		25	4	2	5
Natha: Wales	4	1	..	4	1	..
Rich: Joanes	5	3	21	5	3	21
Widdow Purchase	1	2	28	1	2	28
Rich: Wade	1	2	39	1	2	39
Roger Clap	4	..	..	4	..	..
Robert Elwell	2	2	39	2	2	39
Robert Deeble	2	3	22	2	3	20
Richard Collicot	6	3	38	6	3	38
Thom. Lumbert	3	—	35	3	2	10
Thom. Demicke	3	3	4	4	..	24
Tho. Swift	3	1	12	3	1	12
Tho. Andrews	2	1	30	2	3	10
Tho. Millet	2	3	4	2	3	4
Tho. Hatch	3	1	6	3	1	6
John Pierce	4	..	2	4	1	22
Tho. Tileston	2	3	2	2	3	2
Will. Sumner	5	2	12	5	2	12
Will. Blake	3	2	..	5	..	..
Will. Read	3	3	36	3	3	36
Will. Lane	3	2	16	3	2	16
Will. Preston	3	3	8	3	3	8
M^r. Hathornes House	3	3	26	4	..	30
Will. Gaylor	5	3	12	5	3	12
Tho. Wiswell	5	..	6	5	..	6
Tho. Kimerly	3	2	4	3	2	4
Tho. Sampford	2	1	24	2	1	24
Benjamin Fen	1	3	26	1	3	26
Good: Topley	2	1	4	2	1	4
Jo: Rigby[1]				2	2	12
M^r. Hutchisson	3	3	10	3	3	10
Geo. Way	2	2	17	3	1	13
M^r. Witchfeilds House	3	3	20	3	3	20
John Miller	2	..	20	2	.	20
Bernard Capin	2	..	12	2	2	12
Mathew Sension	3	2	4	2	1	4
M^r. Makepeace	12	2	26	13		6
Richard Hawes	2	3	26	3	1	6
Tho. Tredwell } Robert P .... [2] }	3	3	20	3 3	3	26 2
Somms is				538	3	22

March 18. Mr Holman and Richard Colicot to vew the pale of the great lotts and to see the fence be sufficient.

---

[1] Will. Clarke erased and Rigby added in original. — W. H. W.

[2] Name very illegible. — W. H. W.

John Pierce, John Hull to vew the pale of the lott where they dwell.

Edmond Munnings, George Dyar to vew the pale next them.

Tommas Wiswell, Will Read to vew the feild next where they dwell.

Will. Sumner, Good. Hawes to vew the feild where they dwell.

Roger Clap, Edward Clap to vew that feild.

M^r. Makepeace, John Phillips, to vew that feild.

[**37.**] Robert Deeble is chosen Baylif for halfe a yeere or till an other be chosen and it is ordered that he shall levy all fines rates and amercements for the Plantation by impounding the offenders Goods, and then to deteyne them till satisfaction be made and if the owner of the goods shall not make satisfaction within 4 dayes it shall be lawfull for him to sell the goods and to returne the overplus to the p'ty offending and to be alowed 12^d for euery distresse and 2^d for euery impounding of Cow horse or hogg and for euery goate a penny and if the sayd Baylif shall be negligent in dischargeing his office and delay the takeing distresse he shall be loyable to a fyne as shall be thought fit by the 20 men. It shall be lawfull for the sayd Baylif to recouer any rates or amercements by way of distresse on any goods.

The 3^d of Aprill 1638. It is ordered that the allotment which was formerly graunted on Mannings Moone shall be 8 ake^s to James Priest the rest to Robert Elwell in p'te of his great lott.

It is ordered that Henry way shall have 5 akers and Brey wilkeins 9 akers next to Rich. Rocket and Andrew Hollet in lieue of that was graunted them on Mannings Moone.

It is ordered that Will. Barber and John Starcy shall haue that rest of land which is left between Anthony Newton and M^r. Bates.

It is ordered that for this yeere only the oxen, mares, goates, and young Cattle shall be kep[t] at the Necke and noe man to keepe any Cowes there one payne of Tenn shill. for euery Cow so kept there contrary to this order.

It is ordered that John Smith and Joseph Wilson shall keepe all the Cowes this yeere in the ordinary Cow Pasture and to keepe them from the 15th of this p'sent month till the first of Nouember next, the sayd keepers to blow their horne in the morneing at Joseph Pharneworths and so along the Towne till he come to M^r. Minotts and euery man on the north side of Towne to bring their Cowes before the meeteing house the rest to bring their Cowes be yound M^r. Stoughtons dore or elce the keep' to driue away the heard not to stay for the rest. The sayd keep's to haue for the hier 5 shillings a Cow and to haue their payment one Third at first putting forth another Third at halfe the Tyme, the rest at the end of the Tyme.

Prouided that all which put in cowes to keepe and shall take them away agayne befo^r halfe the Tyme shall pay for halfe the Tyme if they take them away afore halfe the Tyme they must pay for the whole. If the heardsmen shall not drive away the catile at the Tyme appoynted it shall be lawfull for any man to take away his Cattle only paying for the Tyme they have beene kept.

Where as the pennalty for swyne goeing vn yoaked and vnringed was in a former order 5ˢ a swine It is now ordered that the pennalty shall be but 2 shilling and that the Baylif haue one halfe of the fine for his paynes in takeing up such hoggs and the Towne the rest to be leuied by distresse according to the former order. If any other shall pound swine such p'tye to have halfe the fine.

The 23. Aprill. 1638. It is ordered that noe goates shall goe one the Commons or highwayes neere Corne feilds without a keep' but to be impounded and pay doble dammage.

It is ordered that Mʳ. Aderton, Mʳ. Bates, Good. Munnings and Roger Clap shall stake out away to the necke of fower goad broad and dirrectly as may be and to see the mending of the sayd way where it is defectiue and to be payd by that rest of Monyes in Constables hands and what is wanting to be payd by an other rate to be made one euery one that hath land on the necke according to his p'portion.

[38.] It is ordered that Roger Clap, or whome it Concernes shall haue a high way to the medow by Thomas Andrews.

It is ordered that Mʳ. Minot shall haue a little swamp lyeing neere his house about 12 Rodd, from his garden pale along towards Good : Upshalls pale.

It is ordered that whereas 2 akers of Marsh was graunted to John Bingham and Bought by John Pierce. shall be layed out on this side Mʳ. Hawkins 10 goad broad towards the sea so that it be not p'juditiall to other mens lotts.

It is ordered that Nath : Duncan shall have 3 akers of land in euery diuision of about 500 akers wᵗʰin the plantation, except the diuision of the necke and this in lieu of his great lot haueing none formerly graunted him, and besides his formeʳ divisions according to p'portion with others.

It is ordered that Good : Greenway shall have leaue to set out his pale next his garden a goad farthʳ in the Commons according to a former graunt.

It is ordered that Mʳ. Withington shall haue adjoyned to his house that was Mʳ. Sensions the swamp aboue and the swamp beneath the house for which he p'omiseth to leaue out the springs for watering Cattle the Wynter tyme and to leaue the Water with out side.

Whereas Mʳ. Holman and Rich : Collicot were appoynted to see the pales of the great lotts sufficiently fenced. It is now farther ordered that they shall p'cure what is sufficiently fenced and to be payd out of their penaltyes to be leuied by the Baylif according to the former order

Mʳ. Stoughton to furnish 1 bull.
Mʳ. Minot 1 bull.
Good. Munnings 1 bull.
Mʳ. Hill 1 bull.

It is ordered that euery one that hath his cowes serued p' those bulls shall pay 12ᵈ for euery Cow.

It is ordered that the land for Clea pitts which John Binham had vse for makeing bricke shall still lye in Common for the use of the plantation and that there be loose rayles left for the Comming to the pitts. M^r. Glouer, Chr: Gibson, John Moore, John Pierce to see it layd out and dirrect where the rayles are to be left loose.—

It is also ordered that the p'tyes aboue sayd for the laying out of a sufficient high way joyneing to the Creeke for landing hay and other goods and that they appoynt Goo: Starcy to put in his pale where he hath put it too far out on the high way.

It is ordered that the land in Common vnder no former graunt, last giuen by the Court beyound the lyne from Roxbury bounds to the blew hill as it was lately rann shall be disposed as foll. Euery free man at p'sent intresseed in a hoame lot, and in the former diuident shall haue his p'priety and diuident in the new graunt according to the former rates and diuident: And in this diuident all that are not freemen that had in the former diuision a p'priety are there excluded and It is ordered that the same p'portions answerable to the former shall be sequestred and not entrenched vpon by any p'son but remaynes for the freemens power to giue to the sayd houses and inhabitants in them what quantity the freemen shall Judge fit and when and where or to any other freemen as may be. It being intended, that the medow shall be devided by it selfe and the vpland by it selfe. This Comp^rhending all to Plimouth bounds. It was further ordered the one Third of the former land sequestered, shall be cast into the diuision of the p'sent freemen who by the former rule are in the diuision to receaue each man his p'portion according to the sayd former Rule and diuision.

[39.] Mr. Hill marchant of Dorchester hath sould vnto Edward Bricke of the same Towne and to his heires for euer the p'cells foll. viz. All his hoame lot at the Necke, called or known by the name of M^r. Ludlowes necke being 4 acres more or lesse lyeing betweene the lott of M^r. Nathaniell Duncan on the East, and M^r. James Marshalls one the West, together with a p'cell off ground lyeing next vnto Squantom's necke, being a hill valued Nine acres, but taken and accepted by me William Hill for Twelue acres and Eleuen acres of medow vizt: Six acres on the one side of the sayd vpland which was alotted vnto him and fiue acres on the other side which sometimes was alotted to Thomas Marshfeild also one acre of land or there about at the end of M^r. Withingtons lott, together with the house vpon it with fiue acres of stinted Commons at the great Necke and 8 acres and 10 goads in the Cow Pasture and so on to euery fiue hundred acres according to the Towne booke. Together with all his com̄on and priualages in all the land beyound Naponset Riuer, which is 8 acres 10 goad upon euery diuision and also his p'te of the land lately granted by the Court vnto the sayd Towne according vnto the same p'portion as belongs to him as a free man to his p'sons and state according to the order of the Towne booke, and acruing to his sayd hoame lott.

This sale made The 20th of July 1638.

More Thomas Tredwell of Ipswich Sould vnto Edward Bricke of Dorchester all that house and 2 acres of land standing and being one the end of that lott next to the sea that was M^r. Theophilus willsons with it importinances and Also a p'cell of land being a hoame lott that was Thomas ffords next adjoyneing the ends of the great lotts one the one side and one the necke which was sometimes M'. Ludlows Necke one the other side beind the first lot one that necke from the footes of the great lotts and also that medow of the breadth of the sayd lot which runs towards the New ditch towards the sea and also that great lot. Among the great lot[s] conteyneing about 16 acres of land lyeing betweene Goodman Twitchills lott on the one side and M'. Parker one the other side which was once Jonathan Gilletes and also 4 acres of salt marsh neere to fox poynt which was to bee next the 6 akers graunted M'. Meinot with all the app'rtinances to be held p' ther sayd Edward Brick to him and his heirs foreū which sale was made the 20th June 1638.

October the 30th 1638. At a Generall meeteing at M'. Stoughtons there was Chosen 10 men for the ordering the affayres of the Plantation to continue for six monthes or till others shalbe Chosen whose names are vnder written.

M'. Glouer
Na : Duncan
M'. Adderton
M'. Joanes
Ch : Gibson
Jo : Philips

M'. Bates
Will. Sumner
Nicholas Vpsall
John Gapin

At the same tyme there were Chosen Rateis for the next yeere.
M'. Bates.
Roger Clap
Ch : Gibson.

Barnabee ffour
John Gapin

It was ordered that a Towne Rate should be made by them for 35 pounds.

November 14. At a Generall meeteing It is ordered that the Towne Rate for 35 pounds formerly agreed vpon shall be augmented to 40 pounds and the sayd Rate speedyly to be made by the Raters and collected by the Cunstables.

It is ordered that Ña : Duncan and M'. Aderton shall audit the accountes of the Cunstables and receiue from them all the monyes by them collected to dispose of for the Townes vse and to giue account what they haue done therein vnto the 10 men for the Tyme being at the end of the yeare when others shall be Chosen in their place.

[40.] It is further ordered that the Cunstables shall giue vp their account to the foresayd Auditors within one Month after they haue receiued the Rate with the monyes by them receiued in default whereof the sayd N. Duncan and M' Adderton shall haue power to distrayne the Cunstables for their or either of their neglects of not collecting the monyes, or not bringing in the accounts and monyes so collected.

It is ordered that M'. Adderton shall see the high wayes mended and be payed out of the first monyes receiued on the Towne Rate.

It is ordered that euery p'son that hath any Cattle shall euery spring befo' he brings them to grasse bring them to a man chosen by the plantation to marke them with the letter D on the hineder buttocke one the neere side and such p'son as shall make such marke to have for his paynes 1^d for euery head this to be done the last weeke in Aprill and whosoeuer shall not haue his Cattle thus marked they shall be subject to be impounded and for euery inhabitant of Dorchester so offending to pay 12^d for euery head.

It is ordered that if any cattle of other Townes shall trespasse on o^r Commons they shalbe impounded and pay 2^s for euery head halfe for the p'ty that doth impound them the rest to the Benefit of the plantation.

For the better Encouragement of any that shall destroy wolues It is ordered that for euery Wolfe any man shall take within Dorchester Plantation hee shall haue 20^s of the Towne for the first wolfe 15^s for the secound ; and for euery wolfe afterwards 10^s besides the Countryes pay.

For as much as the want of sufficient fence is a cause of great trouble and discontent in the plantation It is ordered that befo^{re} the 20th of March euery inhabitant that hath pale either in any Common feild or p'ticular feild or garden shall make either 5 sufficient Rayles or wale or pale or ditch, such as may keepe out swine and all sorts of Cattle, and because there is great neglect in vewing of pales and so pale lyeth still insufficient It is farther ordered that 2 men shall be Chosen by the Planters who shall view all the fences and where they find any defect shall forthwith make it sufficient, and shall goe to the p'ty whose fence it is and demaund satisfaction which if any shall refuse to make them good payment to there content It shall be lawfull for the sayd 2 men to distrayne any such offenders goods to make themselues satisfaction to the value of 3^s a day for each of their labour herein, moreouer because men are redy to say the pale is sufficient.

It is ordered that no pale be taken for sufficient except they be well set and bound and at least 4 foote aboue ground.

It is ordered that Tomsons Iland shall hence forwards be appropriated for a calues Pasture and none to put any swyne their on penalty of forfiture of such swyne the forfeiture to be taken by any freeman who is to haue one halfe and the other halfe to be to the benefitt of the Plantation.

It is ordered that all Common Corne feilds with all home lotts shall remayne only in Commons to the owner of the sayd feilds. And whosoever in the feild shall make any breach for takeing in their Corne he forth with make it vp or keepe it, or elce be subject to the penalty of pale breakeing according to an ord^r

It is ordered that the Rockie hill by M^r. Hawkins formerly put into p'prietie to the neighbours there shall still bee free for any inhabitant to fech stones for building or other use without impeachment or hinderance of any of the owners of the sayd rock according to the true intent of the first graunt.

[**41.**] *February 5 1638.* It is ordered that M^r. Israell Stoughton shall haue all his devisions of vpland aboue the Cow pasture both in the old and new graunt to be layd to his howse his farme that in the old graunt to lye next to the lyne as most remote frō the Plantation and next to his house beyond the brooke, Comonly called Mother brooks, and that in the new graunt to lye next to the 100 akers hee hath of M^r. Newberys on the same side of the Riuer the same 100 akers to begin at the lyne, and so all to ʒoe on forwards only to leaue high wayes.

February 13th. It is ordered that Alexander Miller shall haue sixe akers fo his great lott next to the 6 aker lotts.

It is ordered that the Cow pasture and all the land in and about the same shalbe measured out and that is free for any that haue p'prietie there to take that in, and that both the Cow pasture and such p'prietie as doth still lye in Commons shalbe be stinted p' the 10 men.

It is ordered that eūy p'son which puts in any Cattle of what kind so eū into the great neck shall giue a note of how many of each sort hee puts in, vnto Roger Clap who shall haue a note of eūy mans p'portion which hee is to put in and if any bee found by driuing the neck or otherwise to put in more then his stint shall forfeit twentie shillings for eūy Cowe or other Cattle so put in aboue his stint p'portionably, such Cattle to be bee impounded till the money be payd the sayd Roger Clap to haue one quarter p'te of all forfeitures in this kind, the rest to bee for the Benefitt of the Plantation.

It is ordered that M^r. Clarke shall haue libertie to take in fower goads of land next his pale towards the meeting howse which is neere the barne that was lately M^r. Trobridgs the breadth to bee as his pale now stands.

Williā Clarke hath made sales of one aker 1 quarter, and 30 goads of land at the great neck (which he had by agreement frō M^r. Williā Hill after the devision) vnto Christoū Gibson.

It is ordered that Williā Sumner shall have fower akers of vpland next to Good: Hull, M^r. Blake and Tho: millet neere the 6 aker lot which was for so much Jo: Binhā was to haue to make vp his great lott.

It is ordered that M^r. Butler and Jo: Wiswall are Chosen to looke to the fences of all hoame lotts and to see them sufficient according to a former order for fence.

Edward Bricke and Jo: Holland are Chosen to looke to the pales of the great lotts the 6 aker lotts and the captyne's necke, and to see them sufficient according to the order for fence.

It is ordered that no inhabitant of Dorchester shall keepe any swyne but within his own p'ptye or vnder a herdsman 2 miles from any Corne feild vnder penalty of Two Shill: for every hogg taken goeing about the Plantation either p' the Baylif or any planter within the Towne contrary to this order: and also any swyne so taken to pay dammige, the dammige to be vewed and Judged by 2 neighbors, and the p'tye that takes any such swyne to impound them or keepe them till the owners of the swyne shall make full satisfaction, if the sayd owners shall refuse to make payment of the sayd forfeiture and dammige within three dayes it shall be lawfull for the p'ty that hath taken vp such hoggs with the helpe of 2

Neighbors to prize and sell one [42.] or more of them to make himself satisfaction, and deliuer the rest of the mony to the own[r] of the hoggs this order to take effect from the first of Aprill next and to Continue till all the Indian Corne be taken in.

It is farther ordered that no swyne shall be kept at the great necke on payne of five shill. to be levyed p' distresse

It is ordered that Good. Deeble shall be baylif for this yeere to execute and haue pay for his labor according to the order of the last yeare.

It is ordered that Jo: Maudsly and Nicholas Wood shall keepe the Cowes for this yeere in the ordinary Cow pasture, and to keepe them from the 15th Day of Aprill next to the first of November next the sayd keepers to blow their horne at fyue of the clocke in the morneing at Joseph Pharneworth and so along the Towne till he come to M[r]. Meinots, and every man one the North side of the Towne to bring their Cowes befo[r] the meeteing house the Rest to bring their Cowes beyound M[r]. Stoughtons dore or elce the keep's to driue away the heard, and not to stay for the rest — The sayd keepers to haue for their hier fiue shill. viij[d] for each Cow and for their wages, and the bulls to haue their paym[t] ⅓ at first putting forth another ⅓ at halfe the tyme the rest at the end of the tyme. Provided that all that put in Cowes to keepe if they take them away agayne befo[r] halfe the tyme shall for halfe the tyme; if they take them away after halfe the tyme they must pay for the whole. If the heardsmen shall not driue away the Cattle within one hower of their first blowing the horne, they shalbe subject to a fyne to be layd on them at the discretion of the 10 men.

Tho: Wiswool is appoynted to marke all the Cattle according to a former order to that purpose.

The great lotts to be stinted 6 akers a Cow, the medow and 8 akers the like, the 20 aker Lotts at 10 akers a Cow.

There was chosen these 7 men vnderwritten for 6 moneths or till other be Chosen to order all the affaires of the plantation, and to haue full power to act and determine any thing for the good of the plantation according to their discretion, except in graunting land.

M[r]. Glouer	M[r]. Joanes
M[r]. Haukins	Jo: Wiswall
M[r]. Duncan	Jo: Pierce
M[r]. Aderton.	

It is ordered that whereas there was 8[d] a Cow alowed for bull money to be 10[d] p' the Cow keepers for this yeere who were to pay that to the seu[r]all men that put in bulls the sayd pay shalbe now augmented to 12[d] a Cow, and the moneys to be gathered p' the sayd Cow keep'rs forthwith when they receiue the first pay for the Cowes the money being Rc[d] they are to pay that in to M[r]. Aderton for the men who ingage themselues to any of the p'ties that put in buls, the Cow keep[rs] with the money they bring in to Treasur[r] a note of those which Refuse or neglect to pay

M[r]. Glouer, M[r]. Aderton, Willia͂ Somner, Jo Wiswol are instructed with the first opportunitie to take a full veiu of the * *

DORCHESTER TOWN RECORDS. 39

* * * ther pt may be fitt for the plantation [43.] or how that may bee otherwyse vsefull.

It is ordered the 20th of May 1639, that there shalbe a rent of 20^{li} yeerely foreu^r imposed vpon Tomsons Iland to bee payd p' eūy p'son that hath p'prtie in the said Iland according to the p'portion that any such p'son shall frō tyme to tyme inioy and posesse there, and this towards the mayntenance of a schoole in Dorchest^r this rent of 20^{li} yeerly to bee payd to such a schoolemaster as shall vndertake to teach english latin and othe^r tongues, and also writing the sayd schoolemaster to bee chosen frō tyme to tyme p' the freemen and that is left to the discretion of the elders and the 7 men for the tyme beeing whether maydes shalbe taught with the boyes or not. For the levying this 20^{li} yeerely frō the p'ticuler p'sons that ought to pay that according to this order. It is farther ordered that somme man shalbe appoynted p' the 7 men for the tyme beeing to Receiue that and on refusall to levye that p' distresse, and not fynding distresse such p'son as so refuseth payment shall forfeit the land he hath in p'prietie in the sayd Island.

Whereas the order for fence last made is found defectiue in regard of the veiuers having but 3^s. a day for seeing the fence sufficient by which meanes there is no execution of the sayd order. It is therefore farther ordered for the better execution of the former order that theise veiuers vnderwritten are appoynted to each feild to see where they fynd any defect, and to p^{r}sent the defect to M^r. Atherton who hath power giuen him to levie p' distresse 2^s. 6^d. on eūy goad where any pale shalbe found defectiue for the first offence in this kind and whoseū shalbe found defectiue a second tyme to levie p' distresse 5 [s.] on each goad. This order to take effect 15th July.

Jo: wiswoll to veiu the feild next his howse
Roger Clap to veiu the feild next him
Jos: Pharneworth the feild next him
Mr Joanes the feild next him
Williā Somner the feild next him
M^r. Glouer, and M^r. Holman to veiu the great lots 6 aker lotts and Capt^s. neck

John Hull is to have 1 aker and half of marsh at M^r. Hawkins neck in leiu of Calues pasture.

It is ordered that no man shall mow any grasse on Tomsons Iland on penaltie of 20^s for eūy dayes mow, and that all that put Calues there shall pay towards the keep^{rs} p'portionably to the Calves they put in.

October 31th 1639. Williā Barber hath made sales of his howse vnto mathew Smith which he desireth to haue recorded.

Thomas Hatch hath made sales vnto John Phillips of Dorchester one great lott with a howse on that 16 akers within and without pale also 6 akers of meddow 4 on this side and 2 akers on the other side Neponset, and all his Comōns except that in the neck.

[44.] Henery Kibbie of Dorchest bought his howse and about an aker of Upland on the North side, and about an aker of Upland and meddow on the south side adioyning to his sayd howse of

Nicholas Butler of Dorchester, and also all the Wood growing or that shall grow on the Comons belonging to the whō Lott wch was M^r. Parkers according to a deed made p' Nicholas Butler vnto the sayd Kibbie of the 22th day of the 8th moneth 1639 as hereunto is Wittnesse Thomas Joanes.

It is ordered that John Pope shall have 2 akers of marsh towards foxe poynt in lew of some land taken frō him for making the way to the neck.

It is ordered at a Generall meeteing in January that the great Lotts without the pale shall run 8 score Rodds frō the pale into the Woods the one halfe neerest the Towne to be allowed 4 Rood fo^r a hie way the rest of the Lotts to haue noe alowance for a high way

It is ordered that Robert Pierce, shall be a Commoner.

It is ordered that M^r. Waterhouse shall be dispenced with concerneing that Clause of the order in the Charge of Twenty pounds yeerly, rent to be payd for Tomsons Iland towards the skoole: where he is bound to teach to write it shalbe left to his liberty in that poynt of teaching to write, only to doe what he can conveniently therein.

It is ordered that Henery Way, Brey Wilkeins, **Richard** Leeds shall take their portion in Tomsons Iland and haue also liberty to buy of any others any greater portion to the value of 9 akers to Joyne with their owne at a convenient place for fishing. Provided that they set forward fishing and also doe satisfie the yeerely rent Charge imposed on that Iland towards the mayntanance of a skoole according to the order made to that purpose, and according to the Number of the akers they shall make imployment of. Provided also that they make so sufficient a fence about their Lands so taken into p'priety that they shall make good any dammage that shall come to any mans cattle through the default of such fence.

There is graunted to Robert Deeble 1 akre of Land joyning to his owne hoame lott and next M^r. Addertons towards the dead swamp in leaueing the wood to the Towne.

M^r. Glouer is alowed to take on of his divisions of Land beyond Naponset next his Cowhouse by the fresh marsh.

[**45.**] It is ordered that the 3 first devisions of land next the mill beyond Naponset riuer shall be devided as one devision to the whole Plantation and put into severall feilds as nightbors shall agree together more or lesse and all the rest of the land there and also on this side the Riuer except the Cow pasture when it shall be devided to be put likewise into severall feilds, as nightbors shall agree more or lesse together.

It is ordered that Richard Collicot shall possese the 40 akers of land which he hath taken in beyond the Riuer in p'te of his devisions there.

Richard Leids and Jeoffry turner haue the 3 akers 3 quarters and 8 Rodes of Comons which was belonging to W^m. Preston devided betwixt them in halfe as they purchased that on each devision.

Richard Leids hath half an aker Comons on each devision of Comons of that which was John whetcome which hee purchased.

It is ordered that no p'son what soeuer shall fell any trees within Dorchester [that] is marked for the bounds of any land either in p'priety or Commons on penalty of 20 shilling for every tree so felled to be levied by distresse.

It is ordered that if any inhabitant of Dorchester shall put any hoggs on the great necke, or any mans hoggs be found there they shall be impounded p' the Baylif or any free man and pay 2 shill. for every hogg ther taken to be levied by distresse the sayd pennalty to be halfe for him that takes vp such hoggs the rest to be for the vse of plantation.

It is ordered that M^r. Joanes shall haue 1 aker of land nere his owne in leiu of an aker which hee bought of M^r. Trobridge which was appoynted him neere the burying place.

It is ordered that those which bring not in their notes to be registred about the transcript of lands before the next court shalbe loyable to any such fyne as shalbe imposed p' the Court for not bringing in the sayd transcript according to order of Court those which haue brought in the[ir] notes to bee free.

It is ordered that Mr. Blake shall haue one aker of land next his eight aker lott in leiu of 1 aker was giuen him neere the burying place.

It is ordered that M^r. Glover, M^r. Holman, John Phillips shall lay out the high wayes according to order of court.

It is ordered that the Raters shall make a Rate of 40^{li} for the Paym^t of Debts and other things to be done for the good of the Plantation.

It is ordered that M^r. Aderton and John Wiswall shall p'cure wheeles to be made and Carriedge to mount the peeces that are at M^r. Hawkins by the sea and to cause them to be mounted and also the drake at M^r. Stoughtons to be mounted the charge to be payd out of the 40^{li} rate.

[**46.**] It is ordered that the 30^{li} Rate made last yeere for the measureing the land beyond the Riuer shall be reduced to 15^{li}.

It is ordered that Natha: Duncan, M^r. Aderton shall take accō: of the 4 barreles of powder that were sold and shall take the money and buy as much powder with it as they can p'cure from the first shipps that will sell any.

It is ordered that no man shall fell any trees in the Commons within Dorchester neithe^r for Timber nor wood to make sales of without the plantation, nor any Timb^r to build houses on penalty of the losse of their labour and 10 shill: for every tree so felled to be levied by distresse.

It is ordered that no p'son that is not a Commone^r within Dorchester shall fell any trees for Timber on pennalty of 5^s for every tree so felled to be leuied by distresse.

It is ordered that M^r. Joanes and W^m. Sommer shall lay out 4 akers of marsh at the neck for M^r. Aderton which was Jo: Kingsleys and 3 akers for M^r. Withington which was mathias Sensions.

It is ordered that Good: Tolmans howse bee appoynted for Receiuing any goods that shalbe brought in whereof the owner is not knowen.

It is ordered that th' order made last yeere about Swyne bee Continued only the Clawse for keeping p' keep' 2 miles fro any Corne feild to be reduced to halfe a mile.

It is ordered that all that haue great lotts shall p' the 25th m^{ch} fence in the ends and the hither side to wards the woods with 5 Rayles or other sufficient fence on payne of 5^s to bee levied p' distresse for eūry goad found defectiue.

It is ordered that Robert Deeble is to be Continued baylif for the yeere foll. with the same power according to the order of the former yeere.

Aprill 1st 1640. It is ordered that no hoggs within 12^s price shall be suffered to goe out of any mans p'prietie on payne of 12^d for eūry within that price found on the Comons and all other hogs shalbe sufficiently yoaked and Ringed or bee vnder the hand of a sufficient keep' on payne of 12^d for every hogg found in the Comons Contrary to this order the sayd fyne to bee levied by distresse and half thereof to bee for any freeman that shall take vp such hoggs the Rest to be for the vse of the towne this order to take effect this p^{e}sent day.

Richard Lyppingcot is Chosen to keepe the pound to haue 2^d for impounding 1 hogg alone and but 1^d if he impound more together and to haue for impounding other cattle according to the order of the last yeere.

It is ordered that all the fence in the hoame lotts neere the towne shalbe made fast sufficiently within 4 dayes on payne of fyue shillings for eūry goad found defectiue and the great lotts to be likewise sufficiently fenced by the 8th of this moneth on the same penaltie of 5^s a Rodd to bee levied p' distresse.

[47.] It is ordered that no man shall put any Cattle on the great neck till the 15th of this moneth on payne of 12^d. for eūry beast found their befo^r that day to bee levied p' distresse.

It is ordered that Thomas Dickerman, Henry Wright and Thomas Sampford shall haue each of them one aker and halfe of marsh in M^r. Hawkins neck which was formerly granted them and not booked.

June 8th 1640. John Holland hath sould unto M^r. mathers all his Commons at the great neck which is eight akers 3 qu^{tr} 79 Rodes beeing his owne p'portion of right there, and also Robt Elwells which he purchased.

For as much as former neglects of lookeing to high wayes hath beene p^{e}juditiall to the Plantation in diuers respects. It is therefo^r ordered that hence forth there shall be yeerely Chosen 2 officers by the name of supveysors of high wayes who shall ouer see and p'cure the makeing or amending such high wayes as are defectiue within the plantation, and to that purpose shall haue power to take any mans teeme or seruants or other workmen or mony, to the effecting of such worke as they shall haue to doe, p'portionablely to such mens portions of lands where such wayes lye and so farre as they are bound to be Chargeable to such workes; and whosoeuer shall refuse to afford such helpe as shall be required p' the sup'-visours as aboue sayd shall be loyable to the pennalty of 3^s 6^d for a mans worke a day so refuseing and 6 8ᵈ for refuseing to helpe with a Teeme to be levied p' distresse a record to be kepte and deliuiered vp supervisors to paye 5ˢ for euery neglect of orders for vse of Towne.

John Eales Junior and George * * are to be Cow keepʳˢ this yeere, and to haue 5ˢ a Cow, and to keep the for the tyme and other Circumstances according to the order of the last yeere

29ᵗʰ 7 mo 1640. there was granted vnto John Eells a small p'cell of vpland ground Lyeinge betweene his marsh and Mʳ. Hawkins ground a Little belowe his house

28 of 8 mo. 1640. mᵈ that John Eells of Dorchester in new England hath sould vnto nathaniell Patten now of Dorchester afforesaid all his Dwellinge houses and other outhouseinge thereto belongeinge with all his Lands in p'priety or comon, and all other appurtenances thereto app'taineinge in witnes whereof I haue herevnto put my hand the daye aboue said

JOHN EELLS

21 of vltmo 1640 Oliuer Purchase hath sould vnto Tho Swift 2 acres in the First Fresh marsh the daye and yeare aboue said.

[**48.**] *Septemb. 29: 1639:* Mʳ. Tho: Clerke: hath sould vnto Henry Wᵗʰingtō : all his Comons at the great necke : at Squantum : which Late he purchased of William Read : beinge ffour acers.

p' THO: CLARKE.

Octob. 20: 1639: William Clerke hath sould vnto Henry Withingtō all his Land at Squantum necke which he Lately purchased of Mʳ. Hill which he doth vphold to be 7 akres and if it Fall short of so much he is to abate of what he hath receaued after 20ˢ the acre

by me WILLIAM CLARK.

mᵈ — that vpon Februaire 22 : 1638 : John Eells sould vnto mʳ mather all his Land in that portiō of Land Called Dorchester necke which is recorded in the Deuision to be 5 acres ½ 20 Rods : mᵈ that upon the 26 Daye of Septemb. 1639 Mʳ. Samuell Newman sould vnto Mʳ. Mather : all his Land in that portiō of Land Called Dorchester necke which is the Deuisiō belonginge to the house that Late was Mʳ. Witchffeilds : beinge as is Recorded in the 36 page of this booke : 3 acres 3 quart 20 rods.

mᵈ That these 2 Last Records should haue beene placed the one in page 41 the other in page 44 had they not then beene Forgotten,

21 10 mo: 1639. mᵈ That the Daye aboue written Dauid Sellecke sould vnto Mʳ. Thᵒ. makepeace 16 acres of Land Lyeing and bounded accordinge to a deed beareinge Date with these pʳsents.

August the 26ᵗʰ 1639. William Read hath sold vnto Thomas

Clarke his Dwellinge house with the grounde behinde it which is 4 acors and likewise 4 acors of comones at Squantum necke; 6 acores 46 Rode at the necke of land a persell of medow 10 acors more or lese as the fence now standes by the necke of lande 3 acors of grounde at the six acors lottes which were Ainciently John Millers: with all the Comines that belounges to mee and likewise the Comenes which belounges to John Millers lott beinge 6 acores and 46 Rode of both in euery deuision and two acores of medow at the second fresh marsh.

WILLIAM **W** READES marke.

[**49.**] The 1ᵗ of February 1641 there was Chosen the 7 men whose names are vnder written to order the Affayres of the Plantation and to haue power according to the former order as was giuen to the 7 men then beeing

    Nathaniel Duncan
    Sargeant Atherton
    Mʳ. Clarke
    Richard Collicot
    John Holland
    Roger Clap
    John Pierce.

The same day the Elders Mʳ. Stoughton and Mʳ. Glouer are intrusted p' the towne to sett Tomsons Iland att a Rent for the best Benefitt of the schoole.

Theise orders vnderwritten should haue been in order recorded aboue that which is aboue written as the dates Doe witnes but for some reasons it was otherwise.

19 11 mo Anno Dm. 1640. It is ordered that, no p'son or p'sons that is not a Commoner within Dorchester shall Fell any tree or trees for Timber on penalty of 5ˢ for euery tree so Felled to be Leuied by Distresse.

It is ordered that hencefforth it shall not be Lawfull For any p'son or p'sons to Fell or take from the Comons in Dorchester as in their owne Comon Right or by waye of buyinge or purchase any Timber or Wood to sell or Carry out of Dorchester Plantatiō into any other place to be imployed, vsed or spent out of the Plantatiō vnder the penalty for Euery tree or Tunn of Timber he shall take and Carry thence 10ˢ to be Leuied by Distresse.

Whereas there hath been and also is at this p'sent much wood Fit for Fewel lyeinge and rotinge upō the Comons in Dorchester, to the Losse thereof and also to the p'uidce of the Pasture there and yet notwithstandinge there is much Fellinge of Timber and wood For Fewell and Fyreinge, it is thereffore ordered that hence Forth it shall not be Lawful ffor any p'rson to Fell any manner of wood vpon the Comons in Dorchester for Fewell or Fyreinge at any Tyme within the space of 12 monthes From the date of theise pᵉsents vnder the penalty of 5ˢ for euery tree they shall Fell to be Leuied by distresse for the vse of the Towne.

1 of 1 mo 1641. It is ordered that wheras there are Certaine

Lotts lyeing and beinge within the Fence of the great Lotts and beare no share at the side nor End Fence that they shall From hence Forth be Lyable to beare theire p' portiō in the Comon side Fence which those that haue beene burdened with it; hitherto and that Bro. Holman & Colecot shall veiwe those Lotts and appoint them how much and where they shall make such Fence.

And Further that all the Fences about the great Lotts shall sufficiently be made vp with good railes or Pailes well bound at or before the 20th of this instant month at the Furthest upō paine of 2ˢ for euery goad that is Faulty to be Leuied by Distresse and we appoint our brethren before named to veiwe them.

It is ordered that all the Fences about the home Lotts shall sufficiently be made vp with good Railes or Pailes well bound before the 20th of this instant month vpō payne of 2ˢ for euery goad that is Faulty and we appoint our Brethren Richard Bar. Fawer. Tho. wiswall. Hope Foster to vewe them.

[50.] It is ordered that the great and Little neckes of Land shalbe kept Fast vntill the 23th of Aprill and that what soeuer Cattell shall be Found there at any before that Daye shall be impounded by any Freeman and the owner to paye 6ᵈ for the first Trespasse and xijᵈ. for the 2ᵈ and to be Augmented and agravated accordinge to the offence from tyme to tyme to be Leaued by distresse the one halfe to the impounder and the other for the vse of the Towne.

It. that whosoever shall Fell any of those trees now standinge behinde Mʳ. Minott House marked with a great S being preserued for shade trees for Cattell in Sommer Tyme shall paye for Euery tree so Felled 10ˢ to be Leuied by Distresse for the Townes vse:

It is ordered that whosoever shall put any Cattell vpō the necke of Land this yeare 1641 : shall upō the 23th of Aprill next or vpō some daye after when they shall put such Cattell or horses or mares vpon the necke, giue in a note in writinge vnto Hopestill Foster appoynted to receaue them of the number of the heades they put in and what Land they put in for, and alsoe that H Foster shall haue power to keepe those notes and to giue publike notice vpō some Lecture Daye that all the inhabitants that haue any Cattell horses or mares there maie come at such tyme as shall be appointed them to Driue the necke and also to claim their owne Cattell to the intent that such as are Delinquent Either in haueing more than their stint there or haueinge not giuen in their note accordinge to the p'misses maie be Found out and whosoever shall offend in the p'misses shall paye 5ˢ for Euery head in p'ticuler for the First offence to be Leuied by Destresse ffor the vse of the Towne, and whosoever shall not come or sende accordinge to the publicke notice giuen shall haue his Cattel impounded and pay 2ˢ 6ᵈ for the First offence beside the Pound chardge to be Leuied by Distresse for the vse of the Towne.

It is ordered that all the inhabitants of Dorchester shall at or before the 22th of this instant march sufficiently Ringe and yoke all their Hogges and other swine and that it shall be lawffull ffor Bayliffe of the towne or any ffreeman whosoeuer of the Towne after the Daye afforesaid to take and to impound any such Hogges or other swine as he or they shall Find vpon the Comons of Dorchester vnringed or vnyoked from tyme to tyme and the owners to Paye for euery Hogge or other swine so impounded 8^d beside the pounde Chardge the one halffe to the impounder and the other to the vse of the towne to be Leuied by Destresse p'vided that if there be any Liuinge neare vnto any Clam bankes where they would haue their hogges to Clam they shall Comitt them vnto the handes of a keep' to driue them to the banke and there attend them and to bringe them backe vnto their Coates or pounds where they keepe such swine and if any such swine be Found not vnder the hands of a keep' and vnringed and vnyoked shalbe Lyable vnto the penalty exp^{r}ssed in the p^{e}misses, the order of yoakinge to continue vntil Indian Haruest and ringinge, in regard of the sad experience we haue of the hurt is Done in and about the Towne and Like to be it is to continue all the yeare.

12 of 1 mo. 1641. It is ordered that Andrew Pitcher shall make 18 Rod of a Crosse Fence that is to goe from the Riuer vpward: in Considerō of his Fence that he was to make for the Land giuen him and besides that soe much as Falls to him by reason of his Lot amonge the rest of his neighbours and to Doe it before the 16 of aprill next vpō paine of 16^d a rod for neglect, the head of the Longe side Fence to begin at the corner of the great Lotts and Allexander Bradfford to be the ffirst.

M^r. Sumner	2		Wm Blake	4
John Phillips	3		Ricd Leeds	5
Tho: Millet	6		Andrew Pitcher	8
John Smith	7		Jonas Humphrey	9
nicho vpsal	10	**[51.]**	Henry Waye	12
Tho. Tileston	11		Aron Waye	13

Braye wilkns 14. the fine is that euery 3 acres is to make 2 Rods of fence also the marsh Land is to bee added to the vpland as Followes

M^r. Howard 4 acre M^r. makepeace 4: John Phillips 4: all to be reckoned for 15 of vpland and so to beare Fence.

It is ordered that they shall paye vnto them that haue set vp the Fence for so much as is to be paid For after 20^d the rod for so we thinke such worke was worth when it was Done.

Jo Holman) are appointed
Jo Pope) ouerseers.

17 of ii mo. 1641. It is ordered that the waye through the great Lots within Paile and without shall be cleared by the 22th of the ii mo. 1641 vpon paine of 12^d for euery tree that shall not be remoued beside the Cor^t order in that case p'vided to be Leuied by Destresse.

It that no p'son or p'sons whosoeuer shall send Forth any Cowes or other Cattell vnto the Cow walke or any p't thereof vnder the hand of any keep' there to Feed vntil the 3^d of the 3^d mo: 1642 (except the towne please to send Forth the heard) vpō paine of 2ˢ for euery head that shall be so sent Forth ffor the First Trespàsse and the 2ᵈ to be agravated by the Discretiō of the 7 men for the tyme beinge the penalty to be vnto any Free man that shall impound any Cattell offendinge against the pᵉmisses: to be Leuied by Distresse.

It is ordered that the Freemen of Dorchester From tyme to tyme yearely at the End of 6 months accordinge to a Former order shall Elect and choose their 7 men without delaye: and in case of Deffault therein it shalbe Lawffull For the 7 men to giue in an accompt of their seruice and to Laye Downe their place.

It. That the Bayliffe for the tyme beinge and so From tyme to tyme hereafter shall make speedy and Faithfull executiō of all busnesses comitted to him vpō paine of 10ˢ to be forfeited For euery Trespasse and also shall giue in a Faithfull accompt vpō Demand vpon paine of the foresaid penalty to the vse of the towne.

Whereas there are Diuers that haue Lotts granted them in the 3ᵈ Fresh marsh beyond mʳ. Stoughtons Farme who now Desire to haue it Laid out ffor them it is ordered that it shalbe Done with what conuenience and expeditiō it maie and For that end we appoint Bro. Holman and bro. Holland to Do it.

9th of the First: 42 Wheareas wee haue hade suffithente experyance of the hurte and damedge that hath bine to the hearde by Reason of the greatnes there of and the hurte that is done by steers and oxen to millch Cattle

It is therefore ordered that there shall noe barren Cattle goe with the Cowes for this p'sente yeare excepte it bee younge hefferes which are like to take the Bull: and no other heard nor stray Cattle horse or mares shall goe within the Cow pastor vpon penalty of 2ˢ for euery head so found to be leuied by destresse.

It is ordered that noe Cattle shall goe in or vpon the Comons of Dorchester vntile the 15ᵗʰ day of the 2ᵗʰ mo: next: and that it shall bee lafull for the Baylife or any freemen of the towne to take and Impound any such Cattle founde vpon the Comones before the day aforesaide and the owners to pay for euery heade soe Impounded 12ᵈ the one halfe to go to the Impounder and the other halfe to the vse of the towne: this order to begine the 20ᵗʰ of this Instant.

[**52.**] It is ordered that the Inhabutance of Dorchester shall suffecyently Ringe and youcke there swine at or before the 22ᵗʰ of this Instante: and that noe piges vnder a quorter old shall goe Abroad therefore it shall be lawfull for the Baylefe or any freemen of the towne After the day Afore saide to take and Impound any swine that shall bee founde defectiue heere in vpon the Comons of Dorchester and the owners to pay for euery swine 8ᵈ besides the pound charges the on half to bee for the Impounder the other halfe to the towne to be leuied by destresse. this order of yoackeinge to bee continued till Indean haruest bee ein.

The order Abought Fenceinge is to Continue as it weare the last yeare those that are chosen to see the execttion of it are theies.

Bro: Smith } are for the great lottes and Captines necke.
Bro: Hull

Bro: Gibson for the lottes behinde his house.
Bro: Farnworth for the feild behinde his house.
Bro: Bates for the feild behinde his house.
Bro: Backer for the feild by his house.
The Order Abought the necke to Continue in al thinges as it were the last yeare.

The 15th of the first 1642. Agreed by A towne meetinge that Richard Hawes shuld haue one acere of grownde aded to his first deuision in the Cow wolke in consideration of on acore that were giuen him Aboue the bureinge place which hee is not to haue now.

Agreed at the same meeting that Brother Whight shuld haue one Acore aded to his First deuision in Consideration of on acore that he shuld A hade Aboue the bureinge Place which now he is not to haue.

Agreed by a towne meeteinge Abought the 10th mo 1641 that Thomas Clarke shuld haue eaight acors of ground laide out at the ends of his 8 acore lottes p'rouided that it may bee done with out any damedge to the highway in Consideration of eaight acors of ground formerly giuen to Robart loucke whose Alottmentes he bought: the towne hath Apoynted to lay it out

    Thomas Jones;   Roger Clape
    Christopher gibson: nico: Upshall

Agreed In A towne meeting that Thomas Clarke shall haue one acore quarter of ground aded to his first deuision in the Cow paster in Consederation of A highway that leyes through his 8 acore lottes which were not Allowed for before.

[53.] *The 4th of the 2th 1642.* George Proctor is Chosen Balife for this p'sente yeare.

Wheare as there are Diuers cattle that are Vn Rulley not apt to bee pounded neither Can bee driuen by on man. It is therfor Ordered that any such Cattle Trancegresseinge Aganst any towne order that The Owneres thereof shall pay the Balife his dutyes Although the Cattle are not Impounded (prouided that the Balife goes and acquantes the Owneres at the time that they Trancegresse) but if the Owneres of the Cattle shall Refuse to pay the baylife: Then it shall be lawfull for him to take one man or more as occasion may Requier to helpe him to driue thoes cattle to the pound and the Owners shall pay the fine and all the Charge of thoes men helpeinge of him and this to be leueyed by destrese.

md That I John Wiswall of Dorchester haue sould vnto Christopher Gibson of the same towne 6 acres of medowe beyond naponset Lyeinge at the mouth of M^r. Huchinsō Creeke beinge the 76 Lot as it is recorded Wm. Rockwell Lyinge on the one side and goodman Hatch on the other.

                             p' me JOHN WISWALL
                                24 of 3 mo 1642.

Agreemente maide betwine John Pope and Christopher Gibson Aboute the Exchange of land, John Pope is to haue the great lott of Christofer Gibson with in the pale Containeing ten acors more or lese : which lyes on the south side of the saide John Pope, with the house wood and timber ; except some woode that is Cut out and some wood that lies in the boundes for the feyor.

And the said Christofer Gibson is to haue all John Popes propriety without the peale excepte Fourty Roodes Aioyneinge to the fence Containeing nineteene Acores and three quarters bee it more or lese which 40 roods hee is to haue for euer ; and the parsell of meddow at the est end of M^r. Israell Stoughtons Lott containing one Acore more or les duering life of Christofer Gibson, the saide John Pope is to haue the old wood that is downe or may be blowne downe Twenty Roodes from the fence and hee is to haue six years to take it Away in and he is to haue the goeinge of Six swine for six yeares after the 29th Septemb next 1642 : for the afore said land.

Memorand Christopher Gibson hath Exchanged with John Phillips the end of his great lott that lyeth without pale that lyeth to John Phillips great lots end that was Hatches for five accres that he hath from John Phillips in the necke of land

the mrke of $\mathcal{A}$ JOHN PHILLIPS.
CHRISTOF GIBSON.

7th of the 4th 1642. Agreed at A towne meeting that Mr Olleuer shuld Rune A head loyne at the heade of brantree Boundes And then to Run the line vp in to the Countrey ffor the layinge out the new grante : there is Apyonted to goe with him Sergante Atherton : Bro : Wickes and Bro : Breake.

Agreed at the same meetinge that in the layinge out of the necke of land they are to begine at the north side of the necke and lay that out First : namely of the north side of the way that is laide out : and when that is laide out ther to begine at the south side of the way and soe forward : that if any land be lefte it may ly at the firthest poynt toward the Castle : and M^r. Olleuer, Bro. Jones and Bro. Wickes are for to giue such Allowance for swampes as they in there wisdome shall think meete and firther it is Agreed that euery lott is to haue an equale p'porssion in the little necke ; namely A little lott as much as A greate, and are to be laide out accordinge to there lott in the great : and are likewise to Begine on the north [side].

[54.] *The 28th of the First 1642.* Agreed By a Towne Meetinge that John Phillipes shuld haue one Acore of grounde in the Comones neare his Owne Lotte in Consideration thereof hee is willing to Allow A way of one Roode and halfe Broade throw his lotte from pine necke vp Into the woodes :

The 18th of the 5th mo : 1642. By a towne meeteinge. It is Ordered that all Oregenale lottes In the necke of Land shall haue their Voates Abought planteinge the Necke : & If any haue bought one : two or three more or les : they shall haue soe many Voates as they haue lottes.

Whereas it were formerly Ordered that when the necke of Land Comes to be planted : if they Can not all Agree to plante then

the minor parte shall fence Aganst the maior: It is now Firther
Agreed that After the Voate is past if any of the minor will doe
as the maior doth they may haue that liborty without mainetayne-
inge any p'te of the fence with the minor:

It were this day Voated whether the necke of land shold be
planted or Fead: and there were sixty fiue Voates for planteinge
and Twenty eaight Voates for Feadinge.

The 23th of the 5th mo: 1642. ordered by the 7 men.

In Regard it is Very P'beble that many of the bounde stake bee
Twixte mens lottes may be put doune by Cattele In the diuissions
In the Cowe pasture; for the Avoyedinge therefore of futer Truble
It is ordered that all that haue lottes in the Cowe pasture shall
vpon the First Fourth day of the Eaight month by nine of the
Clocke in the morneing goe to his lott; the first deuission First and
soe to the seconde and thirde that soe men may together Agree
About the makeinege shure the bounde stakes: and all such
p'sones that neglecte the Comeinge accordinge to this order shall
pay Two shillinges to be leueyed by destres: The one halfe to the
vse of The Towne and the other halfe to thoes that doe justly
suffer by ther not Comeinge.

It is Ordered that noe Inhabitante of Dorchester shall mowe Any
grase In the medowes that are still Com̄ones either salte or ffresh
marsh before the Last of the Fith month: neither shall any haue
Aboue on mower vpon A day one the Com̄ones: and whosoever
shall Offende here In shall pay Fiue shillings for euery dayes
moweinge.

Bro. Atherton and Bro. Deyer are Apoynted to lay out on acor
of Ground For John Capen which were granted to William Lane In
the lew of the Calfes pasture.

Bro: Holland and Bro: Gibson are Apoynted to lay out Two
accores of ground at M^r. Hakines necke For Thomas Clarke which
were giuen unto Robarte Loke In the Booke:

Bro: Gibson and Tho: Clarke are apoynted to lay out Foure
accores of grounde at M^r. Hakines necke ffor Bro: John Holland:

[55.] The thirde of the sixt month 1642 there were Chosen 7
men whose names are heare vnder wrighten: To Order the Affaires
of the Plantation and to haue power acordinge to the former Order
as was giuen to the 7 men then Beinge:

    M^r. John Glouer: Bro: Gibson:
    Bro: Bricke: Bro: Upshall:
    Ensigne Holman: Thomas Clarke
    Bro: m^r. Bates:

The 18 of the 10 month 1642. Whereas it hath beene obserued
diuerse tymes, in our general Towne meetinge, that som Confusion and disorder hath happened in the agitation of our publicke
matters and plantation affaires, by reason that men haue used
thire libertye to p'pound theere matters to the Plantation without
any fore knoledge of the seauen men, and theere matters haue beene
so followed that diuerse things haue beene spoken of and few
matters haue beene issued by reason that new matters haue beene

vpsterted whyles a former hath beene in hearinge and so much tyme spent and lytle worke don, and moreouer the spirits of som men trobled and offended by reason that thire matters Could not be hearde, it is thearefore ordered by the 7 men that al matters and questions which any man hath to be agitated and Petions to be answered by the Plantation shall first be brought to the 7 men or to som tow or more of them, and by them Consydered and orderly p^{r}sented to the plantation who shal follow the busines, together with the Plantation, without any interruption, by any matters incerted, to the Conclusion and determynation theareof, except it be vnreasonably refused by the 7 men otherwyse euery person ofending against this order shal forfeyt for the same syx pence for euery such offenc to be leuyed by distresse for the use of the towne.

It is ordered that if any man haue in his hand any goods of his neybors, borrowed, found, or strayde, aboue the value of 8^d wheareof he knoeth not the owner, he shal repaire to the Constable of the towne and giue him information theareof who is also heareby ordered to record the same in a booke kept of porpese, that so who shal haue any such goods missinge may repaire to the Constable to make inquyry who fynding the true owner the Constable shal giue order for the restoration theareof, and if it be kept aboue three weekes without such information giuen he shal be Counted an offender, and if the owner be not found he shal forfeyt the same thing vnto the towne p'vyeded it be not aboue the value of 20^s.

Whearas it hath formerly beene ordered that al laborers and Teames should abate 3^d at the shilling of such wages as they formerly used to take which order [was] onely intended for summer labor. Now for the better vnderstandinge [**56.**] thearof and equality to be kept. It is ordered that from the 25 day of the first month to the 25 day of the eight month it shal not be lawful for Comon laborers as howers Reapers taylors &c who weare used to take after 2^s the day, to take aboue 28^d a day and from the 25 day of the 8 month to the first day of the tenth month 15^d a day and from the sayd first day of the tenth month vnto the first day of the twelfte month twelue pence the day and from the sayd first day of the twelfte month vnto the 15 day of the first month 25 a day and so an abatement to be made for al other laborers and teames also by lyke p'portion in al the sayde months, and that those that doe other mens work at thire owne houses shal abate by lyke p'portion also, and that al men Com in due tyme to thire labor vppon such penalty as the Court vppon inst Complaint made shal be pleased to inflyct.

Dorchester 2 of 3 month 1642. Wee John Holman and John Holland beinge ordered to appoynt the lyinge of the lots granted in the hyest fresh marshe do hearby appoynt them to be layed out on this syde of the Riuer of Naponset towards Dedham, it beinge so intended in the grant of them, and if theare be not enoughe on this syde then it to be layde out on the other syde.

   Witnes our hands   John Holland.
              John Holman.

It is agreed and bargayned betweene Christopher Gibson and Nicholas Vpsall as foloweth

that the sayd Christopher Gibson shall haue hould and enioy that 3 akers of meddow roayninge to the new Creeke and now in his possession, be it more or lesse and for and duringe his natural lyfe and after the decease of the sayd Christopher Gibson then the sayd 3 ackers of medow shall be had held and inioyed by Nicholas Vpsall his heyres or assynes for euer.

and the said Christopher Gibson hathe granted and bargayned with nicholas Vpsal that he the sayd Nicholas Vpsall shall from and after the decease of the sayd christopher Gibson have hould ocupy and enioy that great lot that was granted mathew Grant that was about 3 ackers within the fence of the great lots be it more or lesse, and also six ackers of land, in the neck of land, now in the occupation of the sayd Christopher Gibson and lying next to Mr Hawkins lot to him selfe and to his heirs and assygnes for euer.

[Here 4 pages (57–61) are gone (2 leaves).]

[**61.**] It is ordered the 20th of 3^d m^o. 1644 by the maior vote of the Towne that the Raters shall make a Rate of one hundred pounds towards the fortifications of Castle Iland and p'viding powder and shot, and other Implements for the great gunnes to be deliuered into the hands of Nathaniel Duncan and Humphrey Atherton Ovseers of the worke who are to bee accoumptable to the Towne of the disposing of that.

Out of the same thirtie two shills: due to James Bourne to be p^d.

The 26th. 3 m^o. 1644. It was ordered that M^r. John Glou shall haue that vpland and meddow he desireth beeing, and lying to the brooke side at the higher end of the great playne beyond his farme, the sayd Jo: Glouer giuing vpland and meddow for the same to the vse of the Towne either out of his own p'prietie of the 3 diuisions there, or out of the next land divisible, or elsewhere to the full value therof, according to the Judgement of Nathaniel Duncan, Thomas Joanes, Willia Sumner, and Hopestill Foster, and Willia Blake or any fower of them.

The 24th of the 7th moneth 1644 at a Towne meeting the 7 men vnderwritten were Chosen to order the Affairs of the Towne till the 1st of the 9th moneth which shalbe in the year 1645 and to haue full power to make orders to bind the Towne as former 7 men haue had except in giuing and disposing of lands, till other instructions bee giuen them by the Towne.

M^r. Glouer Natha. Duncan
M^r. Patten M^r. Atherton
M^r. Haward M^r. Joanes
Tho: Wiswall

this to new recorded in the new towne booke.

John Glouer sould vnto Nicholas Butler the 26th of the 9 m^o

tenne akers of lane lying in the great necke in the further end of his lott togeither with the halfe of the way quantitie, and qualitie Considered lying next the mouth of the neck to haue and to hold to the foresayd Nicho: Butler and to his heirs, for eū and the aforesayd John Glouer doth accknowledge to haue reiceiued satisfaction for the aforesayd 10 akers of land and doth p' thes p'sents for him, his heirs executors and eūry of them warrant the sayd land vnto the sayd Nicho: Butler frō all men Clayming by, and vnder him, that hee shall inioy the same peaceably foreū.

Wittnesse his hand
JOHN GLOUER

Nathaniel Duncan Senior sould vnto Anthony Gulliver the 15th of the 11th moneth 1644 about 4 akers and half of land on Captn neck which was belonging to M^r. James Marshall of Exeter in old England and was late in the possession of Thomas Trobridge of which about two akers three quarters broken vp the Rest fey ground to haue and to hold to the sayd Antho: Gulliuer and to his heirs foreuer and the sayd Nath: Duncan doth p' these p'sents for him his heirs, executors and eūy of them warrant the sayd land vnto the sayd Antho: Gulliuer frō all men Clayming it and that he may inioy that peaceably foreuer.

Witness his hand
NATHA: DUNCAN.

[62.] *The 6^a of the 11^a m^o 1644.* It is ordered that M^r. Joanes, and George Weeks shall see the measuring of the 3^d division of the Cow pasture to make the Rate with the help of the measure and to Collect that, and to haue 2^s a day for there paynes the measurer to haue 5^s a day the sayd Collectors vpon any mans refusall of payment of his p'te to levie it p' distresse.

It is ordered that there shalbe a veiu taken of the best way for a Ferrey to bee setled to Brayntree, and those p'ts and to p'cure the sayd Ferrey from the Generall Court to the Townes disposall for euer. M^r. Glouer, Nathaniel Duncan, and M^r. Atherton desired to take the veiu of the sayd Ferrey and to Consult with Braintree and Inghā men, and Waymouth about that which may bee the most Convenient place, and whither one or 2 ferreis, may bee best and to Informe the Towne a moneth before the next G: Court, what they haue done heerein.

It is ordered that John Smith shall haue passede with Cart or Cattle through Edward Brecks meddow at the end of the great lotts frō the beach to his lott which was once Giles Gibbes.

Whereas their haue bene diuers orders made about felling of trees on the Commons It is now ordered that all such orders formerly made shall bee Repealed except that agaynst felling of trees about the meeting house and the m'ke trees on the bounds, and the trees on the Rockie hill p' M^r. Meinots, and M^r. Holmans, Provided also that none shall fell trees in the Commons to sell or Carry out of the Towne for any use on payne of fyue shillings for any tree so felled to be levied p' distresse to the vse of the Towne.

Md. That the 17th Daye of the First mō. 1645 Thō. Clarke now of Boston sould vnto Thō. Wiswall of Dorchester a p'cell of Land estimated 3 acres and a ½ be it more or Lesse which Late was p't of William Read his home Lott with one Barne and other thinges mentioned in a deed beareing date with thes Record.

witnessed
by JOHN WISWALL
beinge moderator of the
7 men
GEO: WEEKES.

[**63.**] It is agreed at a generall meetinge of the Towne the 26th of the 12 m° 1644 for peace and loues sake that there shalbe a new meeting house built on M^r. Hawards land in the most Convenient place betwixt M^r. Stoughtons garden and his barne and this agreement to stand firme except any Considerable number of such as are absent frō this meeting shall giue any satisfactory reasons vnto the 7 men within 14 dayes for any other alteration of the place.

Upon a generall and lawfull warning of all the Inhabitants the 14th of the 1st moneth 1645 these rules and orders following p^{r}sented to to the Towne Concerning the Schoole of Dorchester are Confirmed by the maior p'te of the Inhabitants then p^{r}sent.

First It is ordered that three able, and sufficient men of the Plantation shalbe Chosen to bee wardens or oūseers of the Schoole aboue mentioned who shall haue the Charge oūsight and ordering thereof and of all things Concerneing the same in such manner as is hereafter expressed and shall Continue in their office and place for Terme of their liues respectiuely, vnlesse by reason of any of them Remouing his habitation out of the Towne, or for any other weightie reason the Inhabitants shall see cause to Elect or Chuse others in their roome in which cases and vpon the death of any of the sayd wardens the Inhabitants shall make a new Election and choice of others.

And M^r. Haward, Deacon Wiswall, M^r. Atherton are elected to bee the first wardens or oūseers.

Secondly, the said Wardens shall haue full power to dispose of the Schoole stock whither the same bee in land or otherwyse, both such as is already in beeing and such as may by any good meanes heereafter be added: and shall Collect and Receiue the Rents, Issues and p'fitts arising and growing of and from the sayd stock, And the sayd rents Issues and p'fits shall imploy and lay out only for the best behoof, and advantadge of the sayd Schoole; and the furtherance of learning thereby, and shall giue a faythfull and true accoumpt of there receipts and disbursements so often as they shalbee thervnto required by the Inhabitants or the maior p'te of them.

Thirdly the sayd Wardens shall take care, and doe there vtmost and best endeavor that the sayd Schoole may frō tyme to tyme bee supplied with an able and sufficient Schoolemaster who neūthelesse is not to be admitted into the place of Schoolem^r without the Generall cōsent of the Inhabitants or the maior p'te of them.

Fowerthly so often as the sayd Schoole shalbee supplied with a

Schoolemʳ — so p'vided and admitted, as aforesayd the wardens shall frō tyme to tyme pay or cause to be payd vnto the saydᵈ Schoolemʳ such wages out of the Rents, Issues and p'fitts of the Schoole stocke as shall of right Come due to be payd.

Fiuethly the sayd wardens shall from tyme to tyme see that the Schoole howse bee kept in good, and sufficient repayre, the Chargs of which reparacion shalbe defrayed and payd out of such rents, Issues and p'fitts of the Schoole stock, if there be sufficient, or else of such rents as shall arise and grow in the time of the vacancy of the Schoolemʳ — if there bee any such and in defect of such vacancy the wardens shall repayre to the 7 men of the Towne for the tyme beeing who shall haue power to taxe the Towne with such somē, or sommes as shalbe requisite for for the repayring of the Schoole howse as aforesayd.

[**64.**] Sixthly the sayd Wardens shall take Care that eūy yeere at or before the end of the 9ᵗʰ moneth their bee brought to the Schoolehowse 12 sufficient Cart, or wayne loads of wood for fewell, to be for the vse of the Schoole master and the Schollers in winter the Cost and Chargs of which sayd wood to bee borne by the Schollers for the tyme beeing who shalbe taxed for the purpose at the discretion of the sayd Wardens.

Lastly the sayd Wardens shall take care that the Schoolemʳ for the tyme beeing doe faythfully p'forme his dutye in his place, as schoolmʳˢ ought to doe as well in other things as in these which are hereafter expressed, viz.

First that the Schoolemʳ shall diligently attend his Schoole and doe his vtmost indeavor for Benefitting his Schollers according to his best discretion without vnnecessaryly absenting himself to the pʳiudice of his schollers, and hindering there learning.

2ˡʸ that from the begiñing of the first moneth vntill the end of the 7ᵗʰ he shall eūy day begin to teach at seaven of the Clock in the morning and dismisse his schollers at fyue in the afternoone. And for the other fiue moneths that is from the beginning of the 8ᵗʰ moneth vntill the end of the 12ᵗʰ mōth he shall eūy day beginn at 8ᵗʰ of the Clock in the morning and [end] at 4 in the afternoone.

3ˡʸ eūy day in the yeere the vsuall tyme of dismissing at noone shalbe at 11 and to beginn agayne at one except that

4ˡʸ euery second day in the weeke he shall call his schollers togeither betweene 12 and one of the Clock to examin them what they haue learned on the saboath day pʳceding at which tyme also he shall take notice of any misdemeanor or disorder that any of his skollers shall haue Committed on the saboath to the end that at somme convenient tyme due Admonition, and Correction may bee admistred by him according as the nature, and qualitie of the offence shall require at which sayd examination any of the elders or other Inhabitants that please may bee pʳsent to behold his religious care herein and to giue there Countenance, and ap'pbation of the same.

5ˡʸ hee shall equally and impartially receiue, and instruct such as shalbe sent and Comitted to him for that end whither their parents bee poore or rich not refusing any who haue Right and Interest in the Schoole.

6ˡʸ such as shalbe Comitted to him he shall diligently instruct as they shalbe able to learne both in humane learning, and good litterature, and likewyse in poynt of good manners, and dutifull behauiour towards all specially their sup'iors as they shall haue ocasion to bee in their p'sence whether by meeting them in the streete or otherwyse.

7ˡʸ euy 6 day of the weeke at 2 of the Clock in the afternoone hee shall Chatechise his schollers in the principles of Christian religion, either in some Chatechism which the Wardens shall p'vide, and p'esent or in defect thereof in some other.

8ˡʸ And because all mans indeavors without the blessing of God must needs bee fruitlesse and vnsuccessfull theirfore It is to be a cheif p'te of the schoolemʳˢ religious care to Comend his schollers and his labours amongst them vnto God by prayer, morning and euening, taking Care that his schollers doe reuendly attend during the same.

9ˡʸ And because the Rodd of Correction is an ordinance of God necessary sometymes to bee dispenced vnto Children but such as may easily be abused by oūmuch seuitie and rigour on the one hand, or by oū much indulgence and lenitye on the other It is therefore ordered and agreed that the schoolemaster for the tyme beeing shall haue full power to minister Correction to all or any of his schollers without respect of p'sons according as the nature and qualitie of the offence shall require whereto, all his schollers must bee duely subiect and no parent or other of the Inhabitants shall hinder or goe about to hinder the master therein. Neuthelesse if any parent or others shall think their is iust cause of Complaynt agaynst the master for to much seuitye, such shall haue liberty freindly and louingly to expostulate [**65.**] with the master about the same, and if they shall not attayne to satisfaction the matter is then to bee referred to the wardens who shall imp'tially Judge betwixt the master and such Complaynants. And if it shall appeare to them that any parent shall make causlesse Complaynts agaynst the mʳ. in this behalf and shall p'sist and Continue so doeing in such case the Wardens shall haue power to discharge the mʳ of the care, and Charge of the Children of such parents. But if the thing Complayned of bee true and that the mʳ. haue indeed bene guiltie of ministring excessiue Correction, and shall appeare to them to Continue therein, notwithstanding that they haue advised him otherwise, in such case as also in the case of to much lenitye; or any other great neglect of dutye in his place, p'sisted in It shalbe in the power of the Wardens to call the Inhabitants together to Consider whither it were not meet to discharge the mʳ of his place that so somme other more desirable may be p'vided

And because it is difficult if not Impossible to give p'ticular rules that shall reach all cases which may fall out, therefore for a Conclusion It is ordered, and agreed, in Generall, that where p'ticular rules are wanting there It shalbe a p'te of the office and dutye of the Wardens to order and dispose of all things that Concerne the schoole, in such sort as in their wisedom and discretion they shall Judge most Conducible for the glory of God, and the trayning vp of the Children of the Towne in religion, learning and Civilitie.

and these orders to be Continued till the maior p'te of the Towne shall see cause to alter any p'te thereof.

Upon a generall and lawfull warning of all the inhabitants the 14^t of the first m° 1645 the rules and orders aboue written p'sented to the Towne Concerning the schoole of Dorchester are Confirmed v' the maior p'te of the Inhabitants.

Deacon Wiswol —
Humphrey Atherton — } chosen wardens for the schoole.
M^r. Haward —

It is ordered the same day that a rate of 250^{li} shalbe made for the building of a new meeting howse and the Raters Chosen are

Edward Breck.   Williā Blake.
Williā Sumner. Roger Clap.
Thomas Wiswol.

The ouseers of the worke in building the meeting howse who are to agree with the workmen Receiue the Rates and pay them and to agree with M^r. Haward about the plot of land where the sayd meeting howse must bee sett.

M^r. Glouer.   Deacon Wiswol.
Natha: Duncon.   Deacon Clap.
M^r. Atherton.   M^r. Haward.
M^r. Joanes.

[**66.**] *Dec: 17. 1645.* Memorand there was given to Edward Brecke (by the hands of most of the inhabitants of this towne) smelt brooke Creeke one the Condiciōn that he doe sett a mill there.

The 7 men chosen the 2^d day of the 10th month for the yeare following

Mr Glooner   John Holland
Mr Jones   Edward Clapp
Edward Breck   Will: Clarke
John Wiswall

Januari 19th 1646. It is agred and voted, that for the Seating of the meeting house in Dorchester, and for the making of the wales warme and Decent within and without, the p'forming of what is requisite for the finishing of the house in such sort as the Seven men shall in there Discreation thinke meet, there shalbe a rate laid vpon the Plantation for the accomplishm^t of the same.

Memorand. that 40^{li} is granted to be Levied for the vses a boue said, to be gathered by Distress.

It is granted by the plantation that Jonas Humfrayes shall haue an acre of Land (which was granted him to haue had elsewhere) at Squantums neck and recompenc for a way laid oū his land in the great lotts Containing 45 rodds.

It is granted by the plantation that John Holland shall haue Sattisfactiō for a sixe acar lott which hee purchessed of Thomas Rawlins.

M^d that the twentieth daye of the eight mō in the year 1646 Richard Williams of Tanton: in New England Sould vnto Thō

Wiswall of Dorchester in N: E. afforsaid all his Lott and Accommodations in Dorchester afforsaid with all the priuiledges and Liberties therevnto belonging accordinge to their bounds and demessions as they are exp'ssed in an Indenture beareinge Date with this Record:
    Witnessed
      By John Wiswall beinge
       moderator of 7 men
        GEO: WEEKES.

[**67.**] [This paragraph on page 67 was crossed out on the original.]

This should have been Recorded in yeare 1644.

It is order^d accordingly by the select men appointed that John Phillips, Willi. Blake, Edw Brecke, shall Laye out a waye from the Towne of Dorchester vnto the Pynne necke now in the occupatiō of John Greennwaye or his Assignes which partyes aboue named haue done it as it is now Recorded : viz that whereas vpon Record in page 54 it appeares that sattisfactiō was giuen vnto John Phillips for a waye from the Comōns to Pine necke we find it most conuenient that he passe vpon that waye and at the end at John Phillips land to enter vpō M^r. minots and goody Bradford land passing alonge betweene them two vntil he come to the Lower end of the ffeild vnto the marsh and then to turne vpon the Left hand vpō the vpland vntill he come vnto goody Bradfford marsh and there to have 2 goads broad vnto the bridge and after that also 2 goad broad till vnto the pine necke.

William Blake Edward Brecke John Phillips beinge by the select men of Dorchester ordered to Laye out a waye from the house of John hill in the great Lotts vnto Rob. Pears house on the pyne necke : Doe make their Returne as followes viz that the waye afforesaid Runnes vpō a streight Lyne on the north side of the Lot that Late was John Phillips vntill it come to the easte end of the great Lotts and soe it goes on in a streight Line vpō the south side of the Land that Allexander Bradfford vntill it Come to the marsh and then it turnes vpō the said Land by the marsh side vntill it Comes to the meadowe that was the said Alexanders and so to Runne in a streight line vnto the pyne : and all alonge to be a Rod and a halfe broad :

Theise are to testifie to whom it maie Concerne that John Ginjion hathe bought of Anthony Gullifford of Dorchester Foure acres and halfe of Land Lyeinge on Captaines necke in dorchester which the Forsaid Anthony bought of M^r. nathaniel Duncan Late of Dorchester : for the Consideratio of thirteene   * * *

[**68.**] *the:* 8 (3) 48   4 of Roxbury selectmen being with us : vpō the Former disagreements : : they

[This page seems to be pasted on page 69.]

DEDHAM TOWNE.

Loueinge neighbors whereas we vnderstand that you haue vnawares tresspassed vpō a swamp Lyeinge within our bounds contrarie vnto a cort order and that you wishe it maie not be offensiue vnto vs and for that end you p'pose vnto vs that you might giue some neighbourly consideratiō for that which is ffallen because it now Lyes vpō spoyle and you haue bestowed some Labour on, theise are to signifie vnto you that we Looke vpō what is Done with as much neighbourly patience as we can and are willinge to correspond with you vpō faire tearmes for which end if you please to beare the chardge of 2 whom we shall send in our steed to consider what you haue Done and to agree with you vpō neighbourly tearmes about it, therefore if you please to appoint the tyme and send vs word at 2 Dayes notice we purpose to attend you in it and in the meane tyme we wishe you to trespasse no further vpō vs and either in Remoueing any ffallen or ffellinge any more:

so we Rest your Loueinge neighbours in the name and with the consent of the 7 men
Dor: 13 9 48

13 9 48 to p'pose about the Rate of captaine Danfforth.
6 Rod for Richard waye and william Ireland p'pose a plot of Land for Barne recd Demand accompt of 48^s from bro smith:
the Fynes in great Lotts about fence: and breach of order, viz: vnseasonable put in notece

We agree that 9^d p' goad be Demanded: and taken of all that pay willingely but if any put vs to Distrayne they must paye whole and such chardges as arise there about.

Looke to nicholas Butler about 9 cattell vpō great necke contrarie to order: 12^d p. head:

Baliffe to Demand for wm Salsbury of Elder minot: for cattell at pond:

sister george accepts 4^s 6^d of Bro Twichell 13 (9:) 48:
Reconed with sister George and Due to her 1 — 12 — 2:
Looke about Deuisiō of Squantum the comō Land
p'pose Reveiw that 3 Deusions the bounds of them   consider the rent of cow walke:

[69.] wheras Captain Atherton Thomas wiswall and Joseph Farnworth were appointed by the select men of dorchester to lay out a towne way by willyam blakes toward the fresh marsh and the three deuissions; which way Is thus appointed to run from the corner of willyam blakes garden to a stump on the side of stony hill and soe to a tree In the bottom and soe allong to a rock in M^r. Jones lott the way lying on the left hand going in the old way vnto a stony ually and soe to a tree where are 4 stones laid and soe allong unto the body of the fresh marshes leauing the old way on the left hand this way was laid out the 9: of the 10: month 1650:

HUMPHRAY ATHERTON.
JOSEPH FARNWORTH.
THOMAS WISWALL.

[Page 70 blank.]

[71.] *Dorchester the 8 of the i mo: 52* It is covenanted and agreed by and betweene the select men of this towne for 3 o^r 5 yers and Robt Stanton of the same towne: That the said Robt Stanton shall and will from the 8th of the 3 moneth next insueing vntill the 8 day of the 8 moneth following keepe all such oxen or steeres or fating cows from yew to Cow for 3 or 5 yers in a heard as shall at their first going forth be deliv̄ed unto him for that inde, by aney of the inhabitants of the said towne, and none of other townes to be received or kept with them; their walke or place of feeding to be on the further side of the river Norponsit, and aboue or beyound the Cow-walke of dorchester, and not suffered to goe amonge the cowes. and also the said Robt Stanton doth covenant to and with the said select men to goe forth with the said Oxen and steeres halfe an hower by sonne, and bringe them to their appointed place or pen so called about sonne sittinge eū̄y night, that so the owners may haue them there if they please to send for them, either in the eveninge, or in the morninge before the said tyme of their goeing forth, and not be dissapointed when they haue vrgent occasions to vse them, and to make the pen sufficient for largnesse of ground that so the Oxen or Steeres may be the lesse injurious or hurtfull one vnto an other, as also sufficient in point of fence, and for his faithfullness and care herein he the said Robt Stanton is to haue twoe shillinges a head to be paid at two paym^{ts} the one halfe within one month after they be put to him and the other halfe at the end of September followinge.

the marke of ROBERT STANTON
in the name of the Select
HUMPHREY ATHARTON:

Dorchester the 8 of the i mo: 52 It is ordered by the Select men of the sayd towne for this p'sent yeare, as also covenanted and agreed by and betweene them for and in the behalfe of the said towne.

And Steven Hopinges and Nicolas George both of the same towne: That the said Steuen Hopinges and Nicolas George shall and will keepe the cowes and heffers that shalbe Commyted vnto to them this p'sent yeare in the ordinary Cowpaster or Cow walke after the vsuall mann̄ from the 18th day of the second moneth next insueing vntill the 28 of the 8 moneth folliwinge; The said keepers one of them to blowe their horne at or about halfe an hower by sonne in the morneinge at the meetinge howse and so along the towne vntill he com to John Minots, and eū̄y man on the north side of the towne to bringe their cowes before the meeting howse within halfe an hour after the horne is their blowed. And that keeper their to take them at the same tyme, the other keeper at or about the same tyme to goe vp to the buring place and take the cowes (and such other Cattell not p'hibited) that are their left for them aney wheare about the Commons between Austyn Clemans lote which was M^r. Makpease, and the said Buringe place, so that both keepers may meete on the rockey hill, or at the gate by John Minots to goe forth with the whole heard and not to stay beyound their appointed tyme of goeing forth viz: one oure and the halfe after the sonne Riseing and bring those cowes that belong to the back side of the Towne, agayne to Law^oo Smiths barne and if any be lost in the woodes they shall doe their indeavour to looke them vp.

And for their faithfulnesse and care herein The said Steven Hopinges and Nicolas George is to haue thirtie poundes to bee [**72.**] proportioned with the bull money vpon so maney Cattell as are put to heard or goeing vpon the Comons or Cow walke aforesaid, one thurd thereof to be paid them at or about the beginninge or first putting forth, an other thurd at halfe the tyme, the remaynder at the end of the sayd tyme.

        HUMPHREY ATHARTON
        ROBT. HOWARD in the name
         of the rest of the select men
        The marke of
        STEVEN **H** HOPPINGES
        The marke of
        NICHOLAS **X** JORGE

To all Christian people vnto whome this p'sents shall come greeting Know ye that I Nicholas Butler haue deputed and ordayned my welbeloved sonne John Butler to be my lawfull Atturny and in my stead to by and to sell to take and to pay and to sew at the law to recover Debtes and make discharges and to act in all lawfull actions in as full and ample mann^r as I my selfe cold doe as well in matter of sale of land as in aney thinge else.

Witnesse my hand and seale dated this 15th of the 8 mo: 5i
Signed sealed and deliūed in the p'sents of vs } NI: BUTLER
THOMAS MAYHEW SENIOR PHILLIP TABOR   }

Entered the 27 of December 165i by Willm̄ Aspinwall Notarius Publ. as also amongst these records p' m^o.

        ROBT. HOWARD Record^r

Dorchester this 28 day of the i: mo: 53 It is covenanted and agreed by and betweene the Select men of the said towne for this p'sent yeare for and in the behalfe of the said towne, And Clement Topley and Beniamyn Bates both of Dorchester That the said Clement and Beniamyn shall and will keepe the cowes and heffers that shalbe comitted vnto them this p'sent yeare in the ordinary Cowpastuer or Cow walke after the vsuall manū from the 15 day of the second moneth next insueing vntill the 28 day of the eight moneth following. The said keepers one of them to blow their horne at or before halfe an hower by sonne in the morneing at the meeting howse and so along the town vntill he com to John Minots and eūy man on the north side of the towne to bring their cowes before the meeting howse within halfe an hower after the horne is their blowed.

And that keeper there to take them at the same tyme, the other keeper at or abought the same tyme to goe vp to the burying place and take the Cowes and such other cattell not p'hibited that ar their left for them aney wheare aboughte the Commons betweene

Augustin Clements lote which was M^r. Makpeace and the said buring place so that both keepers may meete on the Rockey hill or at the gat by John Minots to goe forth with the whole heard and not to stay beyound their appointed tyme of goeing forth Vidēlt one hower and halfe after the sonne riseing. And bring those cowes that belong to the back side of the towne agayne to Lawrance Smith barne. And if aney be lost in the woodes [**73.**] they shall p'sently goe backe and seeke them and if they cannot find them that night, they shall one of them seek for them the next day and so after vntill they find them p'vided the owner of the cattell put a sufficient man to keep the cow heard while the sayd keeper seeke them. And for their faithfullnesse and care herein The said Clement Toply and Beniamyn Bates — is to haue — thirty poundes to bee p'portioned with the Bull money vpon so maney Cattell as ar put to heard on goeing vpon the Comons or Cowe walke aforesaid, one thurd thereof to be paid them at or abought the begining or first putting forth, on other thurd at halfe the tyme the remaynder at the end of the sayd tyme.

CLEMENT TOPLIF
BENIEMAN BATES } herdsmen.

ROBERT HOWARD in the name of the rest of the Select men.

Dorchester the 26 of the second mo: 53. It is covenanted and agreed by and betweene the Select men of this towne for this p'sent yeare and Antoney Newton and Willm Solsbury of the same towne that the said Antoney Newton and Willm Solsbury shall and will from the 9 of the 3 moneth next insueing vntill the 27 or 28 day of 7 moneth following keepe all such oxon or steeres in a heard as shall at their first goeing forth be Deliūed vnto them for that inde by any of the inhabitants of the said towne and none of other townes to be received or kept with them without leeve or lysense from the said towne first had and obtayned, Their walke or place of feeding to be on the further side of the river Norponsit and aboue or beyound the Cow walke of Dorchester and not suffered to goe among the Cowes. And also the said Antoney Newton and Willm̄. Solsbury doth covenant to and with the said Selectmen to goe forth with the said Oxon and Steeres halfe an hower by soun, and bring them to their appointed place or pen so called abought sonn sitting eūy night, that so the owners may haue them their if they please to send for them, either in the eveneing or in the morneing before the said tyme of their goeing forth, and not be dissapointed when they have vrgent occasion to vse them. And to make the pen sufficient for largenesse of ground that so the Oxon or Steeres may be the lesse iniurious or hurtfull one vnto an other, as also sufficient in point of fence and for their faithfulnesse and care herein they the said Antoney and Willm̄ is to haue twoe shillinges a head to be paid at two paym^{ts} the one halfe within one moneth after they be put to them and the other halfe at the end of the 7 moneth following at som convenient place in towne where they doe appoint but if in case they be driven to com for their pay then they are allowed to receive two shillings and two pence a head.

        WILLIAM SALSBOR * *
        ROBT HOWARD in the name
        of the rest of the select men.

[Page 74 blank.]
[Page 75 do.]

[76.] *Dorchester the 30 of the 3 mo. 52:* It is voted that M^r. Mather shall haue one hundered pounds allowed vnto him for this p'sent yeare insueinge to be p'portioned by a towne rater and the Decons to ioyne with the raters in p'portioning.

It is voted the day and yeare abouesaid that Captayne Humfery Artherton shall haue a p'cell of ground on the Comons neere John Kinslyes to set a house on for a sop howse.

Upon the 28 of the 9 mo : 53 it was voted by the Fremen of Dorchester at a publike meeting that Henry Cundlife should gather in by distresse or otherwise divers rates yet vnpaid by seuall p'sons in seuall yeares already past Dve vnto the ministerie according to severall bills to be Deliued vnto him by the Deacons or Select men, and to inable him theirvnto doe by the ensueing warrant vnder theire hand the day abouesaid authorise him.

To Henry Cundlife : you are hereby willed and required to aske and receive of the severall p'sons p'sented to you such sume or sumes as you shall find them charged withall and vpon their default of paym^t vpon Demaund these p'sents shall inable you to distrayne and make sale according vnto order of Court in like causes ; and the sume or sumes so gathered to deliu vpon accompt vnto the Deacons who shall give you a discharge according to what you deliu vnto them for the vse aboue said ; which receipts vnder their handes shalbe accepted as a true returne theirof, which we will you not to faile vpon your perrill at or before the first of the last mo : 53.

        ROBT HOWARD in the name
        of the Fremen as being by vote
        willed and required theirvnto.

It is voted the said 28 day cf the 9 mo. 53 that our Teacher M^r. Mather shall haue a hunderid pounds for this yeare and that the Deacons shall ioyne with the raters now chosen to p'portion eury man according to the rule of proportion.

The said 28 day of the 9 mo. 53 brother John Smith is chosen by a publike vote to repare the meeting howse with groun sells Daubing clabbord and [77.] glasse abought the windows and otherwise as he shall thinke fit, vnto which he the said John Smith, being p'sent frely consentid.
    Test   ROB^r. HOWARD Record^r

This is a postscript entered vnder the aforesaid warrant from the towne vnto Henry Cunlefe Dated the 28 of the 9 mo : 53. as followith

Dorchester the 14 of the 12 mo. 53. Whereas their is a question whether the power of Henry Cunlife bailife in acting accordinge to the aboue said warrant is not endid. We the said Inhabitants Doe by a publike rate will and requier him the said bailife to goe on in acting according to the said warrant vntill all arrerages be brought in according to the intent of the said warrant.

Rob^T Howard in the name
of the rest of the Fre men as
aforesaid.

𝕸 there was given to Bastiane Keane by the Towne a parcell of Land one the Rockey hill from his garden to the Greete Rocke Contayning about 13th rods this 19 of : 7 : mo. 1655.

𝕸 there was giuen by the Towne to Richard Daues 4 feete of Land with out his garden Rayles by the water or bridge by George Procters Close : for the addicon of his shop for his more Conveniencie this : 22th day of the : 7 : mo : 1655.

[Page 78 blank.]

[**79.**] *Dorchester the : 12 : of 10 : m°. 53 :* Whareas it hath been found by sad experience that much hurt and Damage hath been done in Corne feilds and one greate cause is Insufitient fence and allso the Generall Courte hauing imposed vppon the Selectmen the Care to make orders for the repairing of fences in the severall townes as in an order of the 30th of Augus 53 : doth appeare : it is therefore ordered by the Selectmen that all fences in p'ticuler and comon corne feilds except farmes of aboue an 100 Acres shalbe suffitiently fence att or before the 25th of March next with Rayles pales or other good suffitient fence which shall be 4 foot high at the Least and so close as Swine cannot get through or as the Veiwers shall Judge And what p'sons in this Towne shall haue any Defectiue Fence after the Day aboue said he shall forfeit 2^s 6^d p' rod besides paying Damage ; and so p'portionable for a greater or lesser quantỹ which fence shall be good and sound as the Veiwers shall Judge and if any one shall neglect the repayre of his fence aboue said he shall forfiet for every weeks neglect 2^s 6^d beside paying Damage after dew notes giuen them by the veiwers : All which said penaltyes to be taken by Distrayne or otherwise one thierd part to the Baylife the other to the vse of the Towne.

mad by the Selectmen.

This aboue written order is to continue in force vntill the towne se cause to repeale it ; Dated the 8 : 1 : 1657 or 1658.

It is ordered by the select men the 12 (1) 1659 : or 1660 : that noe stoone wall shall be Counted sufficient fence vnlesse ther be a raile put into a Cruch or post put upon the wall.

Whereas an order of Court appoints the Selectmen of every Towne that they should appoint two or more of their Inhabitants to veiw the Fence of every Cornefeild within their Towne.

And they haue further ordered the selectmen to make orders

for repayreing and mayntaing of sufficient feence to each feild within there Towne:

Wee therefore the Selectmen of Dorchester do order and appoint that you whose names are hereafter expressed to be the severall veiwers of each feild shall carefully veiw all and each mans fence and every parte thereof. And soe that it be according to the order of the Selectmen baring date the 12 day of the 10th mo. 53 : And if any mans fence be vnsufficient you are then required forthwith to giue notes to him who shall forth with repayre the same and further you are required who are the severall veiwers of each feild to make returne to the Selectmen or some of them of all such p'sons as are defectiue in ther fences according to the order before expressed one the first day of the 2 mo. next vppon penaltie of 2ˢ 6ᵈ for each veiwers neglect.

You are also to veiw the fence once in each month vntell the tenth of the 8 month next and to make return within one week after you haue Giuen notes to the owners of his defect. If it be not repayred within that weeke vppon the penalty before expressed. And further if any p'son shall enforme you or any of you of any defectiue fence att any tyme you shall forthwith goe and veiw it and make returne as aforsaid vppon the penalty aforesaid. This 12th of the 10 m. 53 by the Selectmen for this yeare

This aboue writen order is to continue in force vntill the towne se cause to repeale it.

Dated the 18 : 1: 165 $\frac{7}{\text{or } 8}$

[1] [Att a meeting of the select men 12 (1ˢᵗ) 166⅝ it is ordered that all defects in fences that are Less then one rodd shall pay 12ᵈ for euery defect, and 12ᵈ p' rodd for all aboue one rodd, and 12ᵈ p' weeke for eury weekes defect beside what damages may Arise and it is alsoe ordered thatt all stone wall off foure foot high shall bee accounted sufficient fence without a rayle aboue itt.

this order to bee obserued from the first of aprill till the 10th of october next, for all comon feilds and then to be cleard or run the aduenture of damadg that may arise for this year Insuing or till the select men doe take further order.]

[80.] *Dorchester this 13th of 12: mo. 53* Forasmuch as Rituousnes amongst men is not only the Comandement of god but the way to Continew Loue and peace amongst men and sad Complaynts being made to vs of vniust practises of Divers in this Towne who distroy mens Corne and Grasse by puting in or at lest suffring there Cattell to feed one other mens Corne and meadow : for the prevention of which is ordered by the Select men of this Towne as followeth.

1. That every man shall fech or cause to be feched out his owne bease or any that hee hath vnder his charge Whether Sheepe, Ruther Cattell Horses and Swine out of all comon Corne feilds meadow and pasture within this Towne of Dorchester one the first

---

[1] Written in margin of p. 79.

2 day of the 2 mo next and soe from time to time, vppon the penantie of 2ˢ the head for every beaste not feched out one that day: to be payde by the owner of such Beast vppon demande to homesoever shall finde and fett out any such beastes aforesayd and if he that ownes the beast or bestes shall refuse to pay vppon demand the Baylife shall take it by distres.

2. That the veiwers of every feild shall not only see the fences to be good according to that order made in the 12 of the 10 mo. 53 but allso that such Gates and fences which ar Comon to the vse of any feild shall be sufficiently made before the day aboue expressed: with gates and if they be not made before the day of Clering feilds, then the veiwers shall forth with make and repayre the same and shall Demand and take of every p'prietor of every such feild one penny for every acker of Broken vp land within that feild and if any refuse to pay as afaresaid the Baylife shall haue warant to take it by distres:

3. If any p'sonn shall Leaue openn any such gate he or his Parents or master if it be a Child shall pay one shilling for every tyme he shall be knowne to leaue it openn: or if any p'sonn shall Lett in any best to any such feild and leaue it there he shall pay as aforesaid 1ˢ for every best lett in or Left there.

4. If any p'sonn shall put in any beast or Leaue any beast Loose in any such feild by night vntell the feild be reid of Corne & haye he shall forfett 5ˢ a beast for every beast so put in or Left Loose there:

5. If any p'sonn Whatsoever shall in Plowing tyme or elce Leave or sefer his or there Cattell to trespas vppon other mens p'prietie in any Comon feild in this Towne he shall forfett for every such offence 1ˢ 6ᵈ p' head to the informer to be taken by distres or otherwise besides paying all damage to the man damnified.

.6. If any p'sonn haue any Just occasion to drive any Cattell in any waye through any Comō feild he shall not suffer them to feed one mens Corne or grase but shall follow them deligently vppon the penaltie of paying six pence for every beast he suffers to trespas besides paying all Damages to the partie trespassed.

These six orders aboue writen are to continue and to be in force vntill the select men se cause to alter them by the order of the select men p' the 11 (3) 1663.

[81.] *This 13ᵗʰ of 12 mᵒ 53.* Wee the Selectmen of Dorchester hauing hard that there are in som Comon Feilds Fences which are not oned by any of the p'priators and allso other places about some Comon feilds which hath no fence and for want of good fence much hurt and damage doth come thereby: wee willing you would agree of some equall way amongest your selues: Desire that the p'prietors of each feild home it Consernes: would of themselues appynt two or more as they shall see meete to veiwe all such

fences as ar not owned and such places as need new fencing: and
would bring in in p'ticaler what some of Rods or footes it is; with
what the Charge will be within Seaven days after they be Chosen:
And wee desire that the p'prietors would appynt within them
selues some to doe it and for the doing thereof to rayse vppon the
erable Land in every such feild so much as shall Defray the Charge
in generall by the eacker or other wise as you shall see good for the
making of it. Which if you doe not by the first day of the first
mounth next then wee the Seelectmen shal doe our best for the
preventing of Damage and hurte and make som order and appynt
men out of your selues for the doing of it.

Whereas M^r. John Glouer was chosen with William Sumner
and William Clarke to Laye out m^{ris} Stotons ffarme, now the said
M^r. Glouer being deceased this 14th day of the 12 m^o 53 att a
Towne meeting the Towne hath Chosen John Wiswall in the Rome
of M^r. Glouer to aioyne with the said William Sumner and William
Clarke for the Doing of that woorke.

This 14th day of 12 m^o 53 Joseph Farworth was Chosen by the
Towne of Dorchester to be Clarke of the markett for the ordring
and sealing of Waits and mesures for this Towne of Dorchester.

[82.] *The 13 of 12 m. 53.* The names of such as are appynted by the Selectt men of Dorchester to veiw the fence in the
Corne feilds for this yeare 1654.

Edward Clapp } Larence Smith }	Imprimus for the neck of Land	{ William Clarke { James Blake
Rich Leeds } Hugh batten }	Item the feild one the Backe side of M^{ris} Stoughtons —	{ Richard Withington { Richard Cortes
Nath Glouer } John Minott }	Item the Great Lots from M^{ris} Hol- lands and so Round westward and end so far as Widow Popes Lott	{ John Smith { John Gurnet
Abram How } Tho: Trott }	Item for the rest of the fence in the Great Lots	{ William Robinsonn { Robert Pearce
Willyam Clarke } Tho: Danforth }	Item Twentie eacker Lots	{ James Hmphres { James Kenion
Henry Kibbey } Henry Woodward }	It. for the Lot behind M^r. Jones,	{ M^r. Blake { Thomas Lake
Isack Jones } Enock wiswall }	It for the Lot behind Thomas Wiswall—	{ M^r. Jones { Joseph Farworth
Georg Dier } Timothy Mather }	It for the feild behind M^r. Mathers —	{ John Wiswall { Ensine Foster
Nico: Clapp } Thomas Andrews }	Item. for the feild behind Thomas Burds —	{ Thomas Burd { John Blackman
Henry Conliffe } Rodger Sumer. }	It. for the Eight eaker Lots	{ Henry Wooddard { William Sumner Jun.
Andrew Picher } Anthony gulliford }	It. for the feild by Elder Kingslys howse —	{ Andrew Picher { Anthony Gulliford

[83.] *This 6th of 2 m^o 53 or 54.* Att a Towne meetine there
was Chossen Deconn Wiswall and Ensine ffoster to treate with the

Comīte Chosen by the Generall Court to veiwe a plantation att Naticke to knowe whate is meete to be Donn and what there Desire is and so to retorne an answer to the Towne of Dorchester.

[Page 84 blank.]

[**85.**] A copie of a Letter sent to the Generall Court this 12th Day of May 1654.

To the Honored Comite appinted by the Generall Court for the setling of the Indian Plantation att Naticke : The retourne of the Inhabitants of the Towne of Dorchester in answer to a litter presented vnto them by order from the Generall Courte baring date the 13th day of September 1653.

It being Desired of vs that wee would further the Indian woorke att Natick What wee may which is our desire as farre as wee see God in the same and for that end that wee would accomidate Dedham with some Land Convenient for them In case they should supply the Indians att Natick : wee doe with all redines acknowledge our selues p'sons and estates and all we haue and are to be the Lords : and hope wee shall therein manifest ourselues When ever hee Call vs : 2ly wee doe with the like redenes acknowledg our selues subiect to this Comonwealth and the Gouerment heare established and therin as instrements in and for God to call sue or" and what we haue in away of god to be Disposed of by them : therefore wee haue attended vnto what was presented vnto vs in that Letter : and adressed ourselues to comply with our Brethren of Dedham for that end choose out two of our beloued Brethren to meete with them and the Comete for that ende who vppon notes attended tyme and place att Roxbury and vnderstanding by them that our Brethren at Roxbury Cann doe litell or nothing toward the accomendation of Dedam in that request In the Letter wee are Willing so fare as wee cann with out to much preiudice to our selues to doe the more for the furtherance of the worke. But the tyme being short sence wee vnderstoode the Case and What may satisfie : and wee meeting with some obstickles in our way to what wee would doe Cannot att Present giue such an answer as wee desire. But if it may not be to prejudicall to the woorke intended wee desire and humbly Craue the patience of this Courte vntell the next sesions which wee conceaue may bee in October hoping by that tyme to be able to answer the honored Court and our Bretherens expectation att Dedham which is the thing wee ayme att or giue : wee hope satisfactory Reasons to the Contrary hoping that wee ourselues In our honest and resonable request shall find Redie acceptance with you in what Lyes in your power to answer vs agayne and so wee humbly take Leaue and rest yours to our power.

Subscribed this 10 of the 3 : mo 1654 by Robert Howard appynted by and in the name of the inhabitants of the towne of Dorchester.

[Page 86 blank.]

[87.] A rate made the 27th day of the 10 m° 1653 for the Towne and Castell of the some of 40li 14s 11d Disbursed as followeth.

	ll.	s.	d.
Imprimus to the Captayne of the Castell	20.	16.	0
Item for Caring of Corne to the Tide mill for Capt. of the Castell	0.	1.	0
Item for driuing up and setting downe and for the keeping of the Cowe that was with Goodman meade	0.	9.	0
Item to the Secretary for writing of Court orders	1.	8.	4
Item for 2 quire of paper		1.	0
Item for a messenger to goe to Mr. Callicots about Tomsons Iland	0.	1.	4
Item for a borde and nayles and worke to stop the Place in the gallery in the meeting howse	0.	2.	11
Item for making the fence by Goodman Toplens	0.	7.	6
Item payd Abraham Howe and Thomas Trott being Constabls to make vp there rate being Short	1.	6.	0
Item payd Thomas Tollman towards a pare of wheles for the Gunn	1.	0.	0
Item payd to a man of Dedham for killing of two woolves	0.	19.	0
Item to Goodman Tollman for killing a woolfe	1.	0.	0
Item payd to John Smith his one rate 14s to Richard Hall 6s 2d and 11s 8d by John Mynett which he should haue Laid out about the meetinghouse is	1.	11.	10
Item to Goode George	3.	10.	0
Item it is Voted that the 19s and 3d that was Dew from Nicholas White for his rate vnpayd should be abated	0.	19.	3
Item for Tomsons Iland the Rate to the Country being 16s 8d and the Towne rate being 8s 4d it is not throfly agreed one only for present we Craue allowance but shal doe the best to gitt it if you cann sett vs in som way to do it sum is	1.	5.	0
Item for Jeremia Rylands his rate no hops to get it	0.	1.	0
Sum totall. Laid out to this 4th day of 10 m° 54: is	34.	19.	2
Item Dew from Thomas Tollman for that Thomas Lakes Child died within two yeares	11.	0.	0

Sum Dew to the Towne is 21. 12. 9

[88.] It is ordered at a towne meeting this 4th of the 10 m° 1654 that Mr. Robart Howard shall draw out a warrant according to the warrant of the last yeare to Henry Coundly for the gathering vp of Mr. Mathers' pay which is behind to this daye.

4 of 10 m. 54. It is ordered or voted att a towne meting that our Decons and John Capen shall make a rate for Mr. Mathers pay for this yeare.

4 of 10 m 54 It is voted at a towne meting that Josufe Farnworth Nicholas Clap and William Clarke shall vewe the waye by the buring place and Larance Smithes barne to conseder whether

there may be ground spared to supply Larence Smith without hurte to the way.

1654. Item there was Coming to the Towne out of the Cuntry rate for the yeare 1653 : 3^{li} : 10^s : which was to be payd to those men to our Capt. 2^{li} 17^s and to Larance Smith 13^s which monys wee Nathaniel Patten and Thomas Lake haue payd being then Counstabls :

9 : 2 : 1655 : Deacon wiswall was appointed by the selectmen to make agreem't with leiftenant Ellis John french and goodman Oldredge of Braintree about a parsill of medow In our bounds which they desire to rent of the towne of Dorchester :

[89.] Wee whose names are here vnderscribed And being appynted by our several Townes and being mett this first day of the 7 : m⁰ 1654 : to Lay out the High Waye through Dorchester Woods from Brauntre Bounds to Roxbury bounds : do agree as followeth :

first that the Waye shall be fowre Rodd Wide from Brantre bounds to Roxbury bounds : secondly beginning neere Hinrye Crane's house the Way to Lye one the Sowthest side of it in the old Beaten roede waye : and so to a Lowe White oake marked on the same side of the waye and so by the marked trees to the Brooke : so from the Brooke the way being Lade in the Winter we agreed to take about a roode wide into Anthony Golliford's lott wheare the fence Interrupts the waye : and so to a marked post to wards John Gill's howse : and from thence to an other marked post against John Gills howse : from thence to a stake in Elder Kingslys yearde and from thence to the mille in the olde beaten roede waye : and from the mille to tow greet rockes one the Lower side of the waye att Robert Spures and Henry Merifelds howses end : and from thence to the new feild by the marked trees in the olde roede waye : and so through the new feld wheare the waye formerly was and from thence by the marked trees one the Left hand to Roxbury bounds :

of Dorchester NICHOLAS CLAPE
———— ——— WILLIAM CLARKE.
of Brantree   MOSES PAINE.
GREGORY BELLCHER.

Item whereas there was dew from John Gurnett for the Cowe that was meads : 4^{li} : 17^s which he sould for the Towne hath paid as followeth

Item paid to Ensine Foster which was dew to Hudson
for our Deputies Diett in the yere : 54 . . . 03^{li} 00 00
Item paid Goode George for the Selectmens Diet . · 01 00 00
Item paid by Nathaniell Patten for John Gurnett to
the Towne 00. 17 00

Sume is $4^{li.}$ $17^{s.}$ 0

Item whereas there was dew to the Towne from Nathañell Patten

John Minott and John Wales one the book in the year: 1654: 5^{li}: 15^s: 9^d paid as followeth.

Item to Mr Jones for mending the pound . . .	00. 12.	00
Item to Leftenant Clape	00. 11.	04
Item to William Pound for mending the Stockes .	00. 01.	00
Item to Thomas Wiswall for the glasiers Diett .	00. 05.	10
It. for Carige of Capt. Damford's Corne . .	00. 03.	09
It. for killing a woulfe in Caues pasture . .	00. 15.	11
[**90.**] Item Nicholas Whites and Tomsons island rats	00. 15.	06
Item for the hire of a horse to goe to Punkepage	00. 01.	06
Item paid towards the 3^{li}: 15^s: to the Capt. of the Castell which was Dew to Phelipes for our Debuties Diett for the yere 1654	03. 02.	03

Sume is 6^{li}: 9^s: 1^d:

So the Some paid and remains to me Nathaniell Patten 00. 13. 04
Now I the said Nat Patten am Debtor to the Towne 17^s. which I vnder tooke to pay for John Gurnett and for a wolfe which I had allowance from the Tresuer: 10^s: and I am to pay 2^s. to the rate mad in the yeare: 1654: which Thomas Burde gathred the whole is 01. 09. 00
So take out 13^s: 4^d remayns 00. 15. 08
Now there is Dew to me Nathaniell Patten from John Minott which I laid out for his part of his rate of the yere: 1654: 16^s. 9^d. which hee will pay wheare you will appynt so all thes somes ar satisfied: and there is Dew to me Nat Patten from the Towne — 00. 01. 01
Now I the said nathaniell Patten doo put over this 1^s. 1^d. dew to me: to pay Richard Evens he being not satisfied for Laing a borde in the west gallery tho as I thofte I had allowed him more out of the former account then it was worth but he demanding it I am willing to allow being . fines 00. 01. 02
of the 16^s. 9^d. fines dew from John minett abousd hee hath paid 12^s. to captaine dauenport . . . 00. 12. 00
Richard Cortes and Thomas Tillestone being Constabls for the yere 55 there rate was 72^{li}: 16^s: 0: and they are to pay the treasu^r 70^{li}: 14^s: 8^d. 3 farthings so they are to retorne the Towne 2. 1. 3
                                                                                                            farthing
12 of 8 m 57 Dew from Richard Hall and Henry Woodard Constabls for the yere 5^s. aboue that they should pay to the Tresuer · 4. 5. 0
Dew from thomas Toleman in all 5. 10. 0

                                                                                      11. 16. 3

Decon Weswall to be accountable for 15 hundred of bords

whereof Left. Clap had 7 hundred   remaynes 8 hundred

[91.] of a rate of Twenty pownds sixe shillinges eleaven pence chardged vpon the Towne of Dorchester by the select men in the yeere 1655 they giue this Accompt of the Disbursment for the towne vse as followeth

Imp^{rs} paid by Thomas Burd vnto p'ticulers here aftermencioned viz Rodger Clap and John Wiswall Deputyes	9 – 3 – 0
It. vnto William Blake ⎱ for the high ⎱ Richard Hall ⎰ waye through ⎰ Peter Lyon ⎰ their great Lotts ⎰	1 – 16 – 0
It. vnto Deacon Parkes of Roxbury For chardges about Tompson Iland	1 – 13 – 6
It. vnto William Clarke For wood to the watch and for Runninge the Lyne	0 – 12 – 6
It. For select mens chardge at sister Georges For the yeare 55	3 – 15 – 8
It. vnto William Pond vpon Accompt For worke to be done at the Meetinge house	1 – 16 – 5
It. vnto Rodger Clap for hay and bords	0 – 2 – 0
Totall is	18 – 19 – 1
Rest due vnto the Towne From brother Burd this 23 (9) 56	1 – 7 – 10
Wherof Brother burd hath paid vnto sister George, towards the select mens chardge this yeare 56	1 – 1 – 0
to balance this Accompt with brō burd Rest due From him	0 – 6 – 10
which we Assigne him to paye vnto sister George vpon Accompt this yeare 56 and so dischardge him of the being the Rate ffor the yeare 54 and 55:	20 – 6 – 11

Wheras the Balif Thomas Burd in the yeare 55 was Charged to pay vnto the liftenant the some of won pound fiftene shiling and six penc: but wee haue found that the liftenant hath bin payd other wayes therfore the Balife is still Charged with so much as detter vnto the towne: the liftenant was payd with seuen hundred of bords.

9 : 12 : 1656 we gaue goodman georg a note for to reō 35^s. 6^d. of Thomas Bird which he should haue paid to the leiftenant: —

Also goodman George had half a hundered of Towne bords.

[Page 92 blank.]

[93.] This : 3 : of the 10 m° 1655 the officers that were Chosen for this yeare ensuing by the Towne &c.

Selectmen John Weswall
Ensine Foster
Edward Bricke
Nathaniell Glouer
Nathaniell Patten

DORCHESTER TOWN RECORDS.

Raters
John Smith
John Mynott
William Clarke
Suporvisors for the highwayes for necke land all so
Anthony Gulliuerd
Nicholas Clape
Baylife Henry Garnseye.

It is voted by the Towne this: 3: of 10: m. 1655 that they haue given Power to the Selectmen to set the Towne for Any rate in wheate Rye peas and Indian or any other graine as they shall thinke Fett for this yeare Insuing both for herds men or other: this order was voted the 7: 10: 1657: that it should continue this yeare alsoe.

[Page 94 blank.]

[95.] Wheareas the Generall Court out of Religious Care of the Education of the youth of this Comonwealth in the prenciples of Christian Religion hath enioyned the Select men of every Towne within there severall Lymetts to haue a vigilent eie to see that mens Cheldren and such as are within their Charge be Catechized in som Orthodox Catechisme in familes: so as they may be redie to answer the Selectmen as they see tyme Convenient to examine them. Wee the Selectmen of this Towne of Dorchester for the tyme being in our obedience to Authoritie and in pursute of so vsefull and p'fitable a worke Do hereby will and require all parents masters and any that haue the Charge and oversight of any youth with in this Plantation that they be diligent to obserue this Iniuntion to Catechize there Cheldren servants and others with in there severall Charge in some sound and Orthodox Catechisme that they may be able to render account heareof when they shall be herevnto required either in the Church or privatly: as vppon advice shall be Judged most conduceing to the generall good of all men. And faile not herein vppon such penaltie as the Court shal see reson to inflict vppon Information giuen against such as shalbe found Delinquent herein: this 11 of the 12: m° 1655.

8-12 m. 55. It is agreed by and betwene the Selectmen of Dorchester for the tyme being one the one part in the behalfe of the Towne and Thomas Wiswall and his sonne Icabod Wiswall as follows:

First that Icabod with the consent of his Father shall from the: 7: of March next Ensuinge vnto the end of three full years from thence to be compleate and ended Instruct and teach in a free Schoole in Dorchester all such Cheldren as by the inhabitants shall be Comitted vnto his Care in Ennglish Latine and Greeke as from time to time the Cheldren shall be Capable and allso in struct them in Writinge as hee shall·be able: which is to be vnderstood such Cheldren who are so fare entred all redie to knowe there Leters and to spell some what: and also prouided the Schoole howse from time to time be kept in good order and comfortable for a man to abide in both in somer and in Winter by prouiding ffire seasonably so that it may neather be preiudicall to master nor Scholer and in cause of palpable neglect and matter of Complaint and not reformed it shall not binde the m^r. to Endanger his health.

Secondly that the Selectmen of Dorchester shall from yeare to yeare every yeare paye or cause to be paid vnto Icabod or his Father by his Assignment the full somme of Twentie Five pounds two thirdes in wheate pease or barley marchantable and one thirde in Indian att or before the first of March dueringe the three yeares yearly att price Currant which is to be vnderstood the price which the generall Court shall from time to time appoint.

EDWARD BRECKE in the name of the rest.
ICHABOD WISWALL

[Page 96 blank.]

[**97.**] *Dorchester the 11th of 12: m°. 1655:* It is Couenanted and agreed betwene the Selectmen of this Towne and Robert Stanton of the same towne for the keeping of the Oxe heard att the Vsuall place aboue the Mill for such a tyme in the yeare for fiue yeares from the Daye of the Date aboue said that is to saye from the 8th day of the 3 mo : to the 8 : of the 8 : m°. following and so from yeare to yeare dewring the terme of five yeares : That the said Robert Stanton doth Covenant with vs to keepe all such Oxen and Steeres being two yeares old or vpward with what Drie Cowes wee shall put a feeding of any of this Towne, and none of other Townes : And to keepe all such Oxen and steeres in a herd as shall be delivered him att the Penn and to take Care of such feeding Cowes or Oxen in some Convenient place where it may be best for the fating of them according to his best discretion : The walke or place of feeding to be one the Sowth side of the River nerponsett and aboue or beyound the Cow walke of Dorchester and not suffred to goe among the Cowes. And that the said Robert is to make and maintaine a sufficent Pen both for Largnes of ground and soficince of fence so that the Oxen and steeres may not hurt one another. And to goe forth with the said Oxen and steeres halfe an howre by sonne in the morning and to bring them in about sonnsett in the Evning that so the honors may haue them there, if the please to send for them, ether in the morning or Evning before the said time of there going forth, and not be disapointed : And for his faithfullnes and Care here in he is to have : 2^s p' head of every beast to be paid the one halfe in Indian Corne and the other halfe in wheat Barly or pease att two payments the first paiment by the : 12th day of the : 4 m° and the Last paiment by the : 30th day of the : 7 : m° following and so from yeare to yeare dewring the terme of five years from the day aboue said : And further the said Robert is to haue the Vse of such penns as ar there or may be there to Improue them to his best advantage Dewring the tyme of the five yeares : And he is to billd an howse by the penn of 12 foote in Length and 9 foote in bredth or such a one as is att the sheep penn and to repaire it and att the end of the five yeares to Leave it to the Towne and for the Dewing of it : the Towne is to giue the said Robert Stanton thirtie shillings in the like paie aboue said to be paide out of the Cattell hee keepes by equall proportion and the howse to be bilte by the tyme he is to beginn to keepe the heard : And what so ever Oxen or steeres shall goe vppon the Commons of Dorchester shall be payable to the Oxe heard according as these that are there : And in case there shall be Just grounde and profe of his niglectt herein, then the bargen to be voide and for the payment of his Corne att the times agreed one if you will not bring it to his howse he will appint some place in the Towne wheare you may bring it which is att Thomas Lakes howse.

The mark of | ROBERT STANTON.

[98.] *10 of: 1 m° 1656.* The names of such as ar appinted to Vewe the fence in the Comon feldes for this yeare 1656 :

Imprimus the neck of Land — { Thomas Jones / Richard Baker

The feld behind M^{ris}. Stotons — { Elder Witherington / James Minot :

The gret Lots from M^{ris} Holland and so round westward and end so fare as Widdow popes Lott — { Richard Leeds / Joseph Farnworth

The rest of the gret Lots fenc — { Elder Minott / Thomas Tollman

Twentie eaker Lots { Thomas Sweft / Clement Toplen

T Lot be hind M^r. Jones { William Clarke / Edward Blake :

The Lot behind Thomas Weswals — { Thomas Jones / Joseph Farnworth

The Lott behind M^r. Mathers : — { William Pound : / Timothy Mather

The Lott behind Thomas Burds { Richard Hawes / Jasper Rush

The 8 eaker Lots { James Vmfres / Henry Woodard

[99.] *Dorchester 2 of the 12 mth 1646*
This is a true copy
For the finall Determining and ending of all matters in controuersy : conserning the fence about the grett lotts, the capttins neck the 6 aker lotts and other proporsions of land now within the same fence : the proprietors who are owners of ther seuerall proporsions of land with in the sayd fence ; haue refered them selfues to the Arbitration ; of M^r. Isach Heath, John Johnson and Wilyam parkes of Roxbury ; binding them selfes heerby to stand to what the sayd Arbitrators shall determine both in respect of what fense shall be mayd ; and wher ; and by whom, and euery won of the proprytors hath liberty if he please to giue information in the case ; to the said Arbitrators ; when the shall com to Dorchester to be informed therin ;

Richard Mather
John Glouer

Nickolas Clap
Thomas millett

Thomas makpeas
Edward Brecke
Robert Howerd
Wilyam blake
Wilyam Clarke
John pearse
Rodger Clap
Edward Clap
James Bates
Thomas Wiswall
Cristofar Gibsone
michaell Willis
Austine Clement
Hopestil foster
Richard Withington
Jonas Humphres
James Humphrey
Richard Hawes
Wilyam Sumner
John Kingsly
Nicholas Buttler
Richard Leeads
John Smith
Wilyam turner
John Hollond
Josepth farnworth
Wilyam layne:

John Hill His mark **1**
Sarah Bradford
John Holman
Richard Calycott
Richard Hall
Wilyam Triscott
Clement toplife
Antony Gulifard
Henery Way
Aron Way
Wilyam Irland
Richard Way
Nickolas George
John Gingine
Nickolas Eline
  His mark **3**
Josepth tuchell
Thomas touleman
Richard Howlbrook
  His mark **R H**
androw picher
Thomas Tilestone
Bray Wilkines
Jane pope
Isabel Rigby
John whiplle

[**100.**] *The 23 of the 12 month 1646.* Wee whose names are under written; being chosen by the inhabitants of Dorchester; to giue in ower determination about the fenses of a parsell of land caled the great lotts; capttins neck and 8 aker lotts and 6 aker lotts and other lands and medowes within the sayd fense; to order and determine as is Hereafter expresed

This fense to begine att a creecke betwixt the new dwellinge House of John Holonds and the mill belonging to Edward Breck as the fense now standeth and so all along vnto the little spott of meado that belongs to John Holand and from that meado all along by the beach Vntill it comes to the ould fense agaynst Edward Breckes Barn and from that last last mensioned place as the fense now stands vnto the corner of this fenc next the towne and as the outsid fense now standeth belonging to the grett lotts all along as now it standeth vntill it commeth att the Riuer commonly caled neponsett Riuer taking in the 8 aker and 6 aker lotts. And if itt be found by experienc that neponsett Riuer be nott a suffisyent fense to secure the corne from damag itt shall be in the power of the mageor part of the proprietors of this fild to secure itt att an equale charge of all the propryetors by ether Keeper or fense as they shall Judg most meett:

And where euer itt toucheth vpon any land of the sd John Holand hee the s^d. John shall make and mayntayne the moyetye of the s^d. fense for euer and the other moyetye to make and **maynetaine** for euer by the propryetors of the s^d filde.

And whereas some medowes are alredy fensed in and others intended to be fensed in at there owne charge and so to mayntayne it for euer.

wee order that if thos partyes or any that shall giue in securyty with in 20 days vnto the 7 men that are chosen to order the prudensiall affayers of the Towne to make up a sufficient fence betwene this and the first of the 3 month which shall bee in the yeare of the Lord 1648 : and to mayntayne itt for euer that then shuch medowes shall nott pay nor make any part of the outside fence but all other medowes to beare part of the fence that is to say 2 akers of medow to beare as much fence as one aker of upland and all the upland to beare an eaquall proporsion of this outside fence to secure this fild that is to say euery aker a like quantity of the said fence to make and mayntayne for euer. And where as wee vnderstand that some perticular men by contracte ether with the Toune or particular persons haue engaged them selfues to make and mainetayne for euer seuerall parsels of this fence wee leaue them to make good ther perticuler bargaines and contractes : wee order that euery mans fence shall lye aganst his owne land as much as may bee and wher itt cannot be layd against ther owne land yett to bee layde as neare to each mans house as conueniently it can bee and wher as some men haue mayd more fence then there proporsion will com now to acording to the number of akers : wee order that who euer shall com in to make and maintayne any part of shuch fence shall giue an equall Value for the ould fence as 2 men shall Judge it to bee worth or otherwise if he or they refuse to giue so much for the ould fence then it is in the power of the owner of this to take it away Vnto his owne proper use and the other to sett up a suffisient fence in the Roume of it : wee order that euery man shall know where his fence shall lye and what quantity euery man shall beare betwene this and the first day of the first moth if possible : we further order that euery mans fence shall be mayd or repayred suffisiently to the satisfaction of shuch as are apoynted to Vewe the fenses betwixt this day and the 10 of the 2 month Vppon shuch penaltys as the afore sayde 7 men shall see cause to Inflict uppon them : Further we order that it shall bee in the liberty of any of the proprietors at there owne charge to fence out any part of there owne land prouided that still he or they maintaine there proporsione of there outside fence and If any man haue or herafter shall fence in any part of ther owne land from the aforesayde fild that what damage soeuer any of the propryetors of the sayde fild shall reseue by ether cattell or swine of there owne or others shuch person or person or persons as shall [**101.**] particularly fence in there land from the sayde fild that what damage the sayde filde shall reseue through the defecte of his or theire fence he or they shall make it good as two Indeferant men shall Judge the damage to be.

And If any cattel or swine that of Right ought to feed in the aforsayd filde shall breake in or doe any hurt or damag vnto thes lots enclosed according to there liberty afore expressed from the aforesayde Generall filde shuch cattel or swine are nott to bee counted trespasers nor pay any damage.

Wee make ownely this exceptione concerninge one parsel of this land caled pine neck if the owner or owners of that land or medow doe giue securyty vnto the aforesayde 7 men within 20 days after the date herof for euer to secure this filde from damage through any part of that land and also secure it selfe from any damage that may com to them by any cattel that have Right to feed in this filde that then this land shall be exempted from any part of this generall fence, otherwise to beare it proporsione Equale with other lands of like qualyty

ISACK HEATH
JOHN JOHNSONE
WILLIAM PARKE

And though the order of feeding was not put to us yet out of ower owne experienc wee think good to aduise that the feeding of this fild should bee acording to there seuerall quantytys in this filde.

A true account of the fence of the grett lotts and the maner of of lynge of itt.

wee began with M^r. Glouer and Brother Brecke:

M^r. Glouer — 75 Rode — 1 foott his began in the side fence

Mr Bates — 8 Rode 3 foott

Richard way — 6 Rod — 13 foot and Halfe it recheth 3 foot short of Brother Breckes

Edward Breck — 38 Rod — it goes to the yonder corner of his medowe:

Then we went to the Creeck at Captins neck

	Rod	foot	Half
Edward Breck	10 Rod	0	0
William Sumner	6 Rod	13	h^1

	Rod	foot	
E^d Brik for Rich^d lot	12	13	h^1
Richard Calycott	12	4	h^1
Jonas Humphres	8 want	6	0
Elder mynot	6	2	h^1
Augustin Clement	4	0	0
Richard Hawes	2	12	0
Edward Breck	4	8	0
Antony Gulyfer	6	2	0
Jonas Humphry	2	15	0
Richard Leeds	3	1	h^1
Bray wilkins	10	4	h^1
william turner	3	2	0
michaell willis	4	1	h^1
Nickolas clap	2 nex beyond the poole		
John Holand	4	13	0
widow way	6	2	h^1
william Blak	4	14	0
m^r makepeas	4 and quarter		
Joseph tuchel	11	6	6

[102.] The Grett lotts next aboue Mr Glouers

| Mr Stoughton | 7 | 4 | 0 |

DORCHESTER TOWN RECORDS. 79

John Wiswall	——	6 —	13 —	0
Mr Haward	——	6 —	14 —	0
John pears about the Gate —		5 —	5 —	0
John Kingsly	——	4 —	0 —	0
M^r. withington	——	6 —	0 —	0
John Smith	——	19 —	0 —	0
Edward Clape	——	2 —	13 —	0
Elder mynot	——	22 —	6 —	0
m^r Buttler	——	2 —	13 —	0
widow Rigby	——	16 —	4 —	0
The last lot next Bro.				
Brik m^r mathers	——	12 —	14 —	0
wilyam layne	——	4 —	11 —	0
Josepth farnworth	——	4 —	0 —	0
Henry way	——	2 —	0 —	0
willyam Irland	——	2 —	13 —	0
John & tho. wiswall	——	5 —	9 —	$\frac{1}{2}$
George Dyer	——	6 —	2 —	0
willyam clarke	——	2 —	13 —	0
widdow pope	——	14 —	3 —	0
Josepth tuchell	——	6 —	14 —	0
Thomas millett	——	4 —	0 —	0
John Hill	——	5 —	5 —	0
John Whiple	——	4 —	0 —	0
Thomas touleman	——	6 —	14 —	0
John philips	——	2 —	0 —	0
The 6 Acre lotts:				
Andrew picher	——	26 —	3 —	0
John phillips for his lott and medowe		20 —	7 —	h^l

Richard Leeds for his 20 Acers lott Thos Hilly's necke 27 and a quar^r

Jo. Grenowway for the pine Neck	20 —	8 —	h^l
m^r makepeace for his 12 Acers of medowe	8 —	3 —	0
willyam Ireland	5 —	1 —	h^l
Robert thornton	1 —	6 —	0
John Gingin	8 —	3 —	0
Thomas Tilstone	20 —	2 —	h^l
Richard Hall	8 —	3 —	0
widdow miller	65 —	1 —	h^l

Andrew picther one length of Rayles by the side of the Gate

Joseph philips begines at the norther part of the Gate and to the corner of his owne lot 2 Rod and 2 foot

M^r patten Betweene Richard Leeds and Jo Grencway 2 Rod 12 foot

Nickolas George next M^r patten 6 Rod and 13 feet

ISACH HETH
JOHN JOHNSON
WILLYAM PARK

We desire the Vewers of the fenses of Dorchester Nickolas Butler willyam Blak and John Smith to aquaynt each man where his fence lyes to the end that damag may be preuented and peace procured and establyshed among them all.

[**103.**] This the work was dune in the yeare 55 ;
Acording to the Court order for the Running of the lines betwene Dorchester and Dedhame we whose names are vnder written being Chosen by the townes of Dorchester and Dedham to renew and settle the bounds betwene the townes did acordingly meette and agreed of the lines betwene the towens and the bounds and the bounds was marked from the hed line of Dorchester and Roxbury to a heap of stones on the lowe playne and so from thens to the Ragged playne and so forward according as itt was formerly rune and marked out ;

For Dorchester	For Dedham
WILYAM SUMNER	JOSHUA FISHER
WILYAM CLARK	DANIELL FISHER
NATHANAEL GLOUER	WILYAM AUERY
MAHALALEEL MUNNINGS	

[**104.**] 1 10 56

at a meetinge of the Towne accordinge to the yeareley meetinge a p'sentment against deffectiue ffence of the great necke beinge Comitted to the Consideratiō of the towne they voted a Remissiō of it vpō this Consideratiō that the proprietors of the necke doe some tyme in the eleauenth month next meet together and take Effectual Course for amendinge seuerall greuances now Complained of viz that such Fence as maie be spered be take of and a new p'portiō of the Fence be made and doe for that end appoint m^r Jones Ensigne Foster and Deacon Clap fforth with to veiw what Fence they iudge meet to be taken of and make Returne vnto the next meetinge of the selectt men who shall then order the meeting of the p'pretors acordingly.

voted Affirmatiue.

for the p'sentment about the necke waye it was suspended and Leiutenuant Clap Ensigne Foster, sergeant Clerke Mr Jones, Joseph Pharnwoorth are aponted a Comitee to Examine the waye and Refforme what in their iudgm̄t they thinke is mistaten and make Returne vnto the select men vpon their Returne or maior part of them : who shall Remit part or all as they see Reason and are Required hereby to be serious in p'vidinge soe amendinge of it without p'tiality and herby we engage ourselues to be thankeffull to them for their seruice therein and not Coutenance any that shall be Discontēd without Cause the Returne is to be the 8 of 10 56

voted Affirmatiue.

In reference to the Order aboue said Mr. Jones Ennsine Foster and Decon Clap were appyntoud by the Towne to vew the fence att the necke which accordingly they haue donn ; And therefore wee the Selectmen Do order and apynt that all the p'prietors of the neckeland doe meete att the meting howse by 9 : of the Clocke in the forenoone one the 7th day of the : 11 : m^o next one penaltie of xij^d for every one failing this 8th of 10 m 56 :

this 8th of : 10 m : 56 John Smith desired vs to pay vnto Robert Pond 12^s which he wil be accountable for which we accordingly did.

At a meetting of the p'prieto^rs of the necke of land   In reference to the order of the towne aboue written it was agreed as followeth:

That what fence may bee spared on both ends bee taken off and a new deuision made according to a dew p'portion and men chosen to p'portion the same. And for the remouing of any part of it, it shall bee at the discresion of those men chosen as they shall see meete.

Mr Thomas Jones, Edward clap, Joseph pharnworthe, willyam clarke were chosen the same time to doe that worke this was Voted and agreed on by the proprietors of the necke the seaventh of the ii month 1656:

[105.]   9 : 9 m. 1657. An account of the Rate of 40^{li} : 9^s : 11^d : made in yeare 1655 : for discharge of severall Expences and Charges for the Townes vse and Scoole Cometted vnto the hands of Henrȳ Garnsey Bailife and

	li	s.	d.
Item to William Pound for mending the Stockes	00.	09.	06
I^t for Selectmens Diett in the yeare 56 : to Goode George 3^{li} 2^s 10. whereof shee receved 22^s of Edmon Blake which he owed the towne for the Scoole house and som of Thomas Burd so we Laid out	01.	12.	11
Item Left Clap as Debute for the yeare 56	01.	16.	06
Item to Deacon Weswall as Debute and other p'ticulers as by bill	02.	16.	06
Item to Nathaniel Patten in severall p'ticulers as by bill of which	00.	10.	06
my rate is 9^s 4^d so remaynes to me 14^d.			
I^t to Goodman Andrus for woorke about meting howse.	00.	08.	00
Item to Edmon Browne for worke about meting howse.	00.	05.	06
I^t to Richard Evens for worke about the Scoole howse	00.	10.	06
I^t to Mr Glouer for running the Lyne and Charge about Bastian Keans wife in her sickness	00.	06.	6
It. to William Somner for Runing the Lyne	00.	05.	
I^t to Mahalaell Munnings for Runing the Lyne	00.	05.	0
I^t to Robert Voce and his two sonns for runing the Lyne.	00.	07.	6
I^t to Robert Badcoke for Runing the Lyne	00.	02.	6
I^t to Thomas Hollman for Running the Lyne	09.	01.	0
I^t to Robert Redman for killing a woolfe .	01.	00.	0
I^t to William Trescott for killing a woolfe	01.	00.	0
I^t to James Minott for his man Pike to Keepe hoggs.	00.	02.	6
I^t to Robert Pearce for mending a gate in the greet Lots	00.	01.	0
Item allowed Henry Gearnsey for lose of Corne for want of Convenient roome and having no order to dispose of it	00.	09.	0

Iᵗ wee allow him the said Henry for his paines att Necke	00. 12. 0
Iᵗ paid the Scoolemaster Icabud Wiswall by the Baylife	20. 19. 11
Iᵗ the Baylife craue allowance for John Smith John Plume Thomas Garnett Samuell Hollway Retorne Munning and Bastian Keane, som of them gonn, other poore, and Mʳ Edward Tinnge tresurer the whole is	00. 04. 10
Iᵗ for Selectmens Diett for: 1657:	03. 00. 0
Sum is	ˡˡ37 6ˢ. 8ᵈ.
Dew from Henry Garnsey, Bailife	02. 09. 3
from Mr. Jones or Anthony Fisher for the farm rate	00. 14. 0

Which soms amounts to 40 ˡⁱ 9 ˢ 11 ᵈ

Item paid by Mr. Jones to Thomas Wesswall for the Scoolemaster	02. 00. 0
Item Henry Garnsey paid to Ensine Foster 2 bushels and halfe of pease att 4s p. bush. is	00. 10. 0
and Henry Garnsey paid Mr. Jones 8 bush.	1. 12. 0
and Henry Garnsey paide Icabud Weswall	0. 04. 0
so Dew from Henry Garnsey this 8ᵗʰ of 12m° 57	0. 03 :

[**106.**] The account of John Smith taken this 11 of the 3 m: 57 of his Disbursments about the meeting howse and recites as fare as we cann by reson he Loosed his notes to this day:

Item to William Pound	3. 16. 0
Iᵗ to the Glasier formerly	1. 17. 0
Item for nayles	0. 05. 0
Item to Henry Ledbetter for a dayes worke	0. 02. 0
Item for Carting of stones to the meting howse	0. 05. 0
Item for a dore to Mʳⁱˢ Stotons and Mʳⁱˢ mathers seate	0. 03. 2
Item to the Glasier in the yeare 56	1. 10. 0
Item for seting the glas from boston and helping the grasier	0. 01. 6
	7. 19. 8
Now of this 30ˢ to the Glasier in 56 he hath not paid anything but restes one the Towne so the whole sum Laid out by the said John Smith is: 6ˡⁱ : 7ˢ : 8ᵈ	
Iᵗ Laid out for nayles and for William pons man	0. 3. 0

Writs of John Smith Item of John Gurnett	00. 18. 0
Item of Thomas Swifte	01. 01. 5
Item of Richard Hall	00. 06. 2
Item his Rate formerly in 54, 55	00. 14. 10
Item his Last rate that Henry Garnsey Baylife should haue gathered	00. 11. 10

DORCHESTER TOWN RECORDS.   83

Item of John minott 00. 11. 8
Item of Thomas Burd 01. 10. 8
Item wee paid for him to Robert Pound by his
 desire 00. 12. 0

     Sum receved by John Smith is 06. 05. 9

   so remaynes to John Smith from the Towne in all 5ˢ 5d
[**107.**] This the furst of the tenth month 56, the offisers that wer Chosen by the towne for the yeare ensuing:
Selectmen Mʳ. patten
   Edward Breck
   Ensine Foster
   Mʳ. Jones
   Nathanael Glouer
Rators Sargent Capen
   William Clark
   Robert Badkok
Super Visors for the High Wayes
      Georg Badkok
      James Humphres
      Richard Hale
Baliffe   Thomas lake

 12 : 11 1646 Ed wiat came and demanded pay for Cow keeping In the yeare 1655 : of mⁱˢ stowghton : 4ˢ and of John wales 15ˢ of Richard davis 4ˢ. we gave him a note to warne the said partys to giue answer at next meetting if they did not pay why they would not or elce they must exspect the bayliff to make distreesse ffor the same : This note was signed by
       Eᵈ. breck in the name of the rest
 This the 12 11 56 there was a warrant Giuen vnto the balif Thomas lake for to warne al the towne perticulerly to meet to Consider of many wayhty things that Consernes the whole towne : the day is the 23 day of the 11 month : about 9 of the Clok in the forenowne ;
 At a generall Towne meetting the 23 of 11 : 1656 It was voted that all the lands In the towne should be recorded in the new booke.
 Brother w Blake senor was chosen recorder for the towne and to take the bookes and mapp &c. Into his keeping, also was chosen clark of the writts for the county of Suffolk :

[Page 108 blank.]

 [**109.**] This the 23 day of the 11 month upon a Generall towne meeting a lawfull meeting thes Vots were Voted and fully agreed upon as followeth :
 Furst that this was voted that the Commons should bee stinted :
 Secondly : they agreed to stinte ownly the three Diuisions that bee nearest to the towne, and all lands within that Compas ;

This was also Voted at the same meeting aboue sayde vpon the 23. 11. 56 that the select men should forthwith send prohibisione to John Aldis or any other that he or they shall not fell or Cutt or Carry away any more timber out of ower seder swampe without any further alowanc from the towne : and giue an Account for what hee or they haue all Redy taken :

That whereas the towne uppon a lawfull meeting did Voted that the Selectt men should forthwith send p'hibyison vnto the sayd John Aldis of Dedham that he should seas from Cutting any more of ower timber in ower Seder Swampe or other wheare : wee therfore by Vertue of that vote and order did send Vnto the sayde John Aldis and hee did satisfy vs, that hee nor none other in his name or by his order hath Cutt up as much as he hath payde for in the tow thousand of bord : for he Came and Gaue up an account of what he had dune namly that hee had but Gott twenty three thousand of shingle and in bords six Hundred : which amounts but to ten shillings eight pens and this account hee Gaue upon the second day of the last month. 56.

This the second of the last month in 56 : a memorandome that the Gran Jurymen were with us to speake with us aboute som things that they thought were lyable to bee presented as namly this that the Chatecysing of Children is neglected in ower towne.

At a Generall Towne meeting the 23 11. 56 Brother William Blake the elder was Chosen Recorder for the towne of Dorchester and to attend the Select men from time to time to scribe and trascribe shuch orders and Records as should by them bee Committed vnto him and for that end wee the Select men doe order that the sayde william Blake doe take the towne Books or Booke into his hands and Keeping as likwise the mapp or mapps Conserninge the towne and Keepe them secuerly and not Deliuer the same to any but by order from some of the Select men.

At a Generall Towne meeting the 23 11 56 itt was Voted thatt the three deuisions and other land in the Cow walke should bee stinted. In refferenc to that Vote wee the select men of Dorchester doe order that all persons within this plantation that haue any lott land or Deuident in any of the aforesayd lands doe bring in a note Vnto some one of the Select men beetweene this and the furst of the furst month next Vppon penalty of forfeyting flue shillings to bee taken by distres or otherwise for the neglect hearof.

Dated the seCond of the twelfe month 56 : —

This the 9 of the last month in 56 Goodman Vose was with vs to desier vus to propose this to the towne vppone some meting of the towne that they would lay him out his 40 akers which he bought of M^r. Glouer up towards the Blew hills.

This the 9 of the last month Goodman touleman doth desire us that wee should p'rose this vnto the towne he hauing a hard bargine of the Child he desiers that they Consider him somthing and abate him somthing of that which is due vnto the towne by his bargaine.

A memorandom to Remember to giue notise vnto the towne that they may bring in ther Votes for the magestrates and County tressurer in the second weeke of the furst month in 57 :

[110.] *The 9 of the last month 56.* The names of sLuch as are appoynted to Vew the fenses in the Common filds for this yeare 57:

Imprimus the necke of land { Richard Withington / Rodger Sumner.

The filde behinde Mr Stoughons { John mynott / Richard Baker

The grett lotts from Mr Hollands and so round westward and end so fare as widdowe popes lott . . . } Geoarge Procter / John Gurnell

For the Rest of the grett lott fence { William Robinson / Thomas Tilestone

The twenty acere lotts . { wiliam clarke / Thomas Dauenport:

The lot behinde Mr Jones . . { Sargent Gapen: / Henery Kebby.

The lott behinde Thomas wisswale . . { John wiswale / william Clarke.

The lot behinde mr mather { Geoarge Dyer / william Ponde

The lotts behinde Thomas Burdes house . { Nickolas Clapp / Thomas Andrewes

The 8 aker lotts . . . { James Humphres / Rodger Sumner

[111.] *This the 9 of the 12 month in 56.* A memorandome that wee the Select men of Dorchester Doe order that the same orders shall stand still in forse as namly that about fenses in all Corne filds, both for the suffycentsy of it and the time when it shall bee vp and the Same orders about hogs that the be so sufisiently yoaked and Ringed: and that John Plume shall see that all hogs bee yoaked and Ringed.

It was Voted by the towne the 21 of the 12mth 56 that it should bee the halifes office to looke that Swine be yoaked and Ringed accordinge to order: and hee is to take the Penalty as is expressed in the order if they be not so Ringed and yoaked:

It was voted by the towne the: 10 of the last mth 56 that Robert Vose was to haue 40 acres of land layd out which was granted vnto Mr John Glouer neare the blew hills adjoyning to the medow of the sayd Vose:

This the 9 of the furst month 57 the Select men Gaue order for the laying of out this sayd 40 acres vnto the sayd Vose in refferenc to the towne vote: and they appoynt william Sumner william Clarke william Robinson to see it layd out:

At a metting of the selectmen the 12 : 4 : 1657:

Thomas Bird brought a note from Henry woodwarde Constable and demanded twentie shillings for a wolfe that his sone and Samuel Hemaway kild within our bounds the 5 : 1 : 57: which we doe order that they shall be payd the next towne rate:

At a towne mitting the first of December: 1656:

Wheras ther was a twentie acre lott that was the inheritance of David Prise Deceased, who gaue the sayd Lott

Mr Eliot p^{e}sented a Letter dated the 4 : 4 : 57 : vnto the selectmen to be p^{e}sented vnto the towne.

Bro. willyam Blake senior Desired to buy a booke for the record of births burialls mariages to be kept in per pe tuam memoriā and be paid for it out of the towe stocke :

Thomas wiswall was here desired In the behalf of the scoole that a flower be laid ouer head In the scoole house and a studdy made In it for the vse of the scoolemaster prouided 5^s toward It and timber In his lott for Juice.

same time Thomas wiswall desired 14 bushells of Indian corne In part of pay for his sons teaching scoole whihh M^r. Jones ordered him to take at Dedham M^r. Jones to haue 4 bushells of M^r. patten 2 of ensigne foster againe and peas of brother brecke for the rest and allowed them In there rates againe.

It was voted by the towne the 18th 6 : 1657 : that Edward Clapp William Clarke and Henry Woodward ore any two of then are appointed to view whether the heigh way by the twentie acre Lotts may be layd by the fence of the twentie acre lotts as maior Atherton doth desire and soe make returne vnto the town : Now the foresaid men hath vewed the waye and retorned there answer this 7th of 10 m. 57 that the way may goe by by the fence of the twentie eaker Lots next to mag^r Athertons Land this was granted voted and agreed one att a Towne meting

WILLIAM BLAKE
Recorded

[**112.**] Wheras the fence at the necke of land and the way vnto it is very defectiue and neglected hitherto to be repaired because of a new devision that was ordered to be made which alsoe hath ben done because of some error in the former : It is ordered that the Veiwers of the fence for the necke and the surveyers of the heigh wayes doe forhwith giue Notice to the p'prietors to repaire both within 14 dayes without faile one the penaltie exprest in the order for defectiue fence and wayes and that they doe veiw and make returne to the select men within 6 dayes after the 14 dayes vpon penaltie of 2^s 6^d for each neglect of veiwers ore surveyors herein : dated the 12 : 4 : 1657 :

Ther was a warrent giuen by the selectmen the 12 : 8 : 1657 : vnto Henry Garnsey late bailiffe and to the Constable to take by Distresse ore otherwise of those that haue not payd the sayd Garnsey ther sum̅s that they are rated vnto as doth appear in the rate that Henry Garnsey hath bearinge date 30 3mo 1656.

[**113.**] We who wer appointed by the p'prietors of the necke of land at the mettinge the 7 : 11 : 56 : to consider what fence might be spared at both ends and alsoe to remoue it one any parte of it at our discression and alsoe to p'portion every mans share : accordingly we haue agreed that the fence shall be remoued to the other side of the waye one the east side from the gate to Mr Jons his meddow ; and one the west from from the gate through Amiel Weekes his land and allsoe we haue agred with Amiel Weekes that the heigh way to the meddow shall ly next his meddow p'vided that the barrs that Cross the way shall be parte of his fence and alsoe that none shall fead in the heigh way to his Damage alsoe we agree that these that haue their share of fence next to the gate shall haue one fourth parte abated : that is to say from the gate to the maiors medow on one side and Amiel weekes barrs on the other side alsoe we haue p'portioned every mans share of fence accordinge to a due p'portion : and because some doe not remoue ther fence we agree and determine that those that doe not remoue shall alow and pay to those that do remoue an equale p'portion as two men shall iudge if any doe desire it of them : 7 : day of the. 3. moneth : 1657 :

      THOMAS JOANS
      JOSEPH FARNWORTH
      EDWARD CLAPP
      WILLIAM CLARKE

At a mettinge one a traininge Day the 28th of the 7mo : 1657 it was Voted and granted, that the select men should add ten pounds vnto the next towne rate to be payd in wheate for the p'curinge and purchasinge of great Gunns for the vse of the towne :

At a mettinge of the select men the 22th 7^m : 1657 : Timothy Mather entred an action of Debt of thirtie and fiue shillings against Nicolas Bolton.

Nicholas Bolton acknowledged twentie and fiue shillings payd for him by lieuteñant Clap in wheate, and two bushells of barley him selfe receiued of the plaintiffe   They finde for the plaintiffe thirtie fiue shillings to be payd in kinde, and Cost six shillings six pence.

Whereas ther was a way Layd out formerly by Nathaneel Walles William Robenson and Nathaneel Patten by the appointment of the Select men of Dorchester from Mr Glouers Farme to Squantomsc Necke of two rodd broad Vntill you come to the way that leads from Mr Hawkens his farme and then to be three rod broad to the Necke aboue sayd, now by Length of time ore for want of Lookinge vnto the way is vnknowne therefore vpon the complainte of some of the towne att a mettinge of the Selectmen they appointed Nathanel Patten and William Robenson to Lay out the sayd way as neare as they can in the same place the way was before, which we the sayd Nathanel Patten and William Robenson haue Done as neare as we can this 17 day of the 6 mo : 1657 :

[Page 114 blank.]

[**115.**]   This 17th day of the : 9 : m : 1657 : Came Henery Woodard and Richard Hall to the Selectmen and gaue Vp there account of there Counstable shipe both of the Country rate or what other they gatherd in the yeare : 56 : and 57 : to this day :

Now the whole Some which they ware to gather of the Towne was : 71^{li} : of which they paid the Tresurer : 66^{li} : 13^s : 6^d : which did appeare by their acquitance from the Tresurer so remains from them 4^{li} : 6^s : 6^d : out of which they paid for a Fine to the Countie Tresuerer : 10^s : and they allowed Mr Edward Tinng being Tresũer for his Country rate 1^s : 4^d : and Abda the Indian which was gonn away : 2^s : 3^d : which was Charged in the Country rate :

and John Wanerites rate who was Charged in the Country rate vppon his master and p'ticularly one himselfe which was 2ˢ : 3ᵈ : which somes ar 15ˢ : 10ᵈ : which wee thinke is Just to be allowed them, so remains from them 3ˡⁱ : 10ˢ : 8ᵈ.

of which some Henery Woodard do } acknowledg him selfe Debter to the Towne . . . . }   2. 19. 10

and Richard Hall Debtor to } the Towne . . }   0. 10. 10

payd to william Blake by Henry Woodward   0. 20. 0

Wee the Selectmen of the Towne of Dorchester taking into Consederation the in Comberances one the wayes in our Towne by laying of Doung wood Tember Stones Billding of hovalls Sties for Swine Sawpits or Digging of Claypitts or any other thing to the annoyance of the inhabitants or strangers : Wee the Selectmen doe order that all the wayes in the Towne be fourthwith Cleared and Wood stones tember Doung Sawpits hovalls sties for swine Claypits be fourthwith taken away and filled vp by the 24ᵗʰ day of the 10ᵗʰ mo. next vppon the penaltie of iˢ for every Loode of Dūng timber wood stones not taken away by the day aboue said : and for every hovall piggstie Sawpitt or Claypitt not taken away or filled vp by the day aboue said hee shall pay 2ˢ : 6ᵈ : to be taken by Disstraine or otherwise of the p'ties so offending this 9ᵗʰ day of the 9mᵒ 1657.

[Page 116 blank.]

[**117.**] The seaventh of the tenth moneth 1657 the officers that were then chosen by the towne for the yeare ensuinge.

Selectmen Leiutenant Clap }
          Ensigne Foster }
          Mʳ Joans }
          Mʳ Patten }
          Edward clap }
Raters Joseph Farnworth }
      William Clarke }
      Richard Withinton }
Baliffe Laurence Smith
Supervisors of the hie wayes
                    Roberte Vose
                    Thomas Tolman
Supervisors of the wayes vnto the necke of Land
                    Richard Baker
                    William Clarke.

The day aboveˢᵈ william Triscott was chosen to suply a constables office vntill the last fourth day In march next and then the towne to choose two new ons for one yeare.

Dorchester Rate made for the vse of the Country by the selectmen and the Commissioner chosen for that end the 24 : 6 : 1657 : the totall sume as the Commissioner hath cast it vpe is 78ˡⁱ 2ˢ 6ᵈ.

At the mittinge of the Church and towne the eleueth Day of

December: 1657: It was voted that they would giue vnto Mr Mather 100^{li} for the yeare that is past to be Rated vpon all the inhabitants accordinge to the p'portion of every mans estate; it was alsoe voted the same time that they would giue Mr Eliezer Mather 10^{li} for his Labour that he hath taken amongst vs already, and the ten pounds to be added vnto the one hundred pounds in the Rate.

The question beinge moued vpon the former vote whether our brethren and neighbours at Vnquetie[1] should pay ore not p'portionable to the one hundred pond to the ministry ——— in regarde they had a minister ther, whervpon it was voted the same time as followeth: That those aboue the riuer of Naponsett (except M^{ris} Glouers farme and M^{ris} feñs farme) are exempted for payinge vnto Mr Mather for this yeare if they Desire it.

At the mettinge of the select men the 14: 10: 1657: then was order giuen vnto the raters for makinge the rate of 110^{li}. for the ministry as is aboue written

Alsoe the same day ther was order giuen for the makinge of a Rate of thirtie pounds for the vse of the Scoole and towne.

The 16: 10: 1657: Ther was a warent sent to the sup'visors of the hywayes that forthwith they should se that the heighway att the north end of the bridge at Naponset betweene that and the hill be made sufficient and to make ther returne vnto the selectmen ore one of them by the 29: 10: 1657: vpon the penalty of fiue shillings for ther Neglect.

At the meetinge of the select men the: 14: 10: 1657: It was orderd by them that Mr Patten should Call vpon Deacon Wiswall to giue an acounte for the 1500: of boards and alsoe whether he hath any writinges ore papers that concerns the towne of Dorchester.

The same Day ther was a warrent granted to the Constable for the gathering vpe of those sums of those that haue not payd ther p'portion for the maintenance of the ministry for the years 1655: and 1656:

[118.] At the meeting of the select men the eleuenth day of the eleventh moneth 1657: was a towne Rate giuen vnto the Constable of 25: 13: 9: the Constables were John Capen and William Trescott:

The same day order was giuen that the Constables in the yeare 1655 to bring in ther accompt of the Countrie rate to the select men the next Day of ther meetinge: the Rate was 25^{li}: 16: 0: the Constables wer Richard Curtic and Thomas Tilestone.

The same day the selectmen did order that the Constable should pay the scoole maister 20^{li} out of the Rate aboue sayd

I^t to Mrs Pecocke	1 . 2 . 0
I^t for a wolfe killinge to leiutenant and others .	1 . 0 . 0
I^t to Leiutenant[2] being the remainder to make vpe that which is due vnto him for beinge due vnto him for beinge Deputie	0 . 8 . 0

---

[1] This was Unquety or Uncataquissett, now Milton. — W. H. W.
[2] Lieut. Roger Clap was deputy to the General Court in 1657. — W. H. W.

I^t to Ensigne Foster . . . . 0 . 9 . 0
I^t to Richard Evans for worke he did at the meet-⎱
inge house . . . . ⎰ 0 . 18 . 0
The same day ther was oder giuen to the Constable to pay vnto Liuetenant Clap and Ensigne
Foster . . . . 2 . 18 . 0

George Procter Doth Desire a plott of Land to sett a house.

At the meeteing of the selectmen the 8 : 12 : 57 : Henry Woodward was apointed to pay Thomas Bird twentie shillings.

The same Day the Constable John Capen was to pay vnto Robert vose for a wolfe . . . . 1 – 0 – 0
I^t the Counstable was to pay John Smith sen^r . 0 – 5 – 5
I^t the Counstable was to pay Thomas Birde . . 0 – 5 – 0

Gamaleel Beman Doth Desire a plott of Land to set a Barne.

[119.] We whose names are subscribed and beinge appointed by our severall townes, And being mett the first day of December 1654 : to lay out the heigh way through Dorchester woods from Brantry Bounds to Roxbury bounds Doe agree as followeth

1. That the Way shall be foure Rodd wide from Brantrey Bounds to Roxbury Bounds.

2. Beinge neare Henry Crans house the way to ly one the south east side of it in the old Beaten Roadway and soe to a low white oke marked on the same side of the way and soe by the marked trees to the brooke soe from the brooke the way being badd in the winter we agree to take aboute a Rod wide into Anthony Gulliford's lott wher the fence interrupts the way and soe to a marked post towards John Gills house and from thence to an other marked post against John Gills house, from thence to a stake in Elder Kingsleys yarde and from thence to the mill in the old beaten Road way and from the mill to two great Rockes on the Lower side of the way att Robert Spurs and Henry Merifeilds houses ends and from thence to the new feild by the marked trees in the old Road way and so through the new feild wher the way formerly was and from thence by the marked trees on the left hand to Roxbury bounds :

	of Dorchester	of Branty
	NICHOLAS CLAPP	MOSES PAINE
	WILLIAM CLARKE	GREGORY BELCHER

Entered and
examined by me
WILLIAM BLAKE
Recorder

At a meeting of the select men the 8 : 1 : 57 ore 58 : It was ordered that those vnder writen are apointed to goe a p'ambelation betweene Brantree and Dorchester and to renew the bounds according to Law and make returne to the selectmen

John Capen
Richard Withinton

The same Day, it was ordered by the select men that those vnder writen are apointed to goe a p'ambelation betweene Roxbury and Dorchester and to renew the bounds accordinge to Law and make returne to the select men. These men are to run the line betweene Dorchester and Dedham alsoe.

     William Clarke
     Richard Leeds
     Enoch Wiswall

At the meetinge of the select men the 8 : 1 : 58 : they Doè Desire that John Capen would warne all the Commoners to meet at the meetinge house the 17 Day of this p'snt moneth to giue ther votes whether they would haue the Commons Devided ore noe.

[120.] *8: 1: 1658.* The names of such as are apointed to veiw the fence in the Common feilds for this yeare 1658 :

Imp'mis the necke of land	John Capen / Nicolas Clap
The field beyond M^ris Stoughtons	Richard Leeds / Hugh Batten
The great Lotts from Mr Hollands and soe Round westward and end soe farre as widdow Popes lott	John Smith / John Pelton
for the rest of the great lott fence	Edward Brecke / Abraham How
The twentie acre Lotts	James Humphrey / Edmund Bowker
The Lot behind Mr Joans	Henry Woodward / Thomas Locke
The feild behind Joseph Farnworth	Joseph Farnworth / Enoch Wiswall
The feild behinde Mr Mather	Timothy Mather / William Trescott
The feild behind Thomas Bird	Richard Williams / Thomas Bird
The eight acre Lotts	Henry Woodward / Roger Sumner

At the meeting of the Select men the 8 : 1 : 57 : ore 58 : ther was bill giuen Nicolas George to receiue of Thomas Tolman 1^l. 10^s. 0.

The same day the selectmen Did apoint Richard Baker, William Clarke, and John Capen to Lay out a heigh way of four Rod broad from Clement Topleafes house vnto the heigh way that is in Mr Thomas Jones Lott in the eight acre Lotts vntill they come to the heigh way that Ruñs betweene Roxbury and Brantry.

At the meeting of the selectmen the : 8 : 9 : 1658 : pay^d Nicolas George for, Diet — 0. 12. 0

[123.] *Dorchester : 8 : 12 : 1657 :* Forasmuch as timber and fire wood is of great vse to the p'sent and alsoe future generations and therfore to be prudently p'serued from wracke and Destroying for the vse of the people interested in the same. And wheras ther is complaint to the select men of this towne of much abuse by some p'sons that take libertie to fall cut and cary ofe the Commons in this towne notwithstanding Diuers orders that haue ben made and are yet in force to the Contrary, To the intent that none may plead ignorance and that such abuses may be restrained: It is therfore further ordered by the select men of the towne of Dorchester aforesayd, that no person ore persons what soeuer whether free men or non free men Commoner ore not Commoner within the towne of Dorchester aforesayd shall fall ore cutt ore cary away any timber ore wood (that is standing ore fallen) from ofe the Commons ore any part of the Lands undeuided in Dorchester, or from any of the heigh wayes, either for ther owne vse or others vpon penalty of forfeitinge fiue shillings for euery tree soe falled ore cutt and for euery load of timber ore fire wood caried offe the Commons aforesayd excepting such as had liberty from such as were apointed ore shall haue liberty from such as shall be apointed to grant Liberty for cutting and feching timber ore wood for mens necessary ocasions. The aforesayd penaltie to be taken by distresse ore otherwise for the vse of the towne: And because this order should not hinder any who haue right in Commons from timber ore wood for mens necessary ocasions at p'sent till such time as Commons may be allotted out we do therfore apoint and athoriz our beloued brethren Joseph Farnworth Nicolas Clap and John Capen ore any two of them to grant liberty to such whose ocasions may necessarily require, p'vided it be not to sell or carie out of the towne either directly ore ore indirectly in which case they shall not grant liberty at all: and for the better and more due obseruation of this order we doe desire our foresayd brethren to keepe a Record of what number of trees wood or timber they grant, and to whom and when it was soe granted that the select men may haue account therof if they se cause to call for it at any time.

[124.] At a Lawfull meetinge of the towne the 9 : 1 : 57 ore : 58 : It was voted that Ensign Foster Nicolas Clap and William Clarke are apointed to veiw the gates at the south ore south west end of the great lotts, whether only one gate may be sufficient ore whether ther then must be two gates maintained continually.

The same day vpon the request of George Proctor It was voted and granted vnto him a plott of land to sett a house vpon, by his now Dwelling house and John Minot and Richard Hall were apointed to lay it out soe that it exceed not seauen Rods.

The same day James Blake and Hugh Batten were chosen Constables for the yeare insuinge.

the : 10th : 3 : 1658 Upon the request of John Pelton and in the name of Edward Brecke John Minot Richard way and others it was granted by the select men that they may haue libertie for the security of Corne of the great Lotts and Captaines Neck to sett vpe a gate at John Peltons Barne for this yeare :

At a Lawfull meetinge of the towne the 9 : 1 : 1657 : or 1658 vpon the request of Gamaleel Beman it was voted and granted vnto him a plott of Land adioneing vnto his Barne to make an adition vnto his Barne and William Blake and William Clarke were apointed to lay it out. John Capen was apointed alsoe because William Clarke was remoued vnto Northamton and William Blake and John Capen hath Done this worke accordinge to this order.

[125.] Wheras ther hath ben and still is Complaint by reason of want of gates ore insufficiente gates leading thorow the great lotts and to the necke of land, for the making and repairing the sayd gates: It is therfore ordered by the select men that all p'sons possessing and improuing any land in tillage in any of the sayd Corne feilds shall pay ore cause to be payd one peny for euery acre in tillage vnto Abraham How for the great lotts and vnto Richard Withington for the necke of land (except such as haue already payd vnto Richard Withington by vertue of a former order) the sayd peny p' acre to be payd at ore before the first of october next and whosoeuer shall neglect as afore sayd shall pay two pence p' acre to be taken by Distresse ore otherwise of all such as shall soe neglect to pay ther peny p' acre, and those that receiue the same are to keepe account what he hath receiued and payd out for the maintenance of the sayd gates and to giue account of the same yearly if called ther vnto by the p'priettors of the sayd feilds; ore by the selectmen:

At a generall towne meeting the sixt of December: 1658: the officers that were chosen for the yeare ensuinge

Select men Maior Atherton
          Leuitenant Clap
          Ensigne Foster
          Mr Joans
          Mr Patten
Raters   John Capen
          William Sumner.
          William Robenson
Bailiffe   Clement Maxfeild

Supervisors of the heigh ways { Thomas Swift sen^r / Thomas Lake / John Gill.

Supervisors of the way to the Necke of land { Nicolas Clap / Timothy Mather

The same day It was agreed and voted by the inhabitance then, that all p'sons shall giue in a true and p'fect accompt of all ther Ratable estates vnto the Raters by the thirtieth Day of this p'sente moneth and soe by euery thirtieth Day of the tenth moneth from time to time, And alsoe to bringe in a true and p'fect account of ther Ratable estates vnto the select men by the thirtieth day of the fift moneth next and soe by the thirtieth day of the fift moneth from time to time vpon the penaltie of fiue shillings for ther neglect of each time from time to time, and alsoe to abide the will and Doome of the selectmen and Raters of them the fine ore penaltie to be put into, ore added vnto the towne Rate:

The same Day it was agreed and Voted that they would giue Mr Mather one hundred pounds for the yeare that is past to be Rated vpon all the inhabitance accordinge to p'portion of euery mans estates.

The same day it was voted that the selectmen should make an order that noe p'son should take into ther houses ore habitations any p'son without the alowance ore consent of the select men vpon such penalty as the selectmen shall se good to lay vpon them :

The same Day it was Voted vpon the motion of John Gill that the Landing place aboue Naponsett Riuer should be altered vpon the veiw of Robert vose William Robenson and Robert Badcocke and they to make returne vnto the select men.

The same Day it was voted vpon the testimony of Diuers that in euery Rung̅ in euery Devission ther should be two Rod wid layd out for high wayes:

[**126.**] At a generall meeting the sixt of December: 1658: It was voted that the landing place by Mr Huchensons Farme should be recorded to be a Common Landinge place and a way vnto it upon the veiw of Robert vose, William Rcbenson and Robert Badcocke and they to make returne vnto the select men.

The same day it was voted that Robert vose, William Robenson and Robert Badcocke should veiw a way to goe to George Badcockes house.

The same Day it was Voted that William Sumner and William Clarke are appointed by the towne to require M^{ris} Goer that shee doe Desist from making any vse of any land at ore neare Wainmans ordinarie or any wher else in Dorchester for buildinge makinge of hay ore any other vse.

At the meetinge of the select men the: 13: 10: 1658 It was ordered by them that Leiutenant Clap is intreated to see speddy repaires of the glasse windows about the meeting house and John Capen is ordered to see other repaires in and about the meeting house as the sayd John Capen shall be directed by the select men ore some of them: and they shall be payd out of the next towne Rate.

The same day ther was a warent granted out that John Capen and William Trescot Constables in the yeares 56: and 57: should bring in ther accoūts vnto the select men 28: 10: 58: vpon the penaltie of 20^s.

The same day ther was twentie shillings giuen vnto William Blake and his Rate the last yeare which was 3^s for his paines for writinge attending vpon the selectmen for time past and for six pence he leyd out for paper:

At the meetinge of the select men the: 10: 11: 1658:

Maior Atherton was intreated to speake with the scoolmaister to know his mind whether he will keep scoole For longer time.

And Mr Patten is intreated to looke vpe what notes and papers he heth that concernes the accounts of the scollers for the two yeares past 56: and 57: and bring them to select [men].

The same day Mr Joans was appointed to warne John Aldis to come and giue an account vnto the select men of what timber he hath fallen in the swamp Commonly Called purgatory swamp.

The same Day it was ordered that William Robenson and Thomas Mekens are appointed to lay out the landing place by Naponset Mill and the landing place in Mr Huchensons farme: And it is further ordered the same day that the aboue sayd William Robenson and Thomas Mekens are appointed [to veiw] the most convenient places for two heigh wayes from the Country heigh way to run into the woods towards the Blue Hill and to make Returne vnto the select men the 14: 12: next.

[**127.**] The same day it was ordered that Abraham How is to bring vnto the select men of whom he hath receiued a peny an acre towards the setting vpe of the gates in the greate lots: and Abraham How and William Robenson are to bring vnto the select men the number of acres of land that is broken vpe and what number of acres every p'prietor hath in the great lotts the 14: 12: next.

Dorchester the 10: 11: 1658: Wheras the generall Court hath taken care what strangers shall Reside in this iurisdiction and how lisenced as by the law title strangers it doth appeare, but haue taken noe order for families ore p'sons that remoue from one towne in this Jurisdiction to an other: Now to p'vent such inconvenience as may come if euery one be at liberty to receiue into this towne whom they please. It is ordered therfore by the select men of this towne that if any maner of p'son ore p'sons in this towne shall intertaine any soiorour ore inmate into his or ther house ore habitation aboue one weeke without lisence from the selectmen ore the maior parte of them first had and obtained, shall forfeit fiue shillings, and for every weekes Continuance three shillings foure pence. And if any p'son as afore sayd shall receiue any family into his or ther house ore habitation longer then the time aboue sayd shall forfeit the penaltie of twenty shillings, and for euery weekes continuance 13^s: 4^d: all which fines shall be forth with taken by distresse ore otherwayes by warent from the select men from time to time;

The account of William Trescott constable taken the 28: 10: 1658 for the yeare: 1657:

	ll.	s.	d.
The whole Rate commited vnto his hands was	78	2	5
	l.	s.	d.
Imp'mis payd vnto the treasurer for the Country rate in the yeare: 1657	52	6	4
I^t more a quarter parte being added	13	1	7
I^t to the treasurer for our parte to the Colledge	5	5	0
I^t to the treasurer for Copies of the Court orders	0	11	0
I^t payd to Leiutenant Clap in part for his Diet being Deputy	1	5	0
I^t payd vnto Ensigne Foster for the same account	1	13	0
I^t payd vnto the treasurer for the Deputies Diet	3	10	4
	77	12	3
So ther is Due vnto the towne from William Trescott Constable	0	10	2
The towne Rate delivered to William Trescott constable for this 1658: the Rate was	40	12	2

Considering his losse and troble the selectmen thought meet to discharge the sayd William Trescott: the 12 (9) 1660.

The: 14: 12: 1658 ther was a warent giuen vnto Clement Maxfeild Balife for the gathering of two pence an acre of euery acre in tillag in the great lotts.

The 8: 1: 1658: or 1659 William Robenson and William pond were Chosen Constables for the yeare insuinge.

At the meetinge of the select men the 14: 1: 1658 or 1659 ther was a warent giuen William Trescot for to gather of those parents and Maisters that sent ther children ore seruants to the free scole those summs that are in his list.

The same Day Leiutenant Clap and Ensigne Foster are appointed to Manage the business of Tomsons yland for the obtaining of it.

[128.] At a twone meeting the: 8: 1: 1658 or 1659: It was voted then that the inhabitants would haue a tryall at the Charge of the towne for to gett Tomsons yland for the towne of Dorchester as they suppose that it is ther by right and it was alsoe voted the same day that the selectmen are desired and impowered to p'secute the triall in the best way and maner as they shall thinke best and most Convenient for the obtaining of it.

The names of such as are appointed to veiw the fence in the Common feilds for this yeare. 1659:

Ipm̄is for the necke of land	Edward Clapp / Lawrence Smith
The feild behind M^{ris} Stoughtons	Richard Withinton / Edmund Bowker
The great lotts from Daniel Prestons and soe Round westward and end so farre as the widdow Popes lot	Richard Leads / Richard Hall
for the rest of the great lotts	Thomas Tolman / Thomas Trott
The twenty acre lott	Thomas Dauenport / Thomas Grant
The lott behind Mr Joans:	William Clarke / William Blake
The feild behind Enoch Wiswall	Isaac Joans / Thomas Swift
The feild behind Mr Mather	Timothy Mather / George Dier
The feild behind John Blackman	John Blackman / Obadiah Haws
The eight acre lotts	Jonas Humphrys / Henry Woodward
The feild aboue Naponsett Riuer at the North side of William Daniels house.	John Gill / Thomas Swift

At a towne meeting the 8 (1) 165 $\frac{8}{\text{or } 9}$ William Robenson and William Pond were chosen constables for the yeare ensuing:

At a meeting of the towne the 28 : 1 : 1659 : It was concluded and voted that they would haue a scoole kept in Dorchester as in former times.

It was voted the same day that Mr Thomas Joanes should haue the pound he paying for it thirty shillings and he doth p'mise to sett vpe a pound at an other place wher the select men shall see fitt he being alowed what charge he is att in setting vpe the New pound:

At the meeting of the select men the 13 : (4) 1659 : Came John Smith sen^r to the select men and Desired libertie of passage through a high way that Runeth by the North east end of the great lotts from the beach by Edward Breckes to the smelt Riuer: which liberty was granted him:

[**129.**] At the meeting of the select men the 12 (7) 1659 : William Robenson was desired by the select men to inquire how long tho Trott hath lived at Vncatte[1] in Nicolas Whits house:

The same day ther was order giuen to the sup'visors of the heigh wayes that they should se the heigh wayes to be made good and sufficient espesially that way by the widdow Battens feild it being p'sented at the County Court.

The same day John Capen was ordered and intreated to se the meeting house repaired according to a former order made the 13 (10) 1658.

The same day Mr Batten was intreated and ordered by the select men that he would se a speedy repaire of the scoole house.

The same day William pond Constable had order to warne Angola the Negar to depart this towne.

At the meetinge of the select men the 14 : (9) 1659 they then desired and impowered William Clarke and Henry Woodward to serch and seeke out a farme of 1000 acres of land granted vnto the towne of Dorchester for the vse of a scoole by the generall Court held at Boston the 18th of october : 1659 :

The same day Mr Patten was appointed to speake with Nicolas George for taking of an Inmate into his house contrary vnto order.

The Country Rate made by the selectmen and the Comissioner for the towne of Dorchester the single rate

the sum is $\overset{l}{51}. \overset{s}{8}. \overset{d}{5}$

in the yeare : 1659 :

At a meeting the 29 (9) 1659 : James Blake Constable for the yeare 1658 : gaue his account as followeth : the sum he was charged with was $\overset{l}{77}\ \overset{s}{16}\ \overset{d}{8}$

Payd of it as followeth to the tresurer as it doth appeare by his acquitance $\overset{l}{74}\ \overset{s}{1}.\ \overset{d}{3}$

I^t mistake in casting vpe the Rate   0. 4. 3

I^t those that follow haue not payd ther Rate John Skriuen

---

[1] Now Milton.—W. H. W.

0. 2. 5 Bastian Caine 0. 3. 2 : the Administrators : of tho : Birch 0. 1. 6 : John Plumb : 0. 4. 3 : Moses Simons 0. 2. 5. I^t for Cariag of Corne to Boston 5^s and other losses 0. 6. 8.

The same day John Capen Constable for the yeare : 1657 : gaue vpe his account and ther is due vnto him 0. 5. 1.

Ther is due from James Blake vnto the towne the 29 : (9 :) 59 1. 19. 9.

[130.] At the generall towne meeting the fifth of December 1659 the officers that were Chosen for the yeare ensueinge.

Selectmen maior Atherton
         Lieutenant Clapp
         Ensigne Foster
         Mr Patten
         Mr Joans
Raters Edward Brecke
     John Capen
     William Sumner
Bailiffe Jacob Huens
Supervisers of the heighwayes { Robert Badcocke
                                    Laurence Smith
                                    John Gurnel

the two last are to veiw the way vnto the Necke of land alsoe : and to se it repaired sufficient.

The same day it was agreed and voted that the select men should take and perfect the account of William Trescott Constable for the yeare 1659.

The same day it was agreed and voted by the inhabitance of the towne that they would give Mr Mather one hundred pounds for the yeare 1659 to be Rated accordinge to p'portion.

The same day it was agreed and voted that the p'prietors of the land beyound the mill vnto the Bleu Hills are to meet the second day of January next to consider about ther deuission of the land ther.

The same day vpon the request of Richard Dauis it voted and granted a litle plott of land vnto him next vnto Henry Conliffe land soe it doe not rech the springe vpon the veiw of Mr Patten, John Capen and William Sumner soe they doe exceed one hundred Rodds and they to make returne to the select men.

The same day Thomas Mekens and James Minott did p'mise to sett vpe a fullinge Mill vpon Naponsett Riuer by the first of December next.

The same day vpon the request of Robert Stanton to have a parsell of land about the ox penn Mr Patten Leiutenant Clapp and William Robenson are appointed to veiw it make returne vnto the select men before the second day of January next :

The same day vpon the request of James Blake to exchange of a plott of Land ioining vnto his fence by the water : it was voted that Ensigne Foster, Joseph Pharnworth Nicolas Clap and Timothy Mather to veiw it and make returne vnto the select men.

The same day vpon the request of Mr Joans the heigh way betweene Roxburie and Dorchester Containing foure Rod broad on the east it begines at Edmund Munings lott and ends on the west vnto Nicolas claps lott: It was voted and granted vnto him in consideration of land taken away from him, by reason of the heigh way layd out from Clement Topleafes to the Country heigh way.

At the meeting of the select men the 12 (10) 1659 they agreed to goe aboue the mill to veiw wher they shall thinke best wher the wayes should be layd.

The same day was an order giuen vnto the Raters for Leuie a Rate of 100^{li} for Mr Mather and alsoe a Rate of fortie pounds for the vse of the towne.

[**131.**] At a generall towne meeting the 16 (11) 1659: the p'prietors of the commons gaue in ther votts by papers and the Maior vote was for Deuidinge of the Commons on both the sids of the Riuer to the Blue Hills.

The same day it was Voted by papers by the Maior parte that euery p'prietor may improue his deuissions as he seeth good.

The same day it was voted and granted vnto Robert Stanton vpon his former request a parsell of land about or neare the oxe pen soe that it Doe not exceed thirtie acres: it being veiwed according vnto former order by Mr Patten, Leiutenant Clap and William Robenson who made ther Returne vnto the select men as they were ordered

16 (11) 59: At a generall meeting of the p'prietors at Maior Athertons house to consider and giue in their votes about Deuiding or not Deuiding of Commons, the question was how votes must be vnderstood in Case one man haue by Contract seuerall interest it was agreed that euery p'prietor putinge in his vote with exspression and Nomination of whose interest they Claime and then in Case of need of Determination the booke shalbe examined and euery mans vote p' or Con shalbe valued according to his Contracted interest:

WILLIAM BLAKE.

At the meeting of the select men the: 13: (12) 1659: they ordered that the Constables should giue out of the towne Rate vnto Beniamine Tuchel fiue pounds for his p'sent necessitie for Clothing of himselfe and his children.

The same day the select men ordered the Constables to pay the Recorder William Blake 1.0.0

At the meeting of the select men the 12 (1) 1659 or 1660: Vrsula Batten desired to haue a plot of land to sett a Barne.

The names of such as are apointed to veiw the fence in the common Corne feilds for this yeare 1660.

Imprimis for the neck of land { James Blake / Enoch Wiswell

The feild behinde M^{ris} Stoughton { Elder Withington / Richard Baker

The feild behinde Enoch Wiswall { Thomas Swift / Enoch Wiswall

The feild behinde Mr Joans { Thomas Lake / William Weekes

behinde Mr Mather { William Trescott / William Pond
behinde Thomas Bird { Thomas Andrews / James Whit.
The twentie acre lotts { Edmund Bowker / Henry Merifeild
The great lotts from Daniel Prestons soe round { John Smith / Henry Leadbetter
westward soe far as the widdow Popes Lott :
The rest of the great lotts { John Minot / Thomas Tilestone

[132.] at the Meeting of the selectmen the 9 (11) 59
Wheras ther were Diuers fences defectiue at or about the 20^{tt} acre lotts [ ] as
Imprmus Robert Stills fined . . . . . . 19^s 6 :
I^t Henry Merifeild . . . . . . :4^s C^d :
I^t James Humphrey . . . . . . :3.0
The select men did then apoint the Baliffe Clement Maxfeild to take of Robert Stills . . . . 0.10.0.
I^t of henry Merifeild . . . . . . :1.6
I^t of Edmund Bowke . . . . . . 0.2.0.
I^t of James Humphrey . . . . . . 0.1.0.
of these fines Clement Maxfeild is to haue for his paines for the gathering of them, and for the driuing of the necke of land and for his paines about the fence about the necke of land . . 0.6.6

At the meeting of the selectmen the 14 :(3) : 1660 :
for the explanation of a towne order respecting viewers of fence and the necessitie of ther twise veiwing of fence before they p'sent it to the select men :
It is declared that what fence they finde defectiue at any time of veiwing fence they shall p'sently giue the owners of the fence notice either by themselues or others that are of age or discresion to witnes the same that the sayd owners shall repaire ther defectiue fence within six dayes, and then p'sently after the sayd six dayes are exspired the veiwers are to veiw the sayd defectiue fence againe, and what fence they then finde defectiue they shall forthwith p'sent the same to the select men : with this addition vnto the p'sentment that they haue giuen the owners notice therof before the last veiwing.

The same day Ensigne Foster and seriant Clarke are desired and impowered to lay out the Common Meddow from the fish house vnto Henry Wayes Creeke.

The same day elder Kingsley requested that the bounds of Mr Huchensons farme may be determined.

At the meeting of the select men the 17 (7) 1660 William Robenson and Thomas Mekins were apointed to veiw a place for a heigh way that may be Conuenient wher John Gill and Robert Redman shall shew you and to make ther returne vnto the selectmen the 24 of this moneth.

At the meeting of the select men the 12 (9) 1660
Mem'dom Laurence Smith Complaint
John Capen request for the exchange of land in the second deuision with the land that was David prises in the second deuision.

Edward Brecks request that hence forth that the way from the beach to the Crecke or whether it shall runn : first that the towne make a sufficient heigh way ther and alsoe to take Care and Charg of the gate that ther be noe Damage by the gate : It. that he may be payd for the land that is taken away from him which is owne p'priety and by reason of the highway.

[133]   An account of the Country rate and towne rate taken of William Robenson and William Pond for the yeare 1659 : giuen the 12 (9) 1670 :

The Country Rate is with addition . . .	77 – 19 – 5
more to be added for persons omitted . . .	1 – 0 – 0
The towne Rate 40ᵗᵗ	40 – 0 – 0
	118 – 19 – 5
The Constables Creditor by paying to the tresurer	77 – 13 – 00
The Constables Creditor to the towne	
Imp'mis payd to Mʳ Pole. . . .	25 – 00 – 00
Iᵗ to Thomas Swift for exspenses . . .	4 – 00 – 00
Iᵗ to Ensigne Foster	2 – 00 – 00
Iᵗ to Leiutenant Clapp	2 – 00 – 00
Iᵗ to William Blake for Recording . .	1 – 00 – 6
Iᵗ for a Wolfe to Joseph Long and Israel Mead .	1 – 00 – 00
Iᵗ to Beniamin Tuchel. . . . ˙ .	5 – 00 – 09
Iᵗ to Richard Euans	0 – 1 – 00
In the Country rate twise Charged vpon the occupiers of John Wiswalls land . . .	0 – 10 – 3
John Scriuen gon out of towne	00 – 2 – 6
The occupiers of Tomsons Iland – 8ˢ 7ᵈ the towne rate that they may require	00 – 8 – 7
Iᵗ for Roome to lay Corne in	0 – 10 – 00
	41 – 4 – 3
The day aboue sayd the sayd Constables were discharged by the select me[n] and ther accounts accepted	77 – 13 – 0
	118 – 17 – 3
Dew to ballance	00 – 2 – 2
	118 – 19 – 5

To Determine about Mʳ Pole at the generall towne meetinge.

Ensigne Fosters request for alowance of land that is taken away from him by reason of the Country way

The Country Rate deliuered to the Constables 1660 the sum is

63¹ 8ˢ 2ᵈ besids Brantry mens rate and two shillings ten pence which is Dauid Joans his rate.

At the meeting of the select men the 26 (9) 1660 John Smith, Thomas Mekens and Richard Hall are apointed to lay out the way from the Country heigh way by the meeting house at Vnquetie through John Gills land and Robert Redmans land that is to Run to the way that Runs to the blue hills: Alsoe John Smith, Thomas Mekens and Richard Hall are appointed to lay out the way from the landing place by the mill through Robert Voses Farme.

[134.] At the generall towne meeting the 3 (10) 1669: the officers that were chosen for the yeare ensuing

 Selectmen Major Atherton
    Leiutenant Clapp
    Ensigne Foster
    Mʳ Patten
    Mʳ Joans:
 Raters William Sumner
   John Capen
   William Robenson
 Baliffe Thomas Andrews Senʳ

Supervisors of the heigh wayes { Steven Minott / John Blackman / Anthony Gulliford:

The same day it was voted that Mʳ Pole is to keepe the scoole vntill his yeare be ended which will be about the 20 (4) 166i

Alsoe it was voted the same Day that the select [men] are to labour to p'vide a scoolmaister by that time that Mʳ Poles yeare be ended:

Alsoe the same day it was agreed and voted by the inhabitance of the towne that they would giue Mʳ Mather one hundered pounds for the yeare 1660: to be rated by p'portion; as the last yeare.

The same day William Sumner and John Smith are appointed to veiw John Capens second devision and the second devision of that which was David Prise and alsoe to veiw the Country heigh way and the land that is to be alowed for the sayd heigh way and make returne to the select men.

At the meeting of the select men the 10 (10) 1660 ther was a warent giuen to the Raters to leuie a Rate of 35¹ vpon the inhabitance of the towne for the vse of the towne; and also to make a Rate of 100¹ for the payment of Mʳ Mather.

At the meeting of the select men the 14: (11) 1660 Thomas Wisall had a bill giuen him to receiue of the Constable eighteene shillings and six pence in satisfaction for lost he sustained by reason of the lost of the prise of Indean Corne which he receiued for that which was due to the scoolmaister:

The same day the returne of William Sumner and John Smith being appointed to veiw the second devision that was Dauid Prises and second devision of John Capens vpon John Capens request for the excange of the sayd Prises lott with Capens lott they doe not see it Convenient for the towne to exchange it:

Ensigne Foster did withdraw his hand from seting it to the towne Rate.

At the meeting of the select men the 14 (12) 1660 Richard Evans request

The same day a warent giuen to the Constable to gather that which is due vnto Mr Mather for the year 58 . . 4 – 9 – 9
and for the yeare 59 . . . . . . 5 – 0 – 3

[**135.**] The same day the Constable is ordered that he should p'vide all those waigts and measures that are required by the law that are not yet p'vided out of the towne Rate and to bring them vnto the select men :

The towne Rate deliuered vnto Constable for the yeare 1660 was 36^l 8^s 6^d.

At the meeting of the select men the 11 (1) 1660 or 166i : Nicolas Lawrence requested a plott of land to build a house near the Crecke :

The same day the select men appointed to runẽ the line betwixt Dorchester and Roxburie and the line betweene Dorchester and Deddam the men appointed for this worke were Richard Leads or one of his sonne William Robenson and Nicolas Clap and Laurence Smith : and to Ruñ the line betweene Dorchester and Brantrey they appointed : Robert Badcocke Anthony Gulliford and Thomas Swift iu^r to doe that worke

The names of such as are appointed to view the fence in the common Corne feilds for this yeare 1661 :

Imprĩ for the Neck of land { Richard Baker / Nicolas Clapp

The feild at the North side of { Samuel Wadsworth / William Daniel
    William Daniels

The feild behind M^ris Stoughton { Richard Leads / Praiseuer Turner

The feild behind Mr. Mather { George Dier / Timothy Mather

behind Enoch Wiswall { John Wilcocke / Isaac Joans

behind Mr Joans { Clement Maxfeild / Joseph Holmes

behind Thomas Bird { James Humphry / Obadiah Haws

twentie acre lotts { Richard Withinton / James White

The great lotts from Daniel Prestons soe round } Edward Brecke
    westward soe farr as the widdow Pope's lott } Richard Hall

The rest of the great lotts { Thomas Tolman / Thomas Trot

At the meeting of the select men the 13 (3) 1661 Thomas Mekings John Smith and Richard Hall are appointed vpon the penaltie of flue shillings of each man to lay out and marke or stake out the way from the Country heigh way by the meetinghouse at Vnquetie through John Gills land and Robert Redmans land that is to Ruñ to the blue Hills : and to make Returne vnto the select men by the one and twentieth day of this p'sent moneth.

The same day ther was giuen warent vnto the Bailiffe to take by distresse or other wise 33^s of Steven Minott for 22 Rod of defectiue fence of his in the feild behind M^rls Stoughtons : p'vided he doe not make it sufficient 21 day of this p'sent moneth.

The same day Isaac Joans was appointed to pay Lawrence Smith seaven shillings and six pence out of the towne Rate for his Runing of the Line.

The same day the select men ordered that the veiwers of the Necke of land shall keepe the gate in sufficient Repaire from time to time vntill all the corne be Caried away and they are to be payd for it out of the towne Rate.

[136.] The returne of John Smith, Thomas Mekings and Richard Hall the 21 (3) 1661 : we haue layd out and staked the way two rodd and halfe broad from the meeting house at vnquetie from John Gills land and Robert Redmans land to John Fennos house leading to the way to the Blue Hills :

At the meeting of the select men the tenth day of Jun 1661 : William Robenson Thomas Trott and the rest of the neighbours ther desired that the way from the riuer vnto the Country heigh way might be layd out.

The same day Edwarde Wyatt and Robert Spurr came to the select men and demaunded satisfaction for land that is taken away from them by meanes of the Country heighway.

The same day the select men did appoint William Robenson and Roger Billinge to veiw and stake or marke the wayes that are in Squantoms Necke and to make returne vnto the select men by the tenth day of the first moneth next.

At a meeting of the select me [n] the 28 (4) 1661 : ordered that Richard Leeds and Richard Hall shall doe within seauen dayes stake a sufficient Cart way by the northeast end of the great lotts from the beach by Edward Breckes to the smelt riuer which sayd way is to be one rod and halfe broad and make returne of the same (to the select men) vnder their hands vpon penalty of six shillings eight pence to be taken by distresse in default and neglect thereof.

We haue layd out a high way from the beach through Edward Brecke his meddow following the Railes and the stone wall a Rod and halfe wide and soe along the end of the great lotts vnto smelt brooke Crecke according to warent : June 29 : 1661.

RICHARD LEEDS his marke o|———)
RICHARD HALL

[137.] Wheras the Inhabitants of Dorchester haue formerly ordered Consented and agreed that a Rate of Twentie pound p' ann shall issue and be payd by the sayd Inhabitants and there heires from and out of a Certaine porcon of land in Dorchester Called Tomsons Iland for and towards the maintenance of a schoole in Dorchester aforsayd. And that vppon experience it is found to be a matter of great labour and difficultie to collect the sayd rent from soe many severall p'sones as ought to paye the same accordinge there seuerall p'portions the p'sones that haue title to land in the sayd Iland and who therfore ought to pay the sayd rent, beinge noe lesse in number than six score or theraboute, And inasmuch as the sayd rent of Twentie pound when it is duly Collected and payd is not of it selfe suffitient maintenance, for a schoole without some addicon thervnto For the augmentinge therfor of the sayd rent and to the intent that the same may hencforth be more readily collected and payd It is heerby ordered and all the p^rsent Inhabitants of dorchester aforsayd Whose names are heervnto subscribed doe for themselues and there heires heerby Covenant consent and agree that from henceforth the said Iland and all the benefitt and p^rfitts therof and all there right and Intrest in the same shallbe wholy and for euer bequeathed and given away from themselues and their heires vnto the Town of Dorchester aforesayd for and Towards the maintenance of a free schoole in Dorchester aforsayd for the instructinge and Teachinge of Children and youth in good literature and Learninge. And to the intent that the better maintenance for a free schoole as is heerby intended may arise from and out of the sayd Iland It is therefore the mynd of the p^rsent donoures that the sayd Iland shall from tyme to tyme be lett, assigned and set ouer by the Inhabitants of Dorchester for the time beinge or theire agents for such yearlie rent or rents as shall in Comon Estimation amount to the full value of the sayd Iland.

And to the intent that the godly intentions of the p'sent donoures may not be frustrated or disapoynted nor the free schoole heerby intended suffer any p^ruidice or damage by insuffitient tenante or Tenants to the sayd Iland, or through none payment of the rent that ought to be payd for the same It is heerby ordered and the p^rsent donoures doe hearby declare that it is there mynd that the sayd Iland shalbe lett assigned and sett Ouer only to such Tenant or Tenants as shall by land or otherwise sufftiently secure the payment of the rent therof for the vse and behoofe of the schoole as aforesayd in such manner and forme and at such time and tymes of payment as shalbe agreed vppon by and betweene the inhabitants of Dorchester or there agents one the one p^rtie and the sayd Tenant or Tenannts on the other p^rtye.

And for avoydinge the Trouble that myght arise in collectings and gatheringe the same Rent by to great a Multitude of Tennante that ought to pay the same, and to the intent that [**138.**] that the rents which shalbecome due for the sayd Iland may be the better and the more redylie Collected and payd it is heerby ordered and declared that the sayd Iland shall neuer be lett out to soe many tenannts as shalbe aboue tenn in number at once.

In witness whereof the p^rsent Inhabitants have heervnto subscribed ther names the Seaventh day of the Twelfth moneth in the yeare 1641.

Memorand. that before the subscribinge of these p^rsents the donours aforsayd did further agree and declare that it was and is there mynd and true intencons that if at any tyme ther shall happen and fall out a vacancie and want of a schoolmaster by meanes of death or otherwis, yet the rents and p^rfitts ishuinge and arisinge of the sayd Iland shalbe converted and applied only to and for the maintenance and vse of the schoole either by augmentinge the stipend for a schoolmaster or otherwise but not for any other vse.

Israel Stoughton George Proctor
Richard Mather Richard Hawes

George Minott
Henry Withington
John Glouer
Natha: Duncan
Thomas Hawkins
Tho: Clarke
John Holman
Nathaniell Patten
Humfrey Atherton
Thomas Makepeace
Henry Wright
Christopher Gibson
John Phillips
John Wiswall
John Capen
Joane Capen Weddow
William Blake
Nicho: Butler
Nicholas Vpsall
Thomas Swift
Thomas Wiswall
Thomas Dickerman
Roger Clap
Joseph Farnworth
Hopestill Foster
William Clarke
Michael Wiles
John Pears
Nicholas Clapp
John P Pope
John Farnham
Barnabas Fawer
Thomas H Andrews

Richard Baker
John Maudelsy

Augustene Clement
Henrie Waye
John Smith
David Sellecke
Bray Wilkins
Geo. Weekes
Jeffrey Turner
John Pearce
Mr Warham
Andrew Pitcher
William X Lane (his mark)
Thomas Jones
Jonas Humffrey
Edmunde W Munings (his mark)
James Bate
George Dyer
Robt Howard
John Grenaway
Edward Brecke
Richard Collacott
Jeremy Howchin
Thomas Tilstone
John Holland
Thomas Millit
Allice the wyfe of }
   Richard Jones }
Nathanael Wales
John Rigbye
Robert Deeble
Edward Clap
Willi Sumner
John O Hill (The sign of)
Clement Toplif

[**139.**] At the meeting of the select men the 9 (7) 1661 they did order and appoint George Procter to repair the Defects of the pound and to p'vide a locke for the doore and to keepe the pound repaired from time to time and what charge and Cost he is at about the pound he shall be payd out of the towne Rate and they doe appoint him to keepe the key of the pound doore and that he shall haue for it one penny the head not exceeding six and if aboue six at a time halfe a penny the head; and not to lett out any Catell or swine vnlesse the parties be agreed:

Memō when the twone Rate is to [be] made they must remember to make the Rate so great that they may pay foure pounds for the laying out of the land that was giuen for the vse of the ministry which was 400 acres: and for the fiue hundered acres to the non-commoners: and for forty shillings that Leiutenant Fisher had for new drawing of the map.

DORCHESTER TOWN RECORDS. 107

The same day they ordered that Leiutenant Clap and Ensigne Foster should se the shingling of the meeting house repayred and what other timber worke that doth want repairing about the house:

Alsoe William Blake is appointed to warne Thomas Andrews to daube the meeting house or else to take the fines that is due for not traininge of him.

At the meeting of the select men the 11 (9) 1661: M^{ris} Stoughton came to the select men to haue to be p'pounded vnto the towne that shee might haue her Deuision layd out in the 500 acres that was giuen vnto noncommoners: Mō that the town chuse Commissioners for the towne to end smale causes:

The Constables account for Rates 1660 taken the 11: (9) 1661:	
The Country Rate was	63 . 11 . 0
The towne was	36 . 8 . 6
for 45 law bookes	5 . 12 . 6
	105 . 12 . 0
Creditor as followeth	
payd the treasurer for rates and bookes	65 . 2 . 2
I^t to Mr Pole for scoole	25 . 0 . 0
I^t to Leiutenant Clap and Ensigne Foster as deputies	1 . 16 . 0
I^t to William Blake Record	1 . 0 . 0
I^t to Lawrence Smith for three days runing of the line	00 . 7 . 6
I^t for one bushell and halfe a pecke	0 . 4 . 6
I^t for carring of pay for law bookes	0 . 4 . 0
I^t for warning the towne	0 . 3 . 0
I^t a ioirny to Dedham	0 . 1 . 6
I^t to Thomas Wiswall as remainder for his sonnes scoolinge	0 . 18 . 6
I^t to Leiutenant Clap as deputie	1 . 0 . 0
I^t to Ensigne Foster the same	0 . 18 . 0
I^t to Thomas Swift for exspenses	0 . 12 . 0
	97 . 7 . 2
I^t to Thomas Swift Ju^r for killing a woolfe	1 . 0 . 0
I^t two law bookes to the towne and Constable	0 . 5 . 0
I^t : 15 bookes returned	1 . 17 . 6
	100 . 9 . 8
I^t payd to Decon Capen for the towne	0 . 5 . 0
I^t payd to Robert Badcocke Anthony Gulliford and Thomas Swift for running the linne betweene Brantrey and Dorchester	0 . 7 . 6
I^t alowance for wares land 6^d and for Daniel Fisher 9^d in consideration of lost by fire and soe to Steven Minot 2^s in regard of his lost by fire	0 . 3 . 3
I^t 1^s which was to be alowed for Mr Joans rate	0 . 1 . 0
Soe ther is due from Constable Isaac Joans to ballace his accountt the 11 (9) 1661 the sum of	4 . 4 . 1

for the Country and towne Rates Isaac Joans discharged the aboue sayd 4 . 4 . 1 . the 9 (12) 1662

[**140.**] At the generall towne meeting the 2 (10) 1661 : the officers the officers that were Chosen for the yeare ensuinge

	Selectmen Leiutenant Clap
	Ensigne Foster.
	Mr Patten
	Mr Joans
	William Sumner
Raters	Richard Baker
	William Robeson
	John Minott
Bailiffe	William Turner

Supervisors of the high wayes aboue the mill and on the north side of the mill
          Thomas Swift Ju^r
          Thomas Trot
          Clement Maxfeild
          Samuel Clap :

The Commissioners then chosen to end smale causes in the towne of Dorchester were Leiutenant Clap Ensigne Foster and Mr Joans.

The same day it was voted that Wiiliam Sumner and William Robenson were apointed to lay out away betweene Dedham and Naponsett mill and they are to bring ther returne to the selectmen by the tenth day of the next moneth they are to giue warning to Dedham and apoint a day and to ioine with them.

It was voted the same day that they would haue a scoole maister in the towne.

It was voted the same day by the inhabitants of the towne that they would haue Mr Poole to be the scoolemaister for the yeare ensuinge :

The same day it was voted that the towne would giue Mr Mather 100^l to be Rated by equall p'portions vpon the inhabitants with M^{ris} fenns farme and M^{ris} Glouers farme the inhabitants of vnquatie excepted.

At the meeting of the select men the 9 (10) 1661 : the select men did Couenant with Mr Poole to keepe scoole for the ensuinge yeare to begine the 23th day of this 10th moneth and the selectmen hath p'mised him for his worke 25^l for this yeare.

The same day the select men did appoint that the Raters should make a Rate of 100^l for Mr Mather and a Rate of 20^{li} for the towne ; by the

At a towne meeting the 16 (1661 :) the vote was that the select men of Dorchester should veiw the heigh way from the landing place by Thomas Tilstones and the new brige or Contrey heigh way leading to the mill and to determine the breadth and Course of it : and it was voted affirmatiuely.

The same day the question was whether all the land in p'priety in Dorchester shall be Rated to the towne Rate and ministrey for the future ; It voted affirmatiue that it should.

The same day it was voted that noe person should fell any tree in the 500 acres giuen vnto the non-commoners vpon the penaltie of 5ˢ for euery tree ther felled:

[**141.**] The Rate for the ministry the yeare 1661 : was 100¹ 5ˢ 1ᵈ the towne Rate for the yeare 1661 was 25¹ 00 3 :

7 (11) 1661 Vpon the request of seuerall of the inhabitance of Dorchester for to erect a vilage at Pole plaine or ther abouts It was voted that the towne of Dorchester was willing to grant sufficient land at the place afore sayd (if it be ther) to accomodate twentie or thirtie families if soe many appeare sufficient to Cary on Church and Commonwealth worke and that the p'pound ther tearmes and agree with such as the towne shall appoint for that end :

Voted the same day that the parties desiringe the village afore sayd repaire to the select men in Conuenient time and p'pound ther termes and the selectmen are desired to attend the same and p'pose it to the towne for full Confirmation.

10 : 1 : 166¼ wheras there is three pounds dew to goodman mead for the bell ringing and cleansing the meetting house, and not sufficient in the towne rate to pay him at present Mʳ patten did promise to pay goodman mead twenty sixe shillings and eight pence, and ensigne foster to pay the rest and both to bee allowed out of the next towne rate : which said three pound was paid goodman mead and by his order in the rate gathered in 1662 by Jams minott constable.

The same day William Pond was Chosen to seale waights and measures in Dorchester and the Constable to p'sent him to a maiestrate to take his oth

Alsoe fence viewers :

for the necke of Land { Richard Withington / John Willcocke / William Daniels / Thomas Swift / Samuel Picher

Mʳⁱˢ Stoughtons { Amiel Weekes / Steven Minott

Enoch Wiswall { Thomas Modesley / Joseph Holmes

Mʳ Mather { Timothy Mather / William Pond

Wᵐ Blake { Thomas Lake / William Blake

Thomas Bird { John Blackman / Thomas Bird

20 acre lotts { Richard Baker / Thomas Dauenport

great lotts from Daniel Prestons vnto popes lott { Richard Leads / John Smith

the rest to the Riuer { Abraham How / William Robenson

The three commissioners appointed to end smale Causes in Dor-

chester haue agreed and appointed to meet for the hearing of Causes if any appeare on these dayes following viz: the first sixt day in the Second moneth the first sixt day in the fifth moneth the first sixt day of the eight moneth the first sixt day of the eleuenth moneth, and the place of meetinge to be at Thomas Swifts sen^r:
Dated the 10 (1) 166½

The 5 (3) 1662 at a generall towne meeting it was voted whether Athony Fisher should have foure pounds alowed out of the towne rate for killing of six wolues the vote was affirmatiue;

The 24 (3) 62 ther was a warent giuen vnto the Bailife to take by distresse or otherwise the fines of those that had defectiue fence in the great Lotts.

[142.] At a meeting of the select men the 9 (4) 1662: Mr Minott request for a way to the meddow that lies by the peny ferry.

Memōd to take order for the repairing of the heighway betwene naponsett mill and Dedham:

Vpon a motion made by leiutenant Joshua Fisher of Dedham to rent the meddows which are in Dorchester neare Dedham bounds aboue Dedham:

It is ordered by the select men the 9 (4) 1662; that William Sumner and Ensigne Capen or either of them haue by this order power and are desired to bargaine with afore sayd Leiutenant Fisher for as many parsells of meddow and for what prise and pay they shall iudg meet; and if the afore sayd Fisher will not giue what in reason they iudg meet: then they to take ther best Chapman only they are to agree or bargaine from yeare to yeare and they shall be payd for ther paines out of towne rate.

Att the meeting of the select [men] the eighth day of September 1662: they intreated and appointed Captaine Clapp and Mr Patten to speake with M^{ris} Stoughton about the laying out of her ffarme that it might be effected forthwith.

The same day ther was a warent giuen vnto Thomas Tolman and Enoch wiswall constables for the yeare 1661 that they should bring in ther accounts of the Rates that were deliuerd vnto them the 19 (7) 62 vnto the selectmen.

The same day the select men did admitt Robert Searle to be an inhabitant in the towne of Dorchester:

The same day ensigne Capen and Wm Blake seni^r were apointed to speake to leift^t william Clarke and demand a barrell of powder of him or pay for that barell which he sold out of the townes stock and make returne the 19 day of this Instant to the select men.

The same day the select men did appoint the Captaine and the leiutenant and the Ensigne to take Care and charge of the Anunation that is the house of m^{ris} Atherton and to remoue it to some conenient place for the vse of the towne.

Memŏ to p'pound vnto the generall towne Meeting whether they would haue the 400 acres of land giuen for the maintenance of ministry of Dorchester and Vnquetie deuided:

I^t whether the towne will giue Beniamin Tuchel .5^l . 0 . 0

DORCHESTER TOWN RECORDS.   111

I^t some order to be taken to gett the Rates that are due from M^{ris} Stoughtons farmers:
Wheras ther was an order giuen to Thomas Tolman and Enoch Wiswall Constables for the yeare 1661 that they should bring in ther accounts of the Rates they receiued: vnto the selectmen the 9 (7) 62: Thomas Tolman cames vnto the select men the 10 (9) 62: and by reason Enoch Wiswall did not appear therfore ther could noe account be giuen therfore the select men doth lay the penaltie of 13^s 4^d vpon Enoch Wiswall for his neglect and [**143.**] And doe further order the afore sayd Thomas Tolman and Enoch Wiswall to bring in ther accounts vnto the select men the 25 day of this present moneth by nine of the clocke in the morning at the house of Captaine Claps vpon the penaltie of 20^s a peice if they neglect: dated the 10 (9) 62:

10 (9) 62: the select men did appoint Enoch Wiswall to gett the glasier to repair the wi[n]ddows of the meeting house before the 25 day of the 9^m 62 and pay the glasier and to be payd againe the next towne Rate, which if he doe the former penalty of 13^s 4^d shall be remitted.

At the meeting of the select men the 25 (9) 1662 the Constables Thomas Tolman and Enoch Wiswall gaue ther accounts of the Rates they receiued the yeare 1661:

The towne Rate was 25. 0. 3$^{li\ d}$

Imp'mis payd Mr Poole —	10. 0. 0
I^t to Robert Pond for killing a Wolfe	1. 0. 0
I^t to Georg Badcocke for killing a Wolfe	1. 0. 0
I^t to Robert Redman for alowance of land taken away by his house for a heighway	0. 17. 6
I^t to John Gill for the like	0. 8. 6
I^t to Nicolas George for exspenses of the Raters when they made the Rates	0. 8. 0
I^t to John Capen for worke aboute the meeting house	0. 16. 8
I^t to the glasier	0. 13. 0
I^t to David Joans	0. 1. 6
I^t to William Blake for Recording	1. 0. 0
I^t to Liutenant Hutson	3. 0. 2
I^t to Captaine Clap	0. 18. 0
I^t to Leiutenant Foster as due from the towne	2. 3. 10
I^t to Nicolas Clap and Joseph Leeds for ruñig the line	0. 15. 0
I^t to Robert Sanders for wood	0. 9. 11
I^t to Deacon Wiswall in parte for laying out the land on both sides the riuer	0. 7. 14
I^t to Enoch Wiswall for glasiers diet	0. 5. 0
I^t for Carring of Corne to Leuitenant Hutson and to the glasier	0. 5. 0
I^t to Thomas Swift	1. 0. 0
	25. 9. 5

At the generall towne meeting the 1 (10) 1662: the officers that were Chosen for the yeare ensuing were

Selectmen	Captaine Clap
	Leiutenant Foster
	William Sumner
	Mr Joans
	John Minott
Raters	Seriant Hall
	Seriant James Blake
	William Pond
Bailiffe	John Blackman

Supervisors of the heighways William Robenson
Thomas Bird

It was voted that if any doe neglect the making of ther way at the necke of land vpon dew warning he shall pay one shilling to be leuied by distresse : for euery foots defect

The same day it was voted that the would giue Mr Mather 95^l for the yeare past and vntill Januari next and vnto Mr Stoughton 25^l vntill Januari next both sums to be rated vpon the towne by p'portion.

[**144.**] At the generall towne meeting the 1 (10) 1662 Nicolas Clap Constable was appointed to se the windows of the meeting house mended, and to p'vide lids or window leaues for the windows and to pay the glasier and for making of the lidds or window leaues and he to be payd againe out of the next towne Rate and it was further ordered and voted that the Constables from time to time to Doe that worke from time to time and to bringe it vpon account from time to time.

The same day it was Voted that the towne would giue Beniamine Tuchel fiue pounds : to be payd out of the next towne Rate :

The same day Ensigne Capen did testifie that Henry Merifeild and his sonne did fell ten trees in the 500 acres that was layd out for the non Commoners : and alsoe the same day Thomas Bird did testifie that John Plumb did confesse to him that he did fell eight trees in the 500 acres layd out for the non-commoners : and that the select men should take order for the getting of the fines of these aboue sayd.

The same day it was voted that noe man should take offe or Cary away any wood from the 500 acres laid out for the non-Commoners vpon the penaltie of three shillings foure pence for euery load without order from the select men.

The same day Captaine Clap Leiutenant Foster and William Sumner were ordered appointed and intreated to seeke out a place or places for a Farme that was giuen by the generall Court in leiue of Tomsons Iland

The same day it was voted, ordered and appointed that William Sumner and John Capen and they are to acquaint Mr Stoughton and lay out his Farme and make ther returne and if Mr Stoughton please he may chuse an other man to ioine with them.

The same day it was voted that the 400 acres giuen for the maintenance of the ministry for Dorchester and Unquety should with the Common swamp to be deuided and Captaine Clap and Ensigne Capen are ordered and appointed to doe that worke and make ther returne.

DORCHESTER TOWN RECORDS. 113

The same day it was voted and ordered that John Minott should be in the place of Maior Atherton to ioine with Captaine Clap Leuitenant Foster and William Sumner to lay out the Farme giuen by the towne for the scoole in Dorchester.

[**145.**] The same day it was voted that those that doe neglect to come to the repairing of the heigh wayes being lawfully warned if a teame vpon the penaltie of six shillings and eight pence, if a man neglect and come not being lawfully warned vpon the penalty of two shillings for euery day and if any send any vnder sixteene yeares of age he is not to be accepted but he that sent him to be liable to pay 2^s for his neglect.

The same day it was voted and ordered that seriant Hall was appointed and impowered to p'secute those that are or haue ben M^{ris} Stoughtons Farmers that haue not pay ther p'portions as they wer Rated for the vse of the ministry in Dorchester.

At the meeting of the selectmen the 8 (10) 1662: they appointed the Raters to make a Rate of 120^l for the maintenance of the ministry and alsoe a Rate of 50^l: for the vse of the towne:

The same day ther was a warent giuen vnto the Raters to make these Rates aboue sayd:

The same day ther was a warent vnto the Bailiffe to gather those fines of those p'sons that felled those trees in the 500 acres that was reserued for the non Commoners:

The Country Rate that the Constable is to gather for the year 1662 was 63–17–9. paid the treasur^r 62–9–4 rest dew to the towne to ballce 1–8–5

The towne Rate Committed to the Constable Mr James Minott is 50^l 14^s

The aboue twenty eight shillings 5^d the balance of the acount of Nicolas clap constable was allowed him for what hee had paid the glasier and other worke done to the meeting house when he was constable: —

At the meeting of the select men the 12 (11) 1662: Phillip Edwards was admitted to be an inhabitant in the towne of Dorchester:

The same day ther was a warn̄t giuen vnto the Constable Nicolas Clap to take by distresse or other wise fiue shillings of John Willcocke for felling of a tree in the Commons:

I^t Mr Stoughton alowed for the p'sent timber for ground sells of his house in the 500 acres layd out for the non-com̄oners

The towne of Milton is to pay for the laying out of the 200 acres of land that was giuen for the vse of the ministry ther: 17^s 4^d and for the heigh way that doth rūn through Robert Redmans land 9^s and 16^s to Anthony Fisher for wolues all which sum̄s the select men doth appoint Robert Redman to receiue.

At the meeting of the select men the 9 (12) 1662: and they did order that John Fenno should haue 16^s for land that was taken away of his by reason of the heigh way that runs to the blew hills to be payd out of the next towne Rate.

The same day Daniel Eliers came to the select men and intreated to be an inhabitant in Dorchester; the selectmen would not accept of him to be an inhabitant vnless he did bring a sufficiant man or men to be bound to secure the towne of him, or to be in couenant for one yeare with some honest man:

John Plumbs fine for felling of trees in the 500 acres is respited vntil the meeting of the towne.

[**146.**] at the meeting of the select men the 9 (12) 1662 the fence viewers appointed were

for the necke of Land	James Blake / Samuel Clap
behind M^ris Stoughton	Richard Baker / Richard Withington
behind Enoch Wiswall	Enoch Wiswall / Isaac Joans
behind Mr Mather	Timothy Mather / Israel Mead
behind William Blake	William Weekes / Joseph Homes
behind Tho: Bird	James White / Obadiah Haws
20 acre lott —	James Humphrey / Henry Merifeild
great lot from Daniel Prestons vnto Thomas Tolmans house	Steven Minott / Samuel Rigbey
from Thomas Tolmans vnto the Riuer —	Thomas Tolman / Thomas Tilstone

The 13 (12) 62: ther was a warent giuen the Constable to take the penaltie of Robert Stiles that is in the order conserning, inmates and soiourners that are intertained into any mans house without lisence from the select men.

At the meetinge of the select men the 9 (1) 1662 or 63: they did apoint and intreat and impower William Sumner, William Blake Ju^r and Richard Hall to veiw and lay out a highway to the great fresh marsh from the Country heigh way; and to make returne by or befor the first of the third moneth next:

The same day William Blake Ju^r and Amiel Weekes did desire that the select men to p'pound vnto to the towne whther they will haue the way continued from Clement Topley vnto Country heigh way.

memor. whether the towne would grant Mr Poole to take 200 of Railes in the 500 acres: layd out for the non-commoners:

The same day the select men did order intreat and impower willia Sumner John Capen and nicolas Clap to lay out a way from the beginning of the lane that R$\bar{u}$ns through that land that was Mr Ludlows to R$\bar{u}$n to the Conntrary high way as way soe to goodman goads: the way to be two Rod broad and to make ther Returne by the 1 (3) next:

Memord. that Mr Stoughtons Request to haue his p'portion in the 500 acres that is laid out for the non commoners.

I^t William Blake Ju^r his request for satisfaction for land that is taken from him by reason of the Country heigh way.

[**147.**] At the meeting of the towne the 11 (1) 1662 or 1663: Richard Baker and James Humfrey were Chosen Constables for the yeare ensuinge.

DORCHESTER TOWN RECORDS. 115

I^t the same day Captaine Clape Leuitenant foster and william Sumner were Chousen Commissioners to end smale Causes in Dorchester:

The same day Captaine Clap and Liuitenant Foster were chosen Deputies for the yeare Insuinge:

The same day at the request of Mr Poole the towne did giue him libertie to haue two hundred of Railes in the 500 acres layd out for the non-Commoners:

I^t it was voted that Joseph long had libertie to take ten trees for the building of a house: in the 500 acres layd out for the non-commoners:

I^t the towne did remit the fines of Henry merifeild John Plumb and John Wilcocke for felling of trees in that parsell of land.

At the meeting of the select men the 11 (3) 1663: John Phillips of Boston came to the selectmen and desired of them that the late devissions drawne by William Robenson of Dorchester might be recorded In the towne booke vpon the sayd Phillips name and as his right but the select men vnderstanding of some difference betweene him and william Robenson about the sayd lands the select men saw no reason to record the same as was desired vntill the sayd difference were Issued.

William Sumner was Chosen Clarke of the trained Company the 15th (4) 1663:

The 10 (6) 63 ther was a warent giuen to the Baliffe for the leuiing of 19^s 6^d of Steven minott for defectiue fence against the feild on the south side of M^{ris} Athertons house and 3^s 9^d of Ursula Baten.

Edmund Bowker debter to the ministers Rate for severall yeares
Imp'mis for the year 1658 0–2–0
I^t for the yeare 1659 1–5–0
I^t for the yeare 1660 1–5–0
I^t for the yeare 1661 0–10–0
I^t for the yeare 1662 . . . .
for his owne estate and for the mill 1–13–2

A warentie giuen to the Constable Richard Baker the 24 (6) 1663: for the leuiing and taking of the aboue sayd sumes by distresse or otherwise:

Ther were three warents giuen to the Bayliffe the 15 (7) 63 to take by Distresse or otherwise the fines that were due for defectiue fence vidz. in the great lotts the necke of land and in the feild behinde Mr Stoughtons house.

[148.] An account of the towne Rate made in the yeare 1662 gathered by Mr James minott constable the rate

	ll. s. d.
is	50–14–00

And the said Rate disposed of as followeth
Imp^s paid M^r pole in parte of his scoole wages . 15–00– 0
Itm̄ to the deacons for Edmund brownes child . . 03–10–00
I^t to Anthony Fisher for wolues killing . . . 04–00–00
I^t to Mr Blake for Recording 01–00–00
I^t to beniamin Twitchill as giuen by the towne . . 05–00–00
I^t to Capt. clap & leift. Foster as deputyes . . 03–06–00

I^t to willyam sumner seni^r for a wolf killing	01-00-00
I^t to goodman mead for the meeting house, (.61.(.62.)	06-00-00
I^t to leift Fisher for towne plott	02-00-00
I^t to Deacon wiswall for soe much paid for the towne for measuring towne land	04-00-00
I^t samuell procter for chardges about the pound	00-12-00
I^t to william turner for labor for the towne w^n baylife	00-02-08
I^t to nicolas clap to pay the glasier and other chardges about the meetting house	03-00-00
I^t to nicolas Georg for Rates expenses	00-07-00
I^t to goodman swift part of select mens exspenses	01-00-00
I^t to John Capen senio^r for Redman dew from the towne Renewing ffor land taken of Redmans for a highway	00-02-08
This account taken the 9th of 9th mo : 1663 :	50-00-04
The selectmen allowed the constable fiue shillings and two pence for losses by some men not paying	00-05-02
	50-05-06
Rent due to towne	00-08-06
Reconed with good wife swift this 9 (9) 1663 and dew to her for expenses this yeare the sum of	4^{lb}-07-04
At a meeting of the select men &c. 30 : 9 : 1663 exspended	0-07-09
paid by James minot of this some 0-8-6	4-15-01
rest due	4-07-01

[**149.**] At a ginerall Towne meeting the 7th of the 10th mo. 1663 It was put to Vote whether Mr William Poole should be Chosen for to be Clarke of the wrights and Recorder for the Towne : The vote was affirmatiue.

The day aboue said the Commite appointed for to lay out or deuid the 400 ackers of land giuen to the vse of the minestry of Dorchester and Melton made ther returne and the vote was whether Milton should haue that end next to the parallell-line and Dorchester the end next the riuer. The vote was afermatiu.

The Day abouesaid It was voted that Mr Mather shall haue fower score pounds paid to him for his worke in the minestry this last yeer which end the last of this p'sent month and Rate free to the minesters Rate. Alsoe that Mr Stoughton shall haue fifty pounds and Rate free for his owne Estate vnto the Minesters Rate.

The day aboue said it was Voted that Jno Capen and William Sumner shall have full power for to lett and set the land appointed for the Scoole and alsoe the two hundred acrs laid out for the maintenance of the minestry on Milton sid : at ther best descretion.

The same day it was voted and granted that william Trescot should have an addition of eight foote of land to be taken in at the end of what he haue already taken in before the hous or land of George Dyer Viz at the east end next to the Calues pasture.

Selectmen. Captin Clapp Liftenat Foster M\u1d63. Joanes William Sumner John Minot.
Raters Jn° Capen Daniell preston Lawrence Smith.
Supuisers of highways for the Towne. Willm Robenson, Tho. Bird.
Sup'uisor for the way to the neck James White.

The day abouesaid Mr Samuell Tory of Milton had granted vpon a petition of his six acrs of Fresh meddow on the south sid of Naponsett riuer aboue or about the blew hills vnto him and his heires or Asignes for euer : being granted by each p'ticuler p'prieter only two excepted.

[150.] mo: 10 : 14 : 1663.
At the meeting of the select men the 14 of the 10 month, 1663, this returne was made.

We whose names are heere vnder written, being appointed to lay out a highway, from the Country highway, leading to the fresh marsh, we mett the 15 of the 1 mo : 1663, and layd out two rods wide from the Cuntry high way, in breadth, by Vrsilla Battens pasture fence, to the brow of a hill, by a rock lying on the East side of the way, of the hill, and from thence crossing ouer to the way that now is.

WILLIAM SUMNER.
RICHARD HALL
WILLIAM BLAKE.

The same day there was a warrant granted for the making of three Rates one for the Ministery, one for the County, and one for the Towne.

A second meeting of the select men. mo : 11. the 11. day. 1663.
This day the Raters doe make returne to us of the 3 seuerall Rates aboue sayd

namely a Rate for the ministry . . . . 130 – 5 –
one Rate for the County . . . . . . 21 – 3 – 4
one Rate for the Towne . . . . . . 40 – 3 – 1

A 3 meeting of the Selectmen the 8 of the 12 month. 1663.
The 6 : of the 5 : mo : 1663 vpon a meeting of the select men of Dorchester, and sundry of the Inhabitants of Dedham and Rocksbery, together with the Committee chosen by the Hon^rd County Court to consider of the difference betweene Dedham and Dorchester, about a Cartway betwixt the said Dedham and Dorchester ; for a finall issue, and according vnto further clayms by Dedham about the sayd way.

It is proposed by the select men of Dorchester that there shall be layd out a Towneway through the lands of Dorchester, from the house of Edward Pason vnto the way that leads from Dedham to Naponsett mill ; in which sayd way now intended the Inhabitants of Dedham shall haue free liberty to pass to and from Dedham to Dorchester, in the sayd way, as Dorchester Inhabitants may doe at any time, and this liberty to be, and is granted to Dedham and the Inhabitants thereof foreuer.

This Bill presented to the Selectmen of Dedham December 31. 1663, by Peeter Woodward; the Select men concurre with what is proposed, provided that it be expressed that the Inhabitants of Dedham haue liberty of a way by the house of Edward Pason, from the way that leads to Dorchester Mill, and that there may be a Record heereof in both Town books.

By order of the selectmen
JOSHUA FISHER.

This Returne of Dedham is consented to, by the Selectmen of Dorchester at thier Meeting this 8. day of the 12 month. 1663.

[**151.**] The Country Rate, with the addition of an half Rate this yeare 1663. comes to . . . . . 65 – 00 – 07

which is to be payd, as foloweth, vnto the Treasurer,
as by his Bill . . . . 56 – 19 – 10
vnto Lieftenant Hudson . . . . . . 02 – 11 – 02
vnto Captaine Clap . . . . . :3 – 6 – : :
vnto Lieftenant Foster . . . . . :2 – 2 – 6
                                                          ─────────
                                                         64 – 19 – 6

The 14th of the 9 mo: 1664. Richard Baker and James Humphreys brought in their Account for the aboue Rate, and are discharged for the same.

At a gineral Towne meeting being orderly assembled the 7th of the (1)6¾ it was put to the vote whether Quarter Master John Smith and William Robenson should be appointed to Joyn with some men of Boston a bout laying out of a high-way from Boston vnto the marsh Cros-ouer the pastuers.

The Vote was affirmatiue.

The day aboue said It was p'posed to the towne viz to the p'prietors whether Mr Stoughton should haue his hundered acres to be laid out on the north sid of the riuer namly beginning at the line of his hundred and fifty acres and soe to come downeward vnto the line soe fare forth as that land will extend, and what is wanting to take it next to his owne land on the South sid: And for the marsh on this Sid of the line viz in the old grant Mr Stoughton granting to accept of it for his deuissions and if his deuissions doe not take it all vp, then to abate soe much on the South Sid and if it fall short of his deuissions then to have it next his other land on the South sid

The Vote was affermetiue.

The same day ther was Chosen for a Committy William Sumner John Capen John Minot for to Ripen and p'pare matters for the laying out of the Common meddow in the fresh Marsh about the blew hils to apoint high ways and wheere to begin and other matters that may Concerne that Bussines And also it was Voted the same time that the Committy abovesaid agreeing with the suruayer for matter of pay whether the p'prietors should not pay each man for his lot according to the Charges that shall be requiset being p'portioned to each man by the Committy aboue said this being put to the Vote the vote was affermatiue.

This last order aboue said is by a uote repealled

[**152.**] This Agreement made the. 1. day of the 2^d month. 1661.

betweene William Blake, and Thomas Davenport.

These men having land lying together on the Hill, west on thier houses, the sayd Thomas Davenport is to sett vp a sufficient fence betweene William Blake his land, and his owne. and to maintaine it for the space of 3 yeares after it is sett vp, and then William is to pay Thomas for one halfe, as two men shall iudge it worth ; and to maintaine the same foreuer ; and for performance heereof, we doe binde the severall lands, vnto the which the fence belongeth : Witness our hands, 1 the day and yeare aboue said. — The fence heere meant, is the middle fence which runneth East and West.

Witnesses
SAMUEL JONES   WILLIAM BLAKE
JOHN KINGSLEY.   THOMAS DAVENPORT

Recorded at a meeting of the Select men the 14 of the i mo : $166\frac{3}{4}$:
p me WILLIAM POLE Recorder.

At a Towne meeting the 11 of the (1 mo :) The Free men chose to serue as thier Deputies, for the year ensuing Captaine Roger Clap, and Lieftenant Hopestill Foster.

It was voted the same day, that Thomas Bird Senior should be exempted from being chosen as Constable for Dorchester, for the space of seuen years ensuing, in regard of much trouble and losses he sustained in the yeare when he was Bailiff, which he was contented to remit to the Towne.

The same day Captaine Roger Clap, Lieftenant Hopestill Foster and William Sumner Se : were chosen Commissioners to end small cases in Dorchester the year ensuing.

Also the same day were chosen to serue as Constables for the Towne of Dorchester Laurence Smith and Clement Maxfild.

[**153.**] At a generall Town meeting the 7th of the (1. mo: $166\frac{3}{4}$) it was put to the vote whether Quarter master John Smith, and William Robenson should be appointed to ioyne with some men of Boston, about laying out of a high way from Boston vnto the marsh cross ouer the pastures.

The vote was affirmatiue.

The same day, William Sumner, Richard Leeds, and John Capen are desired and appointed to view a piece of land about the Clay pitts, desired by Enoch Wizall, and Frances Ball, and to make thier Returne to the Select men, at thier next meeting of the conveniency of the motion.

Also the same day, William Sumner, Richard Hall and William Blake, are desired and appointed to lay out a way to the fresh marsh, from the end of the way formerly laid out by Richard Withington his land vnto the sayd marsh, in the most convenient place, and with the least preiudice to any man.

Also Lieftenant Hope-still Foster and William Sumner are empowered for to procure some pikes for the vse of the Towne; and for that end are granted liberty to contract with such as they see meet for some trees for shingle out of purgatory Swamp, either such as are already fallen, and ly subiect to wast, or others as they in thier prudence and discretion shall iudge meet.

The same day being the 7th of the (1 mo :) It was voted and agreed vnto, between Mr William Stoughton, and the proprietors of the Common land, that Mr Stoughton shall have all that Tract of land, aboue the .100. acres, which he hath for his Farme, vp so farre, as Dorchester hath any common land, lying on the north side of Naponsett riuer, between the riuer and Dedham line, excepting the swamp, called Purgatory Swamp, and any meadow which may lie in this tract of land; And this he shall haue in liew of all his Common rights, both his owne, or purchased within the precincts of Dorchester, on both sides the Riuer, the sayd Mr Stoughton deliuering in, to the Proprietors a iust list of all the proprieties which he hath purchased. Only Mr Stoughton is to haue in Purgatory Swamp 40 Acres, as his full part of that Swamp, and to be liable to any Towne order concerning that Swamp. Also it is to be vnderstood, that the place or extent of this præmentioned Grant, is, at the first crossing the riuer, by the line between Dedham and Dorchester.

Voted, and consented vnto, on both parts and also that Mr Pole shall record this Agreement

By order of the Select men at thier meeting the 14 day of the (1 : mo : 166¾)

Recorded by me WILLIAM POLE Recorder.

[**154.**] At the same meeting (being the 14 of the .1. mo : 166¾) there was brought in, the Returne of a list from Mr William Stoughton vnder his owne hand, of his severall Rights and proprieties in the Lands of Dorchester.

March the 8, 166¾

A true List of the severall Rights in the Land yet vndiued, commonly called the New Grant, made Dorchester, which did vpon the 7 seventh of March, 166¾ belong vnto William Stoughton in every Division

	acres	qrers.	Pole.
1 His owne originall Right.	26	3	20
2 Mr Makepeaces	13	0	06
3 Mr Gilberts	9	1	28
4 Mrs Knights	10	3	0
5 Widow Smeads.	03	0	8
6,7 Mr Jones's & Floods.	09	3	20
8,9 John Pope's & Whetcome's . . .	8	3	28
10,11 Read's & Miller's	6	0	16
12,13 Mr Butler's & Dimmock's . . .	13	0	34
14 Huchinson's	03	3	10
15 Edmond Munnings	10	3	12

16 Mr Holman's to the quantity of 96 acres only.

17 Richard Calacot's to the quantity of 111 Acres and 24 rod.

This Account of my Rights and Dues, is according as I find

them standing vpon my Father's booke. And in pursuance of the Agreement made betweene the Proprietors and my self, March the 7.166¾. I doe now giue in this account, as being exact, to the vtmost of my knowledge. And shall make good all the aboue mentioned Rights and proportions, so far forth as any Record, or bargaine of sale remaining with me concerning the Premises will amount vnto; which I shall be ready at all times to acquaint the Proprietors with, and to produce on thier behalf.

Witness my hand, the day and yeare first aboue written
WILLIAM STOUGHTON.

[155.] 1664.

Dorchester. At a Towne meeting the 1 of April, 1664.

It was then to put to the vote, whether the Towne would suspend the choyce of Lawrence Smith from being Constable for this yeare.

The vote was in the affirmative

The same day Richard Leeds was chosen for to be a Constable for this yeere, and vntill another be chosen.

The same day it was put to vote, whether Mr William Pole should continue teaching of Schoole, for future, as formerly, vntill this yeare shall be expired, which will be the first 2^d day of December next, and then the Towne to consider, whether he shall continue teaching any longer, yea or no. —

It was voted in the affirmatiue.

The same day, there was granted vnto Nicholas Ellin, liberty to take 3. or 4. loads of timber out of the fiue hundred acres toward the building of a Barne.

The same day, it was proposed to the Towne; whether they were willing to haue an Ordinary set vp some where about, or neere vnto the Meeting house.

The vote was Negatiue.

1664.

[156.] At a meeting of the Select men, April the 4, 1664 for Field viewers were appointed as followeth.

For the Neck	Richard Baker / Laurence Smith
for the field behind Mr Mather's	Goodman Dier / William Pond
Mr Stoughtons	Stephen Minot / Mr Withington
Behind Wilcocks	Joseph Homes / Obadiah Swift
On the hill behind Mr Joans	Isack Joans / Thomas Lake
Thomas Bird's	Jasper Rush / John Blackman
20 acre Lotts	Thomas Davenport / Thomas Grant

Great Lotts from Daniel Prestons { Richard Hall
to Tho: Tolemans . . . { John Smith.
From Th: Toleman's { Thomas Tilestone
to the Riuer { Samuel Robinson

The Order of the Select men to the severall viewers.

You are to take notice that you are chosen by the Select men to be viewers for this yeare 1664, of the severall fences committed to your charge to view the same, and to present according to order the severall defects; as also to see the gates sufficiently repaired, that Cattle may be kept off, and dammage for future prevented, and heereof to make a Returne to some of the select men on the 12 of this Instant.

By order of the Selectmen, the 4th of the 2 mon: 1664.

WILLIAM POLE Recorder.

[**157.**] At a meeting of the Select men the 11th of the (5th mo:) 1664.

Robert Stiles is presented for being defectiue in 18 Rod and half of fence belonging to him at the 20 Acre Lotts, for which, by order he is to pay 1^{li} 7^s 9^d But upon consideration had betweene the Select men, they doe remit it to 6^s 8^d provided that he repaire and make good his fence within six dayes folowing, for the which six sh: 8 pence a warrant is granted to the Constable to Recouer it by distress or otherwise.

The same day, Raph Warner, and Thomas Narrowmoore are admitted for Inhabitants in the Towne of Dorchester.

A meeting of the Select men, the 12th of the (7 mo:) 1664.

Whereas there was a motion made by Nicholas Bolton vnto the Select men, for his wifes drawing and selling of Syder, we the Selectmen doe not approue of it.

Upon a complaint made against Thomas Trott for defectiue Fence, the Select men gaue order for the repairing it.

Ensigne Capen and William Sumner are appointed by the Selectmen, to gett the burying place well and sufficiently to be fenced in, and are to demand of John Blake 20 shillings, giuen by his father in his last will and Testament to that end and vse.

Item. It is ordered by the select men that the Constables doe bring in thier Accounts of the last years Rates at thier next meeting the seventh of October, 1664.

The last 2 day in October is appointed by the Select men, for the calling of the proprietors togeither for the deviding of the Common Medow adioyning to Mr Stoughtons Farme.

1664.

[**158.**] At a Meeting of the Select men, the 14th of the (9 mo:) 1664.

This day the constables Richard Baker and James Humphrys for the yeer: 1663 brought in thier Accounts for the severall Rates committed to them.

Imp. the Contry Rate, payd according to order . } . . . . . 65 - - 7

Item the County rate } payd to Mr Ting, Treasurer of the County } vpon this Rate remaines due to the Towne 13 shillings the 15 pences. On the troopers being collected	. 21 – 1 – 3
Item the Towne Rate . . . . . . Payd as foloweth	. 40 – 3 – 1
Imp'mis: Abated to William } Blake ouerrated . }	. 00 – 05 – 04
Itē to Goodman Mede for } his service at the Meeting house }	. 03 – 00 – 00
Itē to Mr Mather, as part of } what was due to him }	. 00 – 6 – 6
Itē payd to Samuel Proctor } for the Pound . }	. 01 – 17 – 11
Itē. to Thomas Damport for } wolf killing . . }	. 00 – 10 – 0
Itē. to Daniel Preston for } wolf killing . . }	. 00 – 10 – 0
Itē. to an Indian for wolf killing .	. 00 – 10 – 0
Item to Goodm: Swift for expences	. 05 – 1 – 1
Item payd vnto John Gill for } land about the high way }	. 01 – 11 – 6
Itē payd to John Fenno for the like	. 00 – 16 –
Itē payd to Obadiah Swift } for work about the Meting House }	. 00 – 02 – 6
Itē Edward Martin 1^s alowed bēc } rated in milton . . }	. 00 – 01 – 0
Item to Mr Pole for the schoole rate	. 25 – 00 – 00
Reconed with good wife swift for the } yeare past this 14th day of the 9mo } 1664 and due to her the some of }	. 03 – 00 – 00
of which is paid by Bro. James } Vmphrey constable as part of } this years chardges . }	. 00 – 16 – 00
rest due to chardges at the house . . .	. 02 – 04 – 00

memōd 8^s 6^d Deb^t from James minot to be enquired after whether paid to goodwife swift or not:

1664.

[**159.**] At a generall Towne Meeting the 5th of the (10 mo:) 1664.

It was put to vote whether Mr Pole should continue teaching of schoole, in Dorchester, for the yeare insuing as he hath formerly. Voted in the Affirmatiue.

The same day it was voted that the Towne did accept of the Selectmens Accounts for the last yeare past.

The same day aboue sayd, It was voted, that Mr Mather for his work in the Ministery shall haue fourscore and ten pounds; and

Mʳ Stoughton, forty pounds. And withall voted that thier Lands shall be rated

The same day were chosen for the
Select men { Capt: Clap, Lieft: Foster, Mʳ Joans } { Will: Sumner, Anth: Fisher Se: }

The same day chosen Raters { John Capen, John Minot, Richard Hall }
The day aboue sayd, chosen Surveyors of the high wayes { Nicholas Clap. Thom: Damfort. }

This day fortnight (being the 19 of this present month) is appointed for a day of meeting of the proprietors about the division of the medows at the Blew hills.

The same day above sayd, vpon the request of Sergeant Hall, for the alteration of the highway lying before his dore, it was voted by the Towne that John Minott, Richard Leeds, and Thomas Toleman should be appointed heervnto; and vpon view thereof to make thier Returne vnto the Selectmen; and as these 3 men doe approue of it; the Select men haue order to record it.

[**160.**] At a meeting of the Selectmen on the 9ᵗʰ of the (11 mo:) 1664.

At this meeting aboue mentioned, Nathaniel Whiting of Dedham appeared, before the Selectmen, and made a motion a litle piece of Common Land belonging to the Dorchester, lying upon the Riuer called Mother Brooks, without the division of Lotts. In order heerevnto the Selectmen haue granted, that it shall be proposed to the Town, at the next convenient Towne Meeting, to have thier approbation, if they see meet, to grant it to him, either by purchase or Rent: and in the meane time, the sayd Nathaniel Whiting shall gett it to be viewed, that so the Towne may be informed both of the quantity and quality of the Land.

At this Meeting aboue sayd, The Raters chosen for this yeere, John Minott and John Capen Se: presented their Rates for the Ministery, and for the Towne, dated the 2ᵈ of the (11. mo:) 1664.

The Rate of the Ministery amounts to an . . . . . 130 – 12 – 6
The Towne Rate . . . . . } 40 – 7 – 7
  to this rate was an addition of 3ˡⁱ – 13ˢ – 1ᵈ } 3 – 13 – 1

the whole is 44 – 00 – 8

This same day Clement Maxfild appeared before the Select men, and desired that his Brother John Maxfild, being arriued lately from England, might Continue in the Towne with him; and that he would secure the Towne, from any dammage, during his residence here. which was granted that he, the sayd Clement Maxfild, might, entertaine his brother as is aboue expressed, vntill such time, as his Brother, shall otherwise settle himself heere, or elswhere.

The same day, vpon a motion made by Joseph Burch he hath liberty to entertaine his Brother Lewis, till the Select men give further order.

Roger Billing his Acquittance for the yeere 1664 recorded.

Receiued by me Roger Billing for the yeere 1664. For running a line, and for killing a wolf the summe of fifteene shillings.

       I say receiued by me
         ROGER BILLING.

[**161.**] At a meeting of the Select Men on the 13. of the (12 mo:) 1664.

At the Towne Meeting the 6th of the (1. mo:) 1665.

Officers chosen for this yeare.

 Deputies { Captaine Clap
      { Lieftenant Foster

 Commissioners { Captaine Clap
       { Lieftenant Foster
       { William Sumner

 Constables { Steven Minott
      { Thomas Trott.

The same day vpon a motion made by John Plum to the Towne there was granted to him 30 Acres of land neere Dedham saw mills vpon such condition as the Select men in thier discretion think meet.

[**162.**] At the Meeting of the Select men the 13th of the (1 mo:) 1665.

At a meeting of the Selectmen the 4 of the (2d mo) 1665.

Roger Billing and William Trescott are appointed and impowred on the behalf of the Towne of Dorchester, to ioyne with some of Milton, and some of Brantry, or such of them, as shall be appointed to attend the work; viz. to lay out, and bound, a sufficient Cartway, as may be most convenient, safe, and easy for passage, between Milton and Squantum Neck, etc, and to doe it, with all convenient speed, and mak Returne of the same to the Select men.

1665.

[**163.**] At a Meeting of the Select men, the 12. of the (4 mo;) 1665.

A motion being made by the widow that, on the behalf of her son in law (lately come from Boggerstow to this Town that he might inhabit amongst us: The Select men see not cause to grant him liberty to Inhabit in Dorchester; and therefore doe order that the sayd Widow Hill, or any other doe not entertaine him vpon the penalty of the order made the 10 (11. mo:) 1658, and that she doe forthwith discharge herself, and the Towne of him. — And that Mr Pole giue the Constable notice hereof, and also a copy of the foresayd Order, that he may acquaint the foresayd widow Hill thereof; and warne him to depart the Towne.

The day and yeere aboues'd It is ordered by the Select men, that John Smith of the Rocky Hill, shall be keeper of the Pound, and that he shall haue for every horse other cattle and swine two pence a piece, and for every sheep an half penny, to be payd by the owners of the creatures so empownded.

At the same Meeting, 12. 4. 1665. Captaine Clap (if he be come home) Deacon Wiswall, William Sumner, John Capen sen: are desired and impowred to meet with Josiah Sachem and others on the 26 of this Instant, and to treat with him, to see what the demand of the Indians is; as respecting any of Dorchester Land; and to make full and compleat agreement, if they see thier demands be but reason; and for that end, they take Copyes of the Deed from Kitshamichin, and other writings; and what other helps they shall think needful to call with them to further the busines; and if they see not cause to issue the matter, then to make report to the Towne for further consideration.

The same day, it is granted, vnto John Capen sen^r that vpon his request made vnto the Selectmen, he shall have the feed of the Burying place vntil April 66. or April 67. which he please; he leaving the place in good repaire at the time expired.

At a Meeting of the Selectmen the 20th of the (5 mo:) 1665.

Wheras there is lately a new Gallery set vp in the Meeting house in Dorchester, without leaue from the Towne or the Select men of the Towne; and the sayd Gallery seemes to proue preiudiciall to the light, and offensiue to many; and therefore that such practice may not be vsed for future, we doe declare that the erecting of the sayd Gallery is disorderly; and therefore doe order that none of the parties that built it, nor any other doe presume to sit in the sayd Gallery vntill such time as the Towns mind may be fully knowne, and declared whether the sayd Gallery, shall be continued, or taken down againe, or how disposed of.

ROGER CLAP, THOMAS JONES, ANTHONY FISHER, WILLIAM SUMNER, HOPESTILL FOSTER.

1665.

[**164.**] At a Town Meeting, the 18. (5) 1665. It was proposed, and put to vote whether the new impression of Mr Mathers Catechismes should be payd for, out of a Towne Rate, and so the books to become the Towns:

The vote was in the Affirmatiue.

At the same day it was voted, that the Elders and Selectmen and Deacon Capen, should have the disposing of the above sayd bookes, to each Famely, according to thier discretion. The vote was in the Affirmatiue.

The 29. of the (6 mo:) 1665. At a Town Meeting.

Wheras Increase Atherton, Thomas Bird, Ju: and Samuel Procter, haue lately erected a Gallery in the Meeting house, without any order from the Towne, or not in such an orderly way as were to be desired. The question was put whether the sayd Gallery so built should stand, and the aboue say[d] persons therein and not be disposed of, to any other person but such as the Towne, or thier Deputy in that matter shall iudge meet. And all this upon thier ingenious acknowledgment of their too much forwardnes therein, The vote was in the Affirmatiue, they p'forming the conditions.

At a Meeting of the Selectmen the 11th of the (7th mo :) 1665.
Whereas there hath beene, and still is great complaints of cattle destroying corne, by persons taking liberty to feed thier cattle, in common corn fields, before the corne is all out. It is therefore ordered by the select men of this Towne, that if any cattle, horses, or swine, be taken in any common cornfield, either in the corne, or out of the corne, except the sayd cattle be within some p'ticular Inclosure, or vnder the keeping of a sufficient keeper, and that within the bounds of the ground of the owners of the sayd cattle; and this vpon penalty of forfeiting 4^d for euery head so taken, as before expressed, beside paying all dammages done by the cattle, horses or swine, and all charges that may arise by Impownding them; and John Smith on the Rocky hill, is, to see to the due execution of this order for the great Lotts.

At the same Meeting was presented to the Selectmen this acknowledgment folowing

We whose names are vnderwritten doe acknowledge that it was our weaknes that we were so inconsiderate as to make a small seat in the Meeting house, without more cleare and full approbation of the Towne, and Select men thereof; though we thought, vpon the conference we had with some of the Select men apart and Elders, we had satisfying ground for our proceeding therein, which now we see, was not sufficient: Therefore we desire, that our failing therein may be passed by: And if the Town shall grant us our seat, that we haue been at so much cost in setting vp, we thankfully acknowledge your loue vnto us therein; and we doe herevpon further engage ourselues, that we will not giue vp, or sell any of our places in that seat, to any person or persons, but whom the Elders shall approue of, or such, as shall haue power to place men in seats in the assembly.
INCREASE ATHERTON
SAMUEL PROCTER
THOMAS BIRD.

Dated the 30. of the (6 mo :) 1665.

[**165.**] At the meeting of the Selectmen the 13th of the (9 mo :) 1665.

Diuers things of the Towne affaires considered of, referred to thier next meeting, the 27. of this Instant.

Only an order taken for the printing of Mr Mathers Catechisme to the satisfaction of the printer.

And likewise an order issued out to the Constables of the last yeere past to bring in thier Accompts of that yeere, 1664 to the Select men at thier next meeting the 27 of this Instant, 1665.

At the meeting of the Select men on the 27th of the (9 mon :) 1665.

The Constables Richard Leed, and Clement Maxfield, brought in thier Accounts for the yeere 1664.

Thier Account for that yeere deliuered to them was
Imp. The Cuntry Rate, with the addition was . . 76 – 09 – 3
The Towne Rate, with the addition, was . . . 44 –   – 6

                                                        120 – 9 – 9

128   CITY DOCUMENT No. 9.

Which is payd as foloweth . . . . .
To the Treasurer of the Countrey . . . . 70 – 7 – 7
By order to the Deputies for that yeare . . . 06 – 0 – 0
                                                    ─────────
                                                    76 – 7 – 7

Payd out of the Towne Rate as followeth.
Imp. to Mr Mather. . . . . . . 01 – 05 – 00
Item to Mr Pole for his work . . . . . 26 – 00 – 00
Item to Captaine Clap . . . . . . 01 – 05 – 00
Ite. to Lieftenant Foster. . . . . . 02 – 10 – 00
Ite. to Goodman Mede . . . . . . 03 – 00 – 00
Ite. to Goodman Swift . . . . . . 02 – 05 – 00
Ite. to Ensigne Capen . . . . . . 01 – 08 – 06
Item to Nicholas Clap; what was due to him . . 01 – 00 – 00
Ite. to Anthony Fisher Jun : for 3 wolues . . 01 – 10 – 00
Item to Henery Ledbetter for a wolfe or Roger Billing 00 – 10 – 00
Ite. to Thomas Bird for a wolf . . . . 00 – 10 – 00
To Samuel Clap . . . . 00 – 05 – 00
Ite to Daniel Prescot for a part of a wolf . . 00 – 02 – 06
Ite to William Sumner . . . . . . 00 – 04 – 06
Ite. to Steven Hoppin . . . . . . 00 – 07 – 06
Ite to Obadiah Swift . . . . . . 00 – 03 – 00
Ite to Roger Billing . . . . . . 00 – 05 – 00
Ite to Samuell Procter . . . . . . 00 – 10 – 01
Ite to Thomas Lake, Richard Hall, and Steuen Minott 00 – 07 – 06
                                                    ─────────
        Summa Totalis   43 – 01 – 01

[**166.**]   At a generall Towne Meeting in Dorchester the 4th 10 (mo :) 1665

Were chosen for Selectmen
Lieftenant Hopestill Foster
Anthony Fisher Sen^{or}
Thomas Jones
William Sumner
John Minott
Supervisors for the high-wayes
   Enoch Wizwall
For the Neck-way
     James Blake

For Raters for the yeare ensuing
Ensigne Capen
Richard Hall
William Pond

Thomas Tilestone

The same day it was put to the question, What should be allowed to the Ministery for the yeare past which ends the first of January next. For Mr Mather it was voted he should have eighty pounds, and his estate Rate-free to the Ministery.

For Mr Stoughton, it was voted he should haue fifty pounds and his estate Rate-free to the Ministery.

At the same Meeting it was put to vote whether Mr Pole should keep on schoole teaching for the yeare ensuing : The vote was Affirmatiue.

The same day, It was voted, vpon the desire of William Sumner, concerning satisfaction for the high way vpon his Land. that lies neere Goodman Goads. That Ensigne John Capen, Richard Hall, and James Humphrey, should view the sayd way, and allow the sayd William Sumner satisfaction out of the same highway lying neere his Land, and they make report to the Select men that thier determination may be recorded.

The same day it was voted, that the Selectmen should consider, of the land that is not yet layd out what is the most equall and righteous way by which it should be layd out, and to appoint a day, when the Town shall meet together to heare what they have considered of.

[**167.**] At a meeting of the Select men the 11th (10 mo:) 1665.

The Rate for the Ministery 130
The Cuntry and County Rate for this yeare is . . 80
Itē for the Towne and Schoole 56

Ordered that a Warrant be giuen to the Raters, Ensign Capen, Richard Hall, and William Pond for the making of these three severall Rates.

At this meeting of the Select men Samuel Hix was sent for, to enquire of him why he had not giuen Bond according to his promise, and also gaue him warning speedily to depart the Towne, or giuing Bond for the time he shall stay.

The same day Nicholas Ellen made a motion to the Select men, to moue the Towne that he might haue Liberty to take in a parcell of ground vpon condition of setting vp, and maintaining two sufficient gates.

The same day the Selectmen were desired to moue William Trescots request to the Towne, for to haue some small parcell of Land (to his Tenement) for English grass about the Ox pen.

At a generall Town Meeting of the Proprietors and the Towne of Dorchester the 27 of the (10: Mo:) 1665.

The Question was proposed, whether there should a Committee be chosen, for to consider and ripen the business, about dividing of the Land beyond the Blew hills and whether there should not be some land disposed of, vnto those that are not for the present accounted Proprietors, provided there be no violation of the former rule vnto the Proprietors.

The vote was in the Affirmatiue.

The Committee chosen are

The Selectmen—Captaine Clap, if he can be obtained. John Wiswall, señ John. Capen sen: William Robinson Richard Hall. Richard Leeds. James Humphryes.

These or nine of them may be a Meeting, and that these men, or Committees may consider of an answer vnto a letter sent by Lieftenant Hudson.

The vote was in the Affirmatiue.

Also the petitions that are presented, are to be considered of, by the same Committee: and all this to be done by the next Town Meeting, which is appointed to be the second fourth day of February next 1665.

[**168.**] At a Meeting of the Selectmen the 8th day of the (11. Mo:) 1665.

The Rates for the Ministry, and for the Towne were returned and brought in to the Select men by the Raters John Capen, Richard Hall, and William Pond signed by thier hands.

The Rate for the Ministery 130–00–05
The Rate for the Towne and schoole . . . 057–05–03

Also the same day was granted to the Constables a Warrant for the gathering of the Towne Rate.

The same day Samuel Hicks was sent for by the Select men to render a reason, why, being ordered by them by the 18 either to depart the Towne, or speedily to giue them security for sauing the Towne harmless during his abode here, which he promised to doe by the 17 of this Instant.

The day following being the 9th of the (11th mo:) 1665 Samuel Hicks according to the order of the Selectmen brought his brother Zachariah Hicks for his security vnto William Pole Recorder of the Towne vnto whom, the sayd Zachariah Hicks became bound in a Bond of twenty pounds for the Towns security on the behalf of his brother the sayd Samuel Hicks.
As followeth.

Wheras Samuel Hicks hath motioned his desire vnto the Select men of Dorchester, to be receiued for an Inhabitant into the Towne, They in the name, and behalf of the Towne, haue so far forth granted his request, as that he giue sufficient Security, whereby the Towne, may be freed and secured from all such costs and charges, as may thereby come vpon it.
Therefore.

I, Zacchary Hicks of Cambridge, his brother, on the behalf of the aboue sayd Samuel Hicks, as his security, by these presents doe binde myself in a Bond of twenty pounds vnto Mr William Pole Recorder of the Towne, in the name, and on behalf of the Select men, to secure the Towne, of what soeuer charges or damages may ensue or folow therevpon, during his abode in the Towne of Dorchester. And herevnto I haue set my hand, this ninth day of January 1665. And deliuered it as my act and deed.
Witnesses   ZACHARIAH HICKS
JOHN ALDIS
JONATHAN HOWARD.

[**169.**] At a Meeting of the Select men on the 12 of the (12 Mo:) 1665:

This day there was presented vnto the Selectmen of Dorchester a note from the Select men of Boston. containing a Request from them, that the Widow Collins might be permitted by us to passe the winter here in our Towne and thereby engaging themselues, that her reception should not disoblige them from the duty they owe her, as one of thier Inhabitants. A Copy whereof is here inserted.

To the Select men of Dorchester.

These are to advise, that if the Widow Collins be permitted by you to pass the Winter in your Towne, that your reception of her, shall not be to disoblige us from the duty which we owe vnto her as one of our Inhabitants.

Boston this 25. (10) 1665.   HEZEKIAH VSHER
              in the name of the
              Select men.

The Selectmen of Dorchester doe accept of the Request of the Selectmen of Boston on the behalfe of the widow Collins, and doe grant her liberty to remaine, and reside here amongst us, till the 1. day of May, 1666.

The same day the Constables had order to appoint a Towne meeting on the 5th of March next for the nomination of Magestrates and choise of Deputies Commissioners, &c.

The same day Samuel Rigby came to the Selectmen, to desire liberty to imploy John Harker at his calling for sometime: which was granted; provided that he engage to secure the Towne from damage by the sayd Harkers residence in the Towne of Dorchester.

The same day Samuel Rigby binds himself, heirs and Executors, in the summe of twenty pounds to the Select men of Dorchester, and thier Successours from time to time, to secure the Towne of Dorchester from all charges and damages, that may arise to the Towne, while the sayd John Harker shall continue or remaine Inhabitant in the Towne by the sayd Harker. To which the sayd Rigby sets his hand the day and yeere aboue sayd.

Witnesses   SAMUELL RIGBEE
WILLIAM POLE
JOHN CAPEN Senr

The same day, there was a warrant granted to the Constable Thomas Trot to levie vpon John Pope, and Thomas Wilkinson, for what they are behind to the Rate of the Ministery for seuerall yeers.

John Pope is behind for 3 years . . . .   1 – 18 – 11
Thomas Wilkison for 4 yeers . . . .   1 – 17 –

1665.

[170.] The same day vpon information, that severall men, that are not Inhabitants of this Towne doe carry away stones from Squantums Neck, without leaue of this Towne; It is therefore ordered by the Select men that Roger Billing, and Henry Leadbetter, shall, and hereby are impowred to forbid any that are not Inhabitants from carrying away any stones from thence vnless for such valuable consideration, as they shall agree with the sayd Billing or Leadbetter or either of them; and they are to demand of, and agree with any, that have already carried away any stones, for such summe or summes, as they shall iudge meet; and they to make Returne, of what they receiue, to the Selectmen from time to time; And they are allowed, the fourth part of what they doe receiue, for thier encouragement in this service, provided this Order shall not be in force to the damage of any proprietor that hath Land in Squantums Neck.

Town Meeting 5th (1. mo.) 1666.

At a generall Town Meeting 5th (1. mo:) 1666.   Officers chosen for this yeere.

Deputies { Lieftenant Foster, William Sumner }   Commissioners { Lieftenant Foster, William Sumner, Anthony Fisher }

Constables { Daniel Preston, Henery Gaunsey }

The same day Deacon Capen, William Sumner, and Samuel Clap were chosen for a Committee to ioyne with Rocksberry men about setting the line of the Bounds betwixt them and us.

The Persons aboue mentioned were sworne Constables for the Town of Dorchester this 8th of March 166⅔.

Before me

DANIEL GOOKIN.

1666.

[171.] At a Meeting of the Select men the 12th of the (1 mo:) 1666, Fence-viewers chosen For the great Lotts: from Captains Neck to Goodm: Tolemans. Richard Leeds Samuel Proctor

For the rest of the great Lotts from Goodm: Tolemans to Naponset Riuer William Robinson Timothy Foster

For the 20 Acre Lotts James Humphrey John Merrifield

For the field behind Tho: Birds. Thomas Andrews se. Obadiah Hawes.

for the feild behind Mr. Joans. Clement Maxfild Isack Joans

For the field before Enoch Wizwall Tho: Modsley Joseph Weeks.

For the field behind Mr Stoughtons Richard Withington Ammiel Weeks

For the field behind Mr Mathers George Dyar William Pond.

For the neck of Land Nicholas Clap.   Joseph Holmes.

Nicholas George is allowed by the Select men of Dorchester to keep Ordinary for the yeare ensuing, if the Court please to accept of the same.

Robert Wills is appointed by the Selectmen to driue the Great Lotts the 2^d Monday of the (2^d mo:) 1666.

The Order.

Wheras there hath been, and still is great complaints of Cattle doing damage in common fields in the Towne, both in corne and meadows, after the time that Cattle ought to be removed out of such fields by Towne Order.

It is therefore Ordered by the Select men of this Towne, that if any Cattle, horses or swine be taken in any common Cornfield or meadow, except the sayd cattle be within some p'ticular Inclosure, or vnder the present care of a sufficient keeper, and that within the bounds the ground of the owner of the sayd Cattle. vpon penalty of paying 4^d p' head for euery head so taken, as before exprest; beside poundage, and what other damage may arise by the sayd Cattle horses or swine; and for what sheepe shall be found in any such common fields, they shall pay one penny p' head. And for poundage we allow for horses, cattle or swine 2^d p' head; for sheep one half penny p' head: And John Smith, on the rocky hill is appointed, to keep the pound for this yeare, and to receiue the ffees abouesayd.

And we appoint John Homes to see this Order duely executed from time to time in the Neck of Land, till the 10. of October next.

And Robert Wills the like for the great Lotts.

1666.

[**172.**] At a Meeting of the Select men the 14. of the (3 Mo:) 1666.

The Cuntry Rate committed to Steven Minott Cunstable for the yeare 1665 was . . . . 80 – 00 – 00

Payd to the Country Treasurer . . . . 64 – 00 – 3
Payd to the County Treasurer . . . . 13 – 06 – 8
Payd to Lieftenant Foster by }
 Order of the Selectmen } . . . . 01 – 00 – 6
Payd to Goodman Swift by order }
 of the Select men . } . . 00 – 09 – 6
by 3^s 1^d lost . . . . 00 – 03 – 1
Payd to Nicholas George for this }
 present yeare 1666 } . . . 04 – 00 – 0

80

Receiued the 17th of April. 1666. of Mr Steven Minot, Constable of Dorchester in full of thier Rate due to the Cuntry for the yeare past the Summe of sixty foure pounds, three pence. I say Receiued as aboue.

According to my Warrant.

                  p' me RICHARD RUSSELL, Treasurer.

Receiued the (9th of May, 1666) of Mr Steven Minott, in full of a County Rate, due from the Towne of Dorchester, the Summe of thirteene pounds six shillings, eight pence. I say Receiued

                  p' me EDWARD TYNG,
        Treasurer for the County of Suffolk.

The day aboue sayd, this Order was made by the Select men, as followeth.

Whereas vpon view, we finde a little piece of Land, partly inclosed vpon the hill aboue Goodman Georges, contrary to order, or leaue from the Towne; We the Select men of Dorchester doe Order that Robert Sanders doe forthwith take downe the sayd Fence, and carry the same away for his owne vse, vpon such penalty, as the Select men shall iudge meet.

Dated the 14. (3. Mo:) 1666.

1666.

[**173.**] At a Meeting of the Select the 11th of the (4 mo:) 1666.

At this meeting the Constable Henery Garnsey brought in to the Select men an Account of six shillings expended vpon the Watch· vpon the Election day.

The same day, John Plumme made a request vnto Select men that they would be pleased to grant him leaue and liberty for cutting of one hundred and twenty Railes and thirty posts, the which vpon due consideration, was granted him.

The same day vpon vew of the Creeke and landing place neere the house of John Wales, and finding both the way and Creeke much damefied by digging of Clay, which otherwise might for time to come be of great vse to the towne for the landing of hay corne and wood, and to serue other occasions of the towne. It is ordered that whosoeuer shall dig or cary away any earth or Clay from the said Creeke or any p^t therof below the dwelling hous of John wales Eastward (vnles for the repaire of the said Creeke or landing place) shall forfit for euery load, or p^t of a load drawne away by horse or other cattle the sume of fiue shillings, and for euery wheelbarow one shilling for the vse of the towne, To be leuyed by distress or otherwise and we appoint Enoch Wiswell Thomas Lake and John Wales to take notice off and accquaint the Select men for the time beeing of the names of those that shall at any time transgress this order, that soe they may be dealt with all according to there demerritt.

At a meeting of the Select men the 8th of the (8th Mo:) 1666.

Wheras there is granted 30 Acres of Land to John Plumb neere to Dedham Sawmills as in the Towne book appears vpon such conditions as the Select men shall think meet; we therfore, the Select men of Dorchester, doe iudge it meet, that John Plumb shall haue, and enioy the sayd land to his owne proper vse, during his residence in Dorchester; but doe not allow him to make sale of it to any, nor other wayes dispossess himself of it, till such time, as he shall haue remoued himself, and whole Famely one whole yeare out of the Towne of Dorchester; Then we doe allow him to sell it to any such; as the Select men, for the time being, shall iudge convenient; and we appoint Ensign Capen and Nicholas Clap to see the sayd 30 Acres of Land layd out. By Order of the Select men.

WILLIAM POLE.

This 11th of the (8) 1666.

I Robert Knight of Marble-head doe acknolige that I have Receaued Two great Gunns from the Select men of dorchester for the Contrys vse at Marble-head. witnes my hand.

ROBERT KNIGHT.

This is a true Coppi of the origenall which is on file entered and examined this 19th (10) 1666 by me JOHN CAPEN Recorder.

The 27 of the 8th M° 1666 Receaued 3 Demiculuerin shott on the Contrys account, and on the towne of Dorchesters account to

be paid for by the towne of Marblehead, one ladle, on[e] spunge, two formers the price thereof 7ˢ a witness my hand
ROBERT KNIGHT.

This is a true Coppi of the originall which is on file entered and examined this 5 (12.) 66 by me JOHN CAPEN Recorder.

1666.

[174.] At a Meeting of the Selectmen the 12. of the (9 Mo :) 1666.

This day Constable Trott appeared before the Select men to giue in his Account of the Towne Rate amounting to 57¹ – 5ˢ – 3ᵈ, which is as followeth.

Payd to Mʳ Pole for keeping schoole and recording	26 – 00 – 00
to Goodman Swift for select mens expenses in 1665	03 – 10 – 00
to Goodman George for Indians Dinner, and p'te of the p'sent year	01 – 11 – 00
to Gabriel Mead for Labour at the Meeting House	03 – 00 – 00
to Captaine Clap, as Deputy for the Towne	06 – 18 – 00
to Lieftenant Foster as Deputy for the towne	06 – 05 – 06
to William Sumner, for Killing a wolfe	00 – 10 – 00
to Anthony Fisher for printing Chatechisms	04 – 10 – 00
to Ezra Clap for killing a woolfe	00 – 05 – 00
to Nathan Bradley for killing a woolfe	00 – 05 – 00
to Deacon Capen for so much pᵈ Leiut. Fisher	00 – 12 – 00
For glass for the Meeting house	03 – 02 – 00
for new hanging the Bell	00 – 02 – 00
Payd to William Trescott for running the Line	00 – 06 – 00
To Thomas Bird for nailes for the Buring place	00 – 01 – 06
	56 – 18 – 6
For som other charges and Losses in Gathering the Rate	00 – 6 – 9

and soe the Cunstable is discharged from the sume off 57 – 5 – 3

This Day Reconed with Nicolas George and the Towne is in Debt to him the Just summe of three pounds for expenses by select men Committee and Raters . . . . 03 – 00 – 00
pᵈ by Henery Garnesy as in p. 186.

At a meeting of the p'prietors the 14 (12) 65. It was voted and agreed vnto, that vpon the deuision of the land beyond the blew hils. If in case ther should be any charges fall on any pᵗ or the whole of that land ther to be deuided, that then all should beare a share by p'portion in that charge.

The same day it was voted and agreed vnto also that purgatory Swamp should be deuided to the anchent p'prietors according to the anchent deuedent

The same day it was granted to John Smith senʳ liberty to take 300 of railes out of the 500 acres.

Further it was voted and granted that the small p'cell of Meddow left Common vpon the last deuission of Meddow at the blew hils it shall be laid to the 200 acres that doe belong to the minestry of Dorchester.

Alsoe the same time the Commitee would p'pose vnto the p'prieters (that in answer vnto Liftenant Foster his petition for a farme) they would grant vnto him that his deuission may ly some where on this sid punkapage and beyond the blew hils, and that his deuission may be augmented vnto twenty acres in a single deuission and one hundred acres to be added vnto it.

This p'posall was voted in the Affermatiue.

[175.] At a ginerall Towne meeting the 5 (10) 1666.

After the directory was read and an account giuen of the Contry and County and towne rates.

It was voted what the Towne would giue to the maintenance of the ministry and the vote was that the towne would giue to the maintenance of the minestry for the yeere now almost past the sume of 130^{li} to M^r. mather 80^{li} to M^r. Stoughton 50^{li}

The Select men chosen the day abouesaid weer as followeth viz. Captaine Foster, William Sumner, John Minot, Anthony Fisher, Deacon Capen.

for Raters Srg^{nt} Hale, Srg^{nt} Clap, Srg^{nt} James Blake.

The same day it was voted that ther should be a yeerly Choice of a Recorder to keepe the towne books and record for the towns vse the same day the Select men are chosen.

This was voted in the affermatiu.

The same time Deacon John Capen was Chosen Recorder for the yeere ensueing.

Superuisors { Enock Wiswall.
{ Samuell Robinson.

for the way to
the neck of Land. } Isack Joanes.

The same day it was motioned by Thomas Dauenport Senr whether he might haue liberty to receaue (as Tenant into his house in Dorchester) Daniell Holbrooke Who lately came from Melton. It was voted in the Negatiue.

The same day it was voted and granted that Srg^{nt} Samuell Clap should haue libertie to set his barne fiue foote out on the high way, from the place where now it stands, and soe to run Narower at both ends till it meete with the fence and to be laid out to him by Liftenant Hopestill Foster, James Blake and Thomas Bird Senr.

The 4th of the (10th) 66. At a towne meeting after some agetations about a Schoolmaster It was put to the Vote whether ther should be a Schole Master enquiered after, and p'curered for to teach Schole in this towne, It was voted in the Afermatiue, and by a Second vote it was agreed vnto that Master Mather and Lift^{nt} Hopestill Foster and John Minot should be desier and empowered to endeauor to p'cuer a Schol-Master.

The same day it was voted and granted that M^r. pole should be spoken vnto to goe on in keepeing Schole vntill another Master be p'cuered, at the same rate as formerly, p'portionablely according to the time he shall soe doe, and William Sumner is appointed to speake to M^r pole about it if he will accept of it soe to doe.

At the same time a vote was whether the teaching and rulling Elders should haue power to seate people in the meeting house, the vote was in the afermatiue.

[**176.**] To the Constables of Dorchester.

You are heerby requiered to giue warning to William Chaplen and Arthur Cartwrigat that they and either of them doe vpon the next Second day Repare vnto the Select men to giue an account of the Strangers or Inmits now entertained by them that they doe not by ther neglect bring themselues vnder the penalty of the towne order in that case p'uided heerof you are not to faile. Dorchester this 6 of Desember 1666.

By order of the Select men.

JOHN CAPEN Recorder.

At a meting of the select men the 10th of the (10) 1666 Arthur Cartwright appeared before the Select men for entertaining an Inmate (who is a Cooper) into his house without ap'bation first obtained who haueing not receaued any certiffecate from the Majestrate for his reception into this Jurisdiction, was not admitted to receaue any Inmate, and therfore noe more was done at that time.

The same day ther was a warrant deliuered for the Raters to make a Rate for the minestry of 130ᴸᴵ – 0 – 0 and a Towne Rate of 45 – 0 – 0

The same day William Chaplin appeared before the Select men for Entertaining Peter Chaplin his brother as an Inmate into his house without the ap'bation of the Select men first had and obtained. The Select men taking it into Consideration doe order that the said William Chaplin doe giue in bond of twenty pounds to secuer the towne from damage soe long as the said peter shall remaine an Inhabetant in Dorchester.

The same day warrant was granted to the Constable to leuy vpon the estate of Thomas Dauenport ten shillings by distress or otherwise, for Entertaining Daniell Holbrooke as an Inmate into his house without order: Also to leuy vpon the Estate of William Chaplin 5ˢ for the like breach of order.

	li.	s.	d.
The Contry Rate for this yeere was	91	– 05	– 11
of which the Treasurer is to haue or his order	85	– 10	– 0
The Deputys both of them	05	– 10	– 0

Wee that are now Constables of Dorchester Daniell Preston and Henery Garnesy being informed by our Selectmen that an Indian being dead of the Smale [pox] in the land of James Minot, we did by thier order goe and see and found it soe, he was dead in an Indian Wigwom in James Minots land a litle a this sid Naponset mill the Indians haueing run away, and left him dead and takeing noe Cource for his buriall (and we weer informed he was a warwick Indian) and we Constables did git an English man John Smith of Dorchester to digg his graue in the wigwam, and we did git an Indian whose name is Joseph. a Mashapag Endian, and William Robinson and John Smith for to put him in his graue, and John Smith did couer him with the earth and this was done vpon the 10 day of Decem 1666.

wittnes our hands.

DANIELL PRESTON.
HENERY GARNESY.

This is a true coppie of the originall which is vpon fill entered and examined this 5 (12) 66.

by me
JOHN CAPEN Recorder.

[**177.**] These p'sens Wittnesseth that we Daniell Preston and John Holbrooke, of Dorchester doe bind o'selues and either of vs our heiers executors and adminestrators vnto the Select men of Dorchester, and thier Successours from time to time in the sume of theirty pound, that wee and either of vs will saue harmless and defend the Towne of Dorchester from all Damages and Charges that may arise by meanes of Daniell Holbrookes Inhabiting in Dorchester or any of his while he or they remaine Inhabetants in Dorchester as witness our hands this Sixt of the tenth Month on thouand Six hundered Sixty and Six.

DANIELL PRESTON.
JOHN HOLBRUK.

In p'sence of vs Viz.
SAUMELL RIGBEE
JOHN DAUENPORTT.

Thes p'sents witnesseth that I William Chaplin of Dorchester doe bind my selfe heiers and executors and administrators vnto the Select men of Dorchester and there Successours from time to time in the Sume of twenty pounds to Secuer and saue harmeless the Towne of Dorchester from all damage and Charges that may arise by meanes of peter Chaplin my Brother his Inhabiting in Dorchester or any of his whille he or they remaine Inhabetants in Dorchester as witnes my hand this tenth day of Desember one thousand Six hundered Sixty and Six.

WILLIAM CHAPLEN

In the p'sence of vs viz.
SAMUELL CAPEN
BARNERD CAPEN

The 14th of the. (11) 66

At a meeting of the Selectmen the Raters p'sented the Rates which they weer appointed to make Viz: the minesters Rate of 130^{li} – 0 – 1 and the towne Rate of 45 – 0 – 4 the which Rates the former was commited into the hands of the deacons the other into the hands of the Constables with a warrant to gather it by distress or otherwis and to make disburstments according to instructions therin giuen them.

The same day William Sumner and Ensigne John Capen was desired and empowered to speake with Liftenant Fisher in reference vnto the plotting and lotting of the land beyond the blew hils and to aduise with him about the manner of laying it out.

[178.] At a meeting of the Select men the 11 of the (12) 1666 Nicholas Bolton came before them and made request for to haue 6 load of fierwood and 60 railes to be granted him out of the 500 acres and it was granted him.

The sam day it was agreed that the Constable should giue notice to the freemen to meet vpon the 4th of the next Month to giue in ther votes for Nomination of Majestrates and Choice of Deputies and Commisioners for the town and Constables and County Treasuerer.

The same day it was agreed That wheras by experience in the yeer 1666 it doth appeare that the Cattell that vssualy goe in the pastuers that are within the Corne feilds in this Towne, doe greate damage in the said feilds either in regard of the insufficiency of the pastuer fences or the vnrulines of the Cattle that are therin. It is therfore ordered, that when Cattell or horses doe vsually goe in any pastuers within any Common feilds in dorchester and shall at any time after the time that Cattell ought to be taken off from Corne feilds (as by a former order may be seene) vntill the feilds be cleered of Corne or hay (or should be by Towne order) be found either in Corne or meddow within any feild, it shall be lawfull for any inhabetant to impound them and to demand eighteene pence p' head for euery beast soe taken, besid poundig, and if any Refuse to pay as abouesaid, the p'ty so takeing the Cattle shall haue warrant from the Select men to the Constable, to leuy the same by distress.

The 4th of the (1) 6$\frac{6}{7}$ at a Towne meeting for the nomination of Majestrate ther was Chosen by the freemen.

Deputys for the whole yeere { Captine Foster
William Sumner

Commissioners to end smal Causes Captaine Foster William Sumner John Minot.

for Constables Joseph Homes and Samuell Robinson.

Joseph Holmes and Samuell Robinson sworne Constable the 7 (1) 6$\frac{6}{7}$ before m^r Thomas Danforth Assistant.

[179.] The 11th of the (1) 166$\frac{6}{7}$.

At a meeting of the Select men John Smith Junr desiered liberty to take timber off from the 500 acres for to build him an house and it was granted him.

The same day it was ordered that the Constable should pay vnto Tho: Swift Senr 7^s out of the towne Rate for a dept due to him from the towne not known till now.

The same pay ther was appointed for fence vewers as followeth:

for the great lots from Captins neck to Goo: Tolmans } Enoch Wiswell and John Smith sen^r and

And for the rest of the great lots from Goo: Tolmans to Naponset } Thomas Trot and Thomas Pearce

for the twenty acre lots } Thomas Dauenport and Thomas Grant

for the feild behind Tho. Birds : } Thomas Bird Senr and James Whit

for the feild behind Mr Joanes Thomas Lake and William Weeks.

for the feild behind Mr Stoughton Richard Leeds and Samuell Palle.

for the feild before Enoch Wiswals Nathaniel Homes and Israell Meade.

for the feild behind Mr Mather Timothy Mather and Daniell Elder.

for the neck of land James Blake and Nathaniell Clap.

for the Clearing the greate lots of Catle John Smith Junr and Robt Wils.

for the Clearing the Neck of land John Homes.

The same day order was giuen to William Robinson and Enoch Wiswall and John Smith Senr to Colect a penny p' acre of all the p'prieters of the great lots and Captains neck both Vpland Meddow and pastuer and ther with to make two gates the one neere Richard Hals house and the other neere William Robinsons house and the ouer plus to make returne to the Select men.

Alsoe James Blake and Nathaniell Clap are appointed to Colect in like maner a half penny p' acre of the p'prieters of the Neck of land and to make a new gate and the ouer plus to returne to the Select men.

[180.] The same day William Sumner John Capen Senr James Blake and Samuell Clap are Chosen to Run the line between Dorchester and Rocksbery and also between Dorchester and Deadham to plimouth line.

And for the lines between Melton and Dorchester punkepage and Dorchester Captaine Foster John Minot and Thomas Tolman Senr for Melton and Joseph Homes to Joyne with them for punkepag.

And for the line between Dorchester and Brantry from the top of the blew Hill to plimoth line was Chosen Daniell preston Steuen Hoppin Samuell Rigby: Ensigne Hall and Richard Withington also added.

The same day Thomas Dauenports fine of ten shillings for Entertaining of Daniell Holbrooke was remitted on condition that he Cleere the water-Cours Cros the way before one Come to the house he bought of William Blake and this to be done by the 10th of Aprill next.

The same day John Minot was desired and empowered for to git the Scholhous repaiered.

The same day a note was deliuered to Nicholas George as followeth.

To the Howrd County Court of Suffolk Whearas Nicholas George of Dorchester hath for diuers yeers kept a house of Com̃on Entertainment, and ther being within the said time, many Clamorous Reports of miscaredges in the same house, which is uery sad (if true) and not to be by any Countenanced and tollerated, yet notwithstanding the Select men haue Indeauored by their best wisdome to find out the truth of such reports, but for ought that we can find they are groundles, and therfore we doe consent that the said Nicholas George may be continued in the same Employment vnless

the honored Court know more against it then we doe : all this with Submition to the Court heerin.
11 (1) 166$\frac{6}{7}$ —

By order of the Select men
JOHN CAPEN Record^r

[181.] At a meeting of the Select men the 13th (3) 67.
Peter Lion requested for liberty to haue some timber for to build him an house out of the 500 acre the which was granted.

The same day in answer to a letter sent by Roger Bellenge and Henery Leadbetter to the Select men, the Sume of it being a query whether that place at Squantoms neck which they call wheelbarrow Iland did belonge to the towne, or to any p'ticular man, in answer heerunto it is resolued that it belongs to the Towne

The same day Timothy Tilston made request to haue liberty to haue soe much timber out of the 500 acrs as will build a house of about 18 or 20 foote square and 9 foote stud the which was granted him.

The same day ther was Isued out a warrant to Joseph Homes Constable in his majestis name to take by distress or otherwise of such p'sons as are heerafter exprest Such Sume or Sumes as are by Towne order due for them to pay, for ther Catle being taken in the great lots, being ther contrary to order, Viz Quarter Master John Smith 6^s Mr Collicot 6^s 8^d Daued Joanes 3^s 4^d Samuell Rigby 12^s – 3^d and to deliuer the aboue said Sumes vnto John Smith Junr or to Ro^{bt} Wils, and if the aboue said John Smith and Ro^{bt} Wils will a bate any of the aboue said Sums it is in their liberty.

The same day it is ordered that (wheras John Smith Junr and Ro^{bt} Wils are for this yeer to Cleere the great lots of Catle as by the order will appeare) If they neglect ther duty heerin, they are to pay each of them 2^s 6^d for euery neglect.

The same day the Constable Daniell Preston gaue vp his account of the Contry Rate for 66 which he gathered.

The Rate being 91^{li}-5^s-11^d out of which he paid the Treasuerer 85^{li}-9^s-11^d– as by the Treasuerers Recept it did appeare Alsoe to Captaine Foster 2^{li}-15^s-0, and William Sumner 2-15^s-0 both of them Deputis soe ther remains due to the Towne 6^s which is alowed the Constable for losses and he is discharged.

Wheras ther was Some time since a Contribution by the church and Towne for the releife of the Reuerend Mr Tomson of Brantry in the time of his weaknes, and the same Committed to the hands of Deacon Jno Capen of Dorchester, to be improued by him for the said Mr Tomsons supply as he had need, and the said Mr Tomson dying before the said Contribution was al disposed off, the Select men of Dorchester (conceauinge it was a free gift for Mr Tomson and therefore to shew o^r further [182.] respect to Mr Tomsons Relations) doe order that the said Deacon John Capen doe dispose of the remainder of the Contrebution as Followeth Viz one theird p^t to the widdow of Mr Tomson and the other two-third p^{ts} to the Children of Mr Tomson.

The same day it was ordered by the Select men that Liftenant John Capen should with what Conuenient speede he can, draw both the towne books into an Alphabittacall order for the more speedy finding of the Towne orders or grants.

The same day Clement Maxfeild requested for liberty to haue some timber out of the 500 acrs soe much as to build a shop for his Sonne and some wood that is ready fallen and timber for 100 of railes.

The same day a warrant was Isued out to Joseph Homes Constable to gather Seuerall fines for defect of some of the p'sons heer named Viz. for the necke of land

Richard Baker 2 rod widdow Smith $\frac{1}{2}$ a rod Obediah Swift 12 foot James Bate 10 foot Nathaniell Homes one rod and $\frac{1}{2}$ for the feild behind Mr Stoughton Richard Baker one rod one foote and halfe

At a meeting of the Select men the 10th (4) 1667.

Wheeras it is found by experience that great hurt and damadg is done in Corne feilds and pastuers by many horses and mares and Colts lying about the Towne, and more is likely to be done when Corne comes to maturety it is therfore ordered by the Select men, that ther shal be noe horses mares or Colts suffered to be a bout the Towne on the Commons or out of enclosuers within the Compas of the west end of the 20 acre lots, except such beasts as are sufficiently fettered according as the law p'uids upon penalty of 1^s a peice besids damages for the first offence, and two shillings a peice for the second ofence besids damages, and 2^s 6^d for the third offence besids damages and soe from to time as often as they shall be found contrary to this order. And in case that any beast be taken vp and noe owner be found then to be p'ceeded with as the law p'uids about strays, and Clement Maxfeild and John Wales are appointed to see to the execution of this order or any other p'ticuler p'son and for ther recompence they shall haue the one halfe of the pay for their paines.

the 13 (1) 70 or 71 it was concluded that this order shall stand in force vntill the Select men see Caus to alter it: p'uided and it is to be vnderstood that this order from yeer to yeer is in full force from the time that Corne feilds should be cleered vntill Corne feilds are cleered of Corne.

[183.] This Indenture made the 8th of October in the yeare 1636 betwixt Richard Collecott and Kitchamakin sachim of Mattathewthes witnesseth theise p'sents that I Kitchamakin do covenant grant and sell vnto Richard Collicott of Dorchester all that p'cell of Land beyound the Mill within the bounds of Dorchester to the vtmost extent ffor the vse of the plantation of Dorchester ffor they and their heires ffor euer only Reservinge ffor my owne vse and my men fforty acres where I Like best and in case I and they Leaue it the same also to belonge vnto Dorchester giueinge some Consideratiō ffor the Paines bestowed about it: moreover Forty acres I haue giuen vnto Richard Callicott Lyeinge next to his Lott by the South side and I the said Kitchamakin do acknowledge to haue Receaued the value of 411 Twenty eight Fathoms of wampam beinge the Full Payement of the Fyne and I the said Kitchamakin do acknowledge myselfe satisfied as witnes whereof to this p^rsent Indenture I haue sett my hand the Daye and yeare aboue written.

Signed in the ⎫
p^rsence of me ⎬ the mke of [symbol] Kitchamakin
Stephen Hopinge ⎭
the mke of S̲h̲

13th (4) 1649

Theise are to Certifie whom it maie Concerne that we whose names are herevnto subscribed were p^rsent when Kitchamakin aboue named did voluntarily signe the Indenture aboue as his owne act and deed at the Request of the select men of dorchester because the old deed was somethinge decayed with ill keepeinge the daye and yeare aboue written.

[Page 184 blank.]

HUMPRAY ATHARTON
JOHN WISWALL

[185.] The 5 of the (5) 1667.

At a meeting of the Select men the day aboue said William Sumner and John Capen sen^r are desiered and empowered to attend the Court in the Towns behalf in that Case respecting James Minot or the Child which is laid to his Charge to see that the Towne be not Charged with any thing as respecting that Case, and they the said William Sumner and John Capen to take any help to asist them therin as they shall Judge meet for attornys or otherwise.

The Same day it was agreed vnto that (whereas the way ouer Naponsit leading to Sea-cunk is remoued from the place that it did formerly ly, by the Tennants of the Schole land, and that this new way doe need some mending) therfore If John Farrington shall mend or Cause to be mended what is needfull in that regard, that hee shall be alowed for it in his Rates that he is to pay till he be satisfied p'uided that the Charges be Considered by vewing it by the feffees of the Schol land or their Compounding afore the work be done or to their Satisfaction.

The Same day it was ordered that James Minot be sent vnto yet once more to demand the pay the Court ordered him to pay towards the Maintenance of the Child of Francis Tree, and that he make a speedy returne for the p^ruention of further trouble ther a bout.

The 9th (7) 1667

At a meeting of the Select men Wheares Nicholas Lawrance brought to vs the Select men of Dorchester a Warrant from the Hon^rd Court bearing date the 19 Feb. 66 requiering vs to order the payment of three pound fower shillings to the foresaid Lawrance for expences laid out one Frances Tree in the time of her Ilnes. Thes are to certefie to the Hon^rd Court or to whom it may Concerne that we haue done nothing in that respect, neither doe we see reason for vs soe to doe, but with Submition to the Hon^rd Court we conseaue that the reputed father of the Child should discharge it.

Dated the 9th (7) 66 by the Select men

JOHN CAPEN, Recorder.

The same day Richard Curtice Came to the Select men, and desiered ther app'bation to Come into the Towne to liue, which was granted on Condition that he doe make ouer his house and land at Melton for the Towns Security that he be not Chargable to the towne.

[186.] The same day William Sumner was desiered to speak with the Widdow Hims (who is lately come into this towne) to informe her that she must returne to the Place from whence she Came.

The same day Anthony Fisher sen' was desiered to speake with Frances Oliuer and to informe him that he is to returne to the place from whence he Came.

The same day it was Concluded that (for the Contribution for the Fleet) M'r Mather should be desired to accquaint the Congregation ther with the next lords day, that they may be in a readyness to bring in ther uotes the Saboth day after.

The same day at the Request of William Trescot, William Sumner and John Capen Sen'r and Amiell Weeks are appointed and empowered to set out the bonds betweene the vpland and Swamp, of that Swamp in Melton giuen to the vse of the minestry.

At a Meeting of the Selectmen the 24 (7) 1667.

Anthony Fisher Sen'r was desiered and appointed to take a Constable with him and to goe to James Minot and demand the remainder of the pay due (by the Court order) towards the maintenance of the Child, which is till the last County Court.

At a meeting of the Select men the 11th of the (9) 67 It was ordered that a warrant should be Isued out to the Constable for to demand and receaue by distress or otherwise ten shillings of Abraham How for entertaining of John Parmiter as an Inmate into his house or habetation without liberty obtained from the Select men which is Contrary to a towne order respecting Strangers or inmates.

The same day Henery Garnesy Constable for the yeere 66 brought in his account of the Towne Rate which he gathered that yeere, the rate being 45ˡⁱ 0ˢ 04ᵈ.

Imp. to M'r Poole	24 – 15 – 00
To Nicholas George for the yeere 66 . . .	03 – 00 – 00
To Captine Foster as deputy for 66 . . .	03 – 05 – 00
To William Sumner as deputy for 66 . . .	02 – 19 – 00
To the Widdow Meade for Ringing the bell .	03 – 00 – 00
To Nicholas George for expenses on the Warders Election day for 66	00 – 04 – 00
To William Sumner toward painters Stockings	00 – 01 – 00
[187.] To John Homes for warning a towne meeting	00 – 03 – 00
To Thomas Swift for losses vpon peass formerly	00 – 07 – 00
Deliuered in at the house of John Capen Sen'r by Seuerall p'sons	05 – 16 – 02
	43 – 10 – 02
Remains due from Henery Garnesy . . .	01 – 10 – 02

the 9th (1) 6¾ Henery Garnesy came and made it appeare that Mr Poole should haue had of Rog Belleng 17ˢ of Jnº Minot 7ˢ and Timothy Tilston 8ˢ 8ᵈ all which was deducted out of thes mens rats for painter which the Select men are to pay Mr Poolle and the said garnesey discharged.

The same day it was Concluded that at the next meeting of the Select men Goodman Leeds should be spoken with about his takeing in apeice of Meddow downe by the Creeke.

The same day Frances Oliuer Came to the Select men and desiered liberty to be an inhabetaut in this towne but he refusing to secuer the towne from damedge was not admitted.

At a generall Towne meeting the 2 10th 1667 after the Directory was read and an account giuen of the disburstments of the Contry and towne Rates, It was p'posed to the towne what they would alow to the maintenance of the minestry. The vote was that they should haue 130ˡⁱ, Viz. 80ˡⁱ for Mr Mather and fifty pound for Mr Stoughton and to be Rate-free to those Rates.

The same day It was put to the Vote as followeth Viz : wheras the last yeere the towne did make Choice of Mr Richard Mather, Captin Foster and John Minot for to looke out for a Schole Master to teach Schole in this towne, and that being not yet attained (although it haue been endeauored after) the towne doe againe renew ther request to those men fore mentioned, to looke out after another Master ; and further they doe giue them full power to agree with such a man as they shall Judge meete not exceeding forty pound a yeere.

The Vote was in the Afermatiue.

The same day it was agreed vnto and Voted that Mr Pole should be spoken vnto (by William Sumner) and desiered that he would continue teaching of Schole as formerly for the yeer ensueing or vntill another be obtained.

The same day Robt. Searle made request to the towne for some Conuenient place to build a house on, some where vpon the Comons. The towne appointed Deacon Humphry Ensigne Hall and John Gornell to looke out a place and make ther returne to the Select men, which if they agree therunto together with the men appointed then hee the said Robt. Searle may Enjoy it vpon such termes as the Select men shall agree.

Voted in the Affermatiue.

[188.] The same day ther was Chosen

John Minot
William Sumner
Samuell Clap } Selectmen
John Capen Senr
Ensigne Hall

John Capen Senr for Recorder

James Blake
William Pond } Raters
Timothy Mather

Sup'uisors of highways } John Blackman
Thomas Peirce

for the way to the neck of land Isack Joanes

At a meeting of the Select men the 9th of the 10th m° 1667.

Wheras ther was lately a Contribution of the Church and towne for John Merrifeild. The Select men doe order that it shall be improued by Deacon Humphry and John Minot, as they shall Judge meete for the accomadation of his necessety or any in his famely, and that the pay shall be brought in vnto the house of Ensigne Hall for the end a foresaid.

At the same time it was agreed that at the next towne meeting it should be p'posed to the p'prietors whether they would exchange the 30 acrs of land giuen to John Plum by the Saw-mils for some land in the 500 acrs neere Robt. Stantons.

The same day it was agreed vnto, that wheras at the last towne meeting bearing date the Second of this Instant, they did at the request of Robt. Searle Nominate and appoint Deacon Humphry Ensigne Hall and John Gornill to looke out a peice of ground for him the said Robt. Searle to build on as by the order may appeare, now those men haueing vewed a place ouer against the house wheer James Robinson doe now liue on the other sid of the pond, and the Select men, together with those fore mentioned doe consent that he shall haue twenty rods of ground, p'uided that he shall not sell it to any vntill he haue emproued it (viz. by building on it and fenceing it) for the space of Seauen yeers, nor after that time shall hee sell to it to any but such as the towne shall approue off. And they doe appoint William Sumner Deacon Humphry Ensigne Hall and John Gornell to lay it out and make their returne to the Select men.

M$\bar{\text{d}}$ this was not accepted by Robt. Searle but returned to the Towne agane.

The same day it was ordered that a warrant should be Isued out to the Raters to make a rate for the minestry of 130^{li} and a Schole and Towne Rate of 45^{li} and returne it to the Select men at ther next meeting being the Second day in January.

[189.] At a generall Towne meting the 1 (11) 67 It was voted and agreed vnto by the Towne that the west gallery in the meting hous should be brought into such a forme as that all the boys may be ther seated and soe ordered that they may be p'uented from p'phaning the lords day.

The same day Ensigne Hale John Gornell and William Pond weer Nominated and Voted for to take Care about ordering the worke about the gallery and likwise a Table before the Deacons seate, and flowering the meeting house where it is needfull and to mend the doars or other worke that is needfull.

The same day ther was granted to John Plum the remainder of the land left out of the late deuission on the North sid of Naponset towards deadham Mill vpon such termes as the Select men and he shall agree vnto leauing the 30 acrs formerly granted him.

The same day it was put to the Vote that the thousand acrs formerly giuen to the vse of the Schole it should neuer be alienated or sold to any other vse or any p^t of it but to be reserued for the maintenance of a free Schole in Dorchester for euer.

The same day it was Voted that ther should be twelue deuissions laid altogether in the good land beyond the blew hils, the first lot to be neerest the towne, and soe each man to haue his lot Successiuely in the good land, the lots lying as neer as may not aboue eight scoare or 200 rods long and if it soe fall out that a smale p'cell of bad land fals in a lot ther shall be an alowance giuen by the Suruayer and those men that the towne shall appoint to goe with him.

The same day ther was granted to Anthony Newton to haue 20 acrs of land taken vp by lot in this deuission.

The same day it was agreed vnto that the next lectuer day after lectuer the Towne should Com togethe to draw lots for the 12 deuissions.

The same day it was agreed vnto that it is left vnto the Selectmen and Comitte to add to the p'sons that are altered since the last meeting of the Comittee in 66.

The same day Richard withington gave vnto Robert Searell a small pece of land Lyen one the norwest corner of said withingtons land and the said robert Searell was to haue it for him and his hears foreuer.

memorancon it was payd for over and above.

[190.] At a meeting of the Selectmen the 13th. (11) 1667.

Whereas ther was latly a Contribution for the Fleete at the kereby [Carribee?] Ilands the Select men doe order that it shall be brought in to the houses of the two deacons by the fowerth day come three weeks which will be the 5 day of February next and the deacons to take Care for the Conuaying it to Boston and to be alowed out of the same.

The same day it was ordered that wheras John Capen Senr is like to haue a sut at Court wherin he desiers to haue Coppies out of the Towne Records, the Select men doe order and appoint Jn° Minot for to take Coppies out which he desier and to Compare them with the originall and to attest to the truth of the Coppies.

The same day Richard Leeds appeared before the Select men to giue a reason of his takeing in a peice of Marsh which was laid out for the landing of hay or Corne or other goods neere the Creike below Jn° Wales, the Conclusion was that Richard Leeds yelds for himselfe and his Successors to pay twelue pence p' yeere to the Towne soe long as it is fenced in If it be demanded which Marsh the said Richard Leeds fenced in supposing it had ben his owne p'priety.

13 (11) 1667. A list of the acrs of land in the feild Commonly Caled the great lots, which is to pay one peny p' acre for the payment Maintenance of gates this yeer 1667 and what remaines to be put in to Some safe to keepe for the vse aforsaid.

	acrs		acrs
Abraham How	51	James Minot.	12
William Robinson.	19	Robt Badcock	05
Samuell Robinson.	07	Jn° Fennow.	03
Richard Leeds	16	Widdow Hill.	18
Thomas Peirce	21	Augustin Clement.	06
Thomas Trott	50	Tho: Tolman Senr & }	44
Thomas Tilston	24	John Tolman }	

	acrs		acrs
Tho: Tolman Junr	10	Enock Wiswall	11
Mr. Patten	04	Jno Wiswall	05
Jno Minot	106	Joseph Long	10
Nicholas Ellen	02	Samuell Rigbe	52
Johnathan Birch	06	[191.] Isacke Joanes	03
Timothy Mather	12	Joseph Weiks	03
Robt Searle	12	John Smith	50
Samuell Paule	12	Anthony Fisher	24
Richard Leeds	16	Daued Joanes	48
Timothy Mather	16	Richard Hale	02
Mr Minot	14	Nathan Bradly	02
Jno Blake	06	Anthony Fisher	12
Willm Clarke	06	Isack Joanes	02
Timothy Tilstone	12	Richard Hale	04
Willm Pond	04	Jno Pelton	04
William Trescot	04	Rich. Leeds	02
		Tho. Lake	02

The whole at one penny p' acre is   03 – 02 – 10

of this was pd to Enock Wiswall for the gate It. by Ensigne Hale   . . . 00 – 17 – 00
It. to Jno Smith Senr for Carting . . . 00 – 02 – 06
It. to John Minot for an old Dept about gates . . . 00 – 07 – 06
It. to Wil{m} Robinson for the gate by his house the yrons 3{s} – 6d carting 1{s} – 6d . . 00 – 05 –
It. to Timothy Foster for the gate by his house . . . 00 – 15 – 00

                                              02 – 06 – 06

This was gathered by the Constable In the towne Rate being aded to each p'prietors Rate and ther remaines to be laid vp. . . . 00 – 16 – 04

this is for plow land pastuer and medow

A list of the acrs of land at the Neck being Rated at a half peny p' acre for the plow land only

	s. d.		s. d.
Captin Clap	0 – 7	Timothy Mather	1 – 2
Joseph Farnsworth	1 – 0	Capt. Foster	1 – 6
Amiell Weeks	0 – 2	Rich: Withington	1 – 1
Obediah Swift	0 – 2	William Clarke	0 – 6
Widdow Smith	0 – 3	Jno Blake	0 – 1
Mr Patten	0 – 2	Samuell Clap	0 – 4
Richard Baker	1 – 0	Widdow Baker	1 – 3
Willm Sumner	0 – 7	Obediah Haws	0 – 1
Jno Blakman	0 – 1	Widdow Munings	0 – 3
Nicholas Clap	0 – 11	Ezra Clap	0 – 6
Augustin Clement	0 – 4	Jno Capen Junr	0 – 2
Widdow Clap	0 – 9	Deacon Wiswall	0 – 8

George Dyer	. .	0 – 6	J mes White	. .	0 – 2
Deacon Capen	.	0 – 3	Mr Joanes	. .	0 – 10
Mr Howard	. .	0 – 7	Ebenezer Williams	.	0 – 3
Jno Moadesly	.	0 – 2	Enoch Wiswall	.	0 – 6
Mrs Stoughton	.	2 – 0	Thomas Lake	. .	0 – 1
Isack Joanes	. .	0 – 6			
Widow Batten	. .	0 – 4	Totall Sume		19^s – 9^d

James Blake   0 – 11^d
Nathanell Clap   0 – 6^d
[These last two names written in afterwards in different colored ink]
Charges laid out for the gate and hinges is 1^l – 2^s – 0^d

This was also gathered in and with the Towne Rate.

[192.] At a meeting of the Select men the 10 of the 12th Mo. 1667.

An order was directed to Samuell Robinson Constable to pay out of the Towne Rate the Sume of twenty shillings vnto Daniell Preston Samuell Dauenport and Thomas Birch for killing of two wolues in this Towne this yeere.

The same day it was ordered by the Select men that for the time to come whosoeuer haue liberty to haue timber for Railes or other vse out of the 500 acrs and shall fale trees and doe not cleane them vp or Square the timber in three months after they are falen, it shal be in the liberty of the Select men to grant other men to take such trees soe fallen to p^{r}uent the spoile of timber.

The same day Thomas Dauenport desiered liberty to haue 200 of Railes and one tree for posts out of the 500 acrs the which was granted him. p'uided that if ther be any trees fallen already a boue three months. he shall take such trees to p'uent Spoill of timber.

The same day was granted to Jno Pelton the like libertie for one hundered of Railes out of the 500 acres.

The same day it was ordered that the Constable should haue notice to worne the freemen to Come together the Second third day in March being our lectuer day after lectuer to giue in Votes for Nommination of Majestrates and Choice of County treasurer and Constables.

At a meeting of the Select men the 9th of the (1) 166$\frac{7}{8}$

It is ordered that all fences belonging to Corne feilds shalbe made vp by the 20th of this month according to the former order made for that end.

The same day Robt. Stanton had granted to him liberty for to haue ground sels, plates, and beams out of the 500 acrs.

The same day James Bird was appointed to haue 10^s for killing a wolfe to be paid by the Constable Samuell Robinson out of the Towne Rate.

The same day ther was appointed for fence Vewers as followeth for the great lots from captains neck to goodman Tolmans . . . . . } Samuell Pale, Thomas Lake
And for the rest of the great lots from Goodman Tolmans to Naponsett . . . } Timothy Foster, Samuell Robinson

[193.] for the 20 acre lots	Richard Withington / Henery Merifeild
for the feild behind Tho. Birds	Tho. Bird / Jn° Blackman
for the feild behind Mrs Joanes	Nathaniell Homes / James Robinson
for the feild behind Mr Stoughtons	Amiell Weiks / Jn° Baker
for the feild before Enock Wiswals	Joseph Long / Isock Joanes
for the feild behind Mr Mathers	William Pond / George Dyer
for the neck of land	Jn° Homes / Obediah Haws
for Cleering the great lots	John Smith / Robt Wils.
for the Cleering the neck of land	Israell Mead

The 10th of the (1) 6⅞ at a Towne meeting Timothy Mather and Jacob Hewens weer Chosen Constables for the yeer ensewing and till others are Chosen.

And for Comissioners to end smale Causes Captain Foster William Sumner and Jn° Minot.

And for Deputies Captaine Foster and William Sumner.

The 30th of the (1) 1668 on a training day the Select men ordered and published that wheras the time for the Cleering of all Corne feilds was appointed to be the 2^d Monday in Aprill; yet now the spring being soe forward this yeere they doe appoint the time to be the first Monday in Aprill for this yeere vnder the former penalty only the time to differ.

Alsoe it was agreed and published the same time that the former order for yokeing and Ringing of hogs and pigs should stand in force being not yet repealed.

At a meeting of the Select men the 11th (3) 1668.

The day aboue said the Select men did fully agree with Anthony Newton of Melton that he should haue the Child of Francis Tree to be his seruant vntill it should be **[194.]** one and twenty yeer old to him and his heiers or Assignes in Case he the said Newton should dy; And the said Newton is to haue that ten pound which is in Aurthor Masons hand as due to him at his receauing the Child, and not to return any of it though the Child should dy: And if the Child liue and that when the said Newton haue kept it two yeers and half which wil be the first of January 1670 then ther shalbe paid to the said Newton fiue pound more out of the Towne Rate, and if the Child liue tell that time twelue month which wilbe 167i then vpon this Consideration that the Child doe at p^rsent want Clothing he shall haue out of the towne Rate fiue pound more and not to returne any of it after the time that it is payable though the Child dy. and the next Second day being the 18 of this Instant the said Newton doe agree to Come and help to fetch the Child to his owne house.

At a meeting of the Select men the 14th (7) 1668 an order was sent to John Blackman and Thomas Peirce Sup'uisors of Contry and Towne high ways requiering them to see the high-ways repaiered by the 20th of Octob next: and the like was don to Isack Joanes for the way leading to the neck of land.

The Same day Tho. Lake and Samuell Pale brought to the Select men a p'sentment of defectiue fence about the great lots: Viz: Tho Trot 6 rod namly 3 rod at Captains neck and 3 rod at the end of Mr Pattens pastuer Samuell Hill 2 rod ther also Isack Joanes on rod and $\frac{1}{2}$ at the end of Steuen Minots pastuer; Deacon Wiswall 2 rod and $\frac{1}{2}$ at the end of Daued Joans pastuer.

The same day an order was sent to Tho: Dauenport Senr Requiering him to Rectefie the streightening of the high way at the bottom of the Hill between his hous and Clement Maxfeilds.

At a meeting of the Select men the 9th of the (9) 68.

It is ordered in respect of the Schole that those that send ther Children to Schole shall the winter time bring for Each Child a load of wood or halfe a Cord of Cord wood; and thos that bring it in log-wood are to cut it after it come to the Scholhous; and for thos boys that goe but a p^t of the winter; we leaue it to the Masters descretion to appoint the p'portion for such.

[**195.**] The Same day Thomas Trot being formally p'sented by the fence Vewers for defectiue fence; Vpon thos allegations which he the said Trot made the Select men did see meete to remite the one halfe of the fine the whole being 6^s.

The Same time Samuell Hils fine for defectiue fence was wholly remitted in regard of his pouerty and the loss which he lately Sustained.

The Same day the Constable Joseph Homes came and made vp his account of the Contry Rate for the yeere 67 committed to him to gather the Rate being 80^{li} – 2^s – 0.

Imp̄. To the Contry Treasurer for which he brought
a recept 64^{li} – 19^s – 0^d of which 27^{li} – 18^s – 6^d was

to the Castle Souldiers	64 – 19 – 0
I^t to Captine Foster as Deputy	4 – 0 – 0
I^t to William Sumner as Deputy	4 – 0 – 0
I^t to Nicholas George	3 – 0 – 0
Some Totall	75 – 19 – 0
Rest due to Ballance	4 – 3 – 0

The 27^{li} – 18^s – 6^d aboue was disposed as followeth

To Captin Clap for Souldiers diet	7 – 15 – 8
To Jno Minot for Cheeses	0 – 8 – 0
To Samuell Chandler	1 – 18 – 5$\frac{1}{2}$
To Robt. Wiles	1 – 16 – 7
To Asahell Smith	1 – 11 – 3$\frac{1}{2}$
To Johnathan Birch	1 – 17 – 9$\frac{1}{2}$
To Johnathan Hill	1 – 7 – 5
To Ebenezer Clap	2 – 7 – 7
To Samuell Bray	1 – 15 – 4$\frac{1}{2}$

To Isack How	1 – 17 – 9½
To John Bird	1 – 18 – 7
To Daniel Ellen	1 – 16 – 7
To Tho: Tolman Junr	1 – 14 – 5
	27 – 18 – 6

Recc the 17 aprill 1668 of the Constabls of Dorchester in full of the Towns p'portion to the Contry Rate for the yeere past the Sume of Sixty fower pounds ninteen shillings I say receued in full of my warrant according to the order of the Generall Court of Joseph Homes

p' me RICHARD RUSSELL
Treasurer.

This is a true Coppie of the Treasuerers Recept as Attest
JOHN CAPEN Record^r

[**196.**] The Same day being the 9 (9) 68 John Gornell was sent vnto and demanded Concerning his Entertaining Ralph Bradice as an Inmate in his hous whos answer was that he would be bound to secuer the Towne from any Damadg that should arise by his being Receaued into the Towne as an inhabetant vpon which the said Ralph was admitted an inhabetant.

The 4th (10) 1668 at a meeting of the Select men for that end Samuell Robinson as Constable appeared and made vp his account of the Towne Rate for the yeer 67 the Sume of the Rate together with the gats was 49^{li} – 6^s – 6^d of which he haue paid by order as follow'th

Imp. to Mr Pole as Schol Master	25 – 0 – 0
It. to the Widdow Mead for the worke at the meeting house	03 – 0 – 0
It. To Nicholas George p^t of what is due to him 2^s 6^s the rest being 3^s the Constable Homes is ordered to pay out of the Contry Rate	02 – 6 – 0
It. To Enock Wiswall for a gate for the great lots	0 – 17 – 0
It. To Jno minot for an old dept about gates	0 – 7 – 0
It. To Timothy Foster for a gate for that pt of the great lots	0 – 15 – 0
It. To Willm Robinson for yrons and Carting	0 – 5 – 0
It. To John Smith for Carting	0 – 2 – 6
It. To Willm Sumner for 4 days hors and man to run the line between Deadham and Dorchester and Rocksbery vp to Plimoth line at 3^s 6^d p. day	0 – 14 – 0
It. To Liftenant Capen 4 days the same line	0 – 14 – 0
It. To Srg^{nt} Samuell Clap 4 days the same line	0 – 14 – 0
It. To Srg^{nt} James Blake 4 days same line	0 – 14 – 0
It. To Captin Foster for Runing the line between Dorchester and Melton one day	0 – 2 – 0
It. Jno Minot the same line on day	0 – 2 – 0

DORCHESTER TOWN RECORDS. 153

It. To Thomas Tolman one day the same line	0 – 2 – 0
It. To Captain Foster for runing the line betweene Dorchester and Punkapag 2 days at — 3ˢ 6ᵈ p' day hors and man	0 – 7 – 6
It. To Jnº Minot for the same line 2 days	0 – 7 – 6
It. To Joseph Homes the same line 2 days	0 – 7 – 6
[**197.**] It To Samuell Dauenport Tho. Birch and Daniell Preston Junʳ for killing 2 wolues	1 – 0 – 0
It. To Captin Foster as Deputy	2 – 0 – 0
It. to Willᵐ Sumner as Deputy	2 – 0 – 0
It. To James Blake and Nathaniell Clap for neck gats	1 – 2 – 0
It. To James Bird for killing a woolf	0 – 10 – 0
It. To Captin Foster 4ˢ for a bl. of malt to pay the Surueigher for runing the line and 3ˢ expence for making the childs coate	0 – 7 – 0
It. To Nathanell Clap for a bl of malt for the same	0 – 4 – 0
It Jnº Minot as pᵗ of what is due to him for expences laid out a bout the Schol-house	0 – 1 – 7
It. To Samuell Robinson himself for windows and Shuts for the Schol-hous	0 – 16 – 2
It. To Jnº Gornell for expences about meeting hous	– 17 – 0
It. To Ensigne Hale for the like worke	0 – 10 – 2
It. To William Pond for the like work	0 – 6 – 8
It. To Richard Euens	0 – 1 – 7
It. To Mathias Euans	0 – 1 – 0
It. To Mʳ Glouer for pᵗ of his bords for the Schole house 17ˢ 6ᵈ which should haue been pᵈ· to Mʳ· Poole, but the Constable Engageth to make it vp to Mʳ· Poole	0 – 17 – 6
It. left in the hands of Samuell Robinson as pᵗ of the gate money to be called for when ther is need of repairing the lote gates	0 – 14 – 9
Sume Totall	49 – 6 – 6

Md̄ of this 14ˢ 9ᵈ ther is pᵈ by Samuell Robinson 3ˢ for work done about the gate in the yeer 73 viz: that gate by Timothy Fosters. the Constable Samuell Robinson is discharged of the account excepting the 14ˢ 9ᵈ left in his hands and ther is due to him from the Towne 3ˢ 10ᵈ as a remainder of what is due to him for his worke about the Schole Windows.

The same day Liftenant Jnº Capen gaue in an account of what had been Comītted into his hands at Seauerall time at first of ten bushells and half of peas brought in to his hous by James Minot which was for the child of Frances Tree the 21 (2) 67: and 4ˢ p. bushel

Imp pᵈ to John Homes 3 bls.	0 – 12 – 0
It. dˡ to Jnº Homes a gaine 3 bls.	0 – 12 – 0
It. pᵈ for Jnº Homes by his order a peck and half for Caps-fare	0 – 1 – 6
It. dˡ 3 pecks to Joseph Long	0 – 3 – 0

[198.] It. p^d againe fore Jn° Homes to the Towne rate 6ˢ 4ᵈ which was for Deacon Wiswall and Hannah Munnings . . .   0 – 6 – 4
It. d¹ a bl. more to Jn° Homes . . .   0 – 4 – 0
It. loss on the measuer on peck and two quarts   0 – 1 – 3

Disburst	2 – 0 – 1
Rest due to the account	0 – 1 – 11

More left in the hands of Jn° Capen of the Towne Rate for the yeer 66 and brought in in peas at 4ˢ p' bl. . . . .   5 – 16 – 2
of which ther was loss on the price they being put off all at 3ˢ 6ᵈ p' ble . . . .   0 – 14 – 6
It. p^d for the Childs Coate . . . .   0 – 9 – 0
It. to Jn° Homes on account . . .   0 – 7 – 1
It. laid out for painter for a pa shooues and for makeing his waistcoat . . . .   0 – 2 – 6
It. laid out for a Catcher for the meeting hous doar . . . .   0 – 0 – 6
It. for attendence at the Court 9 days.. . .   0 – 13 – 6
It. for Recording for the yeere 67 . .   1 – 0 – 0
It. d¹ to Jn° Homes by order from the Select men in shoowes . . . . .   2 – 0 – 0
It. laid out for boards for the Scholhouse . .   0 – 15 – 0
and for nayls . . . . . .   0 – 0 – 6
It. laid out a bl. of malt for the Surueigher for runing the line . . . . .   0 – 4 – 0
It. for a bell rope . . . . .   0 – 1 – 0

Sume Total	6 – 11 – 10

Recc. on the ballance of the other account as aboue. . . . .   0 – 1 – 11
It. Recc. alsoe from Thomas Clap rent for Comon meaddow and the 5ˡⁱ 16.2 as aboue . .   0 – 6 – 0
Rest due to Jn° Capen to ball^nc . . .   0 – 9 – 7
Md Ther was alsoe d¹ into the hands of Jn° Capen by the Relicts of William Blake towards the repaiering the burying place,   0 – 18 – 0

the which was by the Select mens order deliuered into the hands of William Sumner and at this time was by them alowed vnto the said William Sumner for 12 days attendance at the Court.

Alsoe ther was brought into the hands of Jn° Capen by Parker for rent for remote meaddows 3 bls. of Corne but it was dl into the hands of Jn° Minot towards worke done about the Schol house : this rent was for the yeer 67 and also that aboue of Tho: Clap which 3 bls. was paid to Timothy Foster for worke at Schol hous.

[199.] At a generall Towne meeting the 7ᵗʰ of the 10ᵗʰ mo. 1668.

The season being Cold it was concluded generally that the reading of the directory should be omitted, and then the accounts both of Contry and Towne Rats weer giuen in.

The same time it was Voted the Towne would giue vnto the maintenance of the minestry for the yeer now almost past the Sume of 130^{li} Viz to Mr Mather 80^{li} and Mr Stoughton 30^{li} and ther owne estats free from Rateing to that Rate

The same day it was Voted that the Select men for the time being should agree with the School Master for the teaching of the youth; for soe long time as they shall Judg meet.

The same day it was Voted and agreed vnto by the Towne that the next lords day com seauennithht ther should be a Vollentary Contribution for the nesessety of Samuel Hill who is in want of releife and the more by reason that some of his goods was lately Stollen out of his house. And John Minot and Thomas Tilstone are Chosen and appointed to dispos or emproue it for his best Supply.

The same day ther was chosen for Select men.

Captin Foster Liften Capen, Jno Minot Ensigne Halle Srg^{nt} Samuell Clap and for Recorder Lift. Jno Capen   Raters. William Sumner, Srg^{nt} James Blake, Srg^{nt} Willm pond.

Sup'uisors Rich, Leeds Augustin Clement.

And for the neck of land Nathaniell Clap.

It was agreed on by the Comissioners mett at Boston in the yeer 1668 that all earable land and meadow should be rated at ten shillings p'acre and all pasture land at fiue shillings p'acre and that majestrats and minesters should be rated.

This returne was made by James Blake who was Comissioner for the Towne of Dorchester.

[**200.**]   At a meeting of the Select men the 14th (10) 1668.

Henery Mare (bringing a Certifficate vnder the Gouernors hand of his allowance to setle in this Jurisdiction) desiered to be alowed an inhabetant in this Towne the which was granted him.

The same day Samuell Paule Came and desiered liberty to haue about 3 or 4 load of Timber out of the 500 acrs towards the building him an house, the which was granted him.

The same day it was ordered that a warant should be directed to the Raters to make a rate for the mantenanc of the minestry of 130^{li} viz of Mr Mather 80^{li} and Mr Stoughton 50^{li} and a towne Rate of 54^{li} and to make their return to the Select men at ther next meeting which will be the Second Munday in January next.

The same day the Contry Rate was fineshed with the addition the Sume whereof is 76–14–8 being a duble Rate because of the Collidg p'portion and deputys expences but the Treasurers warrant is for a Rate and half besides Colledg p'portion.

The same day Frances Oliuer Came againe and desiered liberty to stay in the Towne and for that end brought Thomas Bird and Joseph Long to be bound for him but they vnderstanding that they must be bound to Cleere him wholly from the Towne for three months after he was remoued, refused soe to doe and therfore the said Oliuer was againe warned to depart the Town.

At a meeting of the Select men the 11th (11) 68

The day aboue said the Raters returned ther Rates Comitted to them to make.

The Sume of the Contry Rate	76 – 19 – 8
The minesters Rate	130 – 11 – 5
The Town Rate	54 – 15 – 2

The same day ther was a warrant directed to the Constables to gather the Towne and Contry Rats: and the minesters Rate was Comitted to the Deacons and the Constables to make disbursment according to orders directed to them.

The same day Captin William Hudson of Boston came to the Select men and made a full agreement with the Select men about Assigning ouer his Court Grant of 500 acres of land granted to Mr Jeffereys for 300 acrs of o^r land about wade-ing Riuer and he to become [**201.**] an inhabetant of Dorchester and lyable to publique Charges and the place or house to be called by the name of Dorchester house.

The 11th of the (11) 1668.

Wheras Captin William Hudson of Boston haue by vertue of the Gen^{ll} Court Grant hath fiue hundred acrs of land which was some time giuen to Mr Jefferys, now know that the said William Hudson haue made this agreement with the Select men of Dorchester that in Consideration of three hundred acres about Wadeing Riuer out of the Towneship of Dorchester hee the said William Hudson will resigne vp his grant of fiue hundred acres vnto the Towne of Dorchester and doe acknowlidg my self to be an inhabetant of the Towne of Dorchester and to become lyable to such dutys as doe belong to other inhabetants and doe further Engage to conforme more fully this exchange in time Conuenient and that according to law.

Wittnes my hand   WILLIAM HUDSON.

This is a true Coppie of that breif agreement vntill more full and ample writtings may be made Entered and Examined by me

              JOHN CAPEN, Recorder.

the originall remaining on file.

At a meeting of the Select men the 8 (12) 1668.

The day abouesaid John Blackman requested liberty for to haue 200 of Railes and 50 posts out of the 500 acrs and it was granted him.

The same day a letter was p'sented to the Select men from Enoch Place for his reseption into the Towne as an inhabetant againe but the Select men saw noe Reason to grant it.

The same day ther was granted vnto Ensigne Hale two trees in the 500 acrs for to make posts for fence.

At a Towne meeting the 9 (12) 68 the Court order about horses was published and notice giuen that such horses as respected that order should be brought that day fortnight after lectuer to some place neer the meeting house that ther may be vewed by the Select men.

[**202.**] The same day Nicholas Bolton did agree to tend the meeting house to keep it in decent order and to Ring the bell the yeer insewing for which he is to haue 3ᵘ of which 10ˢ of it in money if it can be gott or otherwis to haue 3ᵈ vpon the shilling for that 10ˢ Jnᵒ Capen and Samuell Clap made the agreement with him being ther vnto appointed by the Select men at ther meeting the day before.

At a meeting of the Select men the 8ᵗʰ of the (1) 6⅜

It is ordered that wheras by experience it doth appeare that the Comons in dorchester are ouer burdened and one Reason is because of great numbers of sheepe that are taken into oʳ Towne from other townes by some of our owne inhabetants to the great Damadge of the whole.

It is therefore ordered that whosoeuer of oʳ inhabetants shall receaue any such sheepe from any pʼson or pʼsons of other Townes to feede vpon oʳ Comons more then one weeke shall pay to the vse of the towne Six pence p. sheepe or lamb for euery weeke and for soe many as they shall soe receaue to be leuyed by distress or otherwise for the vse aforesaid.

The same day ther was granted to John Pason liberty for three loade of timber towards the building of a barne to be taken out of the 500 acrs.

The same day ther was granted to Thomas Grant liberty for 100 of rails out of the same place.

The like liberty was granted to Quarter Master Smith to take 100 of railes in the same place aforesaid.

The same day Robt. Stanton and Jnᵒ Homes weere appointed to giue notice of Stone Horses runing at liberty one the Comons Contrary to Court order.

The same day ther was appointed a Comittee Viz Captin Clap, Captaine Foster Liftenant Capen Sarg^{nt} Samuell Clap and William Sumner to attend that bussnes about the line between Dorchester and Rocksbery at such time as the Comittee appointed by the Court shall giue notice.

The same time James Bird's request for the Towns ap'bation Concerning a Tann-yard between Anthony Gullifords house and Mʳ Collicots at Melton it was referred vnto some spech with Jnᵒ Gill and Anthony Gulliford.

[**203.**] The same day at the motion of Enoch Wiswall and his Complaint of diuers intrenching vpon the third diuission in the Cow-walke vnder pʳtence of that 500 acrs ther was appointed Liftenant Capen Srg^{nt} Samuell Clapp and Amiell Weeks to Joyne with Enoch Wiswall to run that head line between the 3ᵈ deuission and the 500 acrs and to make the bounds more Vissible and the like between the 500 acrs and the first lote in the late deuission.

The same day Nicholas George is alowed by the Select men to keepe an ordinary if the Court please to admitt of it.

Vewers of Fences

for the great lots the further pᵗ . . . { Thomas Tolman
{ Thomas Peirce

for the pᵗ neerest the Towne . . . { Jnᵒ Smith Senʳ
{ Timothy Tilston

for the 20 acre lots	{ Thomas Grant { James White
for the feild behind the widdow Bird . .	{ Obediah Haws { Thomas Andrews
for the feild behind Mrs Joanes. . .	{ Augusten Clement { Isacke Joanes
for the feild behind M^r. Stoughtons . .	{ Steuen Minot { Benjamen Leeds
for the feild behind Mr Mather . . .	{ George Dyer { William Pond
for the neck of land	{ Nicholas Clap { Joseph Homes
for the feild before Enock Wiswals . .	{ Obediah Swift { Thomas Moadesly
for Cleering the great lots . . .	J^{no} Smith Junr
for Cleering the Neck of land . . .	Israell Meade

Al Corne feilds are to be Cleered this yeere by the first Monday in aprill and fence Vewers are to Vew fences by the first of aprill this yeer.

[**204.**] At a Towne meeting the 9th (1) 6⅜ Captaine Foster and William Sumner weer Chosen Deputys for the yeere Ensewing, but they accepted but for the first Session.

The Same day ther was Chosen for Comissioners to end Smale Causes Captaine Foster William Sumner and Jn° Minot.

And Constables for the yeer Ensewing James White and Samuell Rigby.

The 15 (1) 68 on a training day the Select men granted to the Weddow Baker and Israell Meade liberty for one hundred of railes out of the 500 acres and a bout 30 or 40 posts.

The Same time ther was granted to Benjamen Leeds liberty for 150 Railes out of the Same place.

At a meeting of the Sellect men the 12th (2) 69.

It was ordered at the request of James Whit (who was latly Chosen Fence vewer for the 20 acre lots) that seeing he is Chosen Constable for this yeer, that therfore he shall be dismissed from the Vewing of fence and Jn° Merifcild is appointed for that work.

The day abouesaid the Constable brought in a list of the yong men that where not vnder the Gouernment of famelys according as the law enjoyns, and the same day Thomas Pope, Steuen Hoppen Junr, Samuel Bray and Thomas Dauenport weer spoken with by the Select men in p'ticuler and the Constable ordered to giue notice to the rest of the yong men to appeare before the Select men the next lectuer day being the 20th. of this Instant at Captin ffosters house p'sently after the lectuer.

At a meeting of the Select men at Captin ffosters house the 20th of the (2) 69 the p'sons vnder named weer brought by the Constable before the Select men in referance to the order of Court requiering the Select men to take inspection of ther orderly walking and Submitting to famely Gournment.

Richard Frances	Henery Roberts	Peter Chaplin
Josua Henshaw	Johnathan Birch	Nathanell Wales

Ralph Bradish	Asahel Smith	Edward Martin
Joseph Birch	Thomas Birch	Adam Wright
ffraunces Olliuer	Richard Butt.	Tho : Grant was
Johnathan Hill	Cornelius Morgan	not Worned

[**205.**] At a meeting of the Select men the 10th (3) 69.

It was agreed vnto by the Select men that they or some of them together with the Elder should take Some Conuenient time to goe about to the Seauerall p^{ts} of the Towne to take notice and enquiery of the Seauerall p^{r}sons of ther manner of liueing and of ther p'fitting by public or priuate instruction.

It was agreed on by the Commissioners for the Contry Rate for the yeer 166ꝫ being mett together at Bostcn that all Eareable land and meadow, should be vallewed at 10^s p' acre and all pastuer land at 5^s p'acre : and that all Majestrates and minesters shalbe rated.

This is a true Coppy of that returne which o^r Commissioner James blake did make. Entered by me

J^{no} Capen Record^r

At a meeting of the Towne being orderly called together on the 8 (4th) 69.

A motion being made by o^r Breatheren and freinds liueing at or neer to hadly vnto the Towne for to dismiss Mr Atherton from his engagement to the Schole in Dorchester vnto the publique worke of the minestry with them their.

It is therfore put to the vote whether the Towne will be willing to dismiss Mr Atherton from his Engagement by the 29 Septem. next or sooner if the towne by ther Comittee can p'uid a supply for ther Schole.

The vote is in the Affermatiue.

Ther Same day ther was Chosen a Comittee to looke out and agree with a Schole Master for to teach Schole in Dorchester ther names are Mr William Stouhton Lift^{nt} Jno Capen and Jno Minot.

At a meeting of the Select men the 13 (7) 1669.

The Select men doth order that Mr. Timothy Mather be spoken with all, and he is heerby desiered to Erect a Conuenient and Comely Pillar vpon his fathers graue and for that, and towards the funerall expences he shall haue out of the next towne Rate ten pounds paid vnto him p'uided it be done by the last of Nouember next.

[**206.**] The Same day the Select men vewed the way betweene Clement Maxfeild and Tho : Dauenport and they found it not broad enough and therefore staked out the way two rod broad from the Stone wall in vpon that land which Thomas Dauenport haue taken in.

The Same day the Select men made a Rate for this County by warrant from the County Treasurer the Rate was halfe a Single Contry Rate, for the yeer 1668 the which being Sumed vp Came to 18^{li} – 12^s – 8^d of which the Treasurer is to haue 18^{li} – 8^s – 9^d.

The Same day a warrant was directed to the Constable Samuell Rigby to repaire to Joseph Birch the Contents whereof is as followeth.

To the Constable of Dorchester you are requiered in his Majesties name to repaire to Joseph Birch and requier him (from the Select men) to put himself in an orderly way of liueing, either by placeing himself with some Master that may keepe him in constant imployment soe as may giue Satisfaction to the Court or elce to expect that he wilbe p'sented to the Court for disorderly liueing.

Dated the 13 (7) 69 By the Select men J^{no} Capen Record^r

At a meeting of the freemen the 4th of the (8th) 69 at the meeting house ther was Chosen for Deputies for the Generall Court Captain Hopstill Foster and William Sumner to continue till the next Court of Election.

The Select men on the 27 (7) 69 did agree with Goodwife Carter to let deliuerance Stock abid at her house vntill and in the time of her lying in, for which she is to haue for the month of her lying in 10^s p' the weeke of which 2^s 6^d in money p' the weeke, and for the time before to haue 4^s p' weeke p'uided that deliuerance must worke out as much of this, as she can, and what fall short to be made vp by the Towne and she went to her house the next day.

At a meeting of the Select men the 8th (9) 69.

The day a boue said the Constable Jacob Hewens appeared and gaue in an account of the Towne Rate Comitted to him to gather

	li.	s.	d.
for the yeare 1668 the sume of the Rate being	54	15	2
Imp. to the Schol Master Sir Atherton	25	00	0
It. to Jno Homes for Frances Trees Child	2	3	1
It. to Jno Homes for wokre done at the Schole house	1	15	9
It. to Robt. wils for work at the Schole house	1	5	0
[207.] It. to Nicholas bolton for Ringing the bell and for a days worke to warne a Towne meeting	03	02	00
It. To Nicholas Lawerence for Francis Tree	02	05	00
It. To William Turner for Francis Tree	02	11	00
It. To Timothy Foster for work at Schole hous	02	09	00
It. To Tho: Swift Senr for bords for the metting house	00	03	00
It. To Captaine Foster as Deputy	03	04	08
It. To Nicholas George for expenses	04	03	00
It. To William Sumner as Deputy	03	01	00
It. To Lift^{nt} Capen for a dept due to him for the last yeer	00	09	07
It. To Jno Minot besids what he haue already for Charges about the Schole house	01	05	11
It. To Samuell Robbinson for worke about Schole-windows	00	03	10
It. To Quarter Master Smith for a bushell of Malt for the Surueigher	00	04	00
and for Carrying of bords from Boston for the Schole hous	00	05	00

DORCHESTER TOWN RECORDS.

It. To Mr Glouer for p^t of what was due to him for bords, the other being p^d the yeer before ther being yet due from Mr Glouer 1^s 7^d . . . . } 00 – 14 – 01

It. to Jno Blake for a locke for the Schole hous . } 00 – 02 – 01

It. To William Pond 7^s 4^d and Ezra Clap 1^s 5^d and to Mathias Euens 1^s 3^d and to Richard Euens 1^s 8^d and to Nathan Bradly by Rich: Euens order 1^s 3^d. all this for worke don at the meeting house in p^t of what is due to them . . . . } 00 – 12 – 11

Sume Totall 54 – 19 – 11
Rest due to Jacob Hewens to ballance . . . 00 – 04 – 09

The Same day ther was granted to Tho: Dauenport Junr liberty to take a bout three loads of wood out of the 500 acres to make plows, some Ash and some Oake but the Oak is to be taken of such as is downe already.

Alsoe ther was granted to his father some of the tops of the trees in the same place for fire-wood, but not to fall any nor to take that which is p'uided by other men for theire vse which haue ben formerly Granted

The Same day ther was granted to Sargent Clap to haue 200 of Railes out of the 500 acrs.

[208.] The Same day Israell Mead made a motion for a place to sett a smale frame Joyning to the North p^t of his old building in exchang. for some land neer his barne for the enlarging of that way and for his Conueniency for his frame, vnto which motion the Select men appoints Captaine Foster and Srg^{nt} Clap and Amiell Weeks and Isack Joanes to Vew his request and accordingly they to conclud and determine the matter and make returne.

At a meeting of the Select men the 1 (10) 69 at Captin Fosters hous. Mr Timothy Mather as Constable for the year 68, appeared to make vp his account for the Contry Rate for the yeer 68 Comitted to him to Colect the Sume of the Rate being 76^{li} 19^s 8^d as followeth Viz.

Imp̄ to the Treasurer for which he brought the Treasurers Recept . . . . } 57 – 17 – 04
It. to Samuell Jackson for Glasing 31^{bls} of Endian at 2^s 2^d p bl: but at the Contry price 4^{li} 2^s 8^d . . } 03 – 07 – 02
It. for Carrying the Corne to Boston . . . 00 – 05 – 02
It. for his diett . . . . 00 – 04 – 00
It. for a man to fetch the Glas from Boston . . } 00 – 01 – 00
It. for Nayles to Mr Patten . . . . . 00 – 01 – 06
The Sume of al this as it was p^d in at the Contry Rate is. . . . . } 04 – 14 – 04
It. To Captaine Foster as Deputy . . . . 03 – 12 – 00
It. To William Sumner as Deputy . . . . 03 – 12 – 00

69 – 15 – 08
Rest due to Ballance . . . . . 07 – 04 – 00

Recc of Mr Mather in full of the towne of Dorchesters p'portion to the Contry Rate for the yeer 1668 the Sume of Sixty Seauen pound Seauenteene Shillings fower pence I Say Recc p' me Richard Russell Treasurer . . . . } 57 – 17 – 04

At a Generall Meeting of the Towne the 6 (10) 1669.
After the Derectory was read It was put to the Vote as followeth. Wheras the Select men haue formerly granted to Mr Timothy Mather, ten pound towards the funerall expences and the erecting of a pillar on his fathers tomb. It was [**209.**] p'posed to the towne whether they would consent to what the Select men haue done with out limettation of the time but to be done as sone as Conueniently it may,
The Voate was in the Affermatiue
The Same day it was put agreed by a Vote that ther should be a Rate made 100^{li} for the maintenance of the minestry for the yeer past which ends the last of this Month and this hundered pound to discharge what is due to Mr Mather for fower Months seruice ; and alsoe for a recompence to Mr Stoughton.
The same day it was put to the Vote whether we would haue a house built and p'uided for the Minestry and likewise that a Comittee be chosen to looke out for a Conuenient Place to set it on ; and the house and accomodations to it to remaine to the Towne for such an end, and not to be allenated from that vse from time to time and the house to be such an house as James Blaks house is, namly 38 foote in lenth and 20 foote wid and 14 foote betweene Joynts gert worke.
The Vote was in the Affermatiue.
The same day it was Voted that the Select men that shall be Chosen for the yeere Ensuing, shall be the Comittee for to looke out for a place to set this house on : and to make report to the town for ther ap'bation therof, and likwise for to agree with the workmen for the doeing of the worke, and the Charges to be defrayed by the Towne.
The same day ther was Chosen for Select men ——— Captaine Foster, Srg^{nt} Clap, Lift^{nt} Capen, Ensigne Hale, James Blake.
for Recorder Lift^{nt} Capen
for Raters.   Mr Timothy Mather,
   Steuen Minot, Daniell Preston
for Sup'uisors Richard Baker, Augustin Clement.
and for the Neck of land Nicholas Clap.
At a meeting of the Select men the 13 10 1669.
Daued Joanes made Request that his former Grant to George Procter for a hous plot might be laid out, the Select men appointed Liftenant John Capen and Ensigne Rich: Hale to lay it out according to grant and to make returne.
[**210.**] The same day it was appointed that the Single Contry Rate should be fineshed, with the addition of a quarter p^t for Colledg p'portion and Deputys expences.
Alsoe that ther should be a warrant Isued to the Raters to make a Rate of one hundred pounds for the maintenance of the minestry

for the yeer past, and also for a towne Rate of 55ˡⁱ for the vse of the towne and to pay the Schole Master.

The Same day also it was agreed that ther should be an order sent to John Pope (the Select men vnder standing that a daughter of his is come from Boston into his famely) that he doe forthwith come to the Select men and giue Securety to saue the Towne harmles from Damedg or els to expect the penalty which the towne order lays vpon such as entertaine Inmats.

The Coppie of the warrant which was sent to the Constable Samuell Rigby remains on file.

The Same day it was ordered that Roger Belleng and Tho: Swift of Melton (he being a p'prietor in this towne and being neer ther abouts) that they together with such as they shall take to them to Enform them shall be desiered and empowered to goe forth and vew such Seder Swamps aboue brantry wheer we vnderstand that some doe trespas vpon oʳ land and to take notice therof, and if they find that it is soe to forbid them and Cause them to desist as they will answer it, the Coppe of the order sent remains on file.

The Contry Rate for the yeer 69 amounts to 47ˡⁱ 3ˢ 0ᵈ with the addition of a quarter pᵗ for Colledg p'portion and deputys expence 47ˡⁱ 3ˢ 0ᵈ

This Rate deliuered to Constable James White to Colect and to pay to the Treasurer or his order 37ˡⁱ 2ˢ 11ᵈ being the Single Rate and 3ˡⁱ 1ˢ 7 Colledg p'portion in all 40ˡⁱ 4ˢ 6ᵈ.

Alsoe he is to pay to Nicholas Bolton towards his pay for Ringing the bell . . . . 1 – 0 – 0
Also to Captin Foster as Deputy . . . . 2 – 10 – 0
Also to William Sumner as Deputy . . . . 2 – 10 – 0
Also more to Captin Foster as Deputy . . . 0 – 18 – 0

[211.] At a meeting of the Select men the 10ᵗʰ. (11) 69.

The Raters made returne of the minesters Rate the Sume wheerof was 100ˡⁱ 0ˢ 1ᵈ and Com̄itted to the Deakon.

Alsoe the Towne Rate the Sume wherof was 55ˡⁱ 0 6ᵈ and Com̄itted to Constable Samuell Rigby to Colect.

The Same day the Select men did order that the Rate for the minestry for yeer 69 being 100ˡⁱ should be disposed to Mʳ Stoughton 70 pound and to Mʳ Timothy Mather for his fathers labour 4 months 26ˡⁱ 13ˢ 4ᵈ and the remainder to discharge some former arrears behind to Mʳ Stoughton.

The Same day ther was granted to Mʳˢ Atherton liberty to haue timber out of the 500 acrs to make two ground sels.

Also vpon information of Captin Foster that some p'son haue fallen a tree vpon the highway between the 20 acr lots and goodman pasons farme contrary to order, the Select men vpon his request haue granted and empowered him to take the tree to himself.

At a meeting of the Select men the 14 – 12 – 69

It was ordered that a warrant should be Ishewed out to the Constable to warne a meeting of the freemen the 2ᵈ weeke in March to bring in Votes for Nomination of Majestrates and Chousing deputys and Com̄issioner and the rest of the inhabetants also to Chous Constables and County Treasurer and other bussines that may be then done.

At a meeting of the Select men of Dorchester at Captin Fosters house about some prudentiall affaires of the Towne the 17 (12) 69 It is ordered

That wheras Deacon Samuell Bass of Brantry haue by himself or his order falen some tree or trees in a Swamp within the bounds of o^r Towne (as we app'hend), and wheras the said Samuell Bass, haue made request to the Select men, that he may take a way that which he haue fallen and p'missing to make satisfaction for it, If vpon tryall it proue to be soe. The Select men doe grant that he may take what he haue already fallen, p'uided he fall noe more till tryall of the bounds be made, neither shall this liberty extend to any other who haue not made their address and Condissioned as he haue doun.

[**212.**] At a Towne meeting the 9 (1) 6$\frac{9}{70}$
Ther was then and ther Chosen for Deputys Captine Foster and William Sumner to serue for the whole yeere.

for Comissioners to end smale Causes Captin Foster, William Sumner, Lift^{nt} Jno Capen.

for Constables Thomas Dauenport, Obediah Hawes.

At the same time ther was Chosen William Sumner, Augusten Clement, Richard Leeds, Nicholas George, Enock Wiswall and Jno Wales, for to Vew the Creeke about John Wales his hous, and to Consider the Charges that may be needfull for to make it a Conuenient landing place; and also the manner how; and to make retorne to the Select men that soe it may be p'moted and a Complished by some Vollentary subscription of each man that is willing to disburst towards that Charg, and the Comodety therof to be free to the whol Towne.

The same day it was p'posed to the Towne whether they would Grant liberty to Nicholas Bolton to sell Sider or Victuale in a way of Common Entertainment either Saboth day or elce: the Vote was in the Negatiue.

At a meeting of the Select men the 14 (1) $\frac{68}{78}$
Ther was appointed Fence Vewers.

for the great lots from Captains Neck to good man Tolmans	Rich: Leeds Steuen Minot
for the rest of the great lots to Naponset .	Thomes Trot Abraham How
for the 20 acr Lots	Henry Merrifeild Thomas Pope
for the Feild behind James Bird . .	Elder Humphry James Bird
for the feild behind Mrs Joanes and before Enock Wiswals old hous	Enock Wiswall Joshua Henshaw
for the feild behind Mr Stoughtons . .	Rich Withington Joseph Weiks
for the feild behind Mr. Mathers . .	Timothy Mather Daniell Elders

for the Neck of land William Sumner and Nathaniell Clap.
for Cleering of the Neck of land Jno Homes.
for Cleering the great lots Jno Smith and Robt Sanders or either of them.

DORCHESTER TOWN RECORDS. 165

All Corne feilds are to be Cleered by the 11th day of Aprill and Fence Vewers are to Vew Fences by the 12 day of aprill this yeere.

[**213**] Artecles of Agreement had made and agreed vpon between Captaine Hopstill Foster, Lift^{nt} Jno Capen, Ensigne Richard Hale, Srg^{nt} Samuell Clap and Srg^{nt} James Blake, Select men of the Towne of Dorchester for the time being of the one p'ty: and Henery Merefeild and Margeret his wife of the Same towne of the other p'ty: this three and twentyeth day of March one thousand Six hundred Sixty and nine or Seauenty, as followeth:

Wittneseth that the said Select men on the behalf of the Towne haue put and bound the child of John Stock and Deliuerance his wife vnto the said Henery Merifeild and Margeret his wif their heyers executors Administrators or Assignes, to Nurce, Educate and bring vp vntill it accomplish the age of Sixteene or eightteene yeers (at the liberty of the Said Merifeild to accept off) it being now about the age of twenty weeks, finding vnto and p'viding for the maintenance of the Child now in its Infancy.

And soe forword, as it shall grow vp to more ripnes of yeers and statuer duering the whole terme such sufficient nessesarys for food and rayment &c. as shal bee meete: as alsoe when it shalbe Capable to teach or Cause it to be taught to read p'fitly the English tongue, And also to teach and instruct her in the principles of Christian religion. And in such houswifry employment of Spinning and knitting, as she may be Capable off to learne and her to keep in Sicknes and in helth. And to the premisses the said Henery Merrifeild and Margeret his wife doe bind them selues their heyers executors Administrators or Assignes to p'forme the Conditions aboue mentioned and to Secuer the Towne harmeless from any further Charge, And in Consideration heeroff the foresaid Select men doe in the behalf of themselues for the time being and their Successors on the behalf of the Towne that ther shall be paid out of the towne Rate the Sume of therty pounds: Viz: ten pounds at the end of the feirst yeer after the date heereof whether the Child liue or dy; and ten pound p' the yeer for the next two yeers, p'uided that if the Child dy in any p^t of the Second or theird yeers, then he the said Merrifeild shall haue but p'portionably of the pay according to the life of the Child in witnes heerof the p'tys aboue named haue heer vnto set ther hands the day and yeer aboue said.

Witnes hereof	The mark of HENERY ⊟ MERRIFEILD
AMMIEL WEEKES	The mark of MARGERET ═ MERYFEILD
the marke of	
NICHOLAS N BOLTON	HOPESTILL FOSTER ⎫
	JOHN CAPEN Senr ⎪
	RICHARD HALL ⎬ Select men
	SAMUELL CLAP ⎪
	JAMES BLAKE ⎭

[**214.**] The same day being the 14th (1) $^{69}/_{70}$ ther was granted liberty to Henery Merrifeild to take timber for 200 of Railes and two trees for posts out of the 500 acrs.

The same day it was ordered and appointed that John Homes

and Clement Maxfield should see to the execution of that towne order Respecting yokeing and Ringing of hogs made in the yeer 44 follio 409 in the first book, and for ther paines they are to haue 4^d p' swine for all that are defectiue and if the owners refus to yoke them and Ring them, then they shall doe it themselues, and the owners shalbe lyable to pay them 9^d p swine for soe doeing; If only yokeing them 8^d for a yoke p'uided the owner be first Enformed before they yoke them, but the penalty of 4^d shall be paid and this order to be in force the Eleuenth of Aprill for yokeing and all the yeer for Ringing, and this order extends to all Swine within this plantation; and any other p'son may execute this order also.

The same day Nicholas Georg is a lowed by the Select men to keepe an ordinary If the Court Please to admit of it.

At a meeting of the Select men at Captin Fosters hous the 23 (1) $^{69}/_{70}$ Henery Merrifeild and his wif Came before the Select men and made an agreement about Stocks Child as is recorded in the first book follio 213.

The same day they appointed Amiell Weiks; Roger Belleng, Rich. Withington Samuell Rigby and Daniel preston to Run the line from the top of the blew hill between Brantry and vs; and soe home to Plimoth Line.

And for the line between Rocksbery and vs Captine Clap, Captin Foster, Lift^{nt} Capen and William Sumner.

And for the line between Deadham and Dorchester: William Sumner if he be able Clement Maxfeild, William Pond and Nathaniell Clap.

And for the line between Melton and vs and punkepage and Dorchester Ensigne Rich. Hale, Joseph Homes and Steuen Minot.

The Same day Notice was giuen to Henery Merrifeild to discharge the towne of his daughter Funnell which hath been at his hous about a weeke; vnless he gitt a note vnder the hands of the Select men of Melton that they will receaue her againe if need be and to looke at her as an Inhabetant of their Towne, notwithstanding her residence at her fathers hous for the p'sent:

[**215.**] The same day Nicholas Bolton was appointed to giue notice of a Towne meeting to be assembled the next Second day to publish towne orders and to giue notice therof to the Seauerall Inhabetants.

At a Towne Meeting the 28 (1) 1670 It was Voted that at the next meeting of the Select men in their ordinary Cours being the Second Monday in May they shall appoint a day for the towne to Come together to declare whether they will haue the meeting hous remoued or noe.

Alsoe the same time it was voted that the Selectmen should p'sent against thos that entrench vpon our lands beyond the blew hills.

The same day diuers in the Towne did at the motion of the Select men Engage to lay downe some money and Some Corne and peas for the p'sent supply in placeing of Stocks child to be repaid again out of the next Rate.

Captin Foster 2 bls. of Corne and one bl. of peas
Lift^{nt} Capen one bl. of peas.

Ensigne Hale one bl. of Corne.
Srg^nt Clap one bl. of Corne
Edward pason 2 bl. corne and on bl. of peas.

And in money	s	
Jn° Smith Senr	2	
Augustin Clement	2	
William Sumner	1	
Samuell paale	1	
Rich Leeds	1	& a bl. of Corne
Richard Baker	2	
Tho: Tilstone	1	
Daniell Preston	1	
Thomas Trot	1	
Nathaniell Clap	1	
Jn° Gornell	2	d
Thomas Lake	0 – 6	
Robt. Spur	0 – 6	
Rich Withington	2	
Nicholas Bolton	6	
M̄d merrifeild had also some oats out of the Towne rate of Isack Joans two bl.	4	
and a pair of shows for his wif of Jn° Capen Senr	4 – 6	

The 16 (3) 1670. [**216.**] At a meeting of the Select men vpon an occasionall meeting ther was granted to Ensigne Hale liberty to take 4 or 5 load of timber out of the fiue hundred acrs towards the building of his barne,

the same day ther was granted to Jn° Bird to take a load or ther abouts of timber out of the 500 acres.

The 17 3 70. Richard Leeds and Steuen Minot brought a p'sentment of defectiue fence about the great lots as followeth

According to order wee whos names are vnder writ, haue Vewed the great lot Fence, and haue giuen warning to all whom we found defectiue; Now vpon o^r theird Vewing wee find diuers p'sons defectiue in ther fence.

Joseph long 2 rods defectiue by Toplifs: Timothy Tilston 2 rods 13 foote Joseph long 12 rod defectiue all but 2 lenth of railes somthing good: Timothy Mather 12 rod defectiue by Tolmans

Timothy Tilston 6 rod defectiue by Tolmans

      the mark of RICH c|——> LEEDS
              STEUEN MINOT

The 19 3 70 A warrant was directed to the Constable for the leuying of the aboue said fines the which remains on file with his retorne.

At a meeting of the Select men the 13 (4) 1670.

It was ordered that a Towne meeting should be rated for to Consider and determine whether the meeting house should be remoued in order to the Voate of the towne of the 28 (1) 70 and the Constables to giue notice.

The same day it was ordered that Ensigne Hale should see that the pound be forth with repaiered and made sufficcient to keepe in all sorts of Catle and hoggs.

The same day the Select men vnderstanding that Deliuerance Stock is Come into towne againe from her seruice at Melton; It it is ordered that Captin Foster Srg^{nt} Clap and Srg^{nt} Blake should giue her notice that she put herself in some setled way of liueing under some famely-gouermeut; or elce to expect that the Select men will take further order with her

[217.] The same day Augustin Clement made a motion to the Select men for to remoue his fence at his pastuer about a rod and half wide out, and about ten rod long for his Conueniency of hauing feirme ground to sett his fence vpon, and in Consideration therof he is willing to lay downe forty shillings in money for the vse of the towne and not to be repayed againe; vnto this motion the Select men did agree to p'pose it to the towne for their ap'ba-tion. At which Towne meeting on the 27 (4) 70 it was granted him. And William Sumner John Capen Senr and John Gornell weer appointed to lay it out not exceeding twenty rod of ground.

The same day being the 13 (4) 70 It was ordered (that wheras Constable Thomas Dauenport had taken a gun of Joseph Longs for a fine for his defectiue fence at the great lots) that he should deliuer him his gun againe upon his payment of 6^s besids the Constables fee.

The same day notice was giuen to the Sup'uisors of high ways about the Towne and neck to see that they be sufficciently mended by the first of July next.

The same day it was ordered that at the next towne meeting, the Court order about Horses should be minded.

At a Towne meeting the 27 (4) 1670 the Court order about stone horses was read and diuers Complaints weer made against stone horses as against John Merrifield: Jno Pelton, Tho: Birch two horses: Joshua Henshaw: Jno Wales and Nicholas Lawrence.

The same day It was put to the Vote whether the matter Con-serning the meeting hous of its standing or remoueing whether it should be at this time determined by a Vote.

The Vote was Affirmatiue

The same time it was put to the Vote whether the meeting hous should be remoued from the place that now it stands to the Rocky-hill by the Schole house and be set vp in the same forme that now it is.

The Vote was in the Affermatiue.

[218.] The same day it was put to the Vote whether the house should be remoued to the place formerly mentioned by September 1671 vnless the towne see meet to deferr it longer

The Vote was Affermatiue.

At a meeting of the Select men the 27 (4) 1670 at Captin Fosters hous, at the motion of Ensigne Daniell Fisher of Deadham, ther was granted to him and his Brothers, soe much Seare Ceder as they shall make vse off for Shingle (vnless the Select men p'hibitt him) in a Swamp or Swamps neer pole-plaine and a quan-tity of Greene Cedar for Clobord to the quantety of a thousand or two thousand of Clobord: p'vided he shall not hinder any of o^r owne towne to fetch ther alsoe; but to p'hibbet any of another towne from takeing of any without liberty from o^r towne or the Select men for the time being.

At a meeting of the Select men the 1 (5) 70 Steuen Minot and Johnathan Birch brought two hors Colts before the Select men to be vewed for ther legall goeing at liberty in the Comons a black hors, and a pied hors; the black hors was aproued off but the other was not but was fined 20^s for a month goeing in Comons and Steuen Minot Engaged for the payment of the pied Hors which was Thomas Burch.

The same day Jno Merrifeld was fined 20^s for a hors of his goeing at liberty on the Comons Contrary to law and not bringing him to be vewed.

At a meeting of the Select men the 12 (7) 70 a warrant was Isued out to Constable Tho: Dauenport to take fines for defectiue fence at great lots and ludlows neck of Elder Jno Wiswall for 2 rods and a half, Mr Mather for 8 rods Jno Wales for 3 rod and Joseph Long for 2 rods and half.

The same day order was giuen to Srg^{nt} Clap and Srg^{nt} Blake to p'cuer some man or men to stop the holes of the meeting hous by dawbing of them.

The same day Liftenant Capen and James Blake weer desiered to speak with Lift^{nt} Fisher and to p'cuer him to run the line from the blew hills to plimouth line.

[**219.**] At a meeting of the Select men at Srg^{nt} Blaks house the 27 of the 7th 1670. It was ordered that Ensigne Hale Srg^{nt} James Blake Sir Foster Srg^{nt} Wiswall John Withington and Consider Atherton should (together with Lift^{nt} Fisher and such as Brantry should send,) run the line from the top of the blew hils and soe at the head of Brantry and to plimouth bounds; the time appointed by Lift^{nt} Fisher is the next Second day being the theird of September if that day proue not fit, then the next day, and to meet at the lower end of the blew hill meaddow.

Md it is to be noted that this time appointed aboue said was disappointed by Lift^{nt} Fisher, he being taken off vpon Contry seruice.

At a meeting of the Select men the 14 (9) 1670 Timothy Tilston being formerly fined for defectiue fence 8^s – 9^d some time in the 3^d Mo. 1670 he engageth to pay in at Mr Poles two bushels of Corne in a short time and then he is discharged.

The same day John Wales made Complaint against some that transgressed a towne order about digging of Clay, Viz Clement Maxfeild about 4 or 5 load and Samuell Robinson two loads, John homes for Mr Ting.

The same day James Whit Constable for the yeer 69 brought in his accounts for the Contry Rate which was 47^{li} – 3 – 0 and for the County Rate 18^{li} – 12^s – 8^d.

Imp pd. to the Treasurer for which we haue his receipt . . . . 40 – 04 – 10
It. to Capt. Foster as Deputy . . . . . 03 – 08 – 00
It. to William Sumner as Deputy . . . . 02 – 10 – 00

It. to Nicholas Bolton towards his pay	. . .	01 – 00 – 00
It. to Mr Ting the County Treasurer	. . .	18 – 03 – 07
		65 – 06 – 05

The same day Nicholas Lawrance desiered that it might be p'posed to the Towne, for liberty to set vp a barne about the Clay pits : this was p'posed afterwards to the towne but not granted.

[**220.**] The same day J^{no} Hoppin was rated before the Selectmen to answer for his disorderly liueing.

Also Aurthor Cartwrights Sonne was then delt with all for his disorderly liueing.

The same day Reckoned with Nicholas Georg for expenses for the yeer p'ceeding which Came to $3^{li} - 9^s - 3^d$ besids some remainders of the las yeer which was not then paid by Constable Rigbee vntil he haue brought in his accounts.

At a generall Towne meeting the 5 (10) 1670 after the directory was read, the accounts of the rats was deliuered to the towne.

The same day it was agreed that Mr Stoughton should have 70^{li} alowed him for his labour in preaching for the yeer that is past.

The same day it was p'posed to the Towne whether they would haue William Clarks house and land and all his accommodations in Dorchester purchased to ly for the vse of the minestry in dorchester, and soe to continue for euer, and whether the towne will Engage to pay in specy as shalbe agreed with the said William Clarke, Further that if any p^t or the whole shal be Changed for the bettering of the thing, or more Conueniency of any of it, yet the Chang shall be for the vse of the minestry as aforesaid, and the Chang to be approued off by the Major p^t of the town before it be Changed.

The Vote was in the Affermatiue.

The Same day ther was Chosen for Selectmen } Captin Foster
Liftenant Capen
Ensigne Hale
Srg^{nt} clap.
Srg^{nt} blake

for Raters. William Sumner, William Pond, Daniell preston.
for Recorder. John Capen Senr.
Sup'uisors of high ways. J^{no} Gornell, Richard Withington.
and for the Neck Mr Mather.

[**221.**] The same day ther was Chosen Mr Stoughton, Elder Humphry, Richard Baker, Augustin Clement and Richard Leeds to Joyn with the Select men in the purchas of the house and land of william Clarks.

At a meeting of the Select men the 14th (9) 70.

Samuell Rigbee as Constable for the yeer 69 brought in his account of the towne Rate which was committed to him to Colect, the Sume wherof was $55^{li} - 0^s - 6^d$.

Imp. p^d to Capt. Foster and his Sonne for p^t of the first yeer Schooling Viz two months . } 04 – 16 – 00

It. to Liften^nt Capen for two yeers Recording and for alphabetting the books	04 – 00 – 00
and for Steuen Hoppen a days worke	00 – 01 – 06
It. to Ensigne Hale for Carting Clobord from puncapage	00 – 15 – 00
It. to Thomas Dauenport for the like work	00 – 15 – 00
It. to Timothy Tilstone	00 – 15 – 00
It. to Richard Withington	00 – 15 – 00
It. to Rogger Belleng as soe much ouer Rated	00 – 10 – 03
It. to William Trescots Rate not being due	00 – 04 – 06
It. to Jacob Hewens a dept due to ballance acc^t	00 – 04 – 09
It. to Mr Pole	08 – 19 – 00
It. to Nicholas Bolton 40^s towards his labor to ring the bell the rest p^d him out of the other rate and 30^s one the account of Deliueranc stock her keeping	03 – 10 – 00
It. to Nicholas Georg for expences	04 – 10 – 00
It. to Arthor Cartwright for entertaining of Deliuerance Stock	02 – 10 – 00
It. to William Sumner in p^t as deputy	01 – 11 – 00
It. to an Indian for a woolfe	00 – 10 – 00

[**222.**] At a meeting of the Select men the 12 10 70.

At the request of Incres Turner ther was granted vnto him liberty to haue two loads of timber towards his building out of the 500 acrs.

The same day it was agreed that the towne should be called together the next sixt day at 12 of the Clock to speak together further about the purchas of Willm Clarks hous, and the Constable Tho. Dauenport doe giue timly notice of it to the inhabetents.

At a meeting of the Select men at Capt. Fosters house the 16 10 70 in the morning It was then agreed that a warrant should be Isued out to the Raters to leuy a Rate of 70^{li} for the maintenance of the minestry.

Alsoe a towne Rate of 45^{li} for the vse of the towne and Schole.

At a publique Towne meeting one the same day 16, 10 70 being legally called together by warning from hous to hous it was put to the Vote whether the Select men should agree with a Schol Master for to teach children and youth for the yeer Ensewing.

the Vote was in the Afermatiue.

The day abouesaid It was fully agreed vnto and determined by a Vote that a Comittee should be chosen to buy the house and land which was Hudson Leuerits for the vse of the minestry and to remaine for that vse for euer.

The same day ther was Chosen Mr Stoughton, Elder Humphry Capt. Foster, Rich. Leeds and Richard Baker to be a Comittee for to transact the bussines abouesaid about buying the hous and land which was Hudson Leuerits and what they agree for shall be discharged by a towne Rate both for quallety and quantety.

[**223.**] These p^{r}sents witnesseth that I Timothy Tilston of Dorchester doe bind my self heyers executors administrators vnto the Select men of Dorchester and ther Successors from time to time to Secuer and saue harmles the Towne of Dorchester from all damage and Charges that may arise by meanes of James Bridgman my father in law his Inhabiting in Dorchester or any of his while he or they remaine in Dorchester as witnes my hand this fowerteenth day of Nouember 1670.

TIMOTHY TILESTONE.

WILLIAM SUMNER
THOMAS DEVENPORT senior.

13 of January 1683 : by order of the select men Timothy Tilstone is discharged of the aboue Written bond the party that he gaue bond for being Remoued out of towne.

Thes p'sents witnesseth that I Enoch Wiswell of Dorchester doe bind my self, heyers, executors and administerators vnto the Select men of Dorchester and their Successours from time to time to time to secuer and saue harmles the towne of Dorchester from all damage and Charges that may arise by meanes of John Memmary and his famely ther inhabitting in Dorchester or any of his while he or they remaine in Dorchester witness my hand this sixteenth day of Nouember 1670.

ENOCH WISWELL.

SAMUELL CAPEN
BARNARD CAPEN.

[**224.**] At a meeting of the Select men the 10th (11) 1670.
The Raters returned the Rates for minestry and towne Committed to them to make ; the Sume of the minesters Rate was 70^{li}-6^{s}-0. The Town Rate 46-8-10. The Sume of the Country Rate was 28^{li}-12^{s}-11^{d} being three quarters of a Single Rate.

The same day ther was order giuen out to the Constable to pay out of the Country Rate as followeth.

Imp. to the Treasurer or his order	22 – 08 – 10
It. to Nicholas Bolton for p^t of his labour	01 – 00 – 00
It. to Capt: Foster as deputy a p^t	02 – 00 – 00
It. to William Sumner as deputy a p^t	02 – 00 – 00
It. to Tho. Tolman Senr for p^t of his worke about wheels	00 – 05 – 00
It. to Jno Tolman for the like worke	00 – 01 – 08
It. to Nicholas George p^t of what is due to him for expenses the last yeere	00 – 10 – 00
It. Tho. Moadsly his Rate not p^d being poore	00 – 02 – 06
It. Samuell Minots Rate not p^d	00 – 01 – 00
	28 – 09 – 00
Rest due	00 – 03 – 10

Reckoned with Constable Tho Dauenport this 13 9 71 and ther is to due the Towne to balance 3^s – 10^d which is alowed him for warning towne meetings and he is discharged.

The same 10th (11) 70 the Constable was ordered to pay out of the Towne Rate as followeth

Imp to Mr Jno Foster as Schole Master	25 – 00 – 00
It. to Nicholas Bolton as p^t of his pay	02 – 00 – 00

It. to Anthony Newton towards the Child	05 – 00 – 00
It. to Nicholas George as p^t of his due	02 – 19 – 09
It. to Capt: Foster as deputy	03 – 07 – 00
It to William Sumner as deputy	03 – 07 – 00
It. to Tho. Tolman Senr for work as aboue	00 – 09 – 10
It. to Jn° Tolman	00 – 04 – 06
It. to Tho: Andrews for work at meeting hous	00 – 08 – 00
It. to Srg^{nt} Clap for runing the line	00 – 06 – 00
It. to Clement Maxfeild for the like	00 – 03 – 00
It. to William Pond for the like	00 – 03 – 00
It. to Nathaniell Clap for the like	00 – 03 – 00
It. to Ed. Pason for what he laid downe about stocks Child to Merrifeild	00 – 10 – 06
[**225.**] It. to Jn° Smith Senr for the like	00 – 02 – 00
It to Augustin Clement for the like	00 – 02 – 00
It. to Samuell Pale for the like	00 – 01 – 00
It. to Tho. Tilstone for the like	00 – 01 – 00
It. to Daniel preston for the like	00 – 01 – 00
It. to Robt. Spure on the same acc^{nt}	00 – 00 – 06
It. to Isake Joanes for oates to Merifeild	00 – 04 – 00
It. to Ensigne Hale for mending the pound	00 – 02 – 00
and for his goeing to Puncapag Cart	00 – 14 – 00
It. to William Pond for worke at meeting house	00 – 08 – 03
It. to James Robinson for goeing with stocks Child	00 – 01 – 06

The same day Henery Leadbetter was Caled before the Select men to answer for his receauing Jonathan Birch into the towne contrary vnto a towne order.

The same day ther was granted to Henery Leadbetter liberty to take out of the 500 acrs 20 trees not exceeding

At a meeting of the Select men the 13 12 1670 at the motion of Edward Pason ther was granted vnto him libertie to take two trees in the way between his farme and the 20 acre lots or some wher ther about prouided that he nor any other p'son shall fale that tree about Thomas Grant's house, but it shall stand for shaddow.

At the same time ther was granted to Thomas Grant that on Condition that he pay his fine of 5^s (for faling a tree which he took contrary to order) he paying it by that time Corne is marchentable after the next haruest, then that tree standing by his house shall not bee granted to any man.

The same day ther was granted to Thomas Grant liberty to take a walnut tree for fier wood in the way between his lot and Ed. Pasons farme.

[**226.**] At a meeting of the Select men at Capt: Fosters house the 15 12 70 it was ordered that a warrant should be Isued out to the Constable to giue notice to the freemen to meete the first monday in March to bring in Vots for Nomination of Majestrats and County Treasurer. &c. and to the inhabetants for other bussines.

At the same time it was ordered that ther should be a Rate of about 28 pounds leuyed vpon the proprietors of the land beyond the blew hils for to make good o^r p'mise of a gratuety vnto the Indians for Confermation of Kitchamakins deede of sale, and Lift^{nt}

Capen was desiered to draw it vp at the proportion of $8^d\frac{1}{2}$ p' acre for soe many acrs as each man is to haue in one deuission and the farmers p'portionably Viz: the tweluth p^t of each farme to be rated after that p'portion.

At a Towne meeting the 6 (1) 16 $\frac{70}{71}$ ther was Chosen for Deputies Captin Clap and Lif^t John Capen.

And for Comissioners to end small Causes Capt Foster, Lift. Capen, Willm Sumner.

And for Constables Nathaniell Clap and Timothy Tilston.

The same day at the Motion of some It was Voted and apointed that Elder Humfry, Ensigne Hale, Jno Gornell, James Blake and Steuen Minot should Vew the Way from Goodman Toplifs towards the eight acre lots whether the way may be relinquished or whether gates at the p'tition of each lote may not Suffice, and to make their returne to the Select men to be p'posed to the Towne.

The same day it was p'posed to the Towne whether they would alow any more to Henery Merrifeild than 5^s p' weeke for the keeping the Child of Stock.

the Vote was Negatiue.

[**227.**] The same day It was p'posed to the Towne by Augustin Clement (with reference to a habetation for the minestry) that if the towne will lend him one hundred and fifty pounds Viz: soe much in the first payment as the money p^t comes to, and the rest to make vp one hundered and fifty pound in the Second pay ment, then he the said Augustin Clement will purches William Clarks accomodations; and if in Case Mr Flint liks to haue it, he shall: at the price that it Cost, and if not, then the said Augustin Clement shall be at libertie to sell it againe, and returne to the towne againe the one hundered and fifty pound as soone as Mr Flint refuseth it, vnless the towne will buy it for themselues.

The Vote was in the Affermatiue
noe man discenting

At a meeting of the Select men the 13 (1) $\frac{70}{71}$

John Smith Senr made request for libertie to take 400 of Rails out of the 500 acrs but the Select men thought good to grant but 200 railes.

Wheeras it is found by experience and Complaints being made to the Select men of the great Dammadg that is done by Sheep goeing at liberty, and not being vnder the hand of a keeper or sheepherd, and likewise in the mornings and euenings, before and after they are vnder the hand of the Sheepherd: It is therefore ordered by the Select men that from hence forth what soeuer sheepe or lambs shall be found going at libertie, from vnder the hand or Care of a keeper, Especially being found in any Enclosier of Cornfeild pastuer or Meadow, they shall pay for euery such sheep or lamb two pence besids due damadges to be paid to such as shall find them transgressing this order, and this we Conseaue may easily be p^{r}uented, if the sheep Masters would agree together to make some fold or folds into which the Shepherd may bring the sheepe in the euening, and ther take them in the morning, this order to be in force euery yeere from the first of March vnto the last of October vntill the Select men see Cause to alter it.

[228.] The same day ther was appointed for fence Vewers.

for the great lots from Captins neck to goodman Tolmans	{ John Wales { Samuell Pale
for the rest of the great lots to Naponset .	{ Samuell Robertson { Benjamin Leeds
for the 20 acre lots	{ Jn° Merifeild { Jn° Withington
for the feild behind James Bird . . .	{ Jn° Blackman { Jn° Bird.
for the feild behind Mrs Joanes and before Enock wiswels old house	{ Isack Joanes { Israell Mead
for the feild behind Mr Stoughtons . .	{ Jn° Baker { Amiell Weeks
for the Neck of land	{ James Whit { Joseph Homes
for Clearing the neck of land of Catle .	Tho. Andrews Junr

for Cleering the great lots Robt Sanders and he to keepe the key of the pound till the Select men take furder order.

The same day ther was granted to Jn° Homes libertie to haue timber out of the 500 acrs to build a house of about 20 foot long and 18 foot wide.

Alsoe ther was granted to Tho: Dauenport Senr libertie to take about 12 load of timber from the same place towards the building a barne.

The same day it was agreed that al Cornefeilds should be Cleered by the first of Aprill and fence vewers to Vew fences by the 2^d or 3^d of aprill.

At a generall Towne meeting being orderly caled together one the 17. 2. 1671 to Consider of Mr Flints settlement, It was p'posed to the inhabetants as an incurredgment to Mr Flint, whether they are willing that Mr Flint should be a minester to preach the word to the whole towne, and this without any Violation to the law Concerning Church officcers.

The Vote was in the Affermatiue
not a man against it.

[229.] The same day it was put to the Vote whether ther should be a rate made of one hundred pounds in money and leuyed vpon the inhabetants according to a Just p'portion as in other rates, for the purchassing or p'cuering of a comfortable habetation for a minester, according to that law, title Ecclesiasticall, page 26 and Sec. 26, which Enjoyns eury towne, soe to doe, and if in Casse Mr Flint doe purchas or p'cuer himself such an habetation to his content, and take off the Towne from their engagement to Augustin Clement (bearing date the 6 (1) $\frac{70}{71}$) and take office in the Church, for the carrying on the worship of God amongst vs, then he the said Mr Flint shall haue this hundred pounds for his owne towards his setlement.

The Voate was in the Affermatiue.

Alsoe it was Voated and agreed vnto that a rate should be p'sently made and Colected and paid by the 25 of May next, and those that can to pay the whole, at the day p'rfixt, or at least the one halfe of the hundered pounds, but those that cannot pay the whole now, It is agreed that the remainder shall be paid by the time of the second payment, which will be by September in the yeere 1672.

The same day it was agreed that the former town raters shall make this rate, and alsoe it was agreed that Elder Humperey, and Deacon Jn° Capen should receaue this rate and giue discharges of what they recaue.

The same day Nicholas George was alowed to keepe an ordinary If the Honrd Court please to admitt of it.

The same day It was granted by the towne, that at the returne of the Comittee, appointed for that purpose: Viz That ther should be gates made at each pertition, betweene man and man cross that way which leads from Clement Toplif, vnto the 8 acre lots, for an experiment, which if it proue p'jedicciall to the towne for want of lying oxen, then it shall afterward be fenced out on boath sids.

The same day Nathanell Clap was Chosen Constable in Mr Pattens steed.

[**230.**] At a meeting of the Select men the 8 (3) 71 a p'sentment was brought to the Select men of defectiue fence vnder the hands of Samuell Pale and Jn° Wales, fence Vewers of p^t of the great lots, Viz that part next the towne as followeth

Jn° Blake at Captins neck two rods James Minot one rod and $\frac{1}{2}$ the fence belonging to the pastuer of William Clarke, Willm Pond and Willm Trescot which is wholy defectiue: fence belonging to farnworths land 6 rod at the end of his pastuer Jn° Minot 6 rod, more of quarter master Smith's fence 6 rod Mr Timothy Mather 7 rod: being dated the 8 (3) 71.

The same day it was Concluded that whereas ther is a man that sojornes at John Minots a warrant should be Isued out to the Constable to warne the man that he either dep^t the towne, or elce to come to the Select men and to giue an account of his being heer.

one the same day It was ordered that a warrant should be Isued out to the Constable to take by distress or otherwise of the p'sons whos fence is defectiue in the great lots 6^d p' rod, which is but the one half of what is otherwise by order due. but in Case it be not made vp by the 15th of this Instant then they shall pay 18^d p' rod for as much as they shall leaue vnsufficciently mad vp Viz: of Jn° blake at Captins neck 2 rod, of James Minot for one rod and half of the occapiers of William Clark's lot for 8 rod of william pond and William Trescot for 12 rod, Richard Baker for the fence belonging to farnworth's lot 6 rod and for the fence belonging to butlers lot 4 rod: of Quarter Master Jn° Smith for 16 rod at the end of his pastuer and 6 rod at another place: of Jn° Minot for 6 rod: of Mr Timothy Mather for 7 rod.

The same day it was ordered that a warrant should be Isued out to the Constable to ap'hend Steuen Hoppen Junr and p'sent him before some Majestrate according as the law requiers p 38 Title Idlenes.

The same day it was ordered that notice should be giuen to Joseph Birch that hee for beare frequenting the ordinary according as the order of generall Court requiers in the Casse and alsoe that

Nicholes George be requiered not to suffer the p'son aboue said to frequent his house.

The same day it was ordered that wheras at a meeting of the p'prietors of the land in Dorchester the 14th (12) 65 It was Voted and agreed vnto that vppon the deuission of the land beyond the blew hils. If in Case ther should be any [**231.**] Charges fall on any p^t or the whole of that land, ther to be deuided, that then all should bear a share by p'portion in that Charge. Now wheras ther is already Charges to be expended vpon that land, not only that which is agreed vpon for the Indians, but also for the laying out of the land in p'ticular alotments, Now it is therfore ordered that if any p'son or p'sons (who expect to haue land ther) shall neglect or refus to pay their just p'portion to all Charges vpon seasonable demand, that hee or they soe neglecting or refusing, shall loose or goe without that land which hee or they doe ther expect.

At a publique Towne meeting orderly called together on the 27 (4) 1671 The towne did by a Vote desier and appoint the select men for to p'sent in a Cours of law against such as haue don or shall intrench vpon any of o^r lands beyond the blew hils, and on this sid of the pattent line.

At a meeting of the Select men the 10th 6 71 at Captin Fosters hous, By vertue of a warrant which came from the County Court last, directed to the Constable for the disposing of Steuen and John Hoppen vnto seruice by orders from the Select men. It is ordered by the Select men that the said Steuen and John Hoppen doe take a fortnights time for to p'uid them some Masters, such as the Select men shall a'proue off, and if not then to returne againe vnder the Charge and Custody of the Constable to be disposed off as the warrant expresseth.

At a meeting of the Select men the 11th (7) 71.

Nicholas Bolton made motion againe that he might haue liberty to sell Cider, the answer was Negatiue.

The same day a warrant was Isued out to Constable Tilstone to giue notice vnto Henery Roberts for to depart the towne, who is now abiding at danill Ellens.

The same day the Select men called Steuen Huppen Junr before them and Enquiered how he had disposed himselfe in reference vnto the Courts order, whos answer was that he had agreed with Joseph Long to attend his boate but being not aproued off by the Select men he p'mised by the last day of this weeke to sett himself vnder another man, the which liberty was granted him, p'uided he doe bring it vnder the hand of the man that he agrees with that he haue soe don, and to such a man as the Select men shall ap'ue off.

[**232.**] The same day Frances Bale was called before the Select men, and his fine demanded for Entertaining his Brother in law Phillip Searle and his famely in his house without licence from the Select men, whose answer was that he was speedyly to remoue his dwelling to Rocksbery.

The same day Samuell Rigby was called vppon for the remainder of the Colection of the Rate Comitted to him to gather, the greatest p^t wherof was due to Mr Mather.

The same day petter Lyon being caled before the Select men, and at that time desiered liberty for to entertaine peter Greene of Concord into his famely for one month which was granted him, p'uided he Cleer the towne of him at that time.

The same day a warrant was Isued out to Constable Tilstone the Contents wherof is as followeth.

To Constable Timothy Tilstone of Dorchester.

Wheras we vnderstand that Seauerall tracts of land is laid out to Seauerall p'sons, Viz : to Mr Thomas Kellond and others, to the great p'jedice of our rights if Suffered, you are therfore requiered in his majesties name that with conuenient speede you goe vp to wadeing Riuer and therabouts, and take with you such asistance as shall be needfull, and that you or they, doe demollish any bounds and marks ther made vpon any of the lands therabout wadeing riuer wodcock well, or elce where within our bounds, which are not made by any order of this towne, or any Authorrized by them, and also to seaz any hay or timber cutt vpon any of the said land and to dispose of the same to any p'son or otherwise as the Caus may requier : And also to Sumon any p'son or p'sons whom you shall find trespassing vpon any of o^r lands to appeare before some Majestrate or the Select men to answer it. Alsoe to demand of Thomas Clap and parker and such as by contract haue mowed grass in o^r Meadows, pay for what they haue mowen, and this you are not to faile and to make returne, and in so doeing this our warrant vnder o^r hands in the behalf of the towne shall be yor discharge.

This is a true	HOPSTILL FOSTER.
Coppi of the orige-	J^{no} CAPEN SEN^R
nall as attests	RICHARD HALL
JOHN CAPEN Record^r	SAMUELL CLAP
	JAMES BLAKE.

[233.] These p'sents witnessesth that I Samuell Paule of Dorchester doe bind my self heyers executors and Administrators vnto the Select men of Dorchester and their Successours from time to time in the Sume of theirty pounds to Secure and saue harmless the towne of Dorchester from all damadg and Charges that may arise by the meanes of Alice Morrell her coming in to this towne to inhabit heer as wittness my hand this eighth day of December 1671.

SAMUELL PAULL.

witness heerunto.
SAMUELL CAPEN
BARNARD CAPEN.

At a meeting of the Select men the 13 9 71

Thomas Dauenport as Constable for the yeer 1670 made vp his account as in page 224.

The same day Constable Haws Came to make vp his account but it was not fully Cleered.

The same day Lift^t Jno Capen gaue in an account of recepts and disburstments by him made as in p. 134. 135.

DORCHESTER TOWN RECORDS.   179

The Towne Creditʳ
Imp̄ Recc. by me John Capen Senʳ of Viall of
Deadham for Rent for Remote Meaddows for
the yeer 68 . . . . . .   0 – 6 – 0
It. Recc of Samuell Parker for the same yeer . 0 – 6 – 0
                                                ─────────
                                                0 – 12 – 0

It. Recc. into my hands 44ˡⁱ and half of wooll
at 10ᵈ p ˡⁱ on the Childs accᵗ . . .   1 – 17 – 1
and 12ˡⁱ of tobackoh at 4ᵈ – pˡⁱ . . . .   0 – 4 – 2
It. Recc. 5ˢ in money of Joseph Long a fine for
defectiue fence of which ther was 1ˢ pᵈ to Constable Dauenport and 1ˢ the Captin had to ex-
pend on the Indians and 1ˢ for Liquors for the
Jorney to wading Riuer ther remains .   0 – 2 – 0
It. Recc. of Nicholas Lawrance in money for
1000 of shingls . . . . .   0 – 14 – 0
It. Recc. into my hands 200 of yron which
Came from Tanton for the Church being the
first yeers p'duce and sold for . . .   2 – 8 – 0
                                                ─────────
          Sume Totall . . . . . .   3 – 17 – 3

The 13 9 71 at a meeting of the Select men this accᵗ was p'eused and accepted and ther remains due to Jnᵒ Capen Senʳ nineteene shillings.

[235.]   The Towne Deptʳ
Imp̄. due to me Jnᵒ Capen on ballance of accᵗ
for the yeer 69 . . . . . .   0 – 0 – 9
It. laid out to Merryfeild a bl of peas towards
the keeping the Child . . . .   0 – 3 – 6
It. for a pa of shows for his wife . . .   0 – 4 – 6
It. pᵈ Nicholas Bolton for moneys he laid downe 0 – 6 – 0
It. dˡ to Capt. Foster 4ˡˢ of the Tobackoh .   0 – 1 – 6
It. dˡ to Ensigne Hale 4ˡˢ of the Tobackoh .   0 – 1 – 6
It. dew for my Jorney to Wadeing Riuer two
days hors and man . . . . .   0 – 6 – 0
It. for money laid down to the Sachem .   0 – 8 – 0
It. for money laid out to Tom the Indian and
other neccesary expences besids what we had
at Sister Georges . . . . .   0 – 3 – 0
It. pᵈ for the hier of a hors to goe to Deadham 0 – 1 – 0
It. laid out for a quier of paper for the towne 0 – 0 – 6
It. dew for Recording the yeer 70 . . .   1 – 0 – 0
It. for Runing the line between Rocksbery and
vs two days wᵗʰ the Instruments . .   0 – 6 – 0
It. pᵈ Capt Foster for two bls Corne and one bl
of Pease which he let merryfeld haue towards
the keeping the Child . . . .   0 – 10 – 6
It. pᵈ Ensigne Hale for a bl of pease on the
same accᵗ . . . .   0 – 3 – 6
It. pᵈ broʳ Sumner for 1ˢ money he laid downe 0 – 1 – 0

It. p^d Nathanell Clap on the Same acc^t.	0 – 1 – 0
It. p^d Capt. Foster for money he laid downe to the Sachem	0 – 8 – 0
It. p^d Ensigne Hale for the same acc^t.	0 – 4 – 0
It p^d Nicholas Whit for bringing the yron.	0 – 6 – 0
Totall Debt	4 – 16 – 3
Creddit as on the other sid	3 – 17 – 3
Rest due	0 – 19 – 0

[236.] At a generall Towne meeting on the 4 10 71

After the Directory was read The Confession of Aurther Cartwright (Concerning the wrong done against Quarter Master John Smith and his Sonne) it was published according as the Court Enjoyned him.

The same day William Sumner made a motion to the towne, that they would grant him about 12 or fowerteene rods of ground at the North East end of his bearne, the Towne granted his motion and appointed Tho: Swift Senr Augustin Clement and Richard Leeds to Vew the same and set it out and make returne.

The same day Rich Leeds, Augustin Clement and Richard Withington weer Nominated and Chosen by the towne for to take Care of the repaiering of the meeting hous for the p^{r}esent occasion that we may Comfortably come to gether for the worship of god, and they to be paid out of the towne rate. the glass to be taken care for by the Constable.

The same day it was p'pounded to the towne whether they would haue a rate of one hundred pound to be leuyed out of which for the maintenance of the minestry ninty pound Viz Seaunty pound for Mr Flint and twenty pound for Mr Stoughton for his labour amongst vs for fower months as alsoe rate free for the same rate and the other ten pounds towards the repaire of the meeting-house or the like vse and that one fowerth p^t of the whole to be paid in money.

The Vote was in the affermatiue.

The same day ther was chosen for Select men Mr Stoughton, Captin Foster, Lift^t Capen, Ensigne Hale, William Sumner.

for Recorder Lift^t Jno Capen

for Raters — Srg^{ut} Pond Srg^t Ja Blak Srg^t Preston.

Sup'uisors Jno Gornell, Richard Withington and for the neck Srg^t Clap.

[237.] At a meeting of the Select men the 11th 10 1671.

It was agreed that an order should be sent out to the Raters to leuy on the inhabetants one hundred pound of which 90^{li} for the minestry and 10^{li} for other vses.

Also a towne Rate of 50^{li} 11^d and both thes Rates to be made and Returned vnder their hands by the next meeting of the Select men. also a Rate about pork – 0 – 15 – 8

The same day Joseph Long was sent for to answer for entertaining of a maid or yong woman in his house and seruice which was not of any good report; his answer was she was to depart the towne the next day.

The same day it was ordered that a warrant should be directed to the Constable for to goe vp to Capt. Claps farme wher Henery Merrifeild doe liue and to enquier whether his daughter which marryed funnell be abiding at his hous, which if she be, then to demand or take by distress ten shillings for his Entertaining her Contrary vnto the towne order.

The same day it was agreed vnto that a warrant should be directed to the Constable to Sum̃on Timothy Wales and his wife, and his two lesser boys, to appeare before the Select men at their next meeting, to be enquiered after Concerning their Education and improuement of their time, and peter Lyon and his wife, and Jn° Plum and Arthor Cartwright and Robt Stiles all on the same account they or some of theirs.

At a meeting of the Select men the 8 (11) 1671.

Arthor Cartwright (being formerly Som̃oned) appeared before the Select men; his answer Conserning his Sonne was, that he was about to put him apprentice to a kindsman of his that is a Sea-man and soe was dismissed.

The same day Robt Stiles being Sum̃oned appeared also before the Select men to answer for their Idleness, and vpon examination it was found that both hee and his wife haue not improued their time to the aduantag of their famely as they ought and ther vpon was aduertized to reforme or elce to be further p'ceeded with as the law requiers.

[238.] The same day Peter Lyon appeared and gaue an accoupt that his Sonns did follow their employment and that for the time to come he would looke dillegently after them.

The same day Timothy Wales appeared without his sonns and could giue noe good accoumpt of that for which he was sent for, but his words and answers weer very offensiue and Contemptuous vnto the Select men, and therfore it was ordered, that both he and his two Sons be againe Sum̃oned to appeare and to giue an acompt how he answers the law title Children and youth:

The same day Richard Withington and Thomas Tilstone in the name of others p'sented a wrighting, wherin they did desire, that the remoueing of the meetinghous may be p'moted and taken into serious Consideration, and that the Vote of the towne may not be forgotten, or neglected.

The same day Richard Butt appeared to answer for his entertaining of his father in law Steuen Hoppen, whos answer was, that he did not entertaine him, but haue enformed him that it is not the mind of the Select men that he should continue at Tomsons Iland or elce where in dorchester, but for to turne him out of doares, he could not Considering the relation that is between them, but he would willingly be ridd of him if he could.

The same day the wife of Henery Merrifeild appeared before the Select men, to answer for entertaining of their daughter Funnell, Contrary to towne order, whose answer was, that she was their daughter and Could not turne her out of doars this winter time but she would willingly returne to her husband as soone as a passadg p'sents; But they weer not approued in entertaining her, but the penalty of the town order the Select men would remitt and would leaue it to the County Court to determine the thing, if in Casse she be not gon before;

The same day John Plume appeared to answer for his negligence in his Calling, but Could giue noe good acompt for himself, or for not disposing of his Sonne to some Master.

[**239.**] The same day John Capen Junr made request for to take 150 railes and 30 post off from the 500 acre, which was granted him.

The same day Thomas Swift Junr as Select man of Melton, Came before the Select men, to be resolued in a question Conserning a way runing through Goodman Vose his farme from John Gils barrs vnto the fowerteenth lott, whether ther should not be alowance for the land which the way taks vpp; In Answer therunto the Select men of Dorchester saith, that the vse of the way and the right therunto was long before goodman Vosse, or Mr Glouer had a farme granted or laid out, and therfore we Conclud that when the farme was laid out, ther was alowance in measuer for the high way, and nothing demanded for alowance euer since vntill of late.

The same day Lift^nt Capen and William Sumner weer desiered and empowered to setle the bussines about the Comon Swamp at Melton, and to Issue and determin matters therabouts.

At a meeting of the Select men at the house of Nicholas George the 16 11 1671 Timothy Wales and his Sonns, being Sumoned appeared before the Select men, and upon examination of the boys they weer found to be very Ignorant, and not able to read, and being admoneshed was dismissed at that time, only he made some acknowledgment of his offensiue words and Carridge the last day of meeting and that in wrighting which remains on file.

The same day it was Concluded that Nathan Bradly and Thomas Birch should be sumoned to appeare before the Select men at their next meeting.

The same day it was Concluded that the Elder and Deacon should draw vp a list of the members of the Church, and leauy or p'portion the expences at the ordaination; and the expences for entertaining of Mr Flint on the estates of the said members.

The same day it was ordered that the Rates both for Contry and towne should be deliuered to the Constables and they ordered to disburst out of them such depts as are dew to Contry and towne.

[**240.**] At a meeting of the Select men the 12 12 1671

It was agreed by the Select men that the Scholmaster should be agreed with for to teach such as shalbe sent vnto him, and Lift^t Capen, Ensigne Hale and William Sumner are appointed to speake with Mr Jno Foster Concerning that matter.

The same day it was ordered that ther should be a towne meeting called on the 23 of this Instant Feb: to p'mote subscriptions for the Collidg and to conferr about the meeting hous and Stanton about a dry herd.

The same time it was ordered that Tho. Birch should be Somoned by warrant to the Constable to appear before the Select men at their next meeting to give an acompt of his orderly walking.

The Same day Robt. Stanton appeared before before the Select men and tendered his seruice to keep a dry herd of Catle, and if he haue to the number of Six score he will keepe them for 2ˢ 3ᵈ p' head and in Case he haue not soe many from our towne then he may take in from other towns vnto the fore said number and noe more, but if the towne sends more then Six score he is to keepe them at the Rate of 2ˢ 3ᵈ p' head and to begin at May day next and to keepe to the end of September; and this to be p'posed to the towne at their next meeting.

At a generall Towne meeting the 26 12 71 It was Voted in the Affermatiue that Mr. Stoughton, Captain Foster, Lifteⁿᵗ Capen, Ensigne Hall, William Sumner, Augustin Clement and Richard Withington: Thes men or the Major part of them are appointed to Consider and pitch vpon a place on the Rocky hill for the meeting hous to stand vppon and make report therof to the next towne meeting, and the place being agreed vpon, they shall haue full power to determine all other matters referring to the remoueall of this p'sent hous, or if they see it best the erecting of one wholy ꭥew.

The same day it was put to the Vote that Mʳ Flint might haue ;iberty to take in that Corner of the Com̄on which lys on the backꭥid of Liftenant Capens and Steuen Minots pastuers or feilds, by running a fence ouer from goodman Clements his feild to his pastuer, and the same soe enclosed to improue for pastuer, as long as the town shall Judge it Conuenient, reseruing a drift way for p'sons [**241.**] Concerned and that Liftenᵗ Capen William Sumner and Augustin Clements doe state how the Crose fence shall run most conueniently p'uided and it is heerby vnderstood, that the towne reserues a libertie to digg or take off stones from this said land as formerly.

The Vote was in the affermatiue.

At a meeting of the freemen the 8ᵗʰ (1) 7½ ther was Chosen for Deputys for the yeer Ensuing, Captain Hopstill Foster and william Sumner and Capt. Foster was Chosen Com̄issioner for to carry in the Votes.

The same time ther was Chosen for Constables John Blackman and Samuell pale, but afterwards Jnᵒ Blackman being a Dromer at the Castle got off and Obediah Swift was Chosen in his steed.

At a meeting of the Select men the 11ᵗʰ (1) 7 1 − 2 It was Concluded that the fence about the great lots should be maintained and vpheld for the yeer ensewing as formerly, by the p'ticuler p'prietors of the feild.

The same day ther was appointed for fence Vewers for the great lots

from Captains neck to goodman Tolmans	{ Richard Leeds { John Breck
for the rest of the great lots to Naponset	{ Thomas Tolman Senʳ { Tho: Trot Senʳ
for the twenty acre lots . . .	{ Tho Grant { Robt. Stiles
for the feild behind James Bird . .	{ Obediah Haws { James Whit

for the feild behind Mrs Joans and before Enoch Wiswells old hous	{ Srg^nt Clap { Augustin Clement
for the feild behind Mr Stoughton	{ Jno Withington { Isacke Joanes
for the Neck of land	{ Nicholas Clap { Srg^nt Blake

for the Cleering of the neck of land of Catell: Jacob Hewens.
for cleering the great lots Robt Sanders and he to keepe the key of the pound till the select men shall take furder order.

The same day it was agreed that al Corne feilds shall be cleared by the first of Aprill and fence Vewers to vew fences by the 2^d or 3^d of Aprill.

The same day ther was granted to Jno Farington liberty to take one hundred of railes on the Comons at or beyond the blew hils.

[242.] The same day a letter was concluded to be sent to the Select men of Melton to Enforme them of some abuss that is done by taking in of the way leading to the meddows some wher beyond William Blaks, which is offenciue to vs as well as to some of Melton.

At a meeting of the Select men the 13 (3) 72.

John Smith Senr appeared and desiered to haue his lot laid out about the blew hils, which was omitted through some mistake to be laid out when other lots weer laid out.

The Select men doe order that he shall git some man or men to lay it out according to the same forme that other lots weer laid and according to his p'portion which he should then haue had, and the Select men doe order him to p'cuer Liften^nt John Capen and amiell weiks to lay it out or either of them.

The same day in answer to a letter which is on file sent from Melton in reference vnto the way leading ouer brush-hill, The Select men of Dorchester doe determine, that either the way shall run as it was first laid out, or elce if the way be remoued from the Corner of Ebenezer Claps fence vnto the Corner of William Blaks lott wher his barrs are: then Ebenezer Clapp shall be at the charge to remoue William Blaks fence, and sett it in its Right place, and make it sufficcient as now it is p'uided that William Blake shall be at the Charge of adding soe much fence as is requisit by means of the way runing more angular, and in case that the way run wher it was first laid out, that then William Blake shall sett in soe much of his fence as now stands in the high way.

The same day it was ordered that the Constable should be ordered for to Colect the remainder of the hundred pound money Rate which was for the purchasing of Mr Flints habetation.

The same day at a motion of Henery Garnesy and others about some land at the end of the great lots, it was Concluded that p'sons Conserned should appeare before the Select men at their next meeting for to adjetate that bussiness to which end notice was giuen to Samuell Robinson and Jno Minot and who elce may be Conserned therein the which remains on file.

The 22 4th 1672 the Select men mett att the house of Lift^nt John Capen (in reference vnto the determination of the County

Court) and gaue their ap'bation vnto the placing of Mary the daughter of John Plum vnto seruice with praiseuer Turner of Northampton p'uided it be not for less than one whole yeer or more if they two doe so agree.

[**243.**] At a meeting of the Select men the 28th (4) 1672 at the house of the Hon^{re} Mr Stoughton.

The Select men haueing sent for John Plum and his daughter Mercy, and finding that his said daughter being marryed to Thomas Chub of Beuerlee, and being alsoe neere the time of her deliuery is not p'uided for by her said husband, nor taken home to him, but continues heer with her father, contrary to good order, and to the hazarding of a charge vpon the towne, doe therefore order and requier, that the said Mercy Chub doe spedily within Six or eight days leaue this towne, and betake herself to her said husband. And doe also warne and order the said John Plum that he noe longer entertaine his said daughter, but hasten her to her husband as aforesaid vpon the penalty by the Town order in that Case p'uided, and of being complained of further to Authorety that soe the towne may be saued harmeless.

The same day The Select men did lett vnto Samuell parker of Deadham for this yeer all that Meaddow vp in the Contry neer to woodcocks well, which formerly he did vs to Mow saueing what was laid out latly to Rodger Billeng thes are therfore to licence and authoriz the said parker to Mow the said meaddow, and for what hay he shall ther make he shall pay one shilling p' load and we doe heerby inhibit all other p'sons from intermeddleing with this meaddow to his p'jedice, and doe engage to maintaine him in the vse and improuement of it. Signed by

         WILLIAM STOUGHTON
         HOPESTILL FOSTER
         JOHN CAPEN
         WILLIAM SUMNER
         RICHARD HALE

M^d the Sixt day of the Select mens meeting which was the 10 (4) 72 ther was nothing done which was to be Recorded.

At a meeting of the Select men the 10th of the 7th m^o 72.

It was ordered that Amiell Weeks together with the Asistance of Lift. John Capen, William Sumner and Ensigne Richard Hale should Run the head line of the great lots, with Referrance to Henery Garnesy, Robt Spurr, Edward Wiett and others who are damnefied by the Contry high way which runs through their deuissions, that soe they who are damnefied may receaue Sattisfaction out of that way which was alowed by the town.

[**244.**] The same day ther was granted to Increace Turner liberty to haue 100 of Railes and posts sutabl out of the fiue hundred acrs.

The same day ther was granted to Samuell Capen liberty to take two or three load of timber out of the 500 acrs towards the building of an house.

At a meeting of the Select men the 4th (8) 1672 at Mr Stoughtons house it was Concluded that the Comittee which was appointed to Vew a place for the meeting hous to stand on, shall meet for that end, the first Monday after the Gen^{rll} Court is ended which is now to begin the next weeke, to meet about two of the Clock in the afternoone at the Schole-house.

The same day Richard Butt was Called before the Select men, to answer for his Entertaining of Steuen Hoppin Junr, whose answer was that the said Hoppen was gon from him, and that his Master Paine had sent for him to imploy him.

The same day it was ordered that notice should be sent to the Sup'uisors of the high-ways, that they forth with see them repaired.

The same day it was ordered that a warrant should be Isewed out to the Constable for to Colect by distres or otherwise the remainders of the money Rate which was for the purchasing of a habetation for Mr Flint.

The same day Constable Tilston Came to the Select men to make vp his acc^t of the Contry Rate Comitted to him to gather for the year 1671 the Sume of which Rate was 28^{li} 4^s 4^d.

Imp̄ he brought the Tresuerers Recept for . .	25 – 15 – 10
It. pd to Capt. Foster a dept due to him about Court expences	2 – 0 – 0
It. pd to William Sumner	0 – 1 – 8
	27 – 17 – 6
The Constable Tilston Remains dept^r to the Towne	0 – 6 – 10

[245.] The same day Constable Nathaniell Clape Came to make vp his account of the Town Rate Committed to him to Colect for the yeer 1671 the Summ of which Rate was 50^{li} 3^s 8^d and a smale Rate for pork, 15^s 8^d.

M^d that which the Constable was appointed to discharge did amount vnto 7^{li} 6^s 8^d more then the Sume of the Rate Viz: the glass for the meeting hous . . . . . 4^{li} 14^s 6^d and other Charges.

Imp. paid or ordered to be p^d to Anthony Newton for the child he tooke	05 – 00 – 00
It. to Nicholas Bolton for the meeting hous work	03 – 00 – 00
It. to Nicholas George for Expences . . .	03 – 15 – 00
It. to Capt. Clap as Deputy	02 – 05 – 00
It. to Lift^{nt} Capen as Deputy	02 – 05 – 00
It. to him also for Recording for the yeer 71 .	01 – 00 – 00
and to him also a dept due to him last yeer .	00 – 19 – 00
It. to Ensigne Hale for helping about Roger Bellenges farme 6^s and goeing to wadeing Riuer 9^s to demolesh marks	00 – 15 – 00
Also to him also for another Jorney to the same place	00 – 06 – 00
It. to Roger Belleng for 4 days at Wadeing Riuer	00 – 12 – 00
It. to Timothy Tilston the Constabl 4 days . .	00 – 12 – 00
It. to Samuell Rigbe 4 days	00 – 12 – 00
It. to Thomas Dauenport Junr 4 days . . .	00 – 12 – 00

It. to Amiell Weiks about Rogers farme . . 00 – 06 – 00
It. to James Blake for his Jorney to plimoth . 00 – 05 – 06
It. to Joseph Long for his hors to plimoth . . 00 – 05 – 06
Thus fare he p'ceeded at this time.

[**246.**] The Same day the Comittee appointed for the looking out a place for the meeting hous vpon Rocky hill, did on the day abouesaid (Viz this 11 (9) 72) Vew the place or places ther about and did conclud of a place neer vnto the lime-kilme and soe to make returne therof to the Towne at the next publique towne meeting.

At a publique Towne meeting the 2 (10) 1672.

After the directory was orderly read, ther was some adjetation about changing a day of the Select mens meeting: Viz: Wheras the Second Month by the directory is exempted as one of the fower months; It is now agreed vnto by Voate that the theird month is exempted from meeting, and insteed therof they are to meet the Second Month for the time to come and it shalbe soe ordered in the directory.

The same day it was Voted that one of the Constables for the time being from time to time shall attend the Select men at their Seauerall days meeting for to atend such seruices as the Select meet shall haue occassion for them; and for their encuredgment they shall haue their diners at the towne charge.

The same day it was p'posed to the Towne whether it weer not meete to Chouse yeerly a man to be a Treasuerer, whose worke or office should be to take all accompts from Constables for Rates or fines or what other accompts doe belong vnto the towne, and to make disburstments for the towns vse and in Case of non payments by any, for to Isue out warrants to the Constables to distreine; and the Tresurer to giue an acompt to the Select men at the end of the yeere, or at any time that the Select men shall see meete to requier it and from them to haue discharges.

This being put to the Vote it was Voted in the affermatiue.

The same day Nicholas Clap p'posed whether it weer not good to p'serue the latter feed in feilds vnto the p'prietors.

Also at the same time the towne was Enformed of some damedge that brantree men doth doe vpon o'r Comon Swamps thes two last things and left to the Select men to Consider off.

[**247.**] The same day it was p'posed to the towne whether they would giue to Daniell Elders a peice of ground according as the Select men shall Judge meete for the place or quantety, and one Such Conditions as they shall appoint not entrenching vpon mens p'ticular rights.

The Vote was affermatiue.

The same day it was Voted and agreed vnto that wheeras the Contry highway is taken out of the deuissions lying at the end of the great lots it is agreed that the fower rods laid out at the end of the great lots should be alowed vnto such men as haue the way taken out of ther deuission lots in recompence.

The same day was Chosen for Selectmen.

Mr Stoughton 29, Capt. Foster 24, Lift^{nt} Capen 29, William Sumner 22, Ensigne Hale 17.
for Recorder Lift^{nt} Capen.
for Treasurer Captin Foster.
for Raters Srg^{nt} Clap Srg^{nt} wiswell Srg^{nt} preston.
Sup'uisors of highways Isack Joanes, Timothy Tilston.
and for the neck Amiell weeks

The same day it was Concluded that Mr Flint should haue eighty pounds for his labour in the minestry for the yeere that is past (out of which shall be deducted what each man haue put into the box the Sabboth days) of which one fowerth part to be in money; Indian Corne at 3^s p' bl to the Rates peas at 3^s 6^d Rey 4^s barly 4^s and wheat 5^s

At a meeting of the Select men the 9th (10) 72
George Lyon at his request was granted liberty to take 600 of Rayles out of that land beyond the last deuission one the South side of Naponset if ther be timber enough fallen already lying downe to make soe many, if not then to take them out of that land beyond the line and not otherwise.

The same day it was ordered that wheras great inconuenience Comes to the towne by mens selling and allienating of ther lands and not acquainting the towne or Select men or Raters with the allienation thereof, wherby when Rates are made, and afterward demanded, it fals out that the land was allienated before the Rate was made [**248.**] for the p'vention whereof for the futuer. It is ordered and heerby declared that if any man sell and allienate his land and not acquaint either the Selectmen or the Raters thereof before the next Rate made after the allienation that then he or they or that p'son whatsoeuer that soe allienats, shall be lyable to pay all Rates for such lands (as if not allienated) vntill enformation be made as aforesaid, and this to extend to al lands Rateable within the p'cincts of Dorchester.

At a meeting of the Select men at Captin Fosters house the 23 10th 72 the select men made an agreement with Mr John Foster to be a Schole Master as apears in the new book p. 98.

The same day it was agreed that ther should be a town Rate made for the discharge of such depts as the towne are engaged in, and that the Recorder shall Isue out a warrant to the Raters to make this Rate and alsoe a rate of 80 pounds for the minestry.

The same day at the request of John Blackman it was granted him liberty to take some Cedar trees in some Swamps aboue brantree within the bounds of Dorchester, alsoe he is heerby empowered to take such trees as are ther already fallen although they are already Clouen out, p'uided it be not done by any belonging to our owne towne, and alsoe that he giue a true account of what is ther done, and to forbid any that he shall find ther trespassing vpon or lands.

The same day the Deacon Returned the names of such as had not paid their p'portions to the minesters Rates both the money Rate and the other Rate for the yeer 71 and it was ordered that warrant should be Issewed out to the Constable to Colect the same.

At a meeting of the Select men the 13 11th 72.

Wheras it was Voted at a publique Towne meeting the 2 10 72 that Goodman Garnesy Edward Wiet and others conserned should haue alowance for the Contry highway that goes through ther deuissions out of that 4 Rods laid at the end of the great lots, the Select men doe order and appoint that Amiell Weeks together with Lift^{nt} Capen shall lay out this 4 rods they paying the Charges

[**249.**] The same day it was ordered that wheras Complaint is made against James Minot, of his Cutting and Carting away of wood from the 500 acres Contrary to towne order. It is ordered that the Record^r shall send forthwith an order to p'hibit him from p'ceeding to Cut or to carry away any wood from thence, and that he appear before the Select men at ther next meeting which wilbe the Second Monday in Feburary to answer for what he haue already done.

The same day John Plume Came to the Select men to demand vpon what termes he should enjoy that land granted him by the towne lying beyond the late deuissions on the North of Naponset neer to deadham mille: In answer therunto the Selectmen doe enjoyne the said plum that in Case hee doe enjoy that land he shall build vpon it, and liue theron with his famely within one whole yeer from the date heerof or elce not to expect to enjoy the land any longer, and if in Case he doe build and liue as is aforesaid, the said plum shall not allenate sell or let the whole or any p^t therof vntill that he haue legally remoued and setled himself and his famely in some other towne and if in Case he doe remoue as aforesaid he shall not haue liberty to sell any more then the hous and three acres of land about it, and the remainder to returne to the towne, and if the said John plum shall dy his wife shall enjoy it for her life or ther Children after them but not to allienate or sell any p^t or the whole without liberty from the Select men if they see Cause to grant it:

The same day the Raters returned the Rates which they weer ordered to make for the minestry of 80^{li} and the towne rate 20^{li}.

At a meeting of the Select men the 10th 12. 72.

Goodman Pason had a motion to be p'posed to the towne that seeing his lot fales short for what it should be considering the high way that therfore the towne would be pleased to be satisfied with the way 3 rod broad from his hous west ward soe farr as his land doe extend, this was left to further Consideration.

The same day ther was granted to Thomas Grant to take 100 of Railes out of the 500 acrs.

The same day James Minot appeared to answer for his cutting and carrying away of wood from off the 500 acres, whose answer was that he was Ignorant of the [**250.**] order p'hibbiting the Cutting of wood and that he had not cutt or ordered the Cutting downe of any tree for wood but what the Indians haue done Contrary to his order.

Also the same time he desiered liberty for timber to build a house about 16 foot long and 14 wide and to have about Seauen or eight Cord of wood about Stantons; this is granted p'uided it be not to Carry out of the towne.

The same day it was ordered that notice should be giuen to all the p'prietors within fence of the great lots, Six acre lots and Captins Neck vpland and meaddow to meete together on the next Second day being the 17th this Instant at the meeting hous about 12 of the Clock at farthest for to Consider of the fencing of that feild either in ginerall or p'ticuler as shall then be agreed by the p'prietors and Samuell paule and John Minot to giue notice heerof to p'sons Conserned.

The same day ther was granted to the widdow Minot liberty to gitt one or two hundred of Railes out of the 500 acrs.

The same day it was granted to John Memory liberty to take timber out of the 500 acres to build a hous of about 24 foot long and 16 or 18 wide.

At a meeting of the Select men the 17 12 72 at Mr Stoughtons house It was agreed that the Constables should be ordered to Colect and gather the first payment of the Subscriptions for the Collige and to appoint some place or places for the receaueing of it and transporting it to Boston and to be alowed for it out of the principle.

The same day it was agreed that the Constables should be ordered to giue notice to the freemen to bring in their votes for Nomination of Majestrates and for the Choice of other officers as shall then be done on the 14th of March by ten of the Clock and the inhabetants to meet about twelue of the Clock to giue ther ap'bation or dislike of the place pitcht vpon by the Committee for the meeting hous on Rocky hill.

The same day it was agreed vnto that some distress should be made on the tenant at Captin Hudsons farme for some arrears of Rates which are vnpaid.

[**251.**] The same day the p'prietors of the great lots and six acre lots meet together at the meeting hous the Select men being p'sent and then It was agreed betweene the p'prietors that ther shall be a p'tition fence between the feild Viz: on the North side of that lott which was Mr Makepeas his lot from Timothy Tilstons stone wale to the west end of the great lot within fence, and from the fore mentioned place of Timothy Tilstones easward soe farre as to the sea, and this p'tition fence to be made and maintained p'portionably by the owners of the land that is on this side of it, and by the owners of the land on the other side of it at an equall p'portion according to ther land they doe posess each man makeing ther end fence, the meddow bearing p^t of this p'tition fence according to p'portion: further by the land on this sid as is aboue said is intended only the great pastuer which lys on this side of it, and soe to be freed from all outsid fence which each man did formerly make on this side of the greate lots, the pastuer making the one half of the fence soe fare as their land goe, and the other sid to make the other half, and alsoe a sufficcient gate Cross the way, and all the fence to be made Sufficcient for all sorts of Catle and hoggs: And to this agreement the p'prietors doe bind them

selues and Successors vntill the major p^t shall see Caus to alter it this being put to the voate the Voate was in the Affermatiue.
Signed by vs whose names are heer Subscribed.

RICHARD LEEDS his marke (——|○
JAMES HUMFREY   THOMAS PEIRCE
THOMAS TOLMAN SEN^r   THOMAS TOLMAN
SAMUELL PAULE   JOHN TOLMAN
TIMOTHY TILSTONE   WILLIAM TRESCOT
JOHN MINOT   ENOCK WISWELL
OBEDIAH HAWS   WILLIAM POND.

This is a true Coppie of the original which remains on file As Attests

JOHN CAPEN, Record^r.

[252.] At a meeting of the Select men the 10 (1) 7 2 - 3.
Ther was granted to Thomas Grant liberty to take two trees off from the 500 acres for to make posts and if thos trees doe not p'duce 50 posts then if he find any trees downe out of which he may make up 50 posts he may soe doe p'uided he doe not trespas vpon trees that are fallen lately for spesciall vse.

The same day Mr John Foster, Amiell Weeks, Roger Billeng and Thomas Swift Junr are appointed to run the line betweene brantree and Dorchester from the top of the blew hills all along that line soe neer as they can to the patten line and they to giue notice timely to brantree men.

And for the line betweene punkapage and Dorchester Joseph Homes and Timothy Tilston and the same men to run the line betweene Dorchester and melton, that is to say from Brantry line and the outsid of the last Six deuissions downe towards the Meaddow.

And for the line between Dorchester and Deadham Sarg^nt Clap Srg^nt pond and Srg^nt Wiswell.

And for the line between Dorchester and Rocksbery Lift^nt John Capen, William Sumner and Nathanell Clap.

The same day Ebenezer Clap was granted to take trees for sels and plates for a barne out of the Comons beyond the blew hils and alsoe liberty to take some Cedar trees for Clobords out of some of the Swamps in o^r land beyond the blew hils, or if ther be any trees fallen by men of other towns either brantree men or others he may haue liberty to take such trees or bolts.

The same day the Condition of Daniell Elders was taken into Consideration being in want of an habetation, and the Select men haue appointed Ensigne Hale and Enock Wiswell to looke out a place in the 500 acres neer to Stanton's that may be a Conuenient place for him and soe to lay out a peice of land for him and to make returne of what they doe in the p^rmisses.

The same day ther was appointed for fence vewers

for the Captins Neck } John Wales
                     } John Breck
for that p^t of the great   } Tho. Tolman Junr
lotts beyond Timothy Tilstons } Tho. Tilstone
and 6 acre lots   }

[**253.**] for the feild behind } James Bird
James Bird } John Blackman
for the feild behind Mrs
Joanes and before Enock } Enock wiswell
Wiswells old house } Tho: Moadesly
for the feild behind Mr } Richard Baker
Stoughtons } John Withington
for the neck of land } Timothy Mather
} John Blackman
for Cleering the neck } Isack Joanes
of Catle

All Corne fields to be Cleered by the first of aprill and the fence vewers to vew fences by the 2 or 3 of aprill. All fences to be made vp by the 25 march 73.

At a meeting of the Freemen the 14 (1) 7 2 – 3 ther was chosen for Deputys for the yeer ensewing Captain Clap, Captin Foster.

and william Sumner Chosen Comissinr to Cary the Votes to Boston.

The same day vpon the occasion of warning of a meeting of the towne about the meeting hous it was ordered that henceforth the Constables should haue orders in wrighting vnder the Recorders hand and the Constables to returne what they haue done therin.

The same day the Comittee for the meeting house made Report of the place which they had pitcht vpon on the Rocky hill for to erect a meeting house which was neer to the lime-kclme and being put to the Vote Concerning ther ap'bation of the place by Seuering the Company the Vote was in the Affermatue Viz 41 vots for it besids the Comittee and 25 votes against it :

The same day Amiell Weeks and Henery Leadbetter weer Chosen Constables for the yeer Ensewing.

The same day it was appointed that al p'sons shall bring in a note of the Number of their dry Catle to some of the Select men by the 25 of this Instant that soe an agreement may be made with the herds man.

At a meeting of the Select men the 14 2 73

John Plum was Called before the Select men to giue an accompt of his entertaining his Sonne Chub and his wife, whose answer was that his Sonne in law was gon and the Select men ordered him to discharge the towne of his daughter alsoe forthwith.

[**254.**] The same day Johnathan Birch being Sumoned appeared before the Select men to answer for his being resident heer in this towne seeing he had been out of this towne at Lanchester about fower months. The said Burch is ordered forthwith to Cleere the towne and not to Continue heer.

The same day Lif^{tnt} Capen and William Sumner are appointed to run the line between the 400 acrs laid out betweene Melton and Dorchester and to Joyne with them Some of Melton.

The same day ther was a returne made of thos that did run the line between Deadham and Dorchester to the furthest extent and it is vpon file.

The same day it was ordered that the fence vewers of the neck from yeer to yeer shall take Care to see that the gate belonging to the Neck be hung vp and put in order and they are to be satisfied for it.

The same day in order to the Subscription for the Castle repairation it is ordered that Captin Foster Lift^nt Capen Ensigne Hale and William Sumner shall Each of them take a Sargent with them and goe to the Seauerall Squadrons and take ther Subscriptions.

The same day it was ordered that Obediah Haws and Robt. Spur are appointed to looke after Hoggs that are vnyoked and vnringed; and if they find any such they are to demand and receaue 4^d p' swine for all that are vnyoked and vnringed for the first ofence and for the Second ofence Six pence and if they refuse to pay then to impound them till satisfaction be made and if complaint be made of thes mens neglect vpon any man's Enforming of them, then they shall be lyable to pay such a fine as the Select men shall see meete to impose vpon them or either of them.

The same day it was ordered that John Plum shall look after all horses that goe vpon the Comons Contrary to towne order and hee to haue the one half of the fine for his labour and the other to the vs of the towne.

The same day Nicholas George was alowed to kepe an publique house of entertainement if the Hon^rd Court will admit of it.

At a meeting of the Select men the 28 2 72 on atraining day It was ordered that Robt Stiles and John Merifeild shall be fence vewers for the 20 acre lots.

The same day it was ordered that Joseph Weeks shall haue the keeping of the Lock for the pound (he p'uiding one) and to receaue in and lett out as the Case may requier.

[255.] The same day it was ordered that the Recorder should draw vp some thing which may be p'sented to the County Court respecting Johnathan Birch who remains in our towne notwithstanding warning giuen him to dep^t.

The 10th of the 3 M° 1673 Captin Clape being Chosen formerly to serve as deputy at the generall Court, and the Court finding a necessety of his p'sence at the Castle in thes troublesome times (and vpon their notice giuen to the freemen that they may Chouse another deputy) the freemen being called together vpon the day aforesaid made Choice of Lift^nt John Capen to serue as deputy for the yeere ensewing.

At a meeting of the Selectmen of Dorchester this 9th day of June 1673 The Select men did lett vnto John Farrington of Deadham all that meaddow vp in the Contrey neer vnto the three hundred acres which Captin William Hudson had by Contract of Dorchester Select men; That Farme being excepted, and Roger Billeng his farme lately laid out; the rest of the Meaddow we doe lett vnto the fore said John Farrington; And doe Authoriz the said Farrington or his order to Mow the same, And for what hee or to his order shall be ther gotten he shall pay one shilling p' loade, and we doe heerby inhibit all other p'sons from intermedling with any of this Meaddow to his p'jedice, and doe engage to maintaine him in the vse and improuement of it.

     Signed by   HOPESTILL FOSTER
              JOHN CAPEN SEN^r
              WILLIAM SUMNER
              RICHARD HALE.

This is a true Coppie of that which was deliuered vnto John Farrington as Attests John Capen Record^r

At a meeting of the Select men the 9th 4 1673 Joseph Birch was caled before the Select men to answer for his Idlenes whose anwser was that for the p^rsent he had noe yron nor Coles but he would Endeauer to reforme.

The same day it was ordered that Robt. Stiles should haue some supply made to him in respect of Corne and that the Treasurer of the Towne may deliuer him two or three bushels of Corne at his descretion to be alowed in his accompt.

[256.] The same day a letter was sent to peter Woodward of Deadham and Mr Woodcock beyond Wadeing Riuer to inhibit the faling of Ceder trees in o^r Swamps the Coppies therof remaine on fill.

The same day returne was made of runing the line between Dorchester and Rocksbery at large and is on fille.

As alsoe the line between Dorchester and Brantree from the top of the blew hils soe farre as Tanton path and is on file.

At a meeting of the Select men the 6th (7) 1673.

Mrs Hollaway of Boston Came before the Select men and did desier that it might be p'posed to the towne at their next publique meeting, that they would be pleased to grant her one hundred and fifty acres of land which was formerly laid out about woodcock well or ther about.

At a meeting of the Select men on a training day on the 13 8 73 Samuell Rigby was called before the Select men to giue answer vnto him of his desolute liuing, and neglecting his calling, and other misdemeanors and after seriouse admonition giuen to him of reformation he was requiered and appointed to appeare before the Select men at their next meeting in Nouember to giue an accompt of his maner of liueing or reformation if it may be.

At a meeting of the Select men the 17 (9) 73 being a weeke after their vsuall time vpon some occassion.

The Constable Obediah Swift Came to make up his accompt for the Towne Rate Comitted to him to Colect made for the yeer 1672 the Sume of which Rate was 20^li 8 7.

Imp̄. to Nicholas Bolton	3 – 0 – 0
It. to Nicholas George	3 – 7 – 8
It. to Rich. Leeds for Corne to Merifeld and for ½ a bl. of Malt and runing the line	0 – 6 – 9
It. to Rich. Withington and James Whit for worke and nailes at the meeting house . . .	0 – 5 – 6
It. to Ezra Moss, for a woolfe killing . . .	0 – 3 – 10
the rest was p^d by the other Constable paule.	
It. to Samuell pitcher attendance at Court . .	0 – 1 – 6
It. to William Sumner as deputy	5 – 17 – 0
It. to Tho. Tolman Senr for worke about the Carridg	0 – 3 – 7
It. to John Tolman for the like worke . . .	0 – 2 – 4
It. to Thomas Tilstone for the like worke . .	0 – 3 – 2
It. to Timothy ffoster about the Gunn . . .	0 – 3 – 1

DORCHESTER TOWN RECORDS. 195

[**257.**] It. to Joseph Long for keeping of Frances Bakon . . . . . .   0 – 1 – 8
It. to Capt. Foster and his Sonne in p^t of what fell short for the yeer 71 which was 7 – 6 – 8 . .   4 – 2 – 3
It. to Nathan Bradly for a woolf killing 6^s the remainder p^d by Constable paule . . . .   0 – 6 – 0
It. to Augustin Clement for worke at the meeting house . . . .   0 – 11 – 6
It. to William Pond for work . . . .   0 – 7 – 6
It. to Richard and Mathias Euens the remainder of the 17^s 6^d which was not p^d by Samuell paull .   0 – 7 – 11

                                                                             19 – 11 – 3

    The 27 9 73 Constable Samuell Paule gaue in an accompt of the remainder of the minester Rate for the yeer 71 Committed to him to gather the Sume wherof was 13 – 6 – 9 ther being 10^{li} aded to this Rate for the vse of the towne.
Imp. p^d by Seauerall to Mr Flint 5^{li} 4^s 4^d of which the most of them was Reckoned for by Mr Flint and the Deacon . . . . . . ^{li} ^{s} ^{d}
                                                                            5 – 4 – 4
It. wheras ther was 17^s 6 due to Richard and Mathias Euens for work at the meeting hous the Constable haue p^d them out of this Rate . . .   0 – 9 – 7
The rest p^d by Constable Swift as aboue.
It. p^d to Nathan Bradly, or Hix by his order for killing a woolf 4^s the rest by Obediah Swift . .   0 – 4 – 0
It. p^d to Ezra Moss for a woolf . . . .   0 – 6 – 2
It. p^d to Nicholas George in Malt towards expences for the yeer 73 . . . .   1 – 0 – 0
Also Elder Humfrey his Rate not paid . . .   0 – 19 – 5
and Hudsons farme not paid . . . . .   0 – 13 – 4
It. Jno Merifeilds Rate for which Mr Flint haue giuen Credit for it . . . .   0 – 3 – 10
It. Joseph Garnesys Rate not p^d . . . .   0 – 1 – 3
and James Womsly . . . . . .   0 – 1 – 3

[**258.**] It. Ezra Claps Rate vnpaid but vndertaken for by Deacon Capen . . . .   0 – 1 – 5
It. Robt. Stiles Rate vnpaid . . . . .   0 – 4 – 5
It. p^d to the Towne Treasurer Capt. Foster . .   0 – 13 – 8

                                                                            10 – 2 – 8

Remaines yet behind 3^{li} 4^s 3^d.

At a Generall Town meeting the 1 (10) 1673.
After the Directory was read ther was a petition p'sented by some who weer depriued of their meaddow at the blew hils desiering Satisfaction: after some adjetation it was referred to the Consideration of the Select men that shall be chosen to p'pare an answer against the towne meeting in March next.

The same day ther was chosen for Select men M`r` Stoughton, Capt Foster, Lift`nt` Jn`o` Capen, Ensigne Hale, William Sumner.
and for Recorder Jn`o` Capen Sen`r`
and for Raters Srg`nt` Clap Srg`nt` Blake Srg`nt` Pond.
for Sup'uisors of highways Samuell Robinson Jn`o` Withington.

The same day it was agreed vnto to alow vnto Mr Flint ninty pounds for his labour for the yeer past which will be ended the last of this month: and a quarter p`t` to be p`d` in money of which thos that haue put in Contribution to be alowed.

The same day M`rs` Hollways motion of 150 acrs of land to be giuen her was p'pounded and Voted in the Negatiue.

At a meeting of the Select men the 8 (10) 73.

Nathan Bradly vpon his petition to sell Cider by retaile the Select men considering his low Condition grants him libertie soe to doe with the ap'bation of the Court he obserueing to keepe good order in soe doeing and attending the law therin.

[259.] The same day it is granted to Nathan Bradly liberty to take two or three load of timber off from the 500 acres towards the building him a hous.

The same day Samuell Hix p'sented a letter from his Brother Zackery Hix of Cambridg wherin he requested that his aged mother might be entertained in the house of Samuell Hix and the said Zackery vntertaks for the Secuerety of the towne: the which is granted on condition that the said Zackery Hix doe Come p'sonaly and engage to the Select men for the Security of the towne.

The same day it was ordered that the Raters should be required to make a Rate of 92`li` for the vse of the minestry of which M`r` Flint is to haue 90`li` for the yer past and the other 40`s` is for alowance for some that are low in their estates and it may be not able to pay their p'portions.

The same day at the request of Isack Ryall ther was granted to him liberty to take about 100 of Railes and 30 posts out of the 500 acrs.

The same day at the request of Thomas Daunport Jun`r` ther was granted to him liberty to take 8 loads of timber towards the building him a house out of the 500 acrs.

At a meeting of the Select men the 12 11 73 —
Samuell Hix was sent for to answer for his entertaining of his mother into this towne before securety be giuen to Secuer the towne and he is appointed the next Second day to giue in Securety.

The same day Richard Leeds brought in an acc`t` of expences on Francis Bacon which amounts to 1`li` 9`s` out of which he alows her for her labor and a p'cell of woole he had of her 23`s` and the Select men orders him to receaue one pound Six shillings more out of the towne rate.

The same day the Deacon made returne of Seauerall that had not paid their p'portion to the maintenance of the minestry for the yeer 72 and a warant was Issued for the Constables to leuy the same Viz/ Constable Amiell Weiks.

[260.] The same day Richard Withington and henery Garnesy appeared and desiered that the high way at the end of the great lots might be determined to which end the Sixt day of this week being the 16 instant is appointed for p'sons Concerned to meet on the place but that day proued not fitt in regard of Snow but the 23 12 73.

The same day it was granted that Robt. Stiles should haue 20ˢ in Corne if it can be had for his pʳsent releife.

About the same time the Rates weer deliuered to the Constables to Colect Viz the Sume of the Castle Rate of thos that Contributed and thos that did not Contribute amounted to 52ˡⁱ 10ˢ 11ᵈ and the Contry Rate amounted vnto 37 – 15 – 9

At a meeting of the Select men the 9 12 73.

It was ordered that the meeting hous bell (being broken and it may be dangerous to be rung; it shall not be rung any more but speedily taken downe and meanes vsed to Conueigh it to England that another may be p'cuered either ther or elce wher.

The same day Thomas Dauenport Senʳ brought Steuen Hoppin Senʳ who tooke an oath about high ways to the fresh Marsh and alowance of land about the Marsh to sett hay on the which is on file.

The same day it was agreed that this day fortnight being 23 12 is appointed to meet on the land at the end of the great lots to setle the line and Conclud wher the high way lys.

The same day it was ordered that the Rates of Robt. Stiles, Elder Minot, Mʳˢ Atherton and Samuell Minot for the yeer 70 the Sume of all being 6ˢ 8ᵈ it shal be paid out of the towne Rate.

The same day it was granted to James Foster liberty to take about 15 or 16 loads of timber out of the 500 acres towards the building him an house.

looke for more orders made the same day p 262 omitted heer in order

[**261.**] At a meeting of the Select men the 9 (1) 7¾

Joseph Long pʳsented a petition to haue liberty to sell Cidar the which petition is on file.

The same day Richard Mather, Hopestill Humphry, Isack Humphry and John Trescot pʳferred a petition to haue libertie to erect a seate in the meeting hous at the west end of the pulpitt, the which is granted to them p'uided that if any damedg com to the Window by that means they shall repaire it.

The same day ther was appointed for fence Vewers for the Captins Neck — Richard Leeds, John Breck —

for that pᵗ of the great lots beyond Timothy Tilstones	Thomas Trot Israell How
for the feild behind James Bird.	John Bird Obediah Haws
for the feild behind Mʳˢ Joanes and before Enock wiswels old hous	Srgⁿᵗ Clap. Isack Joanes
for the feild behind Mr Stoughtons,	Amiell Weeks John Baker
for the neck of land,	Nehemiah Clap Hopestill Clap
for Cleering the neck of Catell,	Israell Mead Tho. Moadesly

All fences to be made vp by the 25 March 7¾ and all Corne feilds to be cleered of Catell by the 1 Aprill.

The 16 (1) 7¾ ther was appointed fence Vewers of the 20 acre lots Elder Humphry and Rich Baker

The same day John Tolman and William Weeks are appointed to see to the execution of the Towne order Concerning the yokeing and ringing of hogs as the order expresseth Viz ringing all the yeer and once in euery month they are Enjoyned to goe about to p'secute the order and oftener if any Complaint be made to them of hoges being vnyoked or vnringed as the order expresseth and for euery neglect heerin they are to be fined 5ˢ to be leauyed vpor ther estate half for the enformer and the other for the vse of the towne.

[262.] At a meeting of the freemen the 10ᵗʰ (1) 7¾
Ther was Chosen Deputys for the yeer Ensewing beginning the yeer at the Court of Election.

Captin Hopestill Foster and Liftⁿᵗ John Capen.

Alsoe at the same time ther was Chosen

Liftⁿᵗ John Capen as Commissioner to Carry the Votes to boston at the time appointed.

Alsoe at the same time was Chosen for Constable Thomas Peirce and John Capen Junʳ.

The same day it was p'posed and put to the vote whether ther should be a Schoole Master p'cuered as formerly to teach both English and Lattin and to wright at the Schole-house and that the Select men doe take care therin.

The vote was in the Affermatiue.

The same day the orders formerly made and not yett repealled was read Concerning hogs ther being yoked and ringed and fences and fens vewers power and Care and also the order of Court and Towne respecting horses.

The 9 12 73 ther was granted to Enock Wiswell a liberty to Entertaine Margeret the Seruant of Goodman Sweet of Boston vntill the next meeting of the Select men and that without a penalty the which at the next meeting he did ingage to Secuer the towne as in the new book appears.

The same day it was ordered that the Constabl should giue notice to the Freemen to meet on the 10th (1) 7¾ to bring in Votes for Nomination of Majestrats.

M̄d thes two last orders should haue been placed in p. 260.

[263.] In Referance to an order made the 9 12 73 appointing some to vew the highway at the end of the great lots and to determin wher it shall ly it is as followeth

23   12   73

Viz Mʳ Stoughton Capt. Foster, Liftⁿᵗ Capen, William Sumner, Ensigne Hale, Rich Withington, Samuell Robinson, Mʳ Timothy Mather, Tho. Lake and others Concerned being p'sent, Amiell weeks was desiered with his Instruments to fetch the line from two marks shewed by Ensigne Hale (the first of the marks he did aferme vnto of his knowlidg) to see how that line would direct, the which he did beginning at thos marks in Ensigne hale his pastuer vntill he came past Richard Bakers lot, but saw that line run two much in vpon the deuissions, and therfor gaue ouer that line, then he measuered the lenth of the deuission lots vpon a line between M^r pattens lot and George procters and found it 84 roa and ¾ then he went to the line between Mr Duncans lot and Capt. Foster and found it the same lenth as the other which made vs conclud that the way lay on that side of the line next the deuissions and the former act done as in p. 260 about staking out 4 rods at the end of Wiet Spurs and Garnesys lot ends was nullified and the staks pluckt vp.

At a meeting of the Select men the 13 2 74

Henery Garnesy appeared before the Select men and manifested his willingnes to entertaine Frances Bacon from the day of the date heerof vntell the next meeting of the Select men which wil be in the fowert Month next and in Case he like her he shall be willing to keepe her longer.

The same day it was granted to Increas Sumner liberty to take about 7 or 8 load of timber out of the 500 acrs towards the building him an house.

The same day ther was granted to Nicholas George libertie to keep an house of publique entertainement if the Court p'mitt of it.

[264.] At a meeting of the Select men the 8 4 74.

It is ordered that the burying place shall be fenced in with a stone wall and notice is to be giuen to the towne upon some lectuer day and the time then to be appointed both for teemes and hands for the efecting of it some time the latter end of this Sumer.

The same day an order was directed to the Constable to demand and receaue twenty shillings of John Plumb for entertaining his Sonne in law Chub and his wife Contrary to towne order and alsoe to giue plumb notice that he despatch the said Chub and his wife away and Cleer the towne of them as he will further answer the penalty of the towne order p'scribed therin.

At a towne meeting the 17 4 74 in referrance to the foresaid order made by the Select men the 8th of this Instant Concerning the fencing in of the burying place, the towne did by their Vote referr the matter to the Select men to order the time when to be done and the m̄aner how and anything elce for the efecting of it.

The 19th (6) 74 Roger Billeng was Chosen Commissioner for the Contry Rate.

M̄d. the Sume of the Contry Rate made the 26 (6) 74 deliuered to the Com̄isioner is 39^{li} 0^s 6^d.

At a meeting of the Select men the 14 (7) 74

The Constable was appointed to speake with Willm Chaplin and giue him notice that Complaint is made of some abuse that is Committed at or about his house by playing at kitle-pins and expending of time Idly, and therfore that he reforme such abuse vnless furthe Cource be taken and that he doe forewarne him not to sell beare without licence vpon his perill.

[265.] The same day John Plumb appeared before the Select

men and requested that he might receaue the pay for that timber which he formerly sold to Jonathan farebanks which was taken off from the land vp by Deadham which was forfitted by his neglect.

The same day in referance to a towne Vote wherin they did Commit it to the Select men to order the fencing in of the burying place the Select men doe appoint John Homes and Obediah Haws to see that it be done by calling vpon such men as haue teemes and hands and keepe an accompt of what is done and to be paid out of the towne rate and that the outside be done first and then the sid next to the feild and that it be made fower foot and half high and faced both sids.

The same day at the request of Nicholas Lawrance for a little peice of land by the Clay pits for to set p^t of a barne or Cowhouse vpon it the Select men doe Comite that bussiness to Mr. Stoughton and John Capen Senr to act therin as they shall Judg meete without to much p^{r}jedice to the towne or nightbors Concerned.

The same day John Browne was Called before the Select men to answer for his maner of liueing and was aduised or admoneshed to attend famely Gouerment in the place where he did reside and that he be dillegent in his Calling.

The same day Ensigne Richard Hale was desiered and empowered to see that the Scholehous be repaiered either by Clobording or shingleing the Roofe and to take an acc^t what is done and to be paid out of the towne rate.

The same day at the request of the Select men vnto Richard Baker of Dorchester to lend for the vse of the towne the Sume of three pounds ten shillings in money for the payment of the remainder of the money rate which was due to Mr Flint he the

[looke more of this p. 268]

[266.] A note of the acc^t of William Trescot Concerning the rent of the minestry land taken notice off it heer to gether though Credit be giuen for it in several other places and accounts.

Md. the yeer 1672 was the first yeer that he entered into pay and then he was to pay fiue pounds which was p^d as followeth.

It. dl. to Mr Flint 600 and ¼ of Clobord for which Mr Flint is dept^r dl. by Samuell Trescot . .	1 – 11 – 3
It. by 500¾ of Clobord dl. to Jno Capen Junr for which his father p^d on acc^t with the towne . .	1 – 8 – 9
It. by Ebenezer Withington which by Sam Trescots order he pays to Jno Capen Senr on acc^t also with the towne	2 – 0 – 1
It. by 600 of Clobord left in Lift^t Capens orchyard, of which Lift^t had fower hundred and forty and Capt. Foster had 125 the rest lost . . .	1 – 10 – 0
It. by what he p^d to Capt. Foster by himself and Samuell as by the Captains acc^t appears . .	1 – 14 – 0
It. by 600 of Clobord for the Scholhous which Ensign Hale sold to Jno Bird for money to buy nails for the Scholehous	1 – 10 – 0

It. by John Trescot appointed by Samuell Trescot on acc^t with John Capen Senr which is accounted for between the towne and him	1 –	2 –	0
It. by Samuell Trescot on acc^t with Lift. Capen	0 –	4 –	0
	11 –	0 –	0

Md. the aboue said sume of 11^{li} was p^d by Samuell Trescot for the yeer 72 and 73 which was the two yeers he had it of his father.

Towards the yeers 74 and 75 William Trescot haue p^d as followeth which should be fifteen pound

Recc. of Mr Flint by order of W. Trescot	2 –	6 –	0
Recc. of Tho. Bird by order &c.	1 –	0 –	0
Recc. of Nehemiah Clap p' order of W. T.	1 –	0 –	0
Recc. of Widdow Gornell p. order &c.	1 –	0 –	6
Recc. by Lift. Capen on acc^t with W. T.	4 –	0 –	0

Md al these Sums last mentioned weere p^d to Lift. Capen and discounted by him with the town as by his acc^t doe appear

Recc. of Henry Glouer for p^t of his rent whill he Occupi it p^d to Jno Capen in bark and bill and discounted with the towne as on his acc^t will appeer p. 293 old book	7 –	5 –	0
It. Henery Glouer left in the hands of Obediah Swift 6^{li} 10^s which Obediah haue engaged to pay and Glouer haue a receipt as p^t of his rent	6 –	10 –	0
It. more p^d by Henry Glouer in 4 q^{rs} of beif and a hid	4 –	10 –	0

[Page 267 blank.]

[**268.**] Continued from p. 265.
he the said Richard Baker doe p'mise soe to doe and the Select men for the time being doe Engage that it be repaied to him againe, and Mr Stoughton engageth to see that the Select men doe p'forme what is heer p'mised this dett discharged to Richerd bacor, as acknoliged by me. James Baker. this 14th: 10 :1691 :

Mē. Frances Bakon went to Thomas Moadeslys house the 7th of May 1674 and she lay in about the 2 of (5) 74.

Thomas Moadesly haue receaued of Richard Leeds fower bushels of Indian Corne at 12^s and two bushels of Rey at 8^s also he receaued of John Gornell 1^{li} 5^s and for her work before she lay in 10^s 6^d and Since her lying in 3^s 6^d.

And ther was due to him for 16 weeks boarding at his house, both for her lying in and her diet and attendance and all expences fiue pounds, of which is paid in the p'ticulers aboue said the Sume of 2^{li} 19^s 0

Rest due to Tho: Moadesly this 14 (7) 74 : — 2^{li} – 1^s – 0

At a meeting of the Select men the 9 (9) 74

The Constables Viz : Henery Leadbetter and Amiell Weeks gaue in their acc^t of the rates Comītted to them to Colect the Contry and towne rate both together being 37^{li} – 15^s – 9^d and the Castle rate 52 – 10 – 11 as followeth

Imp to the Country Treasurer	29 – 2 – 4
It. to Captin Foster	02 – 0 – 0
It. to Nicholas George the other 20ˢ he had in malt	02 – 12 – 0
It. to Lift^{nt} Capen p^t of his dew	01 – 10 – 0
It. to Nicholas Bolton and 20ˢ he had in Clobords	02 – 00 – 0
It. to Amiell weeks for runing a line	00 – 10 – 0
It. to M^r Jn° Foster for the same line	00 – 06 – 0
It. to Tho. Swift for the same line	00 – 06 – 0
It. to Roger Billeng for the same line and other Charges	00 – 14 – 0
It. to Srg^{nt} Clap for Deadham iine	00 – 09 – 0
It. to Srg^{nt} Pond for the same line	00 – 09 – 0
It. to William Sumner	00 – 08 – 4
It. to Nathanell Clap	00 – 02 – 6
It. to Glass for the meeting house	00 – 14 – 2
It. to William Nahatton for a woolf killing	00 – 05 – 0
It. to Robt Stiles for his releife	01 – 00 – 0
It. to Obediah Swift for worke	00 – 07 – 6

[**269.**]

It. to Israell Euered of Deadham for 3 wolues	1 – 10 – 0
It. to Timothy Tilston foor a line between puncapage and vs	00 – 06 – 0
It. to Joseph Homes for the same line	00 – 06 – 0
It. to Obediah Haws for rates vnpaid	00 – 04 – 0
It. to Rich. Leeds for Frances Bacon	01 – 06 – 0
It. to Jn° Tolman for worke about wheels	00 – 03 – 1
It. to Tho. Tilston for worke about Guns	00 – 03 – 0
It. to Timothy Foster about the Carredges	00 – 01 – 11
	46 – 15 – 10

also the acc^t of the Castle rate being Colected by the same Constable the rate being 52 10 11

Imp̄ to seuerall men as by bill exprest	23 – 19 – 06
It. to Capt. Foster and his order	13 – 10 – 00
It. to Capt. Foster againe	02 – 12 – 00
It. to Daniell preston	02 – 09 – 00
	42 – 10 – 06

Md̄ the Treasurer of the Castle should haue 44^{li}

It. to Jn° Blackman fell short his rate	0 – 7 – 6
It. to Capt. Hudson paid not both rates	– – 11 – 0

Reckoned with the Constables Viz Henery Leadbetter and Amiell Weeks for the Contry rate and Castle rate and towne rate, and they are accquitted and discharged and their acc^t is ballanced this 9 9 74.

The same day it was Concluded by the Select men for the time being that shalbe, shall Commence an action against some of thos that haue entered vpon o^r lands beyond Wainmans ordinary and about wadeing riuer and bring it to a tryall and p'secut it to effect.

The same day Thomas Swift Junr and Henery Leadbetter is desiered and empowered to enquier after witnesses to p'mote the bussines aforesaid.

The same day the Condition of Frances Bacon was taken into Consideration being destitute of a habetation. It is ordered by the Select men [**270.**] that she shall be p'uided for in the famelys as they are drawn vp in a list and to be fortnight at a place or more if the famely be willing to entertaine her and such a famely is to be alowd 3^s p' weeke and her worke for she and her Child and soe to be p'portioned accordingly out of the towne rate and that which the Court appointed John Gornell to pay is to goe towards beding or Clothing as the Select men shall appoint.

The same day it was appointed that William Sumner and Ensigne Hale shall vew a place for a foote bridge ouer mother brooks riuer in the way to deadham and to appoint the Sup'uisors of the high ways to call vpon fitt p'sons to help as neede requier.

At a publique Towne meeting the 7 (10) 74 —

After the directory was read Capt. Roger Clap made a motion and Request that seeing ther is some differance between himself and some other p'prietors of vpland bordering vpon his Meaddow at the neck of land, he desiers that the towne would appoint some men to determine and state the bounds. In answer to his petition the towne by a vote did appoint Ensigne Hale Richard Baker and Lift^{nt} Jno Capen to be the men for to efect and state the bounds and this is with the Consent of Capt. Clap and William Sumner: The returne is in New book p 103.

The same day it was ordered that vpon the ginerall towne meeting in the tenth Month from yeer to yeer thos that haue not paid their p'portions to the minestry for the yeer past their names together with their Sumes shall be published on that day.

[**271.**] The same day at the request of Nathaniell Clap to exchang that peice of land on which the house stands which belongs to the Church and Schole giuen by John Clap, the towne by Vote doe leaue it to the Select men to act therin as they Judg meete.

The same day at the request of Matthias Euans for a place to set a house on neer to his orchyard the towne leaues it to the Select men to Vew the place and act therin as they see meet.

The same day Henery Leadbetter was Chosen to be aded to the Comittee concerning the meeting house in the steed of Augustin Clement which is dead.

By way of explaination of the Vote Concerning the erecting a new meeting house wherby a Comittee stand appointed for the Carrying on that work. It is declared and Voted that the said Comittee or the Major p^t of them shall haue full power to make all agreements and bargains Concerning the p'mises and what Sume or Sums they agree for and Engage shal be discharged both for quantetie and kind by a publique Rate vpon the inhabetants and p'prietors as in other publique Charges.

The same day it was ordered that Mr Flint should haue ninty pound for his labour in the minestry for the yeer ending the first of January next whereof one quarter p^t to be in money.

The same day (ther was Chosen) for Select men Mr Stoughton, Capt. Foster, Lift^nt Capen, William Sumner, Ensigne Hale.

Raters Srg^nt Clap Deakon Blake Srg^nt preston.

Sup'uisors J^no Tolman, Obediah Swift.

for Recorder Lift^nt J^no Capen.

[272.] Sup'uisors of the Way to the neck, the Comittee that was the last yeer appointed Viz William Sumner, Srg^nt Clap, Isacke Joanes, Deacon Blake and Timothy in the roome or steed of Augustin Clement or the Major p^t of them.

The same day it was Voted that the Sup'uisors of the high ways for the time being and soe from yeer to yeer shall keepe an exact accompt of those that doe afford help either with hands or teemes and deliuer it or a Coppie therof vnto the next Sup'uisors that soe equallety may be attended.

The Vote was Affermatiue.

At a meeting of the Select men of Dorchester the 14th of the 10th Mo. 1674

It is ordered by the Select men that wheras ther is much hurt and damedg done in o^r Comon lands both in our Swamps and vpland both Cedar and other timber notwithstanding all former orders that haue been made to p^ruent the same. It is therfore ordered that Ensigne Richard Hale, Srg^nt William Pond, Richard Withington, Roger Billeng, Henery Leadbetter, Timothy Tilstone and Samuell pale thes are Nominated and appointed and empowered to take speccall Notice of any that shall fale or take any timber either Oake or Cedar or any other wood or timber by any within o^r towne or by any out of o^r towne vnder p^rtence of their owne or freinds Rights, except they haue speccall leaue from the Select men of Dorchester or such as they shall appoint, And if thes men or any of them shall know of any breach of order it shal be lawfull for them or any of them to Seaz or take or Cause to be tooke, for the vse of the towne such timber or stufe as they shall find taken Contrary to order, and further thes men or some of them (as they shall agree together) shall goe and take a Vew once euery Month or oftener as they Judg meet, not excluding any other p'son in the towne from doeing the like.

[273.] Further it is ordered that noe man shall imploy any Indian to Cutt or gitt bolts or Clobord or shingle except they leaue the order or Coppy of the order with him, which the p'sons who doe employ them haue obtained from the Select men Signed by the Recorder, that soe it may appeare (to such as are to take a Vew) whether they doe it by order or not, and that noe timber or Clobords or Shingle in bolts or otherwise or wood or barke shall be sold or disposed to any out of the towne, either directly or indirectly, and if thes men or any of them can make any discouery or proofe of any that doe or any that haue done any thing contrary to this order they are to make report therof to the Select men, that some Cours may be taken with them by Way of action or otherwise, and this doe not repeale former orders Concerning wood or timber.

The same day it was granted to Thomas Andrews liberty for to take timber off the 500 acrs for to build him a barne of 24 foote in lenth and 20 foote wide p'uided hee tak what timber his fathers lots will afford.

The same day at the motion of Nathaniell Clap, and in referrance to the Voate of the towne the 7th of this Instant in order to the Exchange of land that lys wheer Mr Sensions house stood, the Select men doe appoint Richard Withington and Daniell preston to Vew the house and land and the land that he will giue in exchange, and as they doe Judge meete soe it shalbe determined.

At a meeting of the Select men the 25 10 1674 vpon some other occassion Richard Withington was granted libertie to take 100 and halfe of railes off from the Comons.

The same time ther was granted to Samuell and Barnard Capen libertie to take about 4 or 500 of Railes off from the 500 acres or other Comons and Posts sutable.

The same time it was ordered that the Raters should be called on to make a Rate for the minestry of Ninty pounds and a Rate for the Schole and Towne of fifty pounds and to make their returne to the Select men at their next meetinge in January.

[274.] At a meetinge of the Select men the 11th of the 11th Mo. 74.

The Raters made Returne of the Rates Comitted to them to make, Viz the minesters Rate of 90 pound and the Schole and towne Rate of 50^{li}

The same day it was granted to Thomas Holman of melton power to fetch away any bolts or Clobord that are gotten by men of other townes, especcialy brantry men out of the Swamps belonging to Dorchester and bring them to his owne house and if the bolts or Clobord be more worth than his Cost in fetching them then to be Countable to the vse of the towne, and the said Thomas Holman doe engage to be Countable for the same.

The same day at the request of Thomas Holman ther was granted to him libertie to take 3000 of Clobord out of the Swamps that are belonging to Dorchester p'uided that he doe not make sale of them to any out of o^r Towne of Dorchester for their owne vse.

The same day ther was granted to Thomas Swift of Milton libertie to take two load of Clobord for his owne vse.

The same day ther was granted to Mr Stoughton libertie to git Clobords for to Clobord his house about.

The same day Captin Foster send word to the Select men of his non acceptance of the place of a Select man.

At a meeting of the Select men the 8th 12 74

Thomas Moadesly came and demanded pay for keeping of Francis Bacon Six weeks after his last reconing for which he demands twenty Shillings of which he receaued fiue shillings in money of Mr Stoughton and fower shillings 9^d in money from seauerall p'sons on a training day Remains due to him ten shillings 3^d besids the former Ballance of acc^t which was 2^{li} 1^s 0

M$\bar{d}$. — ther is charged on Jno Gornels acc^t 2^{li} 11^s 3^d which is due Tho Modsly.

The same day William Chaplin p^{r}esented a petition to haue leaue to keepe an ordinary but it was not granted.

The same day it was ordered that the Constable shall giue notice to John Pope that himself and such of his Children as are of Capaccetie for learning doe appeare before the Select men at their next meeting.

[**275.**] The same day Richard Withington and Daniell preston being ordered the 14 10th 74 to Vew the house and land which was Mr Sensions to Change it for land at neck of land they make returne that they Judge meete that when the house and land fall to the towne then he shall giue one acre of land for it Joyning to the Church land at the Neck to which the Select men doe agree that it shal be as they haue p'posed.

The same day ther was granted to Increas Sumner libertie to git 4 or 500 of Railes out of the 500 acrs.

The same day ther was granted vnto Ensigne Hale libertie to git one or 200 of rails in the same place and Sixtie posts to be taken of trees already fallen.

The same day ther was ordered that the Constable should deliuer out of the towne rate 3 bushels of Corne to Samuell Hill for his p'sent Supply.

And if the Constable can p'cuer a litle meale for the supply of Daniell Elders he is ordered for to doe.

At a meeting of the Select men the 8 (1) 7½

Consider Atherton was granted to haue 3 or 4 load of timber out of the 500 acrs for the repaiering of his house.

The same day it was appointed that the line from the top of blew hils and soe at the head of Brantree shall be forth with run and that brantree men shall haue notice of it to Joyne with our men and the men Chosen for or towne are Amiell Weeks Roger Belleng and John Capen Junr

The same day the Select men did (in referance to a towne Grant to Mathias Euens) lay out a peice of land for his hous to be set vpon Viz: ten foot from the backsid of his Seller vnto a Certaine rock neer about his wall and from the Corner from thence to a popler tree standing in or neer a bout the wale.

The same day the Deacons p'sented a list of thos that had not paid their p'portions to the minesters rate for the yeer 73.

the next in order is in pag 277.

[**276.**] Capt. Fosters Acct when Treasurer 1663 and the next yeer 64.

Capt. Foster Deptr to the Towne.

1673 (1) 28 Imp. by Jno Farington 4 bls wheat 4 bls Rey and 8 bls Endian	03 – 01 – 6
Thes for ye yeer rent 1672 same day of John Pigg 2 bls wheat 13 bls and 1 peck Indian 23 (3) 3 bls Rey all is	03 – 01 – 9
Recc. of Srgn Elice on the same acc. of rent 3 bls wheat	00 – 15 – 0
	06 – 18 – 3
of Samuell Trescot by his fathers order a pt of his rent the yeer 72	00 – 17 – 0
1673 (12) 7 of goodman Trescot as pt of his rent 73	00 – 17 – 0

An acct. of what is disbursted towards the maintenance of the Child of Frances Bacon.

Imp. by what was p^d by Jn° Gornell to Tho. modsly . 1 – 4 – 0
It. p^d to Tho. Mosly againe . . . . . 2 – 11 – 3
It. p^d to Nicholas Clap for 5 weeks . . . . 0 – 15 – 0
It. p^d to Capt. Foster for 2 weeks . . . . 0 – 6 – 0

[**277**.] The same 8 (1) 7⅙ It was granted to Thomas Pope libertie to git about 2 or 300 of railes out of the 500 acrs.

The same day ther was appointed for fence Vewers for the Captins neck Jn° Wales and Jn° pelton.

for that p^t of the great lots beyond Timothy Tilstons	{ Tho. Tilston { Samuell Robinson
for the feild behind James Bird . . .	{ James Bird { Jn° Blackman
for the feild behind Mrs Joanes and before Enock Wiswels	{ Israell Mead and { Joshua Henshaw
for the feild behind Mr Stoughtons . .	{ Rich Baker and { Rich Leeds
for the Neck of land	{ Nicholas Clap and { Jn° Withington
for Cleering the Neck of Catle . . .	{ James Foster and { Hopestill Clap

All fences to be made vp by the 25 March 7⅙ and all Corne feilds to be Cleered of Catle by the 1 Aprill

Fence Vewers for the 20 acre lots { Thomas Grant
and
James Whit.

And Wheras it is found by experience that notwithstanding all former orders that haue been made, for the Ringing and yokeing of Swine, yet great Neglect haue been obserued to the great damedg of pastuers and of the Comons &c. it is therfore ordered that ther shall be yeerly Chosen two men who shall once euery Month, or oftener if need be goe about within the Compas of o^r Towne and if they find any Hogs vnyoked or vnringed, they shall yoke and Ring such as are not efectually done before, and for euery hog or Swine that they doe yoke and Ring, the owner therof shall pay vnto him that doe it Six pence for Each Swine and if they only ring them then three pence for each, and if only yoke them fower pence for each, and the owner of the Swine is heerby enjoyned to help to take the Swine, and the men appointed for the yeer Ensueing are John Homes and Thomas Tolman and all hogs to be yoked and ringed by the first of aprill and soe to be ringed all the yeer. Further it is ordered that if any other p'son shall find hogs vnyoked [**278**.] or vnringed, the owner of Such Swine shall vnto such as find them soe, soe much as the former order Concerning Swine Recorded in the 409 pag of this booke doe p'scrib and soe alsoe for pigs vnder half a yere old the which order is not repealed by this but stands in full force.

The same day it was ordered that it being found by sad experience that notwithstanding all former wholsome and prudent laws and towne orders Concerning horses goeing on the Comons, yet little efect it haue taken but that still great damedge and hurt is done, it is therfore ordered as an adition to the former orders, that all p'sons within the p'sincts of this towne that haue or doe keepe any horses, Mares or Colts of what sort soe euer, they shall bring in a list to the Record' by the first of Aprill next, of the number of horses Mares or Colts, that each p'son doe keepe alsoe each p'son is required, (besides the brand mark) to set an eare marke vpon his or their beast and together with the number soe alsoe the mark to be Recorded, that soe when any hors mare or Colt is taken vp it may be knowne whos beast it is.

And if any p'son shall neglect to eare mark his beast, or to bring in the number of such hors kind as he doe keepe he shall be lyable to pay three shilling fower pence for euery such beast to the p'son finding such neglect, and if any beast be taken vp whos owner cannot be known then in that Cas to be delt with as strays, Further it is to be vnderstood that this order Concerning eare-marking extends also to such beast as men doe keepe in their enclosiers.

At a meeting of the freemen the 12 (1) 7½

Ther was Chosen for Deputies for the yere ensueing Capt Hopestill Foster and Lift^{nt} John Capen.

Alsoe for a Comissioner to Carry the Voter to the sheirtowne for Nomination of Majestrats &c. Lift^{nt} Jno Capen.

The same day William Weeks was Chosen Clark of the wrights.

[279.] The same day was Chosen for Constables Timothy foster and Jno Bird, but ther being a motion made that Jno Bird was a Castle Souldier he was suspended for the p'sent till inquiery be made by o^r deputies or otherwis Afterwards Timothy Foster aleaged his incapacetie by the law Concerning Rateing and soe got off ther was then Chosen Isack Joanes and John Withington.

The same day ther was granted by a Major Vote that ther should be a Rate of ten pounds Leuyed vpon the inhabetants for the payment of that which is yet behind towards the purches of Mr Flints habetation and some other arears that are yet due from the towne to be paid in money.

At a meeting of the Select men the 29 (1) 75 on a training day it was ordered that Thomas Hoppen should be warned to appeare before the Select men at their next meeting in Aprill to giue an accompt of his liueing.

The same day it was ordered that John Pope should be warned to Come before the Select men at the same time with such of his children as are of Capacetie to be Cattechised.

And John plum is then to appeare alsoe.

The same day it was ordered that Robt Stiles should appeare at Mr Stoughtons hous the next Second day at two of the Clock before the Select men to order the disposall of one of his Childern.

Alsoe that Capt. Clap and Roger Billeng should be desiered to meet the Select men in order. to o^r Court bussines about o^r lands.

Also the same time it was ordered that William Sumner and Lift^{nt} John Capen should attend the next County Court to make their adress on the behalfe of Mr Gibson will respecting his legacie to o^r Schole.

The same day it was granted to Samuell Robinson libertie to git two loads of Clobords out of our Comon Swamps.

[**280.**] The same time it was ordered that the Sup'uisors of the highways should be Caled on to looke after the bridg at mother brooks before the next Court.

The 29 (1) 75 Samuell Blake of Millton enformed of some that haue taken Clobords or bolts out of our Swamps without order as petter Woodward of Deadham and Samuell Whiting.

The same day at the request of Samuell Blake of Milton ther was granted to him libertie to git fower loads of Clobords in the Comon Swamps of Dorchester wherof he saith two loads of them are for James Whit of o^r towne and the rest for his owne vse at Melton.

Alsoe it is granted to him power to take any stuff that he can find gotten by any without order p'uided that he giue in a true accompt to the Select men of what he take and he to be fully satisfied for his labour out of the said stuff and the towne of Dorchester to haue the rest.

The 5 (2) 75 at a meeting of the Select men at Mr Stoughtons hous It was ordered that Nicholas Clap should be a fence Vewer at the neck of land insteed of Isack Joanes who is chosen Constable.

The same day at the request of Mr Stoughton it was granted to him the exchang of a peice of land at the North Corner of the training place at the head of the meaddow which he had of John Withington Viz one rails lenth to the South of the barrs that goes into the meaddow and soe on a streight line ouer a certaine Rock lying neer towards Elder Wiswels fence.

At a meeting of the Select men the 12 2 75

William Chaplin did againe renew his motion to haue libertie to keepe a hous of publique entertainement, but it was not granted.

The same day John Pope appeared before the Select men to giue an acc^t of the Education of his Children by way of Cattechizing who p'mised to Endeauor for time to come to be more dillegent that way to attaine instruction for them.

The same day Nathaniell Glouer requested that he might haue libertie to set vp two gates cros [**281.**] the high way by his hous, which was granted him for the p^{r}sent vntill the nightbours or Select men for the time being doe see an inconuenience in soe doing, which if they doe then to ly open againe.

The same day Nicholas George was granted libertie to keepe a publique hous of entertainment with the app'bation of the Honrd Court.

The same day ther was granted to Ensigne Hale libertie to git fower load of Clopboard out of the Comon Cedar Swamps and Shingle for his house.

The same day ther was granted to William Sumner libertie to gitt three loads in like maner.

28 2 75. The Select men of Dorchester haue granted libertie vnto Nathan Bradly to sell Cidar by retaile he attending to keepe order in his house according to law and with the ap'bation of the Honrd Court.

At a meeting of the Select men the 14 4 75.

It was granted to Timothy Tilston libertie to gitt two load of bolts for his Vse to make Vessels out of some of the Comon Swamps.

At a meeting of the Select men the 19 5 75.

Ther was a duble Contry Rate made according to the last yers Rate the Sume wherof is 82^{li} 14^s 1^d it being for the expences for the warr against the Indians and this besids the yeerly Contry Rate.

At a publique Towne meeting on the 13 (10) 75 being one wecke after o^r Vsuall time by reason of exterordinary publique Contry bussines.

After the directory being read it was p'posed to the towne what they would alow Mr Flint for his labour in preaching the yeer past ending the first of January 75. The Vote was for eighty pound a quarter p^t money. The same day ther was chosen for Select men — Lift^{nt} Jno Capen, Srg^{nt} Clap, Deacon Ja. Blake, Rich Withington, Daniell preston.

[**282.**] for Recorder Lift^{nt} John Capen
for Raters William Pond Mr Mather Roger Billeng.
Sup'uisors of highways John Bird Tho. Tolman

At a meeting of the Selectmen the 20 10 1675

It was ordered that Srg^{nt} Samuell Clapp and Deacon James Blake should see to the mending of the meeting hous by p'cuering William pond or some other man doe it and to be paid out of the next towne rats.

The same day it was ordered that a warrant should be sent to the Raters to make a rate of 80 pounds for the minestry and a rate of 15 pound for the vse of the towne.

At a meeting of the Select men the 12 Janu. 75 being a weeke and more beyond their vsuall time, on a publique accompt.

It was agreed with Mr James Minot Junr to keepe the Schole and to teach Such as shall come as in his agreement may appeare.

The same day the Select men appointed Richard Withington and daniell preston to see that the Schole-hous be fitted vp with seats and a lock and key for the doare.

The same day the Raters made a returne of the minesters Rate of 80^{li} 9 – 1 which was Comited to the deacons and a towne rate of 15 – 6 – 10.

[**283.**] The 14 12 75 William Sumner Came to the Select men with the Request which he had from Mr Jno Faierwether as followeth.

17 January 1675 Rec$\overline{cc}$ of Mr William Sumner fiue Sut of Armor markt one N, one R, one y, one W, one X, I say Recc. by John Faireweather Comisary the head peice belonging to the sute markt R is markt with 4 notches.

This is a true Coppie of the Receipt brought to the Select men to be recorded and the originall is left in the hands of the said William Sumner as Attests John Capen Record^r the 14 12 75.

At a meeting of the Selectmen the 14 12 75.

The Deacons p'sented a list of the names of thos that haue not paid their p'portions to the minesters Rate for the yeer 74 and the same was Comitted to the Constables Isack James and Jn° Withington to Colect and gather.

The same day the Select men tooke an acc^t of Constable Thomas Peirce and John Capen Junr for the rates Comitted to them to Colect both Contry and towne.

The same day the Select men appointed Daniell Preston to p'cure 600 flints for a town stock and the Select men doe engag to see them p^d for.

At a meeting of the freemen the 6 (1) 7⅛ ther was Chosen for deputys for the yeer eusueing Capt. Foster and Lift^{nt} John Capen and for Commissioner to Carry the Votes to Boston Capt. Foster if he be able, if not then Lift^{nt} Jn° Capen.

The same day ther was Chosen for Constables John Bird and John Breck.

[284.] The acc^t of Constable Peirce and Constable Capen Junr of the Contry Rate of 40 – 2 – 6: and the towne rate of 51 7 11 committed to them to gather.

Imp. to the Treasurer for which he gaue a receipt .	39 – 0 – 6
It. to Nicholas Bolton	3 – 0 – 0
It. to Lift^{nt} Capen as deputy and Recording and for what was due to him formerly	6 – 9 – 10
and to him ouer paid for which he giues Credit .	0 – 3 – 4
and to him out of the Contry rate	0 – 5 – 8
It. to Nicholas Georg	3 – 4 – 0
and to him ouer paid towards next yeer . . .	0 – 11 – 5
It. to Rich Leeds p' order	1 – 0 – 0
It. to William Sumner	0 – 9 – 7
and to him for frances Bakons tableing . . .	0 – 6 – 0
It. to Nicholas Clap for Frances table 5 weeks .	0 – 15 – 0
It. to Nicholas Georg for bord and a bl of Rey .	0 – 6 – 0
It. for Glass 19^s besides the bl rey p^d by R. Hale .	0 – 19 – 10
It. to Nathanell Clap	0 – 3 – 0
It. to James Whit for francks table . . .	0 – 6 – 0
It. to Samuell Hill a bl of Corn	0 – 3 – 0
It. to Tho. Swift for franks table 4 weeks . .	0 – 12 – 0
It. to Jn° Capen Junr for work for the town . .	0 – 6 – 0
and to him for runing the line	0 – 6 – 0
and to him for expenses about frances . . .	0 – 5 – 6
It. to Israell Euered for a woolf	0 – 10 – 0
and to Capt. Foster p^t of what he should haue .	24 – 15 – 11
rest due to him 2 – 17 – 6	83 – 19 – 1

[285.] At a meeting of the Select men the 13 (1) 7⅛
Ther was appointed for fence Vewers for the Captins neck } Ensigne Hale / Rich Leeds

for that p^t of the great lots beyond timothy Tilstons } Jn° Tolman / Tho. Trot Senr

for the feild behind Mrs Joanes and before Enoch Wiswels } Srg^{nt} Clap / Isack Joanes

for the neck of land . . . . . } William Sumner / Nathanell Clap

for the Cleering of the neck . . . . } James Foster / John Withington
for the feild behind James Bird . . . } Tho. Andrews / Obediah Haws
for the feild behind Mr Stoughtons . . } Srg^{nt} Weeks / John Baker

And all fences to be made vp by the 25 March 7⅛ and Corne feilds to be cleered by the first of aprill.

And the men appointed to look after the yokeing and ringing of hoggs are John Homes, and Nathan Bradly according to the order made the last yeer as in the old booke p. 277.

At a meeting of the Select men the 10th 2 76

It was granted libertie to the Widdow George to keepe a hous of publick entertainment with the ap'bation of the Honrd County Court p'uided she doe not draw Cidar any more then is p'duced out of her owne orchyard.

The same day it was granted to Nathan Bradly libertie to Draw Cidar with the ap'bation of the Honerd County Court.

At a meeting of the Select men the 13 4 76 It was ordered that Richard Withington doe take Care to see that the Pound be repaiered.

The same day ther was granted to goodman Moss and Samuel Maxfeild libertie to take one tree for heading out of the 500 acres p'uided that it is not to [be] [286.] sold out of the towne and this is besids three trees latly granted to goodman Moss for Staues with the like p'uiso.

The same day it was agreed that wheras Jno Bird was formerly Chosen Sup'uisor of the high ways for this yeer 1676 but now he being chosen Constable the Select men doe order and appoint James Bird to attend that seruice.

The same day It was agreed with Nicholas Bolton that seeing half the yeer is expired in which he should Ring the bell therfore for the other halfe yeer he shall haue twenty shillings for the other half yere for Sweeping the meeting house.

At a meeting of the Select men the 18 7 76 being one weeke after the ordinary time vpon occasion.

It was then agreed and ordered that Lift^{nt} Jno Capen Mr Timothy Mather and Richard Withington shall sett out the Contry Way by stakes or bounds from the Corner of Mr Stoughtons land which is fenced in vntell one Come to Henery Leadbetters which is Fenced in and make their returne to the Select men at their next meeting.

The same day it was ordered that the Constable should giue notice to the wife of Funell that she gitt some p'son to giue securetie to the select men for her abiding in the town or to dep^t the towne.

The same day ther was an agreement made with James Foster Conserning Frances Bacons Child Viz the said James foster is to haue the Child till it com to the age of one and twentie yeers for which the Select men doe engage that he shall haue ten pounds Viz fiue pound at p'sent and if the Child doe liue aboue half a yeer then to haue the other fiue pounds and that the Child be Competently Clothed.

The 7 8 76 ther was granted to Jn° Fennow libertie to get three or fower load of Clobord out of the Cedar Swamps which are in o^r Comon land.

[287.] At a metting of the Select men the 13 9 76
Ther was granted to the widdow Smith on the Rocky hill to haue fower loads of wood vpon the town account.

The 18 9 76 the deacons p'sented a list of thos that haue not paid their p'portions to the minesters Rate for the yeer 1675.

At a generall Towne meeting on the 4th 10 1676 after the Directory was read the matter Concerning the Ringing of hogs all the yeer it was Voted that it should be left to the descression of the Select men to make such orders as may reach the end of p'uenting the rooting vp of any of o^r Comons pastuers or Meaddow

At the same time it was also Voted that the Select men should alsoe make orders Concerning Sheepe that they may not goe without a keepper any time in the yeere becaus of the damedg they doe to fences &c.

The same day at the motion of the Widdow long for a hous-plott the towne did appoint Richard Leeds, Richard Baker, Ensigne Hale, William Sumner and Srg^{nt} Clap to be a Comittee to looke out a place that may be conuenient not exceeding a quarter of an acre of ground and they to determine the thing and they to make returne to the Select men.

The same day it was ordered that Mr Flint shall haue eighty pounds for his labour this last yeer ending the last of this month and one quarter p^t of it to be paid in money.

The same day ther was Chosen for Selectmen Lift^{nt} Jn° Capen, Srg^{nt} Clap, Deacon Blake, Daniell Preston. Rich: Withington and for Record^r Lift^{nt} Jn° Capen.

for Raters Mr Timothy Mather Srg^{nt} Pond, Srg^{nt} Wiswell.

Sup'uisors for the towne and County { Thomas Tilston
                                      John Baker

Sup'uisors for the Neck { William Sumner
                          Srg^{nt} Weeks.
                          Isack Jones.

[288.] At a meeting of the Select men the 11th 10 76
Jacob Hewens Came and demanded pay for some trees taken out of his lott to mend the bridg and alsoe for work at meeting hous 1^s and for a load of wood Carted in for Daniell Elders.

The same day ther was granted to Samuell Paule libertie to haue two load of Cloboard out of the Comon Swamps.

The same day ther was appointed Ensign Hale Henery Leadbetter and Srg^{nt} Wiswell to be a Comittee to lay out the high Way from the Country Way by Samuell Chandlors or ther about to the twenty acr lots and soe towards the Comons, and to giue notice to p'sons Conserned of the time and to make returne to the Select men at ther meeting in May next.

The same day ther was granted to Daniell preston and Tho. Swift to each two loads of Clobords to be taken out of the Comon Swamps belonging to Dorchester.

The same day it was granted to Ebenezer Williams libertie to gitt 100 of railes out of the 500 acrs and 30 or 40 posts.

The same day it was granted to Jn° Minot to gitt two thousand of Clobord out of the Comon Swamps.

The same day it was granted to Jn° Garnesy liberty to gitt one load of Clobord and some loggs to saw about one thousand of bord p'uided he doe not take such stuff as will make Clobords and this to be in the Comon Swamps.

The same day it was Granted to Jn° Plum libertie to gitt eight or nine hundred of Clobbord in the Comon Swamp.

The same day it was granted to Samuell and Barnard Capen to each liberty to gitt Clobord out of the Comon Swamps to couer each of them a barne.

The same day the Raters weer ordered to make a Rate for the minestry of eighty pounds and a towne and Schole Rate of forty fiue pounds.

[**289.**] At a meeting of the Selectmen the 8 11 76 ther was liberty granted to Srg^{nt} Robt Badcock to git fower loads of Clobords at beare-Swamp.

The same day it was granted to Srg^{nt} Daniell Preston libertie to git three or fower load of Posts out of the Comons.

The same day it was granted to Thō Grant liberty to gitt one hundred of railes and 20 posts out of the Comons.

The same day the Raters made return of the minesters rate Consisting of 81^{li} 9^s 9^d and the towne rate of $45^1 - 18^s - 0$.

At a meeting of the Select men the 15 11 1676 at Lift^{nt} Capens house.

The Select men did (in referance to the law Concerning Idle p'sons, and priuate houses entertaining of p'sons contrary to good order) appoint Henery Leadbetter Ensigne Hale and Srg^{nt} wiswell together with Constable Breck to inspect that matter as the law directs about p'uoking euels.

And Mr. Mather Nathaniell Clap and Jacob Hewens to be joined with Constable Bird and soe to the Constables that shal be chosen in their steeds for to Inspect as abouesaid.

The same day it was ordered that Thomas Batle of Deadham should haue out of the Comon Swamps bolts or shingle two loads at least for his expence for the towne by way of testemony.

At a meeting of the Selectmen the 12 12 1676.

Joseph Birch was called before the Selectmen to answer for his Idlenes and neglecting to come to the publique ordinances on the lords days and for abusing himself by drinking to the which he answered as formerly that he hoped to reforme and to that end he was granted liberty to Cutt wood about ten Cord on the 500 acrs in the Swamps or woods that is already down to make Coales for his calling.

The same day ther was granted to John Fuller of Deadham libertie to take two loads of stuff for Shingle out of our Comon Swamps which is for his labour and incuredgment to inspect ouer such as shall gitt stuff without order.

[**290.**] The same day George Lyon made request for libertie for three load of Clobord which was not granted but left to the towne meeting in march to be p'pounded to the towne but afterward granted by the towne as in p. 291.

The same day ther was granted to william Blake sen[r] libertie to gitt fiue load of Clobord out of the Comon Swamps.

The same day it was granted to Jn[o] Spurr libertie to git two thousamd of Clobord out of the Comon Swamps for to enclos a smal hous in Dorchester.

The same day it was granted to Jn[o] Minot libertie for two thousand of Clobords this was Recorded in p. 288.

The same day ther was appointed for fence vewers for the Captins Neck Jn[o] Pelton Sen[r] and Jn[o] Breck.

for that part of the great lots beyond Timothy Tilstons	Timothy Foster Samuel Robinson
for the feild before Enoch Wiswells	Srg[nt] Wiswell Tho Moadesly
for the Neck of land	Hope Clap Nehemiah Clap
for the feild behind Jn[o] Bird	Jn[o] Bird Jn[o] Blackman
for the feild behind Mr. Stoughton	Richard Baker Isack Joanes
for Cleering the Neck	James Foster Jn[o] Withington

At a meeting of the Select men 14 12 1676.

It was ordered that the former order about Swine shall stand in force and Clement Maxfeild James Robinson, Nathan Bradly and Tho Moadesly are appointed to looke after them, and for the first time to giue the owners warning of their Swine that they are not according to order, and if they find hogs defectiue afterward, then the owners of such Swine shall be lyable to pay three pence p' Swine though the Vewer doe not yoke or Ring them, which he is not enjoyned to doe, without the owner of Such doe agree with him, and the men aboue mentioned are enjoyned hereunto one the penaltie of fifteen Shillings if they neglect their duty, and that they Vewe euery month or oftener if therunto Called vppon.

[**291.**] At a meeting of the Select men the 23 12 76 at the hous of Richard Withington.

It was granted to William Trescot three load of stuff for Clobord for his hous at the minestry fearme.

The same day Roger Willice was warned and had notice giuen him that he should Cleer the towne of his Sister Mehittabell.

The same day Lift[nt] Capen had liberty to git two load of Clobord out of the Comon Swamps.

At a meeting of the freemen the 7 (1) 7$\frac{6}{7}$ ther was Chosen for Deputies for the whole yeer ensewing Lift[nt] John Capen and Deacon James Blake.

Also for Comissioner to Cary the Vots to Boston Lift^{nt} John Capen.

And for Constables James Bird and Tho. Tolman Junr. Same day it was granted to George Lyon of Melton Libertie to gitt fower loads of Clobord out of the Comon Swamp at 700 by the load :

At a meeting of the Select men the 12 (1) 7$\frac{6}{}$ It was granted to Israell and Isack How libertie [to gitt] fower loads of Clobord at 700 a load out of the Comon Swamps.

The same day Daued Joanes was appointed to keepe the key of the Pound.

The same day it was granted to Samuell Blake libertie to git soe many Clobords as he haue promised Viz for Daniell preston 2i00 Mr. Mather 1000 and obediah Haws. 1400 on Condition that he bring in his former order for gitting Clobord, and not to git any more but what is abouesaid without any further order; also Elisha Foster 1500 and the widdow Long 1400 more besids 700 that is brought hime already.

The same day ther was granted to Joshua Henshaw libertie to gitt 3000 of Clobord out of the Comon Swamps towards the building him an hous.

The same day it was granted to Ezra Clap to haue 1400 of Clobord out of the Comon Swamps.

The same day ther was granted to John Tolman libertie to take Six Maple trees out of the flue hundred acres or 4 maples and two Oaks.

[292.] Towne dept$^{r\,1}$ to Lift^{nt} Jno Capen.

Imp. p^d to Nicholas Waymouth a pa of shows towards worke at Scholhous	0 – 5 – 0
It. for his hors to draw the bell to boston	0 – 1 – 0
It. mended for Frances Bakon	0 – 0 – 6
It. for a quier of Paper	0 – 0 – 6
It. for Frances againe	0 – 0 – 8
It. for attendance at Court Deputy 26 days	3 – 18 – 0
It. for Entertaining Frances Bacon 13 weeks for my self and others.	1 – 19 – 0
It. for Recording yeer 75	1 – 0 – 0
It. for attendance at Court Feburary Sessions yeer 75 6 days	0 – 18 – 0
It. for a quier of paper	0 – 0 – 6
It. for attendance at Court as deputy in May Court 76 2i days	3 – 3 – 0
It. for a pa shows for frances Child	0 – 1 – 6
It. for attendance at Court in August 10 days in order to the messengers goeing for England	1 – 10 – 0
It. for Recording yeer 76	1 – 0 – 0
It. for attendance at Court as deputy Octo Sixteen days	2 – 8 – 0

---

[1] The credit side of this account may be found on the next page.

It. for pa shows for frances Child . . .	0– 1– 7
It. for a pa of bodys for Frances . . .	0– 4– 0
	16–11– 3
This acc^t was made vp with the Select men the	14– 6– 6
11 10 76 and ther was due to ballance 2 – 4 – 9	2– 4– 9

Towne Dept^r[1] to Lift. Jno Capen

Imp' for what he should haue had out of the towne Rate yeer 77 as by that acc^t will appere the Sume of 11^{li} 11^s out of which must be deducted his owne rate 16 – 16 : Samuell Capens 6^s and Barnard Capens Rate 5^s Jno Masons rat 3^s and by his order for Jno Burg his rate 13^s – 6 : remains	9 – 6 – 1
It. for 24 days attendance at Court as Deputy both Sessions	3 – 12 – 0
It. for what he p^d goodman parker of Cambridg Villedg for Horsly's Child the first payment	4 – 0 – 0
It. for a pa shows giuen by the Select men to parke at his cleering the towne of Widdow Horsly	0 – 5 – 6
It. for a quier of pap'	0 – 0 – 6
Dept	17 – 3 – 3
Cred.	9 – 18 – 8
Ballance	7 – 4 – 7

Made vp this acc^t with the Select men the 18 12 78 and the ballance is ordered to be p^d by the Constable out of towne rate for the yeer 79 which is 7 4 7

[293.] Towne p Contra[1] Cred^r

Imp. by Ebenezer Withington by order of Samuell Trescot p^t of his rent . .	2 – 0 – 0
It. by Samuell Trescott 440 Clobord left at my yard 22^s : Capt. Foster had the rest .	1 – 2 – 0
It. Rec͞c. of my Son John as Constabl out of the towne rate ouer p^d	0 – 3 – 4
and by him out of the Contry rate same yeer ouer p^d	0 – 5 – 8
It. Rec͞c. of Mr Flint by Willm Trescots order as p^t of his rent 27. 4 75 . . .	2 – 6 – 0
It. Rec͞c. of him also by Tho. Bird on acc^t as p^t of his rent	1 – 0 – 0
and of Nehemiah Clap	1 – 3 – 0

---

[1] The debit side of this account may be found on the previous page.

It. Recc. of Jno Trescot for Samuell Trescot 22^s as p^t of his rent	1 – 2 – 0
and more at another time by S. Trescot	0 – 4 – 0
It. Recc. of W. Trescot by widdow Gornell	1 – 0 – 6
It. Recc. of W. Trescot on acc^t with myself for makeing Cidar towards his rent p^t for 74 & 75 which should be 15 pounds for thos two yeers but he expects some abatment becaus of the trouble by the Endians	4 – 0 – 0
	14 – 6 – 6

Towne p Contra[1] Credit^r

Imp. by 6 bl^s & ½ Corne brought in by Jno Farington for former rent of Schole land Recc the 15 – 1 – 7⅛	0 – 19 – 6
It. by 3 bl. wheat of goodman Elice of Deadham being p^t of rent for Schole land	0 – 15 – 0
It. by shows left at his Son Jno Capens when he was Constable which he could not put off	0 – 19 – 2
It. by what he receaued of Henery Glouer p^t of his first yeers rent for minestry land in bark and other bils	7 – 8 – 0
and 3^s added to Henry Glouers Sume	0 – 3 – 0

[294.] At a meeting of the Select men 9 2 77

It was ordered that Thomas Trot Senr Samuell Robinson and Ezra Clap are appointed a Comittee to lay out the Contry high way about Naponsett Mill Espesally about the Coming vp of the hill one this sid the Mill and likwis the Way leading from Deadham vnto their landing place at Naponset and also to lay out the Contry way vnto the New bridg which lys below Robt. Spurr and heerof they are to make their returne to the Select men.

The same day it was ordered that Georg Minot should be sent vnto to enquier his reason of entertaining of an inmate into his hous Viz Henery Robts.

The same day it was granted to Srg^{nt} Clap libertie to haue one load of Clobords out of the Cedar Swamps.

The same day it was granted to George Sumner vpon his fathers acc^t libertie to take two or three hundred of railes off from beyond the last Six deuission and the line of the blew hils.

The Same day ther was granted to William Pond libertie to gitt 1400 of Clobord out of the Comon Swamps.

The same day it was ordered that Thomas Dauenport should be added to William Sumner and Ensigne Hale in the steed of William Blake who weer formerly appointed to lay out a way to the fresh Marsh beyond Richard Withingtons lot vnto which place it is already laid out.

The 15 3 77 at a meeting of the Select men It was granted vnto

---

[1] The debit side of this account may be found on the previous page.

John Trescot libertie to gitt 14 or 1500 of Ceder Clopords out of the Comon Swamps belonging to Dorchester.

The 11 4 1677 at a meeting of the Select men

It was ordered that William Sumner Isack Joanes and Enock Wisweell should lay out the bredth of the way from goodman Boltons house toward the Corner of Amiell Weeks orchyard and to make returne to the Select men.

The same day it was Concluded that in the makeing the next Six rates it shall be made soe much the greater as to pay Mr Mather thos rearedges that is due to him [**295.**] for his father p'uided he doe first discount what he is behind for his towne rates for seueral yeers.

The same day Joseph Birch was Caled on who Came before the Select men to answer for his being lately drunke, and being owned by him he was ordered to pay his fine according to law or to sitt in the stocks.

At a meeting of the Select men the 9 5 1677.

Ther was granted to Increas Sumner liberty to take three thousand of Clobord out of the Comon Swamps belonging to Dorchester.

The same day Constable John Bird had order to pay Mr Mather nine pounds one Shilling which is the Sume of his p'portion for the ten rates and Six rates for the yeere 76 being in consideration of rearedges due to his father.

The same day ther was a list deliuered by the Deacons of the names of Seueral that had not paid their p'portions to the maintenance of the minestry for the yeer 76 and it was Comitted to Constable James Bird and Thomas Tolman with a warrant to impower them to Colect it.

The same day it was granted to John Merefeild libertie for 1400 of Clobord out of the Comon Swamps.

At a meeting of the Select men the 16 5 77 for to make the Contry Rate of Six rates.

The same day ther was granted to Charles Dauenport libertie to haue two loads of timber one for fenceing and another for his trade out of the 500 acres.

The 20 (6) 77 Ensigne Richard Hale was Chosen Commissioner to make the Contry Rate with the Select men.

At meeting of the Select men the 31 (6) 77 —

It was granted to Jn° Pelton Senr to git timber out of the 500 acres towards the building him an hous about 26 foote in lenth and 18 foot wide and 2100 Clobord.

The same day it was granted to John Smith Senr libertie to git 2100 of Clobord out of the Comon Swamps.

[**296.**] The same day haueing receaued a note from Robt. Tucker in the name of the Select men of Melton Enforming vs of a Comittee appointed by the Countie Court for to Vew the way ouer brush-hill, and that the Select men of Dorchester may be ther if they haue a mind to it, The Select men doe Nominate and appoint Lift^{nt} John Capen Ensigne Richard Hale and William Sumner to be present at the time appointed.

The same day it was granted to John Minot libertie to take wood already downe to make one kilne of Coales out of the 500 acres beyond the Swamp by Daniell Elders.

At a meeting of the Select men the 10 7 77

It was granted to Samuell Rigbey libertie to haue 1400 of Clobord out of the Comon Swamps of Dorchest'.

The same day it was granted to Mathias Euens libertie to haue fowerteen hundred of Clobord, &c.

The same day it was granted to Richard Euens libertie for one and twentie hundred of Clobord.

The same day Thomas Tilston was appointed Sup'uisor of high ways in steed of Tho. Tolman which is Chosen Constable.

The same day Srg^{nt} Clap and Deacon Blake are desiered and impowered to looke to the repaiering of the meeting hous for this winter, by stopping some holes and puting vp some seates that are fallen and the staires that goe vp to the pulpit and to be p^d out of the towne rate.

The same day Ensigne Hale and Enock Wiswell are desiered and impowered to looke to the Comon Cedar Swamps and if any are ther taken at any time without order, to Seiz them for the vse of the towne or shingle or bolts or the like.

The same day it was granted to Enock Wiswell libertie to gitt 1400 of Clobord.

The same day it was granted to Frances Bale libertie to haue 1400 of Clobord.

[297.] At a meeting of the Select men the 12 9 77

It was ordered that the Constables who haue been appointed to gather in the remainders of the minesters rates, formerly vnpaid shall meet at the house of Lift^{nt} John Capen on the 28 Instant at 4 of the Clock in the afternoone, to giue in and to Cleer ther acc^{ts} and the two Constables for the time being to giue timely notice to the former Constables for 73 74 75 and 76.

The same day it was granted libertie to Jn° Breck to haue one and twentie hundred of clobord out of the Comon Swamps.

At a publique towne meeting the 3 10 77 —

After the directory was read it was p'posed to the towne an inconueniency in the directory which tys vp the Select men that they cannot make a Rate for the vse of the towne aboue twentie pounds till an acc^t be made of the disburstments formerly, therfore it was p'posed that the Select men should make such rates for the towns vse as they in their discretion shall think fitt not exceeding fortie pounds for this yeer : the Vote was in the affirmatiue.

At a motion of William Trescot for an abatement of his rent for the yeer 75 and 76 becaus of the troubles of the warrs, wherby he deserted his place at brush-hill the towne leaues it to the Select men to Consider of the motion and to doe therin as they thinke fitt: The Vote was in the affermatiue.

The same day it was agreed and Voted that ther should be a rate of two hundred pounds made for the carrying on the worke of the meeting hous, one theird p^t to be paid in money, the other two theird p^{ts} to be paid in Corrant Contry pay.

The same day ther was Chosen for Select men Lift^nt John Capen
Daniell Preston
Richard Withington
Srg^nt Samuell Clap
Deacon James Blak
for Recorder Lift^nt John Capen
for Raters Enock Wiswell
John Breck
Samuell Robinson

[298.] At a meeting of the Select men the 10th (10) 1677.
It was granted to Richard Mather libertie to git 1400 of Clobord out of the Comon Swamps towards building him an hous, and two load of bolts to make shingle of such trees as are not fitt for Clobord or of such as are already downe.

The same day Doctor Snellen of Boston Came to the Select men to obtaine libertie for to bring his wife and famely into this towne for some time because of the pox increasing in Boston which libertie was granted him for two months but if he stayed longer to giue bond to secure the towne.

At a ginerall towne meeting the 17 10 77 being legally called together at Mr. Flints house on the occasion of the shortnes of the day before

It was Voted that Mr. Flint should haue 80 pounds for his labour in the minestry for the yeer that is past, one quarter p^t in money.

The same day it was Voted that for the yeere following the minesters pay shall be paid by weekly contribution each lords day and that thos that doe not Contribut they shal be rated according to former p'portion.

The same day Deacon James Blake was Chosen Clarke of the wrights in the roome and steed of William Weeks who is dead.

The same day ther was Chosen for Sup'uisors of highways John Baker and Samuell Paule.

At a meeting of the Select men the 21 (10) 77 at the hous of Lift^nt John Capen It was ordered that order should be sent to the Raters to make a Rate for the minestry of eighty pounds, a quarter p^t money and a Rate for the towne and Schole of Sixtie fiue pounds, and a Rate for the meeting hous of two hundred pounds according to the Vote of the towne of the 10th (10) 77 the which Rate is to be paid one theird p^t in money and to make their returns to the Select men at their next meeting in January which will be the 14th of that month.

The same time it was ordered that Srg^nt Preston should speak with Samuell Paule to looke after our Purgatory Swamp, Concerning damcdg that is done therin by Peter Woodward of Deadham as we are enformed, and to act therin as is meete when he vnderstands how it is.

The same time it was ordered that the Recorder should Isue out orders, Concerning Robt Sanders and the Widdow Horsly who stand in neede of wood that whosoeuer they can p'cuer to git them some they shal be paid out of the towne rate not exceeding fower load for Sanders and three load for the widdow, vntill further order.

At a meeting of the Select men the 14th 11 77

It was granted to James whit libertrie to git 200 of railes and 40 posts out of the 500 acrs.

At a meeting of the Select men the 11 12 77

It was granted to Robt Stiles libertie to git some timber towards building him an house out of the 500 acrs.

The same day Goodwif Horsly was called before the Select men and admoneshed Concerning her entaining p'sons at her hous and warned against it for future.

The same day ther was granted to Henery Leadbetter libertie to git 2800 of Clobord out of the Comon Swamps.

The same day it was granted to John Trescot to haue a load or two of shingle or bolts to make soe many.

The same day it was granted to Ebenezer Williams libertie to git two load of timber to make a Cidar press.

The 6 (1) 7⅛ at a meeting of the Select men at Lift^{nt} John Capens hous it was granted to Thomas Swift libertie for 700 of Clobord out of the Comon Swamps.

At a meeting of the Select men the 11 (1) 7⅛ ther was appointed for fence vewers as followeth

for that p^t of the great lots beyond Timothy Tilstons — —	Benjamin Leeds and Tho. Tolman Junr
for the Captins neck —	Ensigne Hale John Wales Senr
for the feild before Enock wiswels and the hill feild	Srg^{nt} Clap and Isack Joanes
for the feild behind Jno Bird — — —	James Bird and Obediah Haws
[**300.**] for the feild behind Mr Stoughtons —	Richard Leeds and John Baker
for the neck of Land —	William Pond Nathaniell Clap
for Sup'uisors of the way to neck — —	James Foster John Withington
for Cleering the neck —	Jno Blackman and Comfort Foster

And all fences to be made vp by the 25 march next and fence Vewers to Vew fence and the Cleerers of the neck to be vewed and Cleered by the 1 Aprill.

The same day ther was appointed Srg^{nt} Clap Amiell Weeks and Ebenezer withington to run the Line between vs and Rocksbery.

The 13 (1) 7⅛ at a publique towne meeting ther was Chosen for

Deputies for the yeer ensueing Lift^{nt} John Capen and William Sumner.

And for Comissioner to Cary the Votes Lift^n Capen

The same time ther was Chosen for Constables John Tolman and John Baker.

And John Wales is Chosen Sup'uisor of highways in the steed of John Baker.

The same day William Chaplins petition Concerning the keeping a hous of entertainment was read which was not granted.

The same day Mr Flint made a motion for a plot of land on the Comons for to set a smale hous on and a garden; The towne appointed William Sumner and Lift^{nt} Capen to take Vew of the place and make report of the Conueniencie or inconueniency of the motion at the next towne meeting or training day.

The same day it was granted to Teag Crohoar liberty for 2800 Clobord.

At a meeting of the Selectmen the 8 (2) 78

Ther was granted to Samuell Hale libertie to git 150 railes and post Sutable out of the 500 acrs or out beyond the line of the blew hils.

The same day thos that did run the line between vs and Rocksbery made their returne which is on file

The same day it was granted that the Widdow Georg should haue her licence renewed if the Court approue of it.

The same day vpon Complaint that the Way to the landing place by Thomas Tilstons is straitened the Select men doe appoint William Sumner and Henery Leadbetter to Vew it and rectefie that matter and make returne.

[**301.**] The same day Ensigne Hale was appointed to looke after the repairation of the Pound

At a meeting of the Select men the 10 4 78

It was granted to Joshua Henshaw libertie for 2100 of Clobord.

At a meeting of the freemen in the 6 mo. 78 Ensigne Richard Hale was Chosen Comissioner for the Contry Rate

At a meeting of the Select men the 9 Sep. 1678

The same day it was ordered that the Constable should giue notice to Jno Brown and John Hopen to dep^t the Towne as being noe inhabetants

Alsoe that the said Hopen be Sumoned to appeare before the Select men to giue an acc^t of his maner of liueing and to appeare at the house of Deacon Blake the 18 Instant being wednesday an hower before son sett.

The same day it was ordered that the tithingmen in their seuerall p^{r}sincts should inspect all inmats that doe come into each of their p^{r}sincts, either single p'sons or famelies, and to giue spedy information therof vnto the Select men from time to time or to some of them that order may be taken about them.

The same day it was ordered that Deacon Blake and Srg^{nt} Clap should see to the repairation of the Pound and Richard Withington to looke out after a lock for the Scholehous doare.

The 13 7 78 It was granted to Lawance Smiths Widdow libertie for 1400 of Clobord.

At a meeting of the Select men at Deacon Blaks hous the 18 7

78 Thomas Hoppen appeared to giue an acc^t of his manor of liueing, which did not satisfie that which he did mostly follow was guning but noe setled place of abode for famely gouerment.

The same time John Brown appeared and thought that he might Come into town to be inhabetant becaus born in the town and that he might be an help to his father and mother, the Select men did Respit the full determination at that time to know the towns mind therin and in the meane time his warning out of town to continue in force.

[302.] At a meeting of the Selectmen the 11th 9 78 Georg Lyon had a note to goe to James Bird or Thomas Tolman Constables for the yeer 77 for 25s. – 10d. and 16s. – 8d. for James Tucker which was their rats when they weer in Dorchester

Also William Blake Senr for himself and his Sonn Samuell had a note to goe for 3^{li} – 10^s – 4^d which weer their rats to be p^d back againe.

The same day it was ordered that all Constables for 75 76 and 77 should be Sumoned to appeare before the Select men at the hous of Rich. Withington on Monday the 25 Instant to make vp their acc^{ts} for the Rates which they weer to Colect in their seuerall yeers haueing not been made vp afore

At a meeting of the Select men the 25 No 78 at the hous of Richard Withington for to take an acc^t of the Constables for 75 76 77

The same day Isack Joanes and John Withington did appear to make vp their acc^{ts} for the yeer 75, Viz for a duble Rate and the eight rats and towne rate which is as followeth

The Sume of the duble Rate was	^{li} 82 – 7 – 8
out of which the Treasurer is to haue	78 – 1 – 0
the ouer plus is	4 – 6 – 8
out of which is deducted as not to be gathered	1 – 5 – 10
The ouer plus remaining is	3 – 4 – 10
The Sume of the Eight rates is, with the aditions and deductions Considered	326 – 9 – 2
out of which the treasuer is to haue for one of the eight rats	37 – 7 – 3
and out of the other Seauen Rates the treasurer haue	280 – 0 – 0
and the troops and Castle men out of the single rate as in the Margent of the rate	1 – 18 – 1
the ouer plus of the eight rates is	7 – 3 – 10
Soe that the Totall ouer plus of all the ten Rates is	10 – 8 – 8
Also more deliuered to them in shows after they weer prized	7 – 0 – 10
Toatall ouerplus is	17 – 9 – 6
out of which was deducted as desp'at depts not to be gathered	6 – 6 – 2
Rest due to the towne	11 – 3 – 4

look more of this days work p. 306.

DORCHESTER TOWN RECORDS.

[**303.**] out of the which $11^{li} - 3^s - 4^d$ was p^d to Widdow georg p^t of her bill of expences on souldiers at their goeing forth not alowed of by the Contry Comitte . . . . 5 – 11 – 0

and to Capt. Foster for a dept due to him from the towne . . . . 4 – 4 – 8

9 – 15 – 8

Rest yet due to the towne . . . 1 – 7 – 8

The towne Rate Comited to them to Colect the Sume was 15 – 6 – 10 . . . . 15 – 6 – 10

out of which they p^d as followeth
Imp. to Nicholas Bolton	2 – 15 – 6
and to him for frances for 2 weeks . . .	0 – 6 – 0
It. to Widdow Georg	2 – 19 – 1
It. to William Pond for work at meeting hous .	0 – 2 – 6
It. to William Trescot for bord . . .	0 – 1 – 6
It. to Srg^{nt} Clap	0 – 3 – 0
It. to Ensigne Hale for work at Scholhous .	0 – 4 – 5
and to Benjamen Leeds for Carting bords .	0 – 1 – 8
and to Ensign by Samuell Toplifs rate .	0 – 2 – 2
It. to Amiell Weeks p^t of his pay for runing the line at blew hils	0 – 3 – 4
It. to Roger Belleng which Jno Withington must pay for the same line	0 – 6 – 0
It. to Jno Capen Junr which Isack must pay for the same line	0 – 6 – 0
It. to Samuell Paull for the same work .	0 – 6 – 0
It. to Capt. Fosterr his towne rate by Isack .	0 – 4 – 0
It to Henery Leadbetter for frances . .	0 – 4 – 0
It. to Jno Homes for his widdow for frances .	0 – 6 – 0
It. to Clement Maxfeild for frances . .	0 – 6 – 0
It. to Obediah Swift his rate and mothers .	0 – 3 – 10
It. to James Foster for frances . . .	0 – 2 – 11
It. to Rich. Withington for frances . .	0 – 5 – 0
It. to Srg^{nt} Wiswell for franck . .	0 – 3 – 7
It. to Quarter Mr. Smith for frank . .	0 – 3 – 8
It. to Samuell Robinson for frank . .	0 – 4 – 0
It. Srg^{nt} Preston	0 – 4 – 9
It. to Tho Trot Senr for franck . .	0 – 5 – 0
It. to Thomas Tilston for frank . . .	0 – 3 – 4
It. to Samuell Paule for frank . . .	0 – 1 – 6
It. to Timothy Foster for frank . . .	0 – 2 – 9
It. to Timothy Tilston for frank . . .	0 – 3 – 4
It. to John Breck for Frank . . .	0 – 3 – 4
It. to Nathanell Glouer for frank . .	0 – 2 – 2

11 – 8 – 0

look ouer leaf due to ballance . . . . 3 – 18 – 10

[304.] Made vp this acc^t with Isack Joanes and John Withington this 25 9 78 and on the ballance of all their Rates ther is due to the towne five pounds two shilling Six pence 5 – 2 – 6

the one half of this 5 : 2 : 6 was after p^d by Isack Joanes and he discharged.

This was all could be don that day but the Select men appointed another day Viz the 29 day of Instant Nouember at the hous of Lift^{nt} Capen.

The 29 No 78 John Bird and Jn° Breck made vp ther acc^t Viz the ten Rats which they Colected the Sume wherof all deductions being Considered Remains good . . . . 399 – 5 – 0
The Sume of the first Six rates deductions being Considered is . . . . . . 243 – 15 – 11
but of both thes Sumes the Tresuerer is to haue . 636 – 0 – 6
And Mr Timothy Mather had out of thes Rates towards his fathers rearedges . . . 009 – 1 – 0

The Sume of the Towne rate Comited to them to Colect was . . . . . . 43 – 3 – 1
made vp the acc^t this 29 9 78 for all the Rates aboue said, and there is due to John Bird 14^s 3 vntill the bils ar ouer lookt of disburstments out of which ther is a dept due to the town . 0 – 14 – 3

John Withington's further acc^t from aboue wheras ther was the half of 5 2 6 due from Jn° Withington at our last acc^t as aboue said

Hee haue p^d more to Tho. Tilston or Jn° Pason for frank 2^s 8^d besids the former . . . 0 – 2 – 8
It. he p^d more also to Jn° breck for frank . . 0 – 2 – 8
It. he p^d more to benjamin Leeds for fetching a load of Clobord for the Schol hous and 18^d p^d for a days work at the meeting hous . . 0 – 3 – 0
It. he was als alowed for Ferrey to Charlestowne . 0 – 2 – 0
more James Molts rate remitted . . . 0 – 3 – 4
and Jn° Sanders Rate remitted by towne Vot . 0 – 16 – 0
and Petter Talbuts rat remitted by the towne Vote 0 – 15 – 0

2 – 4 – 8
10 11 80 yet rest due to the towne . . . . 0 – 6 – 5
this was p^d by the Select mens order to Lift. Capen as p^t of what towne ows him and John Withington is discharged:

[305.] The 29 Nouember.

The 17 and 18 days of February 1678 the Selectmen meet at the hous of Lift. John Capen to make vp acc^{ts} of the Rats Comitted to them to Colect viz., the Second Six Rates: the 3 single rats the Towne rate and the first meeting hous rate all for the yeer 77 namy [sic] James Bird and Tho. Tolman, but their accounts weer not ready at the time soe left to an other time.

An account of what was Committed to Jn° Bird and Jn° Breck to pay out of the Towne rate which they weer to Colect.

Imp. to the Widdow Foster for her husband being deputie in the yeer 75 and 76 . .	7 – 19 – 0
It. to Lift. Capen as deputie the ballance of his acc^t	2 – 5 – 9
It. to Widdow Georg for expences . . .	5 – 1 – 10
It. to Nicholas Boltons work at meeting hous .	2 – 10 – 0
It. to Dauid Joanes for half yeer ringing the bell	0 – 15 – 0
It. to Ensigne Hale for looking after the Swamp	0 – 3 – 0
It. to Samuell Blake at the same time . .	0 – 3 – 0
It. to Srg^{nt} Clap Deacon Blake, Jacob Hewens and Incres Modesly worke at meeting hous	0 – 4 – 0
It. to Daniell Preston for Bords for Scholhous .	0 – 5 – 6
It. to Israel Euered at the farne for 7 wolues .	3 – 10 – 0
It. to Obediah Swift for worke about the bell of which Isack Joanes p^d 1^s – 8^d rest due to him	0 – 2 – 4
It. to Ensigne Hale Srg^{nt} Clap. Deacon Blake and Rich. Withington to each 4^s – 6^d for wood for the Widdow Smith	0 – 18 – 0
It. to Jacob Hewens for a load of wood for Daniell Elders	0 – 4 – 6
It. to the Scholmaster Mr James Minot .	20 – 0 – 0
It. to Isack Ryall for work about the bell . .	1 – 10 – 0
It. to Rich. Withington for work about the pound and nailes	0 – 4 – 0
It. to Comfort Foster for a wolf . .	1 – 10 – 0
It. to Israell Euered for a wolf . . .	0 – 10 – 0
and to Shocho the Indian . . .	0 – 10 – 0
It. to Mr James Minot more . . .	0 – 16 – 0

[306.] The same 25 Nouember 78 It was granted to Barnard Capen libertie to git 3 or 4 loads of timber on the Comons towards the building a barne.

The 29 Nouem 78 the Select men met againe to take acc^{ts} of the other Constables but their acc^{ts} weer not ready Viz. James Bird and Tho. Tolman.

The same day it was granted to Jn° Trescott libertie to git 4 or 5 load of timber out of the Comons towards the building him a dwelling hous.

At a ginerall towne meeting the 2 10 78 After the directory was read there was an acc^t giuen of all rates for the yeer 75 and 76 except the minesters rate.

The same day it was p'posed to the towne whether Jn° Brown should be admitted inhabetant into this town, being put to the Voted the Vote was affermatiu.

The same day it was p'posed to the town, wheras formerly for the supply of Mr Flint for wood, Seuerall haue on their owne acc^t freely brought in wood which they Judg not equall that some should be at the Cost and others bear no p^t of it. It is therfore p'posed to the towne whether they will alow Mr. Flint 5^{ll} to be anexed to the town rate the next yeer if the towne see meet, and Mr. Flint to p'uid wood for himself. the Vote was negatiue.

The same day it was Voted in the affermatiue that the Elders and Select men should haue power of seating p'sons in the meeting hous.

The same day it was Chosen for Select men Lift. Capen Deacon Blak, Srg^{nt} Clap, William Sumner, Srg^{nt} Preston

for Record^r Lift Capen

for Raters { Srg^{nt} Wiswell, Srg^{nt} Pond
John Breck

for Sup'uisors Joshua Henshaw, Benjamen Leeds
looke more of this days actings p. 307

[**307.**] The 20 4 79
It was Voted at a towne meeting Whether they would alow Mr Flint one hundred pounds for this yeere Sixty pound in money and forty pound in other Currant pay. Mr Flint p'uiding help for supply in the minestry as ther shall be need;
The Vote was in the Affermatiue.

The same ginerall towne meeting It was voted that the old meeting-hous should be disposed off by the Select men for the best good of the towne also the trees that grow ther about shall be by the Select men from time to time soe ordered and disposed as they shall Judg meet either for standing or disposing some of them when and to whom they Judg meet.

This hous was afterward sold to Isack Ryall for ten pound and he alowed it as p^t of his pay for building the new hous. Also the trees, some of them weer sold one to Nicholas Bolton, for 3^s: two of them to Eb williams and Jno Capen Junr for 5^s, two or 3 more to William Cheny and Peter Talbut for 5^s 6^d one to William Trescot for 5^s and one to Elisha Foster for

look more of this p. 325, and for the bill of disbursements —

At a meeting of the Select men the 9 10 78
It was granted to Jno Smith Quarter Mr Son libertie to git two load of Clobord more, Viz: 1400 out of the Comon Swamps and a tree or two out of the 500 acrs to make ribs for their barne.

The same day ther was an agreement with Mr James Minot to be a Schol Master as in the booke will appeare.

The same day ther was an agreement made with Dauid Joanes to Clens the meetinghous and to ring the bell and to p'uid water for baptisme for which he is to haue three pounds a yeer out of the towne rate the yeer to begin the first of January.

[**308.**] At a meeting of the Select men the 13.11.78
It was granted to Thomas Pope libertie to git out of the 500 acrs soe much timber as to build a hous of 18 foot long and 16 wid.

The same day the Raters made returne of the rats Comitted to them to make Viz: a meetinghous rate amounting to 188 pounds 7^s and a towne rate of 23^{li} 12^s 10^d

The same day it was granted to Joseph Skilton libertie to git Six loads of wood out of the 500 acrs: p'uided he doe not fall any trees but take of that which is downe.

The Same day the Constable Jno Tolman was ordered to warne Robt. Stiles to appear before the Select men at their next meeting to know how he improue his time and his Children.

At a publique Towne meeting the 15 11 78 being legally warned and Come together. It was Voted in the affirmatiue that (at the motion of Roger Belleng) the Select men shonld Sige a deede vnto him of the farme he had of the towne lying about Wainmans Ordinary and to secuer it to him as from the towne and their Successors.

At a meeting of the Select men the 10 12 78 Robt Stiles Came vnto the Select men (being Sumoned afore soe to doe) to answer or giue an acc^t how he did improue his time for himself and Children the Conclusion was that he should look out for a place for one of his Children at least, or elce the Select men would p'uide a place.

The same day it was granted at the motion of Simon Peck that he should haue libertie to gather vp some of the old rotten wood in that 50 acrs reserued out of the minestry land at Melton which belongs to Dorchester.

At a meeting of the Select men the 17 12 at the hous of Lif^{nt} Capen John Parker Came and Engaged to secuer the towne of Dorchester in behalf of his daughter Martha Horsly if she might be let [**309.**] out of the hous of Correction, which engagement is one file.

The same day Thomas Dauenport had libertie to take 200 of railes out of the 500 acrs.

The same day Ebenezer Hill Came before the Select men and was aduertized Concerning Idleness.

The next day at the same place the Select men mett againe and made a rate for the minestry vpon such as did not Contribut on the lords days.

Also the same day they made vp acc^{ts} with Constables James Bird and Tho. Tolman for Contry towne and minestry and meeting hous rate soe farr as they had gathered.

At a meeting of the Select men the 10 (1) 7$\frac{8}{9}$ at the hous of Deacon Blake.

The same day Joseph Birch had libertie granted to git 100 of railes out of the 500 acrs.

The same day the Select men Signed to Roger Billeng Senr a deede of the farme about Wainmans Ordinary.

The same day at the petition of Desier Clap James Blake Jno Blake and others for to build a seat in the new meeting hous as in the petition on file will appear, the Select men granted their petition.

The same day Daniell Preston Senr and Srg^{nt} Clap are appointed to run the line between Milton and Dorchester in the outside of the last Six deuissions towards the blew hils and make returne their returns ar on fill.

The same day Willm Sumner Lift Capen and Ezra Clap to run the line between the 400 acrs and at the Swamp by Anthony Gullifords: the return is on fill.

The same day Srg^{nt} Pond Srg^{nt} Wiswell and Nathanell Clap weer appointed to run the line between Dorchester and Deadham but did not doe it that yeer.

and for the line between Dor. and Punchapage Timothy Tilston and Henry Leadbetter: returne is on file.

and for the line between Brantre and Dor. from the topp of the blew hils and soe towards the Patten line, Roger Belleng Samuel Paule and Jn° Minot: return on fille.

The same day was appointed for fence Vewers as followeth

[**310.**] for that part of the great lots beyond Timothy Foster } Timothy Foster and Samuell Rigbe.

for Captins neck . . . . . } Jn° Breck
Jn° Pelton Senr

for the feild before Enock Wiswell . } Joseph Weeks
Tho. Modesly.

for the hill feild . . . . . } Isack Joans and
Joshua Hinshaw

for the feild behind Jn° Bird . . } Jn° Bird and
Tho. Andrews

for the feild behind Mr Stoughtons . } Rich. Baker and
Amiell Weeks.

for the neck of land . . . . } William Pond
Nathanell Clap

for Sup'uisors of the way to neck . } Isack Joanes
Hopestill Clap

for the Cleering the neck . . . } Tho. Bird
Jn° Withington

And all fences to be made vp by the 25 March next and fence Vewers to Vew fence, and the Cleerers of the neck to be vewed and Cleered by the 1 Aprill.

The same day ther was appointed to looke after the boys in the meetinghous on the lords days : Clement Maxfeild Tho. Modesly Timothy Tilston and Jn° Tolman, each to take the Care of the boys orderly caredg in the publique meeting, each of them a quarter of a yeer the first to begin the first Saboth after the 25 march next.

The same day ther was appointed Thomas Modesly and Nathan Bradly for the North end of the towne and Clement Maxfeild and James Robinson for the South p^t of the towne, thes men are appointed to looke after the Swine that they be yoked and ringed according to former order as in p. 277 with referance to that order p. 409 with this addition of 1^s for each Swine that they yoke and ring and also vnder the penalty of 15^s fine for their neglect according to that Claus in the order p. 240 : the order Comitted to them it is on file.

the next in order is in p. 316.

[**311.**] An Order Regulating Swine made by the Select men the 11 12 79.

It is ordered that wheras ther haue been formerly great neglect of ringing and yokeing of hogs notwithstanding all orders that haue ben formerly made to p^ruent damedg. As an adition to former orders, It is now ordered that all Swine shall be sufficciently Ringed by the 18 day of this Instant Feburary and to be sufficciently yoked by the first of Aprill and soe to be kept yoked till the 12 of October, and to be ringed all the yeer, and this order to extend to all Swine from two months old and vpward and for the execution heerof ther shal be men appointed who shall goe a bout once a week or oftener If complaint be made to them, and if they find any such pigs or greater Swin either without a ring or yoke hee shall demand and receaue of the owner three pence for want of a ring, or three pence if they be without a yoke, and if without both ring and yoke then Six pence and if the owner doe not pay, or to the mens satisfaction then he shall take notice in wrighting the owner of the Swine, and the number therof, a list wherof shall be transmitted to the baylif which shall be Chosen, who shall once in euery month goe and take by distress what is due, that is to say, if the owner of the Swine doe not satisfie to satisfaction of the men first finding them defectiue, the which baylif if he be put vpon it to distraine, hee shall duble the fine and shal haue the one half for his labor, and if any man appointed by the Select men refus to looke after the Swine, and doe not giue a satisfiing reason he shall pay as a fine the Sume of therteen shillings fower pence, and he that is Chosen in his steed shall haue the fine, and if he that is Chosen for a baylif shall refus the place, and cannot giu[e] a satisfiing reason to them that Chose him, he shall pay the like fine, and he that accepts the place shall haue the fine, and if thos that are to looke after the Swin cannot find an owner for them then to impound such Swine either in the Comon pound or in some enclosuer of their own, and if noe owner doe appear then to yoke and ring such Swine and let them goe when they haue first paid themselues their due that is to say twelue pence a peice for such Swine.

[312.] The Town Dept^r to Lift. Jno Capen.

Imp. to the Ballance of his acc^t the last yeer as in p. 292	7 – 1 – 7
It. to 5 lbs. of Corne dl. to Daniell Elders . .	0 – 15 – 0
It. to Parkers Second payment	4 – 0 – 0
It. to Recording yeer 79	1 – 0 – 0
It. to a days work of his man the last Spring at Scholhous	0 – 1 – 6
It. to what he laid out a bout the Pound to Jno Trescot and his man and for stuff nails and help	0 – 5 – 0
It. to a days work to run the line between the 400 acrs and the Swamp . . .	0 – 2 – 6
It. to 3 days expences of the Select men at his hous	0 – 1 – 15
It. to nailes for the boys Seat and a quier of pap^r	0 – 10
Dept.	14 – 1 – 6
Cred	6 – 6 – 6
Ballance	7 – 14 – 0
Made this acc^t with the Select men the 11 12 79 and ther is due to Ballance . .	7 – 14 – 0

[313.]   p' Contra Credit[r]

Imp. sister Fosters Rate 2 bls. Corne dl to Tho Modesly	0 – 6 – 0
It. my owne rate yeer 78	0 – 6 – 7
It. Philip Demonzaday by Joshua Henshaw	0 – 0 – 9
and Joshias own rat and p[t] of his Grandmothr	0 – 3 – 3
It. of James Whit	0 – 4 – 10
It. by 16[s] he appointed Jn° Tolman to pay to his bro. T. Tolman for Jn° brecks rate in that yeer	0 – 16 – 0
It. Recc. of Jn° Tolman 1[s] money which was Sam Peltons rate which in Contry pay was	0 – 1 – 6
It. by Samuell Capen his rate	0 – 2 – 11
It. by Barnard Capen	0 – 2 – 6
and by Barnard for William Ryall	0 – 1 – 0
It. by Jn° Capens rate appointed by Jn° Baker	0 – 1 – 6
It. by Enock Wiswell	0 – 5 – 6
It. by James Bird	0 – 4 – 9
It. by Jn° Bird	0 – 2 – 9
It. by James Foster	0 – 4 – 4
It by widdow Farington	0 – 0 – 6
It. by Widdow Blackman	0 – 3 – 3
It. by Corne and Rey brought in by Jn° Pig of Deadham p[t] of former rent of Schol land bought in about May '79	3 – 0 – 0
	6 – 7 – 6

[314.]   The acc[t] of the Ireron M[r] Withington Legacy.

Imp Recc. 200 of Iron which Came from Tanton Octo. 1670	2 – 8 – 0
It. Recc. 100 of Iron May 72 but it was the p'dus of 71	1 – 4 – 0
It. for the yeer 72 Obediah Swift Recc one Hundred of Iron for which he made axes and hows for the Endian gratuetie by Capt. Fosters Order	
It. another 100 & ½ of Iron was left in the hands of Obediah Swifts hands to discharg a debt of the towns which yet he is to be Countabl for it: he p[d] 4[s] 6[d] money for Caredg of it	1 – 10 – 0
It. the next 100 & ½ of Iron Obediah Swift discounted with the Comittee for Ire work about the meeting hous he p[d] for caredge of it 4[s] 6[d] money	1 – 10 – 0
It. another 100 & ½ of Iron left in the hands of Obediah Swift, the begining of winter 1679 he p[d] 5[s] for bringing it rest due yet to the towne	1 – 10 – 0
It. another 100 & ½ of Iron left in the hands of Obediah Swift yet due	1 – 10 – 0

[**315.**] An acc^t of the Schole land
Imp. Recc. into the hands of Lift. Capen from Jn° Farington for rent of Schol land for 5 acrs at 6^s 6^d p acre for the yeer 71 . . .   1 – 12 – 6
It. Recc. of Jn° Pig on the same acc^t for 5 acres the same yeer . . . . . .   1 – 12 – 6
It. Recc. of Srg^{nt} Elice of the same acc^t for almost 3 acrs . . . .   0 – 17 – 8
It. Recc. of Srg^{nt} Elice 20^s left in Mr Flint's hands towards rent . . . . . .   1 – 0 – 0
Thus far acc^t was made to Captin Foster as Tresurer and ther was then 3^{li} 2^s 4^d in the hands of Jn° Capen Senr as by his acc^t will appear p^d to him
It. since Recc. Jn° Farington 6 bl. Endian . .   0 – 18 – 0
and of Jn° Pig 2 bl. Endian . . . .   0 – 6 – 0
and of Srg^{nt} Ellice a bl. of Rey . . .   0 – 4 – 0
all this was for rent formerly due.
It. Recc. of Srg^{nt} Elice a bl. of Rey . .   0 – 4 – 0
same time of Jn° Pig 4 bl. Endian . . .   0 – 12 – 0
M^d all this was dl. to Mr. James Minot to make vp what he fell short in the rate Viz: 10 bbls. Endian 2 bls. Rey besids two bls of Endian he left in the hands of Jn° Capē for a dept due from Mr Minot.
It. Recc. of Jn° Farington 6 bl & ½ of Endian .   0 – 19 – 6
It. Recc. by Lift. Capen 3 bls. wheat of Sr: Elice.   0 – 15 – 0
It. Recc. by Lift. Capen of Jn° Pig in Corne and Rey . . . .   3 – 0 – 0
all this haue been discounted with the Select men as by the acc^t will appear.

[**316.**] At a meeting of the freemen the 14 first m° 7$\frac{8}{9}$ William Sumner was Chosen Deputie for the year Ensewing and also Comissioner to Carry the Vots to Boston.

The Same day ther was chosen for Constable Hopestill Clap and Samuell Toplif.

The same day at the motion of Jn° Lewice for a peice of Comon land beyond the last deuissions on the North sid of Naponset neer Deadham mill it was granted that it should be left to the Select men to Conclud it on such Conditions as they Judge meete.

The same day the Elder published the list for the seating p'sons in the meeting hous, and also gaue an acc^t of the disbursment of the Contributions for the releef of the distressed for nurses and other expences for thos that had the pox Viz Samuell Chandler and widdow Rogers &c.

At a meeting of the Select men the 14. 2. 79 at the hous of Srg^{nt} Samuell Clap.

The same day Jn° Lewice Came to the Select men and Concluded Conditions about the land granted by the towne which is recorded in the New book p. 120 and libertie to git 2 or 3 load of Clobord to Couer his house.

The same day it was granted to Clement Maxfeild libertie to

git 1400 of Clobord and two or three trees for groundsels out of the Comon land.

The same day James Whit and James Robinson was appointed to vew the 20 acr lot fence.

The 22 2 79 It was granted to Ebenezer withington libertie to git two loads of Clobords out of the Comon Swamps.

At a meeting of the Select men the 9 4 79 at the hous of Lift. Capen.

The same day it was granted to John Trescot libertie to git 1600 of Clobord besids his former fowerteen hundred.

[317.] The same day it was granted to Henery Merifeild libertie to git 1400 of Clobord.

The same day it was granted to Samuell Robinson libertie to git 700 Clobord more besides what he had formerly granted and a few bundles of lasts.

The same day it was granted to Timothy Tilston libertie for 2 or 3 trees for to make Vessell timber.

At a meeting of the Town the 30 July 79 it was by a Vote granted to the widdow Salsbery libertie to git 2100 of Clobord out of the Comon Swamps.

The same day Ensigne Hale was Chosen Comissioner for to help make the Contry rate.

At a meeting of the Select men the 6 6 79 at the hous of Deacon Blake to make the 4 Contry rates and to take the Valiewation for the next Contry rate.

It was then granted to Charles Dauenport libertie to get 2100 of Clobord out of the Comon Swamps.

At a meeting of the Select men the 8 (7) 79 at the house of Srg^{nt} Clap

It was granted to Samuell Capen libertie to gitt 700 of Clobord out of the Comon Swamps besids his former grant.

The same day the Select men ordered that Constable John Baker shall pay to Nicholas Bolton ten shillings more to the 40^s formerly ordered him to pay to him which is for his worke at the meetinghous.

This ten shillings was afterward appointed to be p^d by Constable Hopstill Clap because Jno Bakers rate would not reach to doe it.

The same day It is ordered or granted to Samuell Joanes to haue libertie to gitt 1400 of Clobord.

At a meeting of the Select men the 10 9 79 at the house of Lift. Capen.

It was granted to Benjamin Leeds libertie to gitt 700 of Clobord out of the Comon Swamps and some bolts for Shingle.

The same day vpon Consideration that Hopestill Clap who was appointed Sup'uisor of the way to the neck and afterward was Chosen Constable, and now ther is more then ordinary Occasion to haue that way mended being [318.] vnpasible for man or beast to goe comfortably therfore the Select men appointed James Foster to Joyne with Isac Joanes to vew that way, and call vpon p'sons whose way is defectiue and see that it be repaired and made pasable with as much speed as possible can be and if any neglect their duty then to make returne to the Select men that the penalty which the order mentions may be taken : our intent is all such ways as are at p'sent very bad and vnpassable.

At a generall Towne meeting the 1 10 79 after the directory was read ther was Chosen Lift. Capen Richard Baker and Thomas Dauenport to Vew the way that the Widdow Weeks desiereth to haue changed and make ther returne to the Select men who are impowered to Isue it as they shall see best.

The same day a petition was p'ferred by Tho Tilston and others about stoping vp a way, the Petition with the answer to it is on file.

The same day Mr Flint made a motion for to haue a piece of land on the Comons a litle beyond the Corner of his Orchyard to set a barne on if he see meete to set it ther the which was granted but none then appointed to set it out.

The same day Jn° Capen Junr made a motion to buy that peice of land on the Comons a little beyond the end of his Orchyard and soe to Enock Wiswells land which was not granted at that time.

The same day was chosen for Select men —

	Lift. Capen William Sumner	⎧ Select
	Deacon Blake Ensigne Hale Srg^{nt} Clap	⎩ men
for Recorder	Lift^{nt} Capen	
for Raters	⎧ Srgent Pond ⎨ Srg^{nt} Wiswell ⎩ John Brick	

At a meeting of the Select men the 8. 10 79 at the hous of Srg^{nt} Clap The Select men ordered and apointed Lift^{nt} Capen and Srg^{nt} Clap that they should call vpon John Mason for the legacy giuen by John Gornell towards the Schole, and take it into their hands and the legacy of 5^{li} for the yeer past which the Widdow ¹Burg gaue to the poore of Dorchester.

The same day Nathaniell Johnson of Rocksbery came to the Select men and did accknowlidg that he had gotton 1300 of Clobord without order out of a swamp belonging to Dorchester, and that some body had taken them away, but he knew wheer they weer, his request was that the Select men would grant him that libertie as to haue thos which he haue already gotten, if he can recouer them, the which was granted him p'uided he git noe more without order from the Select men.

The same day Jn° Minot was granted libertie to git 2800 of Clobord out of the Comon Swamp.

A list of the names of thos which weer remoued to other towns in the time of the warr which ought by law to pay in this towne.

Henry Garnesy for his p'son	0 – 16 – 8
William Chaplin .	1 – 1 – 0
Mr Beale .	0 – 16 – 8
Henery Mare .	1 – 13 – 4
John Gill as in the third Collom of the County rate yeer 76	1 – 10 – 10

At a meeting of the Select men at Mr Flints hous the 22 10 79 John Bird made vp his acc^t for the rearedges of Mr Flints rat Co-

---

¹ Jane Gornell, widow of John Gornell, married John Burge. Inscription on her gravestone reads: "Jeane Gornell." — See N. E. Hist. & Genea. R   Vol. 4, p. 166. — W. H. W.

mitted to him for his pᵗ of the Rate, and he haue Cleered all for the yeer 75 he engaging to Mʳ Flint, to satisfie him for what is yet vnpaid which is 6ˢ and he is discharged for that part of the rate which was Comitted him to gather.

At a meeting of the Select men the 12 11 79 at the hous of Deacon Blake

The Raters Viz William Pond and Enoch Wiswell made returne of the rates Comitted to them to make Viz the ministers rate Consisting 101ˡⁱ· – 1ˢ· – 8ᵈ· and the towne rate amounting to 50ˡⁱ· – 7ˢ· – 0.

The same day Frances Bale Came to the Select men being formerly ordered soe to doe that the Select men might enquier of him Concerning his outward Estate, the Select men aduised him to dispose of two of his Children, his answer was that his wife was not willing the Select men p'swaded him to p'swad his wife to it

The same day the Select men agreed with Nathan Bradly to ring the bell and Clens the meeting hous and to carry water for baptisme, and while the bell stands on the hill, he is to haue fower pounds a year and after the bell is brought to the meeting house 3ˡⁱ· – 10ˢ· – 0.

[**320.**] The same day it was granted to Mr. Flint libertie to gitt 200 of railes in the Comons aboue the blew hills.

The same day Isack Joanes had a discharg of his worke as Constable for the yeer 75

At a meeting of the Selectmen the next day being the 13 11 79 at the hous of Deacon Blake after noone

It is ordered by the Select men that the day appointed for each p'son to bring in their pay to the minestry this yeer shall be the last Second day in January being the 26 day of the Month, and to bring it in to Mr. Flints hous and make vp their accᵗˢ, and thos that cannot doe it that day, then the therd Second day in Feburary being the 16 day of that month.

Also the same days to bring into the Schole Master wher he shall appoint.

The same day ther was libertie granted to Nehemiah Clap to git a load of timber out of the 500 acrs.

Also granted to Timothy Tilston libertie to take fower trees on the Comons about Puncapag.

At a meeting of the Select men the 9 12 79 at the hous of Lift. Capen a warrant was sent to the Constables to take a fine of John Jackson for fower weeks Entertainement of Op'tunetie Lane Lane his daughter in law Contrary to towne order, and also to warne the said Opertunetie to depᵗ the towne or giue in securetie to secur the towne from damedg and also that if the said Jackson entertaine her longer he must expect to pay 3ˢ· – 4ᵈ· p' weeke for euery weeke after the date heerof: Shortly after the said Jackson came and he and William Cheney entered into 30ˡⁱ bond to secuer the towne. the bond is on file.

The 11 12 79 After lectuer the Select men meet and made an Order to regulat Swine the which order is in p. 311 and Chos men Viz John Pason Ebenezer Withington and Samuell Hix for to look after the Swine on the west sid of Widdow Georges brooke and Nathan Bradly and Tho. Modesly for the North side therof.

The 12 12 79 John Mason brought to the Select men fiue pounds in shows which was Jane Burges her legacy to the poor of this towne the first payment which was for the yeer past; and the Select men appointed who should haue them as followeth.
The next in order is p. 336.

[321.] Henery Merifeild . . . . . . 0 – 7 – 0
Daniell Elders a pa . . . . . . 0 – 7 – 0
Robt. Stiles a pa . . . . 0 – 3 – 6
Tho. Pope . . . . 0 – 7 – 0
Samuell Hill a pa . . . . 0 – 7 – 0
Merriam Wood a pa . . . . . . 0 – 5 – 0
Jnº Plum . . . . 0 – 5 – 0
Robt. Sanders a pa. . . . . . . 0 – 5 – 0
Frances Bale a pa . . . . 0 – 7 – 0
Nathan Bradly a pa . . . . . . 0 – 7 – 0
Jnº Lewice a pa . . . . 0 – 7 – 0
Giles Barg a pa . . . . 0 – 7 – 0
Widdow Lawrance . . . . 0 – 4 – 6
William Turner . . . . 0 – 7 – 0
Edmond Brown . . . . 0 – 7 – 0
Joseph Weeks . . . . 0 – 7 – 0

The 16 day of January which was the day appointed to bring in Mr. Flints Rate, the Constables formerly that weer to giue in their acc^{ts} of the rearedges due to him came that day and all of them except Henery Leadbetter Cleered their acc^{ts} by engaging to Mr. Flint for what was behind and Mr. Flint gaue discharges to them to deliuer to the Select men for the Cleering of the towne, and before this time the Select men had vewed the desp'at depts of each rate Viz. for the yeer 72 vnto the end of the yeer 78 and is to satisfie that to Mr. Flint on acc^t with him, and shortly after Henery Leadbetter did also engage to discharg thos that he was to gitt in: Mr. Flints discharges are on file.
A list of the Seuerall p'sons that are lookt vpon as desp'at depts of what should haue ben paid to Mr Flint for the Seuerall yeers which is to be paid or made good to Mr Flint some other way is as followeth.
for the yeer 72 Henery Leadbetter Constable
    Administrators of Major Atherton Estat . 0 – 3 – 2
    Isable Fisher . . . . . . 0 – 14 – 4
    Hudsons Farme . . . . . . 0 – 16 – 8
    Nathaniell Wales . . . . . . 0 – 1 – 10
    Robt. Pelton . . . . . . 0 – 1 – 8
for the yeer 73 Tho. Pierce Constable
    Susana Breck . . . . . . 0 – 2 – 0
    Hudsons Farme . . . . . . 0 – 13 – 5
    Jeremiah Haws . . . . . . 0 – 1 – 8

[322.] For the yeer 74 Mr Flint did owne that Isack Joanes had Cleered his p^t to Colect and John Withington vndertook for his part except the desp'at.
for 74 desp'at dept look on the right hand *

for the yeer 75 Jn° Bird Colector
James Horsly	0 – 2 – 6

for the yeere 76 Tho. Tolman and James Bird Colectors.
Robt Sanders	0 – 5 – 3
John Merryfeild	0 – 3 – 6
Timothy Wales Junr	0 – 2 – 6
James Horsly	0 – 1 – 6
Tho. Williams	0 – 2 – 6
Robt. Pelton	0 – 2 – 0
Tho. Lawrance	0 – 2 – 6
Jn° Wales Junr	0 – 2 – 6
Tho. Beaman	0 – 2 – 6
John Spur	0 – 2 – 6
William Chaplain	0 – 3 – 6
Henery Merifeild	0 – 3 – 3

for the yeer 77 Jn° Tolman & Jn° Baker Colectors
Robt Sanders	0 – 3 – 0
Jn° Merifeild	0 – 3 – 3
Timothy Wales Junr	0 – 2 – 6
Tho. Williams	0 – 2 – 6
Tho. Lawrance	0 – 2 – 6
Nathanell Osburne	0 – 2 – 6
Jn° Wales Junr	0 – 2 – 6
Samuell Lawrance	0 – 2 – 6
Jn° Beaman	0 – 3 – 0

for the yeer 78 Jn° Baker Colector
Widdow Farington	0 – 1 – 8
Goo. Whitting at the farme	0 – 9 – 9
Israell Euered	0 – 6 – 9

[**323.**] for the yeer 74
*Robt Sanders	0 – 6 – 1
Henery Merifeild	0 – 7 – 0
Tim Wales Junr	0 – 1 – 8
	7 – 4 –11
William Chaplin for 76 T. Tolman Constable	0 – 3 – 6
The Totall Sume of all the desperat depts for the Seuerall yeers to the end of the yeer 1678 is Seauen pounds fower shillings eleuen pence besids William Chaplin 0 – 3 – 6	7 – 8 – 5
The ouerplus of those rats in the Seuerall yeers coms to six pound and ten pence	6 – 0 – 10
besides the yeer 71 at which time ther was a towne rate of ten pounds added to the minesters Rate and ther was carryed in to Mr Flint ouer and aboue what was appointed to him to the vallew of 3 – 11 – 3	3 – 11 – 3
and a load of Clobord which he had of Samuell Trescot being part of his rent for minestry land the which Clobords came to 1 – 11 – 3	1 – 11 – 3
	11 – 3 – 4
	7 – 8 – 5

Rest due to the towne from Mr Flint at the end
of the yeer 1678 the Sume of . . } 3 – 14 – 11

[**324.**] A list of the Tithing men that are appointed (for the yeer 1680) by the Select men 14. 10. 79

Jacob Hewens,	Tho. Tolman Senr
William Trescot,	Roger Belleng
John Capen Junr	Henery Leadbetter
Isack Jones	James Whit
John Baker	Richard Withington
Nathaniell Glouer	Obediah Haws
Thomas Tilston	

[**325.**] from p. 307.

An acc^t of the trees about the meeting hous as in p. 307.

It. d̃ to me by Srg^{nt} Clap 3^s from Nicholas bolton . . 0 – 3 0
It. from William Trescot Rec̄c̄ . . . . . 0 – 1 0
the rest he gaue a reason why not p^d
It. from William Cheny . . . . . 0 – 2 – 9
and Petter Talbut and Widdow batten should pay 2^s 9^d more but the towne was in his dept about the meeting hous in which the Select men set it off that way

Md one shilling of this was p^d to Nathan Bradly
for a bell rop. . . . . . . } 0 – 1 – 0
13 2 80 and p^d Hen. Thomas for glazing at
Scholehous . . . . . . } 0 – 5 – 8
It. more rec̄c̄. of Srgnt Clap from Eb. Williams 0 – 2 – 6
13 2 80 It. Rec̄c̄. of Jno Baker in moneys for the
bill of disburstment for towne powder bullets } 0 – 12 – 0
flints, &c . . . . . .
12 5 80 It. Rec̄c̄. of Elisha Foster for a tree . 0 – 4 – 0
It. Jno Trescot p^d for his tred in his worke about Mr Stoughton's Seat in meetin hous.

[**326.**] An account of Samuell Toplif as Constable for yeer 79 that p^t of the Rate which he was to gather the whol Rate Consisting of 5 } 25 – 7 – 2
pounds 5^s – 0 his p^t to gather is . .
Imp. p^d to Mr James Minot in money . . 4 – 0 – 8
and to him in Contry pay . . . 09 – 0 – 0
It. to Rich. Withington for what he laid down to
wards the hundred pound rat . . } 0 – 19 – 0
It. Danell Preston for what he laid downe for
widdow Horsly 8^s and for runing the line between Milton and Dorchester 2^s – 6 – and 6 } 0 – 11 – 0
pence more . . . . . .
It. to William Sumner for runing the line 2^s 6^d
and 5^s 7^d towards his deputyship . . } 0 – 8 – 1
It. to Ezra Clap for the line between Milton and
Dorchester . . . . . . } 0 – 2 – 6
It. to Timothy Tilston for the line between Puncapag and Dor. . . . . . } 0 – 2 – 6
It. to Henery Leadbetter for the same line . . 0 – 2 – 6
It. to Jno Minot for the line between brantree
and Dor. . . . . . . } 0 – 6 – 0

Roger Billeng for the same	0 – 6 – 0
It. to Samuell Paull the same line	0 – 6 – 0
It. to benjamin Leeds for bringing Clobords to the Scholhous	0 – 1 – 6
It. to James Robinson for two days Cutting wood for Nathan Bradly	0 – 3 – 0
It. to Nathanell Glouer for keeping frances	0 – 3 – 0
It. to Daued Joanes for keeping of frances 3 weeke	0 – 4 – 6
It. to Widdow Minot for Frances	0 – 3 – 0
It. to Samuell Toplif for frances 3 weeke	0 – 4 – 6
It. to Clement Maxfeild for frances 20 weeks	1 –10 – 0
It. to Timothy foster for work at the boys seat	0 – 3 – 0
It. to Samuell Maxfeild for Wading Election day	0 – 1 – 0
It. to Sam Toplif for the sam	0 – 1 – 0
It. to Rich Euens for a days work at Schol hous	0 – 2 – 6
	20 – 7 – 3
	Rest due 4 – 19 – 11
It. p^d of this to Widdow Georg for former expences	0 – 13 – 0
It. p^d to Roger Billeng (besids his money p^t) for Clobord and other things for the meeting hous	1 – 18 – 4
It. p^d to Daued Joans for Ringing the bell	3 – 16 – 0
It. p^d by Hope Clap as in p. 327	0 – 2 – 9
It. to John Guile for an Woolfe	0 – 10 – 0
It. to M^r flint for worke at schole house	0 – 4 – 0
It. Samuel Topliffe for a dayes worke schoole house	0 – 2 – 0

[327.] An acc^t of Hopestill Clap Constable for yeer 79 that part which he was to gather of the same rate with Sam Toplif the whole Rate Consisting of 50 pounds 5^s 0 his p^t is 24 – 17 – 10

Imp. to Mr James Minot in money	4 – 0 – 0
and in Cuntry pay	11 – 0 – 0
It. to Lift. Capen as p^t towards Recording yeer 79	0 – 18 – 1
It. to William Sumner as p^t of deputyship	1 – 10 – 11
It. to Deakon Blake for expenses of Select men	0 – 13 – 11
It. to Srg^t Clap 17^s for expences of Select men and for runing the line between Milton and Dor. 2^s 6^d	0 – 19 – 6
It. to Rich Leeds for keeping Frances formerly and rest due to him yet 13^s 2^d	0 – 16 – 4
It. to Tho. Moadsly for a Load of wood for Nathan	0 – 4 – 0
It. to Jno Wales for keeping of frances	0 – 3 – 0
It. to Nicholas Lawrance for frances	0 – 3 – 0
It. to Srg^{nt} Wiswell for frances 3^s and for killing her Cow 2^s	0 – 5 – 0
It. to Timothy Whiting for killing an woolf	0 – 10 – 0

DORCHESTER TOWN RECORDS. 241

It. to Jacob hewens for a days work Carting for wood for Nathan bradly	0 – 5 – 0	
It. to Tho Andrews Carting for Nathan wood	0 – 5 – 0	
It. to Samuel Wales for frances	0 – 3 – 0	
It. to Sam Trescot for frances	1 – 7 – 1	
It. to Joseph Weeks for Warding Artillery day	0 – 1 – 0	
It. to Hopstill Clap for the same	0 – 1 – 0	
It. to Nicholas Bolton for what he should haue had formerly for ringing the bell	0 – 10 – 0	
	23 – 15 – 10	
Rest due to ballance	1 – 2 – 0	
out of this ther is Gamalliell Beamans rate abated which is 6ˢ	0 – 6 – 0	
and hopstill Clap p^d the same time in money	0 – 4 – 0	
desp'at dept John Jackson	0 – 1 – 0	
It. p^d to Lift^{nt} Capen	0 – 5 – 7	
It. p^d to William Sumner	0 – 9 – 10	

p^d – 2^s – 9^d to much which is
Credit giuen for it to Samuell Toplifs acc^t

[**328.**] An acc^t of Thomas Tolman as Constable for the yeer 77 for that Contry rate of Six rats and that p^t remitted to the said Tolman to Colect the whole rate amounting to 241 – 10 – 2

Imp. the Tresurer is to haue out of this rate	236 – 0 – 6	
remains	5 – 9 – 8	
Desp'at depts out of the Six rates comitted to T. Tolman his p^t		
Robt Sanders	0 – 6 – 0	
Jno Merifeild	0 – 16 – 0	
Widdow Georg abated	0 – 5 – 0	
Joshua Georg being a Castl man is abated one Single rate	0 – 1 – 8	
Jno Sanders	0 – 11 – 0	
Walter Euerington on p'son taken off	0 – 10 – 0	
	2 – 9 – 8	
	1 – 16 – 6	
	4 – 6 – 2	
Rest due to Towne from both Constabls	1 – 13 – 9	
The acc^t of the Contry rate Consisting of three rats comitted p^t of it to Tho Tolman the Sume of the wholl rate is	105 – 18 – 4	
of which the Treasurer is to haue	96 – 14 – 0	
Remains	9 – 4 – 4	
Desp'at depts out of the 3 rates		
Robt. Sanders	0 – 1 – 6	
Jno Merifeild	0 – 8 – 9	
Widdow Georg abated	0 – 2 – 6	

242   CITY DOCUMENT NO. 9.

Jn⁰ Sanders	0 – 5 – 9
Gamalliell Beaman Junr	0 – 5 – 0
	1 – 2 – 9
	0 – 11 – 0
	1 – 13 – 9

Rest due to Towne from both Constabls out of the thre Rats . . . . }   7 – 10 – 7
It. p^d to John Tolman by order being over rated   1 – 9 – 2
made vp this acc^t with the Select men the 15 9 80:
M^d this of T. Dauenport is to be put on the meeting hous disburstments.

[**329.**]   An acc^t of James Bird as Constable for the same yeer of 77 that p^t which he was to Colect of the Six rates.
Deducted out the rate 20^s for Enock Wiswells Sons rate being another man's seruant . }   1 – 0 – 0
Widdow Long p^t of her rate . . . .   0 – 6 – 6
Nathanell Osburne . . . . .   0 – 10 – 0
                                            1 – 16 – 6

The acc^t of the three rate that p^t which James Bird was to Colect
Desp'at Dept. Widdow Long . . . .   0 – 3 – 0
Nathan Bradly . . . . . .   0 – 3 – 0
Nathanell Osburn . . . . .   0 – 5 – 0
                                            0 – 11 – 0

M^d wheras on the other sid ther is due from both Constables to ballan to the town 7^ll – 10 – 7 ther is as on the other sid to be seen p^d to John Tolman by order . . . . . }   1 – 9 – 2
and to Georg Lyon his Contry rate . . .   1 – 5 – 10
and to James Tucker . . . . .   0 – 16 – 8
                                            3 – 11 — 8

This 3 – 11 – 8 is to be taken out of the 7 – 10 – 7 and now remains due to the town 3 – 18. – 11 . . . . . . }   3 – 18 – 11
mor desparat debts brought in by the Constables James Bird and Tho. Tolman

	s. d.	
Joseph Birch	16 – 6	
occup'· of henery mars . . .	4 –	
John Memory	3 – 9	
Thō. Birch . ; . .	10 – 0	
Anthony hancoke . . .	10 – 0	
henery Roberts . . .	10 – 0	
Robert Stanton	3 – 0	2 – 17 – 3
Lose in measure of Corne		0 – 4 – 0

[330.] An acc⁺ of Tho. Tolman of the towne rate Comitted to him to Colect yeer 77 the wholl rate is . . . . . . 64 – 12 – 9
that p⁺ which he is Colect is . . . . 33 – 4 – 9
Imp. pᵈ to Mr. Minot . . . . . 15 – 0 – 0
It. to Widdow Georg . . . . . 4 – 3 – 8
It. to Daued Joans for the bell ringing . . 1 – 10 – 0
It. to James Robbinson for digging a Childs graue 0 – 2 – 6
It. to Corp'all tilston for 3 days at Swamp and ½ a bl. Corne to an Indian . . . . 0 – 7 – 6
and to him for 2 weekes keeping frances of which he had 3ˢ of Isack Joans . . . 0 – 3 – 0
It. to Goody wiet for laying frank and Horsly . 0 – 5 – 0
It. to Rich. Withington 20ˢ money as p⁺ of what he laid down to Mr. Flint . . . . 1 – 0 – 0
and to him for two load of wood for Sanders and the widdow Horsly . . . . 0 – 9 – 0
and to him for what he lent the town in shows to make vp their acc⁺ with the Treasurer . 3 – 0 – 0
It. to Siluester for a wolf in 74 . . . 0 – 10 – 0
It. to Samuell Robinson for Frances left due . 0 – 2 – 0
It. to Thomas Tolman for Frances . . . 0 – 4 – 8
It. to Henery Leadbetter for Franck 5 weeks . 0 – 15 – 0
It. to Mr. Glouer for frank 2 weeks . . 0 – 6 – 8
It to Daniell Preston for the bords formerly for the Scholhous 6ˢ and for frank 2 weeks 6ˢ and for 22 foot of bord for shuts for the Schole hous 1ˢ – 4 and towards a load of wood for horsly 8ᵈ . . . . 0 – 14 – 0
and more towards the wood . . . . 0 – 3 – 10

28 – 15 – 4

It. more pᵈ to Tho Dauenport for Carting timber for the bell . . . . 0 – 7 – 6
It. to Timothy Foster besides 2ˢ 9ᵈ pᵈ in a former rate . . . . 0 – 3 – 3
It. to Samuell Paull for his worke at the Swamp 0 – 5 – 5
It. to Lift. Capen pᵈ by his Sons Samuell and Barnard . . . . 0 – 11 – 11

30 – 3 – 5
Rest due yet . . . . 1 – 2 – 1

Desperate Debts.		Joshua Atherton .	ˢ – ᵈ 2 – 0
	ˢ – ᵈ		
henery Merefeild	2 – 6	Thomas Williams.	2 – 0
lift. holbrooke	0 – 8	James houghton .	2 – 0
John sanders	2 – 0	Isaac how .	3 – 4
John stanton	2 – 0	billing for Woolfe.	10 – 0
John Pelton	1 – 8	vpon the account of money to Richard Withington .	10 – 0
Gamaleel Beaman	2 – 0		

payed more . . . . . 2 – 0 – 2

Made vp the account with Thomas Tolman 22 : 11 : 82 of his

	li	s	d
town Rate and he is detter to the towne	1	1	2

[**331.**] An acc^t of James Bird for his p^t of the town rate yeer 77 . . . . 31 – 8 – 0

Imp. to Mr. Minot	15	0	0
It. to Nicholas Bolton for the bell . .	2	0	0
It. to Amiell weeks p^t of his due for runing the line at blew hils	0	6	8
It. to Consider Atherton for frances 4 weekes .	0	12	0
It. to Deacon Blak as Deputie . . .	4	7	0
It. to Richard Leeds for Frank . .	0	18	6
It. to Srg^t Pond for two weeks of franck and mending the stocks	30	9	6
It. to Srg^{nt} Clap for frances 2 weeks and for 2 load of wood for Sanders and Horsly and to him for nails and boards and work about meeting hous and stocks	0	19	7
It. to Deacon Blak for frances 2 weeks and to him for wood for Sander and the watch and work at meeting hous and for Carting Daniell Elders goods	1	1	6
It. to Nathaell Clap for Carting goods . .	0	5	0
It. to Isack Joanes for the lik . . .	0	5	0
It. to Hopstill Clapp for frank 2 weeks . .	0	6	0
It. to Widdow Clap for the lik . .	0	6	0
It. to Nicholas Clap for the lik . .	0	6	0
It. to Joshua for on load of wood for the watch	0	4	6
It. to Srg^{nt} Clap for the lik . . .	0	4	6
It. to Israell Euered for a woolf . .	0	10	0
It. to Ezra Mos for a wolf . . .	0	10	0
It. to Jno Bird for keeping frances 2 weeks .	0	4	0
It. to James Bird for bords for a Coffen for Horsly and for paper . . .	0	3	9
It. Widdow Foster the remainder of what she should haue had the last yeer of John Bird .	3	12	2
It. to Jno Trescot for a Coffen for Horsly .	0	5	0
It. to Nathanell Clap for two weeks frank .	0	4	0
It. to Obediah Swift and mother for 6 weeks keeping frances formerly . . .	0	18	0
It. to Thomas Bird two weeks frank . .	0	6	0
It. to William Trescot 2 weeks frank and for Carting for Daniell Elders and to him for a bord for old meeting hous . . .	0	12	6
It. to Srg^{rt} wiswell for frances	0	2	6
[**332.**] It. to Amiell Weeks for 2 weeks for keeping frances	0	6	0
It. to Widdow Foster for two load of wood for the watch brought by Jos. Homes . .	0	8	0
It. to Rich. Baker for two weeks frank . .	0	6	0
It. to Mrs Foster for 2 weeks	0	6	0

It. to Widdow Blackman for frank	0 – 6 – 0
It. to James Foster for frank	0 – 6 – 0
The Totall of all that James Bird haue p^d out of the p^t of towne rat which he was ordered to pay is	36 – 17 – 8
and Tho. Tolman haue p^d as on the other sid	28 – 15 – 4
both Sums is	65 – 2 – 4
Rest due to the towne	0 – 16 – 7

by James Bird payed as followeth

Since that account was made more payed to Widdow George	0 – 00 – 0
to lift. Capen and for his owne Rate and Burge and Mason	1 – 13 – 0
Debts that can not be gotten widow Longe	0 – 4 – 0
John Memory	0 – 4 – 4
Thomas Lawrence	0 – 2 – 4
John Wales iu^r	0 – 2 – 0
John Beaman	0 – 2 – 6
Samuel Lawrence	0 – 2 – 0
occup' of henery mares	0 – 1 –11
	2 – 11 – 9

Constable James Bird hath payed	39^li 9^s 5^d
he towne Debter to him	8 1 5

this account was made with the Select men the 22^d : 11 : 82 :

[333.] At a meeting of the towne the 27 7 1680 being legally called together.

It was p'posed to the Church and town to p'pos a Comittee for to look out for a supply in the minestry vntill it pleas god to p'sent a man whom the Church may thinke meet to Cale to office, thos that are p'pounded are the Elder and Deacons and the rest of the Selectmen and Richard Baker. It being put to the vote it was declared in the Affirmatiue.

It was further put to the Vote whether the Rate of ninetie pound p'mised to Mr. Flint for the whole yeer, be fully made vp to Mrs Flint. the Vote was in the Affermatiue.

It was further p'posed to the town whether the minesters that are p'cuered to help vs should be satisfied out of the weekly Contribution, and an account therof keept by the Deacons and at the end of the yeer such a Sum be aded to the ninetie pound Rate. The Vote was in the Affermatiue.

It was further p'posed whether the town would bear the Charges of Mr Flints funerall which coms to about ten pounds in money.
    The Vote was Affermatiue.

[334.] At a meeting of the Select men the 8 No. 1680 John Tolman and Ju^o Baker came and made vp ther acc^t for the Contry and Towne rats comitted to them to Colect the Sume of

the Contry rate is	111 – 10 – 7
the Sum of the town rate is	23 – 12 – 10

for the yeer 78 —

Out of the Town rate p^d by Jno Tolman.

Imp to the Widdow Georg	3 – 3 – 10
It. to Ezra Clap	2 – 7 – 4
It. to Daued Joanes	1 – 15 – 0
It. to Gamaliell Beaman	0 – 6 – 0
It. to Roger Belleng for a wolf	0 – 10 – 0
It. to Samuell Toplif for work schol hous	0 – 2 – 0
It. to William Sumner as Deputie	0 – 7 – 1
It. to Widdow Minot	0 – 3 – 0
It. to Lift. Capen of Seuerall p'sons	0 – 11 – 3
and to him for what was p^d to Thomas Tolman for Jno Breck	0 – 16 – 0
and to him for Sam Pelton	0 – 1 – 6
It p^d to Ebenezer Clap for what should be repaid to him for his rate	1 – 1 – 8
	11 – 4 – 8
The totall of what is p^d out of the town rate by Jno Tolman is	11 – 12 – 6
Rest due to the Towne	0 – 8 – 6

Desp'at depts on his p^t of towne rat is

James Mott	0 – 0 – 6
Henery Merrifeild	0 – 1 – 3
Robt Sanders	0 – 0 – 6
John Sanders p^d his rate	0 – 0 – 0
	0 – 2 – 5
Robt Pelton 8^d Tho Pop 8^d Robt Stils 1^s	0 – 2 – 4
Soe that Jno Tolmans acc^t of what he haue p^d out and desp'at depts Considered is	11 – 12 – 6

The Sume of the Contry Rate was	111 – 10 – 7
The Tresurer was to haue	105 – 8 – 6

Desp'at dept on Jno Bakers

p^t Gamaliell Beaman Junr	0 – 5 – 0
Jno Browne — 5^s	0 – 5 – 0
Anthony Hancock	0 – 6 – 0
Nathan Bradly	0 – 3 – 0
	0 – 19 – 0
Recc. for the Town of Jno Baker in money 16^s – 6 insteed of 1^{li} – 4 – 9 as it was in the Rate	1 – 4 – 9

This sume of 16 – 6 is toward
   Jno Tolmans p^t
      look more of this p. 342

the 13 (1) 8½ Jno Tolman fineshed the acc^t of his Towne rat and he is dept^r to the towne 8^s – 8^d which he ingageth himself to pay it to the Town or Select men and then he is discharged of the towne rate. this 8^s 8^d is payed and John Tolman is discharged.
Desp'at Dept on the Contry rat of John Tolman p^t

DORCHESTER TOWN RECORDS. 247

Hen Merifeild	0 – 8 –	9
Jn° Merifeld	0 – 8 –	0
Lift. Holbrook	0 – 0 –	9
	0 – 17 –	6
Robt Sanders 18^d Th° Pope 3^s 4^d . . ⎫		
Walter Eueringdon 2^s . . . . . ⎭	0 – 6 –	10

the 13 1 8½ John Tolman made vp his acc^t for the Contry Rate and he is discharged therof.

[**335.**] The acc^t of Jn° Baker as Constable for the yeer 77 that p^t which the said Jn° Baker was to Colect of the Towne rate.

Imp p^d to Samuell trescot for frances. . .	3 – 0 –	0
It. to Nicholas Bolton	0 – 17 –	10
It. to Deacon Blake	0 – 5 –	0
It. to Srg^{nt} Clap	0 – 5 –	6
It. to Jn° Withington for frank 2 week . .	0 – 6 –	0
It. to Jn° Baker himself for frank 2 week . .	0 – 3 –	0
It. to Richard Baker for frank . . .	0 – 3 –	0
It. more to Samuell Trescot for frank . . .	0 – 3 –	0
It. to Nicholas Bolton more	1 – 2 –	2
It. to Lift^{nt} Capen p^t of what he should haue as ⎫		
deputy . . . . . . ⎭	2 – 0 –	5
It. to Isack Joanes	0 – 3 –	6
It. to Joshua Hinshaw for frank . . .	0 – 3 –	0
It. to Joseph Weeks for goeing to parker . .	0 – 1 –	6
It. to Samuel Whiting for a woolf . . .	0 – 10 –	0
It. to Israell Euered p^t towards a wolf . .	0 – 6 –	0
It. to William Sumner p^t as deputie . .	0 – 12 –	0
It. to Widdow Georg by Jn° Wals his rate . .	0 – 3 –	2
The totall of what Jn° Baker p^d is . . .	10 – 5 –	1

Desp'at debts on his p^t of the rate is

Frances Bale	0 – 1 –	0
Thomas Leichfeild	0 – 1 –	2
Nathan Bradly	0 – 1 –	0
Jn° Beamen	0 – 0 –	10
Gamaliell Beaman Senr	0 – 3 –	0
Gamaliell Beaman Junr	0 – 0 –	8
Peter Talbut	0 – 0 –	8
Jn° Wales Junr	0 – 0 –	8
Nathanell Osburn	0 – 0 –	8
	0 – 9 –	8

Jn° Bakers acc^t of what is p^d and desp'at is ten pound 14 – 9

The Totall of both Constable acc^t is . . .	22 – 2 –	10
Rest due from both Constable . . .	1 – 10 –	0

made vp this acc^t the 8 9 80.
Look more of this acc^t p. 342.

[**336.**] At a meeting of the Select men the 8 (1) 7 $\frac{9}{80}$
The same day ther was appointed for fence Vewers for that p^t of the great lots beyond Timothy Foster . { Samuell Robinson
{ Tho Trot Senr

for Captins Neck . . . . { Rich Leeds
{ John Wales Senr

for the feild behind Tho. Modesly . . { Elisha Foster
{ Isack Joanes

for the hill feild . . . . . { Srg^nt Clap
{ Joshua Henshaw.

for the feild behind John Bird . . { James Bird
{ Hopstill Humphry

for the feild behind Mr Stoughtons . { Joseph Leeds
{ John Baker

for the Neck of land . . . . { Srg^nt Wiswell
{ Nehemiah Clap

for Sup'uisors of the way to Neck . , { Jno Withington
{ James Foster

for Cleering the Neck . . . . { Tho. Bird
{ Nathanell Clap

And all fences to be made vp by the 25 March 167 8/9 and fence Vewers to Vew fence and the Cleerers of the neck to be Vewed and Cleered by the 1 Aprill next.

The same day as an adition to the order about horses as in p. 182 it is ordered that all the pay for horses taken vp as that order expresseth shall goe to the man or men that doe take them vp, and if it can be sufficciently proued that any hors be so vnruly that notwithstanding being fettered yet they will break down sufficcient fence and doe damedg such horses or Mares shall pay duble damedg

At a publique towne meeting being legally warned the 10' (1) 79 or 80 ther was Chosen for a baylif for the yeer ensewing Clement Maxfeild.

The same day the town did by a vote remit the Widdow Euerits Second meeting hous rate.

The same day ther was Chosen for Constables for the yeer Ensewing Samuell Capen and James Foster.

The same day it was Voted that the Schole hous shall be repaiered wher it now stands and John [337.] Breck and Timothy Tilston to see that it be repaired.

The same time ther was Chosen Mr Mather Rich Baker and Isack Joanes to see that the buriing place be fenced in with stone wall by the last of June next.

The first of the Second M^o 80 It is granted to the widdow Weeks libertie to git three thousand of Clobords out of the Comon Swamps.

At a meeting of the Select men the 12 2 80 It was ordered that William Sumner Lif^nt Capen and Timothy Tilston shall acquaint and warne the Select men of Melton to appoint some men to renew the line at the Swamp in Melton which Could not well bee Isuewed the last time we ran that line becaus of the wett, the day appointed is the 26 Instant Aprill 80.

At a towne meeting the 13 2 80 ther was Chosen for a deputie William Sumner for the whole yeer with a reserue of libertie to send another deputie for another Sessions if the freemen see meete.

The same day at the motion of James White to Chang the way by his twenty acr lot, ther was appointed Ed Pason Tho Tolman Senr and Richard Withington to take a vew therof and make report to the towne: the return is on p. 340

At a meeting of the Select men the 24 April at Mr Stoughtons hous Haueing Receaued an order from the Honrd Countie Court requiering the Select men of Dorchester to Nominate and p'sent some meet p'son to keepe a publique hous of entertainement, In order heerunto the Select men mett together on the 24 Instant and appointed William Sumner and Ensigne Richard Hale to appeare in Court and make answer heerunto, that we would Nominate Rich Worthington or Ensign Richard Hale if we could p'uaile with either of them to be willing to accept of it and some of vs doe Nominate Isack Joanes whos habetation is Very Conuenient.

The 10 3 80 It is granted to John Pope libertie to git 1400 Clobords out of the Comon Swamps belonging to Dorchester.

[**338.**] At a publique Town meeting the 2. 4. 80 being legally called together It was put to the Vote that wheras ther was granted by the Church and towne the 20 4 79 as in p. 307 that Mr. Flint should haue on hundred pounds for that yeer, he p'uiding help in the minestry himself, and some vnderstanding the yeer to end at January, and others that it should extend till the full yeer com about therfore it is now put to the Vote whether the last yeer should end in January, and that Mr. Flint should pay Mr. Minot or others out of the hundred pound but vntill January.

The Vote was in the Affermatiue noe man by Vote dissenting.

The same time It was Voted by the Major Vote that Mr. Flint should haue for his labour in preaching this yeer 1680 which end at January the Sume of Nintie pounds the one half money and the other half Contry pay.

The same time it was Voted that if Mr Minot can be p'cuered to preach once a fortnight (his yeer begining in January last and end next January) that he should haue twentie pounds half money & half other pay.

The same time ther was Chosen for a Comitte to treat with Mr Minot, Mr. Flint Elder Humphry and the p'sent Select men and John Breck.

At a meeting of the Select men the 14. 4. 80 an order was sent to James whit and Timothy Foster sup'uisors of the high ways to ster them vp to mind the ways.

The same day it was granted to Joseph Weeks libertie to git 200 of Clobord.

The same day it was granted to Nehemiah Clap libertie to git 700 of Clobord out of the Comon Swamps.

The same day an order was sent to Roger Belleng Senr to discharge the towne of Thomas Painter or to giue bond to secure the towne.

granted to Mr. Flint libertie to get 3000 of Clobord out of the Comon Swamps.

[**339.**] At a meeting of the freemen the 28 July 1680 ther was chosen Roger Bellang Senr for a Comissioner for the Contry rate.

At a meeting of the Select men the 13 Sep. 80

The same day it was granted to Israell How libertie to git 2100 of Clobord besids his former 4 load, also libertie to git 4 or 5 load of wood out of the 500 acrs p'uided he fale none but take of what is downe.

The same day it was granted to James Barbor, liberti[e] to git 100 of railes and some posts out of the 500 acrs.

At a meeting of the Select men the 8 Nouember 1680

It was granted to Daued Joanes libertie to git 200 of railes out of the 500 acrs.

M$\bar{\text{d}}$ the Widdow euered Came to the Select men the same day and demanded 40 shillings for 4 wolues of which she haue receaued of Jno Baker 6^s and of the Widdow Smith q^r 4^s also she haue had on acc^t with Isack Joans 4^s which must also be p^d to him, and if James Bird doe demand anything, she would haue that p^d to him, and the rest the Select men doe order that she should haue a bill to the tenants of the Schole land to discharg it.

M^d it is ordered that Six and twentie shilling shall be p^d her by Srg^t Ellice.

The same day an acc^t was made with Jno Tolman and Jno Baker of the towne Rate yeer 80 as in p. 334 335 and the Contry Rate in p^t

At a meeting of the Select men the 15 Nouem 80

The same day the Select men tooke an acc^t of Thomas Tolman and James Bird for the Six Rats and 3 Rates and towne rate for the yeer 77 as in p. 328 329 330 331

The same day Ensign Richard Hale requested for three or fower load of Clobord or Shingle and some timber to repaier his barne, and it was granted.

At a generall towne meeting the 6 10 80 At the Motion of John Withington Constable for the yeer 75 it was granted that Peter Talbuts Contry rate and Jno Sanders Contry rate (the same rate) should be remitted.

The same time it was granted to the Widdow Gill (at the motion of Roger Belleng) libertie to git 4 trees on the Com̄ons beyond the blew hils towards the repaieration of her mill.

The same time it was granted to Roger Sumner, libertie to git 3 or 4 trees of Pin or Cedar to make bords out of the Swamp beyond the blew hils.

[**340.**] The same time was chosen for Select men. Lift. Capen Deacon Blake William Sumner Ensign Richard Hale Srg. Samuell Clap

for Record^r Lift. Capen

for Raters Srgnt Wiswell Jno Breck Samuell Robinson

Sup'uisors Ezra Clap Elisha Foster.

The same day a returne was made by the Com̄itte appointed to Veiw and take notice of the motion of James Whit which is as foleth as in p. 337.

Wee who weer appointed by the assembly mett together the 13 2 80 and sent to Vew and returne o^r ap^{r}hentions about the request of bro^r James Whit Concerning the alteration of the way, haue Vewed it, and doe Judg that if the way that now is made vse of into the woods be stated wher now it is for euer then it seems but reasonable to be granted, but if the towne way must be between Rocksbery and Dorchester, then that the way be as it was to to which we subscrib o^r names that weer sent and we did this the 17 2 80

a postscript

on this Condition the old way that now leads into the woods be recorded and that both White and his heirs make the way pasable for euer, and this of bro^r Whits be recorded in the towne book

This retorne is on file.

THO. TOLMAN Senr
The mark of ED PASON
RICH WITHINGTON

The same day at the motion of Lift^{nt} Capen and William Sumner (feffees for the Schole land and minestry land) that they may be dismissed of that work and others Chosen in ther roome, the towne granted their request, and made Choice of Timothy Tilston and John Breck to be feffees in their steed to take acc^t of what is past and to transact for the town for the time to com, not disanulling any former Contract which haue been made. and wheras at the same time William Trescot made motion to be dismissed of his Contract, the towne made Choice of Daniell Preston Senr and Henry Leadbetter to be added for that motion, and all to confer together and make report to the towne what they Judg of his motion.

[**341.**] At a meeting of the Select men the 13 10 80 John Breck desiered libertie to git a sute of Masts and yards for a Vessell which he haue vndertaken to build in this towne in some Swamp about puncapag. the Select men granted his request, he giueing Satisfaction according as the Select men shall Judg meete when they call for it.

At a meeting of the Select men the 17 10 80 vppon Occasion, It was ordered that Orders should be sent to to the Raters to make a rate for the minestry to Mr Flint, and expences on the minesters that haue and shall help vs to the end of December, and for funerall expences to the Sume of one hundered and twelue pound of which Sixtie seauen pound in money the rest in Contry pay. Also a Rate for the towne and Schole and Mr Minots help in preaching this yeer past to the Sume of Seauenty three pounds of which a theird p^t to be in money, the rest in Contry pay.

At a meeting of the Select men the 10 (11) 80 The same day James Whit tithing man made Complaint of Rob Stiles and his famely liueing Idly.

At a meeting of the Select men the 22 (11) 80 vpon occasion this returne was drawn vp to send to the Court

Wheras the Honrd Court in December last ordered that the Select men of Dorchester doe p^{r}sent to the next Court some meet p'son that is both able and willing to keepe a hous of publik enter-

tainment under a penalty Thes are to certefie to the Hon^rd Court, that we the Select men of Dorchester, haue not been neglectiue heerin, but we cannot find such a p'son to be willing, whom we Judg fitt, but the widdow George is willing, and is a Comodated for such an employ, and if the Court pleas to alow her libertie for one yeer more to keep an hous of publik entertainment : William Sumner who is one of our Select men, will Engage for one yeer to doe the best he can to inspect into the Gouerment of the house if he be impowered soe to doe by the Hon^rd Court
22 11 80
          JOHN CAPEN
          WILLIAM SUMNER
          RICH HALE
          JAMES BLAKE
The warrant is on file.   SAMUELL CLAP

[**342.**]   from p. 334

The 14 12 80 Jn° Baker as Constable for the yeer 78 Came to the Select men to make vp his acc^t of the Contry rate that he was to Colect Viz his p^t which Came to . . . £0 – 5 – 7

of which p^d to the Treasuerer money 32^{li} 12 – 8
which being drawn vp into Rat pay which ads 48 – 19 0
a third p^t more maks . . . .

Also it was alowed to him for John Masons goeing to Boston for Memrys Childrens Nurs and Samell Trescots hors and Cart for all is alowed in money — and 4^s in steed of 6^s rate pay — . . . . . . 0 – 4 – 0

and he p^d in money 1^s insteed of . . . 0 1 – 7
which maks all euen for his p^t of the Contry rate.

his p^t of the Towne Rate the Sum is . . 11 – 8 – 1
of which he haue p^d and in desp'at dept as in p. 334 . . . . 10 – 14 – 9
   Rest due to Ballance . . . 0 – 13 – 4

the which he is ordered to pay Lift Capen 12^s and John Baker is discharged of his p^t of town rate.

[Page 343 blank.]

[**344.**] The Town Dept^r to Lift. Jn° Capen.

Imp. the ballance of the acc^t the last yeer as in p. 312 313 the Sume of . . . . 7 – 14 – 0

It. dl to Isack Joanes 2 bls of my Corne towards the towns dept to him besids 18 bls he had of the Corne that Came from the tenants of Schole land as in my book p. 97 will appeare . . 0 – 6 – 0

It. for Recording the yeer 80 . . . 1 – 0 – 0
It. for a load of wood for the watch neuer yet Counted but seeing others haue it . 0 – 4 – 6
It. for Expences of Select men . . . 0 – 5 – 0

              9 – 09 – 6

DORCHESTER TOWN RECORDS.

Made vp this acc^t with the Select men the 14 12 80 and due to balance the Sume of fower pounds Sixteen shillings and three pence	4 – 13 – 3
	4 – 16 – 3

[**345.**] The Towne Cred^r from Lift. Capen.

Imp. by 4 bls of wheat which was brought from Ellice of Deadham as in p. 97	1 – 0 – 0
It. Recc. if Israell Hils goods Viz a Chesell and other Smale things	0 – 1 – 6
It. Recc. by Constable Hop Clap my owne towne rate	0 – 11 – 1
It. of the widdow Batten by Widdow Weeks	0 – 1 – 4
It. of my Son John his rate	0 – 3 – 0
It. of James Barbor	0 – 1 – 6
It. of Phillip Demonzaday	0 – 1 – 1
It. of William Chaplin	0 – 1 – 1
M^d thes 3 last the Constable p^d me him self in money abating the theird p^t.	
It. Recc. a hid from Henry Glouer	0 – 14 – 9
It. Recc. of Jno Farington as p^t of his rent 3 bls of Corne	0 – 9 – 0
It. Recc. Jno Masons Town Rate for the yeer 77 James bird being Constable	0 – 3 – 0
and of him Goodman Burge his rate for the same yeer	0 – 13 – 6
It. Recc. the ballance of Jno Withingtons acc^t as in p. 104	0 – 6 – 5
It. Recc. of Jno Farrington 2 bl. Corne as p^t of his rent	0 – 6 – 0
	4 – 13 – 3

[**346.**] The acc^t of Samuell Capen as Constabl for the yeer 1680 of the town rate Comitted to him his p^t amounting to 38 – 6 – 4. The whol Rate being . . . 73 – 8 – 7

Imp. to Mr. James Minot in money	9 – 15 – 0
and to him in Contry pay	10 – 1 – 6
It. to Nathan Bradly	2 – 5 – [ ]
It. to Tim Tilston for work at Scholhous	0 – 4 – 0
It. to Daued Joanes for Wading	0 – 1 – 0
It. to Rich. Euens for Wading	0 – 1 – 0
It. to Samuell Capen for Wading	0 – 1 – 0
It for keeping Frank at Sam Capen a month	– 6 – 0
It. to barnard Capen for 2 weeks	0 – 3 – 0
It. p^d the Widdow Smith for Widdow Euered	– 4 – 0
It. to Clement Maxfeild for Franke	1 – 8 – 8
It. to Hen. Leadbetter for runing a line	0 – 2 – 6
It. to Samuell Paul for what was left by Jno Tolman	0 – 7 – 1
It. p^d to Elic Wood for Jno Hunting of Deadham for a wolf	0 – 10 – 0

It. p^d to Ensigne Hale for expences	. . .	0 – 5 – 0
and to him for the pound	. . . .	0 – 2 – 5
It. p^d to Danell Elder 3 bl of Corne	. . .	0 – 9 – 0
It. laid out for a marking Iron for the measuers in money	. . . . . .	0 – 1 – 6
It. p^d to Jno Breck for bords for the Schole hous in money	. . . . . .	0 – 9 – 0
It. p^d to Elic wood in money	. . . .	0 – 3 – 4
It. p^d in money towards Danell Elders Cow	.	15 – 0
It. p^d to Widdow Georg of which money 2^s- 6	.	0 – 16 – 5
It. p^d to William Sumner	. . . .	1 – 18 – 2
It. p^d to Mr Minot p' order to him and John Breck	. . . .	2 – 9 – 3

looke more of this Town acc^t p. 354 . . .   32 – 19 – 8
his p^t of the rate made for W. Turner was Six pound
4 4
It. p^d of this to Thomas Modesly . . . .   2 – 18   1

[**347.**] An acc$_t$ of James Foster as Constable for the yeer 1680 of his p^t of the town rate Comited to him to Colect amounting to the whol rate being   73 – 18 – 7

Imp. to Mathias puffer for 2 wolues	. . .	1 – 0 – 0
It. to Richard Leeds for frank	. . . .	0 – 13 – 2
It. to Srg^t Clap .	. . . . .	0 – 5 – 0
It. toNathan Bradly .	. . . . .	0 – 14 – 0
It. William Sumner in ordinary pay	. . .	1 – 16 – 9
It. to Mr Minot in ordenary pay .	. . .	13 – 0 – 0
It. to Mr Minot in money .	. . . .	0 – 0 – 0
It. for carieng the measures and pay for sealing .		0 – 2 – 6
It. more to William Sumner as deputy .	. .	4 – 9 – 3
It. more to Mr Minot in ordenary pay .	. .	3 – 0 – 0
It. to Mr Minot in money .	. . . .	10 – 10 – 0
It. more to Nathan Bradley for Ringing the bell .		0 – 8 – 7

[**348.**] At a meeting of the Select men 14 12 80
It was then Concluded that Nathan Bradly should haue 4^{ll} a yeer for the work he is appointed to doe as in p. 319.

The same day Daniell Preston Senr assigned ouer the deede of the land he bought of Samuell Rigbe for the vse of the Schole being the legacy of Christopher Gibson and left the deed to be Coppied out into the town book.

The same day it was ordered that the Constabls for the yeer 80 should pay out of the Contry rate 3^s 4^d money to Ellice Wood, being rated formerly both heer and at Deadham.

The same day Granted to Jno Blackman libertie to git 3 or 4 trees out of the 500 acrs.

The same time granted to Timothy Foster libertie to git a thousand of Clobord and ten thousand of Shingle out of the Comon Swamps

At a ginerall meeting of the freemen the 8 of March 80 81 ther was Chosen for Deputie for the whole yeer Ensewing William Sumner alsoe he was Chosen to Carry the Vots to boston.

The same day ther was Chosen for Constabls John Pason and John Wales Senr.

The same time the towne did by Vote desier Elder Humphry to Cattechiz the youth and Children that he should call to him when and wher he should appoint.

The same day the Comittee that was appointed to confer with William Trescot about his petition to leaue the minestry land, of which he took a leas, they made report by word of mouth that if the towne would give William Trescot fiue pound besids the rent due from William Trescot which was as they said twentie two pounds then they should haue the building that was vpon it, only William Trescot should haue libertie to [**349.**] take off twentie Cords of wood. this returne being put to the Vote the towne did by their Vote accept of it, and William Trescot is discharged of it.

The same day also the Comitte made returne which p^t of the Swamp at Melton they had asigned to Dorchester for the minestry Viz the westerly end for Dorchester and the Easterly end for Melton.

At a meeting of the Select men the 14 (1) 80 81 ther was Chosen for fence Vewers

for that p^t of the great lots beyond Timothy Foster . . . . { Samuell Robinson / Israell How.

for Captins Neck . . . . . { John Breck / Joseph Leeds

for the feild behind Tho Modesly . . { Joseph Weeks / Thomas Modesly

for the hill feild . . . . . { Isack Joans / Joshua Henshaw

for the feild behind John Birds . . { Obediah Haws / John Blackman

for the feild behind Mr Stoughton . . { Rich Leeds / Richard Baker

for sup'uisors of the Way to the Neck . { Srg^{nt} Wiswell / Thomas Bird.

for Cleering the Neck . . . . { Isack Joans / Rich Mather

And all fences to be made vp by the 25 March 1681 and fence Vewers to Vew fence and the Cleerers of the Neck to be Vewed and Cleered by the first of Aprill next.

The same day it is ordered that the former Order Concerning Eare marking of hors kind and bringing in the Number of horses stand in force as in page 278.

The same day an addition was made to the order regulating of Swine Viz wheras ther was an order made by the Select men the

11 12 79 regulating of Swine as in page 311, It is Ordered that that order stand in force, with this Variation, that Wheras ther weer (in that order) men appointed to look after the execution therof, and finding by experience that such men haue Neglected their duty therein, Now it is ordered that any p'son that finds Hogs or piggs contrary to that order, he may execut that order vpon such Swine, and take the fine ther exprest [**350.**] and in Case of trespas to haue duble damedg, and the select men doe Engag to assist to the vtmost of their power, and if any refus to make due satisfaction, the names of the p'sons soe refusing, shall be transmitted to Clement Maxfeild, who is appointed baylif in this Case, who shall haue Warrant from the Select men to Make distreine.

The same day ther weer Chosen for tithing men for the yeer Ensewing

John Bird	Samuell Hix	Incres Sumner
Nathaniell Clap	Tho. Trot Senr	Samuell Toplif
Thomas Modesly	Jn° Tolman	Ralf Houghton.
Henery Garnesy	Roger Belleng	
Joseph Leeds	Barnard Capen	

At a meeting of the Select men the 11 (2) 81

At the request of Tho Swift Senr of Melton and Ezra Clap of Dorchester. It is granted to them a libertie to Catch fish at Naponsett below the mill, and to make a stage for this yeer, p'uided that they doe not any way Obstruct or hender the ancient Cart way ouer the Riuer, which lys between the Mill and the timber bridg nor the Way leading to the Mill, between the Riuer and the barne that now is ther on the vpland.

The same day it was granted to William Blake (who is a p'prietor) libertie to git 1400 of Clobord out of the Comon Swamps for his own vse.

At a meeting of the Select men the 13 (4) 81

It was ordered that an order should be sent to Samuell Rigbe to order him to Come to som of the Select men within Six days after the date heerof and giue securetie for the man that he entertains at his hous or elce to expect the Constable to come and take by distres the fine of 3^s 4^d p' week for euery weeks entertainment of him since he came to his hous.

The same day ther was granted to Hopestill and Isack Humphry libertie to gitt 2100 of Clobords out of the Comon Swamps, p'uided they git them within fower months time from the date heerof and then to returne the note to the select men againe.

[**351.**] The same day Joseph Weeks Came to the Select men and desiered libertie to take a nurst Child of one Mr Steuens of Boston, Answer was returned that though the man may be sufficcient, yet becaus it may not be a p'sedent vnto others he was ordered to appoint the man to guie some thing vnder his hand to some one of the Select men to secure the towne.

The same day the Select men appointed William Sumner and Deacon Blake to enquier after a Schole M^r

The 10th of August 81 at a meeting of the freemen being Called together, Ralfe Houghton was Chosen Comissioner for the makeing the Contry Rate.

At a meeting of the Select men the 19 7 81

The same time Ensigne Hale was desiered and appointed to enquier after a Schole Master, which some say ther may be one at bridg water.

The same day it was ordered that notice should be giuen to Robt. Stiles, that he dispos of one of his Sons by the next meeting of the Select men which will be in Nouember, elce the Select men must doe it as the Court haue ordered.

The same day it was granted to Thomas Trot Junr libertie to gitt 1400 off Clobord in the Common Swamps.

At a meeting of the Select men the 14 (9) 81 It was left to Lift^{nt} Capen William Sumner and Srg^{nt} Clap to Confer with Bro^r Pason about disposing of Robt. Stils boy vnto him If he be willing and to make report to the rest of the Select men.

The same day it was granted to the widdow Wodsworth libertie to gitt one and twentie hundred of Clobord out of the Comon Swamps belonging to Dorchester, and to returne the note againe by the 25 March next.

The same day it was granted to Samuell Capen libertie to gitt Seuen hundred of Clobord.

The same day returne was made by Constable Pason of Robt Stils answer to the Select men which is on fille.

[**352.**] The same day it was granted to Deacon Blake libertie for one and twentie hundred of Clobord —

The same day it was granted to Samuell Hale libertie for fowerteen hundred of Clobord.

The same day it was granted to Ensigne Hale and William Blake Senr of melton libertie to take some trees that haue been formerly fallen and lys vpon the Commons beyond the blew hils.

At a generall Towne meeting the 5 of December 1681 after the directory was read.

In Referance to the supply in the Minestry. It was p'posed to the towne whether they would be willing to allow Mr. Danforth one hundred pounds by the yeer, he taking the worke wholly vpon him the one half in money and the other half in Contry pay the yeer beginning the first of January next.

The Vote was in the affermatiue
Nemo Contradictione

Alsoe the same day it was p'posed to the towne whether they would haue a place purchased for to build or buy an hous for the ministry and to remaine from time to time for that vse and not to be allenated or disposed off any other way.

The Vote was in the afermatiue.

The same day it was Voted that Mr. Stoughton Richard Baker Richard Withington and John Breck should be a Comittee to look out and treat with p'sons about such a thing and to accquaint the towne with p'possessions at the next towne meeting or if need requier to call the towne together to accquaint them what is likly to be don.

The same day it was Voted that the Select men are empowered to looke out and to agree with a Scholmaster at the best termes that they can p'cuer one.

The same day ther was Chosen for Select men.

[353.] Select men for the yeer 82
- Deacon Blake
- Srg^nt Clap
- William Sumner
- Lift^nt Capen
- Ensigne Hale

for Record^r Deacon Blake

for Raters
- Srg^nt Pond
- Srg^nt Wiswell and
- John Breck

for Sup'uisors
- Samuell Capen
- Elisha Foster

The same day Thomas Leichfeild p'sented a petition to haue liberty to sell his wiues hous and ground the petition is on fill: The town by a Vote determined that it should be left to the Select men for to Consider and determin the matter: The petition is on file.

The 12: day of the 10th moneth (81) in Answere to the petition of Thomas Leichfield the Select men doe order that the land that was given to the Widow Long shall not be sould nor alienated to any person or persons whatsoeuer Either by him or any of his successors without the Consent of the select men of Dorchester or there sucsessors from tyme to tyme neither doe the select men that now are Consent that the sayed Leichfeild should sel the land to any person whatsoeuer vntill he doe first ataine the Consent of his wife therin;

At a meeting of the select men the :12 : 10 : 81 : it was appointed that there should be a Rate made for the minister of 60^li pounds money for the yeer: 81:

The same day it was agreed by the select men that Robert Stiles his Eldest son should be put out as an apprentice to Edward Pason.

these may Satisfie anney whom it may Consarn thatt the present Selectmen of Dorchester Doe giue Free Consent that the Land that was Giuen to the wid Long as in page 267 the said Land may Bee sould to Ephefrom Houerd or ony other whome the Selectmen shall approue of this (7) Day of June 1703

ROBERT SEARLE
Towne Clarke.

[354.] p^t of the acc^t of Samuell Capen as Constable yeer 80 from p 346.

More p^d to Mr Minot besids what was formerly p^d in money	0 –15 – 0
Mr Minot sent a receipt	
It. p^d to Mr Minot more in Contry pay and he gaue a discharg	3 – 9 – 3
It. more p^d to William Sumner	1 – 2 – 3
It. p^d to Lift^nt Capen in Corne	0 – 4 – 6
and to him in 2 bl. barley to Widdow Smith .	0 – 8 – 0

It. due to me for what I p^d for Roger Belleng ⎫ Rates which should be p^d to Capt Clap p^{t}ly by ⎬ Joshua Henshaw ⎭		0 – 19 – 7
It. p^d more to my father in Corne		0 – 3 – 0
and to my father for Samuel Toplif		0 – 6 – 9
and more to him in 2 bls barly		0 – 8 – 0
		7 – 16 – 4
and in p. 346		32 – 19 – 8
and Remitted out of the town Rate		40 – 16 – 0
Isack How	0 – 4 – 10	
Widdow Pelton	0 – 4 – 9	
Samuell Hill	0 – 1 – 8	
Henry Merifeild	0 – 4 – 4	
	0 – 15 – 7	0 – 15 – 7
Remitted on the town rate and on W. Turner rat		0 – 9 – 3
		42 – 0 – 10
More p^d to Tho Modsly and remitted out of ⎫ William Turner Rat ⎬		2 – 18 – 1
Isack How		0 – 1 – 0
Widdow Pelton		0 – 1 – 2
Robt Stanton		0 – 1 – 0
Henry Merryfeild		0 – 0 – 4
Samuell Chandler		0 – 0 – 6
Jno Plum		0 – 0 – 3
Jno Sanders		0 – 0 – 3
Samuell Pelton		0 – 0 – 10
Tho. Pope		0 – 0 – 3
Robt Stils		0 – 0 – 3
Buck and Chamberlen		0 – 0 – 6
Rich Euens		0 – 0 – 8
Tho. Dauenport		0 – 2 – 0
Jno Pelton		0 – 0 – 3
		0 – 9 – 3
M^d the towne Rate of his p^t to gather Comes to		38 – 6 – 4
and William Turners p^t of his rate		6 – 4 – 4
Totall		44 – 10 – 8
the Constable is Creddit^r as aboue		44 – 18 – 11
Due to Samuell Capen this 13 9 82 and he is hereby discharged		0 – 8 – 3

[355.] At a meeting of the select men the 9 : 11 : 81 : there was liberty granted to Samuel Maxfeild to get 4 or : 5 : loads of timber out of the : 500 : acres and 300 : of Railes : allso there was liberty granted him to get : 1400 : of Cloueboord out of the Comon Swamps.

The same day the Raters made a Returne of a Rate for the ministry for the yeare past.

The same day there was liberty granted to Dauid Joanes to get: 1400 : of Clouebourd.

The same day it was agreed by the select men that there should be notice giuen to the Constable to warne a towne meeting on the 16 : day of this instant:

The : 16 : 11 : 81 : At a generall towne meeting it was passed by a Vote that there should be a towne Rate made of : 40^{li} :

The same day at the Request of John Browne the select men doe free him from all Town Rates Excepting only such Rates as shall be made for the ministery : p'uided the towne be at no charges towards the maintenance of his father or mother Except it be in case of sicknes or any Extraordenary Exigent ; but in case the Constable doe Require of him his country Rates he shall then be allowed the same out of the towne Rates.

At a meeting of the Select men the : 13 : 12 : 81 : then there was liberty granted to preserued Capen to get : 200 : of Railes and some postes in the : 500 : acres ;

The same day it was agreed that Robert Sanders should haue one Load of Wood.

The same day there was liberty granted to Richard Withington to get one thousand of Clouebourd or 3000 : of shindels.

28 : 12 : 81 : order was giuen by the Select men to the Constable to demand a penalty according to the towne order of John Spure James Robinson and Robert Stilles for Entertaineng of inmates.

The : 16 : day of the 12th : mo : 81 : A towne Rate deliuered to the Constable to Colect : which was   40^{li} – 9^s – 8^d

[356.] A Towne Rate Comited to Constable John Wales and John Payson consisting of 40^{li} – 9^s – 8^d in the yeare : 81 : to be Colected by them ;

And the account giuen by the Constables of the towne Rate is as followeth

	li	s	d
Inprim. payed to Nathan Bradley as part of what is due to him for his worke at the meeting house	00	17	11
It. to Nicholas Boulton for Expences	03	00	00
It. to William Trescote as part of that which is due to him from the towne	03	19	01
It. to William Sumner as deputy being part of what is due to him for the yeare 80 : and 81 :	05	18	11
It. to William Deane for killing a Woolfe	00	10	00
It. for Warding	00	03	00
It. to Thomas Andrewes for keeping of francis	00	04	04
It. to Samuel Clap for wood to sanders	00	06	06
It. to Desire Clap for keeping of francis	00	02	05
It. to Isaack Joanes in part of what is due to him from the towne	00	04	06
It. to Rodger Billing for two laders for the meeting house	01	02	09
It to lift. Capen as part of what is due to him for Record^r	00	13	11

DORCHESTER TOWN RECORDS.

It. to James Blake Senr as part of what is due to him for Expences in the yeare : 79 : and for timber for the bridg at Roxbury brooke	00 – 06 – 08
It. to John Brown he being free from all towne Rates	00 – 01 – 02
It. to Elisha Foster to p'cure weights for a towne standard	01 – 00 – 00
It. to Robert Sanders one bushel of Corne	00 – 03 – 00
It. payed to the select men 20^s money	01 – 00 – 00
It. discounted with him for Rates that can not be gotten	00 – 06 – 02
widow Cheny 4^s : 2^d : John Pelton : 1^s samuel Rise : 1^s	
payed by Constable Wales	20 – 00 – 04
Constable John Pasons account of that part of the towne Rate collected by him : payed to Nathan Bradley	03 – 02 – 01
It. for killing of foure woolues	02 – 00 – 00
It. to Ensigne hall[1] for wood to Nathan Bradley and to francis Ball for new makeing the pound and carting timber for the Cage	01 – 17 – 04
It. to Timothy Foster for to p'cure weights for the towne	01 – 00 – 00
[357.] It. for keeping of francis	02 – 12 – 00
It. for Warding	00 – 03 – 00
It. to William Ryall for building the Cage	04 15 – 00
It. to lift. Capen as part of what is due him for Recording and for Runeng the line betwene the 400 Acres and Vose his farme	00 – 10 – 02
It. to William Sumner in part of what is due to him as deputy	03 – 02 – 05
It. to Widow George for Expences for the Raters	00 – 05 – 00
It. for Daniel Preston for killing a woolfe and for francis	00 – 13 – 00
It. to Samuel Paul	00 – 03 – 00
It. discounted with him for Rates that can not be gotten : Robert Stanton : 3^s 8^d : henery merefeild 1^s 8^d and John Sanders 1^s	00 – 06 – 04
payed by Constable Pason	20 – 09 – 04
by both Constables the towne Rate fully payed	40 – 09 – 08

The same day the Constables gaue an account of a quarter part of a single Countary Rate which was Comitted to them to Collect the Rate was	09 – 02 – 09
treasurers Warrant	08 – 02 – 06
Remaineth to the towne	01 – 00 – 03
payed to the select men : money	00 – 15 – 00

---

[1] This name has been heretofore in these records written Hale, but it is beyond doubt that the name is now called Hall. — W. H. W.

the remainder which is : 5ˢ : 3ᵈ :
Remitted vpon account of desperate Debts ; And
the Constables are discharged . . . . 309 – 02 – 09

[**358.**] February the : 11 : 1683 : Timothy Foster and Nehemiah Clap Constā. gaue an account to the select men of the seuerall Rates that were Comitted to them to Collect :

	l	s	d
A schoole Rate in the yeare : 82 : which is money	20 –	5 –	4
payed by the Constables to Mʳ Deneson money .	20 –	0 –	0

the remainder of this Rate to the select men
A Rate for the vse of the towne one fourth part } 32 – 18 – 7
of it money . . . . . . }

payed by Constable Clap.

to Mʳ Glouer in money	01 – 00 – 00
to nicholas Boulton money	00 – 18 – 06
to Capt. Capen money	00 – 03 – 07
to John Trescote and the select men vpon the balance of an account aboute house Roome for francke	00 – 01 – 06
to Nicolas Boulton Country pay	02 – 01 – 02
to Nathan Bradley for Ringing the bell . .	00 – 18 – 02
to Capt. Capen	01 – 17 – 00
to Deacon Blake as part of what is due to him .	02 – 04 – 10
to Sergᵗ Wiswel for Runeng lines . . .	00 – 05 – 00
to Ensigne Clap vpon the same account . .	00 – 04 – 06
to Nathaneel Clap for francke & Runeng lines .	00 – 15 – 00
to hopstill Clap for lines	00 – 02 – 00
to John Trescote for francke	00 – 01 – 04
to John Guile for killing a woolfe . . .	00 – 10 – 00
to William Nahaton for killing a woolfe . .	00 – 10 – 00
to William Sumner as deputy	01 – 01 – 03
to James Bird as part of what is due to him .	01 – 02 – 00
By Constable Timothy Foster payed to Nathan Bradley	03 – 09 – 08
to Mʳ Glouer for schoolemasters diet . . .	05 – 10 – 00
more to Mʳ Glouer money	04 – 00 – 00
to Timothy Tilstone for Runeng lines . . .	00 – 02 – 06

	s d		
to Samuel Capen	2 – 6		
John Brecke	5 – 0		
henery Leadbetter	3 – 0	all those for Runeng lines the whole sum is	01 – 07 – 06
Ebenezer Withington	3 – 0		
John Minot	6 – 0		
Samuel Robinson	6 – 0		
Obediah hawes	2 – 0		

To John payson for his labor in takeng account } 00 – 05 – 00
of Comon Lands Rateable . . . }
to Ensigne hall for a load of wood for sanders . 00 – 05 – 00

[**359.**] to the widow George for intertaine-
ment of Raters . . . . . .   00 – 06 – 00
to Robert Mamuntauge for a woulfes head . .   00 – 05 – 00
to samuel Sumner for a debt due to him. . .   00 – 01 – 08
        Debts that cannot be gotten . .   01 – 14 – 01
        to John Tolman . . . .   00 – 01 – 04
        to Timothy Tilstone . . . .   00 – 05 – 06
        for woolues heads . . . .   00 – 12 – 00
        A rate for building a house for the
          minestry which is . . .   104 – 14 – 11
        paid of this Rate by Constable
          Foster to Isaack Ryall . . .   54 – 02 – 06
        by Nehemiah Clap to John Bricke   20 – 00 – 00
        to Isaak Ryall . . . . .   07 – 10 – 00
        to Timothy Tillstone . . .   07 – 00 – 00

Constable Foster's account see more in p: 371:
[**360.**] fence vewers for the yeare: 1662: } Thomas Trott Senr
    for that part of the great lots .   and
    beyound Timothy Fosters . .   Henery Roberts.
    for Capt. necke . . . } Ensigne hall and
                             John Wales
For the feild behind Thomas modsleys serg^t Clap and Isaac Joanes
For the hill feild Joshua henshaw and the occup' of Mrs Flintes.
    for the feild behind John Birds } Thomas Andrewes
                                  James Bird
    for the feild behind Mr Stoughtons } henery Garnesey
                                  and Amiel Weekes

At a meeting of the selectmen of the 13 : 1 : 8½: there was appointed for tithing men for the yeare Ensueng;
                              Hopstill humfrey
                              Hopstill Clap
                              Joseph Weekes
                              Isaac Joanes
                              Samuel Trescot
                              Daniel Preston iun^r
                              Thomas Tolman iun^r
                              Roger Billinge
                              Ebenezar Withington
                              Israel How
                              William Ryall
                              petter Lyon
                              Desire clap
                              serg^t Wiswel

   The same day there was chosen sup'visers for the necke way John Withington and James Foster.

   The same day Jacob huens and Joshua henshaw were appointed to cleare the necke: and the necke is to be cleared by the first of aprill:

   The same day there were men appointed to Run the bounds betweene townes as foloweth;

For the line betweene Milton and Dor- } Timothy Tilstone
chester from the outside of the last: } Samuel Capen
6: deuissions towards the blew hils

    for the line betweene Dorchester } Sergt Wiswel
    and Dedham . . . } Nathaneel Clap
    } and John Bricke.

    For the lines Round aboute } Henerey Leadbetter
    Punkapauge the indian } Ebenezar Withington
    plantation . . .

    For the line betweene brantree } John Minot
    and Dorchester from the tope } Samuel Robinson
    of the blew hills towards the } John Tolman
    patent line . . .

[361.] For the line betweene the 400 } Lift. Capen
    Acres and the meadow of } William Sumner
    Robert Voses farme. .

    For the line betweene Roxbury } Serg^t Clap
    and Dorchester . . . } Obediah Hawes
    } hopstill Clap.

    The same day there was Chosen } John Withington
    sup'visers for the necke way } James Foster

    The same day there were men
    chosen to cleare the necke } Jacob Huens and
    and the necke is to be Cleared } Joshua Henshaw
    by the first of Aprill by .

At a general towne meeting the 14 : 1 : 82 : Mr Timothy Mathers Request was granted for liberty to hang vp a gate at the Corner of John Minots pasture in the great lots.

The same day it was passed by a vote that the Comittee chosen for to p'uide an accomadation for the minestry should purchase that house and orchard which was formerly Richard Dauis with a littell peece of meadow which lyeth on the other side of the way if it may be obtained for sixty pound.

The same day it was passed by a vote that there should be a Rate made of the same Sum that was made for Mr Danforth for his labour in the minestry the yeare past: for to purchase the house and land aboue mentioned;

The same day Timothy Foster and Elisha Foster were Chosen Constables:

The same day Deacon James Blake was chosen deputy for the whole yeare.

The last day of march: 82: there was deliuered to Constable Elisha Foster and his partner three Rates to Collect.

A Rate for the schoole . . . . 20 – 5 – 4
A Rate for the Country which is for the agents }
    Consisting of halfe a singel Country Rate } 18 – 07 – 11
A Rate for the vse of the towne which is to }
    purchase accomodations for the minestry } 60 – 9 – 7

At a meeting of the selectmen the 10 : 2 : 82 : lift Capen William Sumner and Timothy Tilstone were appointed to ioyne with brantree men to Run the line betweene brantree and Dorchester, from milton bounds to the sea:

[**362.**] The same day James Bird was appointed superviser in the Roome of Elisha Foster:

The same day the select men agreed with Thomas Modsley to make and maineteine a sufficient fence against the burieng place for seuen yeares and to keepe it vp all the tyme and then to leaue a sufficient fence at the end of the terme And the fence which he is to make and maineteine is all that which was his p'portion and and he is to haue ten shillinges for his labor and liberty for to get post and Railes out the 500 acres for to doe the one halfe of the fence

Aprill: 82: the Widow George had the ap'bation of the select men to keepe ordenary for this yeare p'uided that John Bricke doe ingage for her that it shall be performed and kept as the law directs; 22: 3: 82 it was passed by a Vote of the Church that there should be a Rate made of ten pounds and that Each one should pay in there p'portions to the deacons on the 2^d day of June next and if that be not sufficient to discharg what is layed out for the ordenation then to be made vp by p'portion afterward.

Weights are p'uided by Constable Elisha Foster; for to be a standard for the towne according as the law Requireth; by which all other weights are to be sized and sealed; diuers of which are bell fashoned viz: one 56: one 28: one 14: one 7: one 4: one 2: the Rest are flat weights and are one pound: one halfe pound: one quarter: one eight part: one ounce: as allso one halfe ounce: one quarter of an ounce: one eight: one 16 part of an ounce:

These were all deliuered to William Pond the: 23: 3: 82:

At a meeting of the select men the: 12: 4: 82: it was then agreed by the select men that a warrant should be sent to the Constable to require a penalty according to the towne order of those that did Entertaine inmates without giueing bonds for the townes security;

The same day there was liberty granted to William Ryall to get 2500: of Cloueboards in the Comon swamps.

The same day was granted to Philip Withington liberty to get Rangeng timber for a dwelling house in the Commons beyound the blew hills;

The same same day Elder Humfrey Mr Mather James White and Jacob Huens were appointed a Comittee by the select men to find out a high way in the most Conuenient [**363.**] place from the Country high way that goeth through the Eight acre lots to the high way that lyeth betweene Roxbury and Dorchester;

the 13: 9: 82: this Comittee make a Returne of what they haue done and it is Consented to by the select men: there Returne is vpon file.

At a meeting of the select men the: 11: 7: 82: there was liberty granted to James White to get 1400 of Cloueboards in the cedar swamps;

The same day William Danforth was called before the selecmen and was admonished by them to forbeare frequenting ordenaryes and to set himselfe in a way of Constant Employment in some lawfull Calling;

23: 8: 82: At a generall towne meeting Nehemiah Clap was Chosen Constable in the steed and Roome of Elisha Foster to doe that worke which he should haue done.

The same day it was passed by a vote that there should be a house built and finished for the ministry by the: 29th day of september next;

the same day it was put to the Vote whether they would chuse a Comittee to agre with a workeman to build sayed house and finish it: the Vote was in the afirmatiue;

the Comittee Chosen at the same tyme; was } Isaac Joanes
Timothy Tilstone
John Bricke

At a generall towne meeting the 4th day of December 1682: after the directory was Read; it was put to the vote whether there should be a schoole master hired for an other yeare; the vote was in the affirmatiue.

the same day it was put to the vote whether they would appoint some set dayes for the bringeng in and receiueing of that part of the minesters salery which is to be payed in Country pay and that there be thre dayes in the yeare appointed for that purpose Viz: the first Munday and the third Monday in february and the first Munday in March:

the vote was in the afirmatiue

The same day there was Chosen for select men
James Blake: Record[r]
Serg[t] Wiswell
Serg[t] Clap
Timothy Tilstone
Ensigne Hall

Raters { William Pond
Samuel Robinson
John Bricke

Supervisers { Samuel Topliffe
Joshua Henshaw.

[364.] The same day it was put to the vote that whosoeuer should be chosen to take an account of the minesters salery should atend vpon that worke on the dayes that are appointed; to take an account of what shall be then brought in and by whome and allso Returne the names of those that are defectiue vnto the select men; who shall forthwith ishue out a warrant to the Constable to take it by distress or otherwise:

the vote was in the affirmatiue

The same day it was passed by a vote that there should be a Collector anualy Chosen;

The same day James Blake sen[r] was chosen Collector for one yeare:

11: 10: 82 At a meeting of the select men order giuen to the Raters to make three Rates: —

A Rate for the minester of one hundred pound the one halfe of it to be payed in money the other in Country pay

A Rate of one hundred pounds for building a house for the minestry to be payed in money.

A Rate of thirty two pounds for the vse of the towne and to pay for the schoole masters dyet : a fourth part money

The same day Joseph Weekes had liberty granted for to take two or three trees by Roxbury line ;

12 : 1 : 83 : liberty granted to Timothy Tilstons to get timber in the Commons beyound the blew hills : to build a barne

[**365.**] 13 – 1 – 83 : At a generall towne meeting James Blake sen^r was Chosen Deputy for the whole yeare ; the same day at the Request of Mrs Poole for liberty to set her orchard fence a little nearer to the high way ; there was Chosen for a Comittee William Sumner Richard Leeds and John Wales se^r to veiw the place and to determine where the fence should stand :

The same day Nathaneel Glouer and Joseph Leeds were Chosen Constables for the yeare Ensueng :

fence veiwers appointed by the select men for the yeare : 83 : —

for Capt necke	John Brecke
for the feild behind Thomas Modsleys .	{ Thomas Modsley { John Capen
for the hill feild	{ Isaac Joanes { Serg^t Clap
for the feild behind John Birds . .	{ John Bird { John Blackeman
for the feild behind M^r stoughtons . .	{ John Baker { Richard Leeds
for the feild behind Mr Mathers . .	{ Mr Mather { William Trescote
for that part of the great lots beyound Timothy Fosters	{ Samuel Robinson { Israel How

Tithing men appointed by the select men for the yeare : 83 : —
Jacob huens
William Trescote
John Capen iu^r
John Wales sen^r
John Baker
Samuel Hix
John Tolman
Roger Billing sen^r
Samuel Capen
John Pason
James White
Clement Maxfeild
Obediah Hawes
James Foster ;

12 : 1 : 83 : the select men granted liberty to Robert Stanton to get 1400 : of Cloueboord in the Common swamps ;

The same day an order giuen to Constable Wales to forbeare the getting of Richard Mathers Rate to the Minestry for the yeare 81 : vntill further order from the select men :

all fences to be made sufficient by the : 25 : day of march :

men appointed to Cleare the neck : . . . { Isaac Joanes and Richard Mather :

sup'vizers for the necke way . . . { nathaneel Clap and Richard Mather.

The same day granted to Thomas Modsley liberty to get one load of timber in the 500 Acres;

[366.] At a meeting of the select men the : 11 : 4 : 83 : at the Request of Samuel Williames in the behalfe of some of Rentham for the hire of meadow : it was granted that they should haue the benefit of that meadow according as is Expressed in the agreement made with them in writing : which is vpon file ;

The same day there was liberty granted to Timothy Tilstone to get 200 of Cedar Clouebooord in the Comones :

July : 27 : 83 At a generall towne meeting it was passed by a vote that there should be a barne built for the minestry of twenty foot square :

At the same time there was a Comittee Chosen for to agree with a Workman to doe it : the Comittee was Capt Capen Samuel Paul and John Breake :

18 : 6 : 83 : At a meeting of the select men it was agreed that order should bee giuen to the Raters to make a Rate of 100^l for a house for the minestry.

10 : 10 : 83 : At a meeting of the select men it was agreed that order should be giuen to the Raters to make a Rate for the minestry of 100^l : and a Rate of 60^l : for the vse of the towne

13 : 11 : 83 : Daniel Eldars came to the select men and requested that the land giuen him by the towne might be Recorded :

the same day there was liberty granted to Joseph Weekes to get timber in the Commones to groundsel his house

10 : 1 : 84 : the select men granted liberty to James Bird to get a : 100 : of Railes and 50 postes in the 500 : Acres

[367.] At a generall towne meeting December the 3^d : 1683 : Towne oficers Chosen

Select men	Raters	Super Visers
lift. Hall	William Pond	Hopstill Clap
Ensigne Clap	Samuel Robenson	Bernard Capen
James Blake	John Brecke	
Enoch Wiswell		
Timothy Tilstone		

The same day it was passed by a vote that the select men shall haue full power to hire a school master for the yeare Ensueng :

The same day there was Chosen for
Collector   Capt Capen
Recorder   James Blake

The same day at the request of Joseph Weekes there was a Comittee Chosen to veiw a little peice of land (which he desird the grant of) and to make there Returne to the towne the men Chosen was Elder Humfrey and Isaac Joanes :

The same day it was passed by a vote with Reference to the

schoole land which is granted by the generall Court in leiw of Tomsons island that the worshipfull Mʳ stoughton Enoch wiswell and John Brecke would looke after and take Care for the layeng of it out:

The same day it was passed by a vote that Timothy Foster should Collect the Remainder of those Rates that were Comited to Nehemiah Clap to Collect.

The same day it was passed by a vote that the select men should haue liberty to Raise or leuie such Rates as will discharge the towne debtes

the same day it passed by a vote that the select men should Consider of some way for the layeng out of the land beyound the blew hills so as might be for the townes aduantage:

The same day Capt. Capen Richard Baker and John Brecke were Chosen to setle the fence p'portioneable betweene Isaac Joanes and the minestry land:

March: 11: 84 at a generall towne meeting at the Request of John Trescote for liberty to set vp a saw mill there was a Comittee Chosen to Veiw the place and it was left to them to determine as they se Cause p'uided he take in none as partners with him that are not inhabetants of this towne: the Comittee Chosen was Capt. Capen Mʳ Mather and Henery Leadbetter: who were allso to veiw the land that he did Request for: by the Riuer side for to accomadate that worke: and to determine aboute it:

The same day at the Request of John Trescote it was granted that he should haue liberty to set vp a shop at the West end of his dwelling house and for his Conueniecy they did grant him a little peice of land which the shop now standeth vpon.

[368.] The same day it was passed by a vote that Ensigne Clap and Joseph Weekes should haue a litle parcel of land at the End of their home lotes as it was layed out by the Comittee Chosen for that worke: which was: Elder Humfrey and Isaac Joanes.

for Capᵗ. necke	{ Daniell Preston sen { Joseph Leeds
for the feild behind Thomas Modsleys	{ Obediah swift { Joseph weekes
for the hill feild	{ Ensigne Clap { John Garnesey
for the feild behind John Birds	{ James Bird { Obediah hawes
for the feild behind Mʳ Stoughtons	{ Richard Baker { Amiel Weekes
for the feild behind Mʳ Mathers	{ Sergᵗ Pond { Ebenezer Williams
for that part of the great lots beyound Timothy Fosters	{ Thomas Trot Seʳ { Beniamen Leeds

Tithing men for the yeare: 84:

John Bird
Thomas Modsley
William Pond
Isaac Joanes

Samuell Trescote
John Breck
Timothy Foster
Thomas Peirce
Ebenezar Withington
Samuel Robenson
Increase Sumner
Charles Dauenport
John Trescote
John Withington

all fences to be made suficient by the 25 day of March : —

The men appointed to Cleare the necke { Nathaneel Clap / hopstill Clap

the necke is to be Cleared by the first day of Aprill

sup'visers for the necke way . . { John Withington / Richard Mather

Nathan Bradley is appointed to looke after swine that they be yoked and ringed as the law derects.

The same day it was passed by a vote that the fence aboute the minestry land adioyneng to the house should be made vp and set in Repaire at the towne Charges :

[369.] The same day the towne did by a vote manefest there acceptance of what the Comittee had done in deuiding the fence betweene the land of Isaac Joanes and the minestry land ;

The same day the Committee for the meeting house gaue vp theire account of what was Comitted to them and theire account was accepted and they are discharged :

The same day there was a liberty granted to John Wales to Cleare the Creeke by his house for his owne benefit p'uided he doeth no damag to high wayes nor no other Conserne : the same day it was passed by a vote that a swampe which lyeth in milton and is part of the minestry land should be sould by Capt. Capen and the Comittee :

the same day

Henery Leadbetter ⎫ were Chosen to take Veiw of all the Comon
John Minot ⎪ Land beyound the blue hills that is within the
Samuel Robinson ⎬ towneshipe of Dorchester : in order to the lay-
Ebenezar Billinge ⎭ eng of it out : and make Report to the towne :

The same day

Capt Capen and William Sumner were appointed a Comittee to Veiw a peice of ground which John Garnesey desireth to haue libertie to set a barne on :

The same day

Capt Capen ⎫
William Sumner ⎪ were Chosen a Comittee to looke out and take
Lieu^t Hall ⎬ notice where there is or may be a nesessity of
Ensigne Clap ⎪ high wayes for the vse and benefitt of the towne
Samuel Topliffe ⎭ and to make there Returne :

The same day at the Request of Mathias Puffer it is granted that he should haue two thirds of his Rates to the minestry abated

The same day William Sumner was Chosen deputy for the yeare Ensueng :

The same day Ebenezar Williames and Bernard Capen were Chosen Constables;

Dor: 15: march: 8¾: wee whose names are subscribed being appointed by the towne of dorchester to veiw a place vpon Naponset Riuer aboue the house of Daniel Eldars at the litle Island in the Riuer to set a sawmill vpon; with aboute: 40: Rod in length by the Riuers side to make a trench for the water of the Riuer to come to the mill and aboute halfe an acre of land against the Island [**370.**] to lay there timber vpon: wee see no Cause to deny there Request p'uided theire damme be not so high as to preiudis the mills below by stoping the water aboue: and vpon Condission the person petitioneng goe on with the designe to Erect a saw mill vpon these Condissoins wee grant theire Request as iudging it not preiudiciall to the towne.

       JOHN CAPEN sen[r]
       TIMOTHY MATHER sen[r]
       HENERY LEADBETTER

  This is a true Coppy as
   attests James Blake Record[r]

Receiued March 16th 1684[b]: from Ebenezar Williams and Bernard Capen the summe of seuenteene pounds Eleuen shillings and Eight pence in money in full of Dorchester in behalfe of my master m[r] James Russell treasurer

I say Receiued p' William Welsteed Jun[r]:

Receiued December 22th: 1685: from Ebenezar Williams and Bernard Capen the summe of thirty three pounds in money and the same summe in Country pay being in full of two Rates for the towne of Dorchester for the last yeare

I say Receud: p' James Russell late treasurer.

[**371.**] Constable Fosters account of A Country
Rate which is . . . . 108 – 09 – 06
              l s d

[**372.**] An account of the Rates that were
Comited to Nathaneel Glouer and Joseph Leeds
Constables for the yeare 1683: A schoole Rate   26 – 18 – 11
payed by Joseph Leeds to M[r] Deneson money . 12 – 00 – 00
payed by M[r] Glouer to M[r] Deneson . . . 09 – 00 – 00
and to himselfe for M[r] Denesons diet . . . 05 – 00 – 00
abatements for Rates that Can not be gotten

        s d
John Browne   0 – 8 ⎫
Waching Atherton   1 – 6 ⎪
John Sanders   1 – 6 ⎬ Totall of what
Thomas plum   0 – 6 ⎪ is payed   26 – 06 – 00
Walter Eueringden   1 – 4 ⎪
payd to Widow Georg 0 – 6 ⎭

The Constables aboue mentioned debter to the ⎱
 towne vpon the account of this schoole Rate ⎰   00 – 12 – 11

9: 9: 85: Receiued of M[r] Glouer: in money   00 – 08 – 00

A Rate for building Comitted to the same Constables to Collect which is to be payed in money   £ s d
110 – 16 – 10
Constable Leeds his part is . . . . .   44 – 04 – 04
payed to the Comittee and the select men . .   48 – 06 – 08
Abatements for Rates that can not be gotten

John Weekes	5 – 0
Widow Farington	1 – 0
John Browne	2 – 6
Nathaneel Lyon	2 – 6
Richard Mather ouer Rated	5 – 0
hudsones farme	9 – 6
Rate short of the sum	8 – 2

the whole sum of these abatments . . .   01 – 13 – 08
to Ensigne Clap 6^s 6^d . . . . .   00 – 06 – 06
to the select men . . . . . .   01 – 00 – 00
abated the Widow Battens Rate . . .   00 – 02 – 06
and so Constable Leeds hath payed the whole of his part of this Rate and hee is discharged by the select men : 9 : 12 : 84 : —

[**373.**] Nathaneel Glouers part of the Rate payed to Isaake Ryall or the Comittee . . .   51 – 00 – 04
payed to the select men . . . . .   01 – 02 – 00
to Isaak Ryall . . . .   02 – 18 – 03

abated to widow George:	. 2 – 6
Joseph hoppen . .	. 2 – 6
henery merefeild .	. 2 – 6
Robert stanton . .	. 2 – 6

Item payed to the Comitee . . . . .   01 – 00 – 00
to the select men . . . . . .   02 – 08 – 00
abated John Browns Rate . . . .   00 – 02 – 06
and payed to the select men . . .   00 – 17 – 06
Mr Glouer hath payed the whole of his part which   59 – 17 – 03
and the Constable is discharged by the select men 9 : 12 : 84 :

Account of a towne rate in the yeare : 83 Comitted to the same Constables to Colect :   which is
60 – 04 – 10
payed by Constable Leeds to Widow Boulton   02 – 13 – 00
to Ensigne Clap for intertainement . .   00 – 05 – 00
to Nathan Bradley for Ringing the bell .   01 – 05 – 01
to William Sumner as deputy formerly due .   01 – 15 – 06
to Capt Capen . . . . . .   00 – 11 – 03
to Mr Deneson for his last quarter teaching : money . . . .   04 – 00 – 00
to John Trescote money . . . .   01 – 01 – 01
to Ensigne Clap for wood : & Corn to John Pelton . . . . . .   00 – 12 – 06
to Richard Baker money . . . .   00 – 10 – 00
to Deacon Blake as part of what is due to him as deputy in the yeare : 82 and 83 . .   07 – 11 – 09
abated for Rates that Can not be gotten .   00 – 03 – 11
Thomas hoppen 1^s – 8^d willlam Trescote . .   00 – 04 – 03

DORCHESTER TOWN RECORDS.   273

Joseph hopen   1 – 4 to John Pelton   .   .   .   00 – 03 – 00
John Weekes   1 – 4
to widow Clap for Joshua Sanders   .   .   .   01 – 00 – 00
to Deacon Blake as deputy .   .   .   .   .   01 – 11 – 06
to Nathan Bradley   .   .   .   .   .   .   00 – 02 – 11
[374.]   to Deacon Blake   .   .   .   .   00 – 17 – 03
to Thomas Modsley for fencing at the burieng }
   place   .   .   .   .   }   00 – 05 – 09
to William Trescote   .   .   .   .   .   .   04 – 05
the whole sum payed by Joseph Leeds is   .   .   24 – 13 – 09
of this sum payed in money   .   .   .   .   06 – 09 – 10
Joseph Leeds Debter to the town   .   .   .   03 – 14 – 04
8 : 12 : 1685 : Joseph Leeds gave an account to ⎫
   the select men of the Rates that were Comitted ⎬   02 – 00 – 07
   to him to Collect : and he is Debter vpon the ⎬
   account of the towne Rate   .   .   . ⎭
and vpon the account of the building Rate, money   00 – 09 – 06
but as for that part of the minesters Rate that is Comitted to him
   he hath giuen no account ; of it ; 14 : 12 : 168$\frac{7}{6}$ Joseph Leeds
   pay^d the full of his towne rate, being   .   02 – 00 – 07
and likewise is discharged his ministry hows rate

   An account of what Constable Nathaneel Glouer hath payed of
this towne Rate :
to William Sumner as deputy   .   .   .   .   05 – 11 – 05
to John Lewes for a woolfes head   .   .   .   00 – 10 – 00
to James Bird   .   .   .   .   01 – 14 – 00
to Nathan Bradley   .   .   .   .   .   .   02 – 06 – 01
to leiut. hall for wood to John Pelton and for ⎫
   which he layed out for glase for the Meeting ⎬   00 – 08 – 06
   house   .   .   .   . ⎭
to Timothy Foster   .   .   .   .   .   .   00 – 05 – 00
to John Brecke   .   .   .   .   00 – 06 – 00
Serg^t Tilstone   .   .   .   .   00 – 02 – 00
William Nahaton for wouelues   .   .   .   .   01 – 00 – 00
to Nathaneel Glouer for schoole masters diet   .   06 – 10 – 10
to Deacon Blake .   .   .   .   01 – 10 – 02
John Trescote money .   .   .   .   .   .   00 – 03 – 00
to Mr Deneson money .   .   .   .   .   .   03 – 10 – 00
to Nathaneel Glouer money   .   .   .   .   01 – 00 – 00
to John Minott for a woolfe .   .   .   .   .   00 – 10 – 00
abatement for Rates that can not be gotten .   .   00 – 11 – 02
to Deacon Blake .   .   .   .   00 – 16 – 04
to lift. hall .   .   .   .   00 – 02 – 00
   [375.]   Nathanel Glouer payed of this Rate .   26 – 16 – 06
of which sum $\overset{1}{5}$ payed in money .   .   .   .   05 – 00 – 00
Mr Glouer debter to the towne   .   .   .   .   05 – 09 – 00
of which sum $\overset{1}{1}$ is to be payed money .   .   .   01 – 00 – 00
which Constable Glouer payed to Joseph Leeds   this account made
   by the Constables with the select men : December the 15th : 1684
   the 9th of Nouember Mr Glouer payed by order of the select men to

Timothy Foster money : 5̊ : to Nathan Bradley money : 8̊ to Daniel Eldars money : 6̊ : and money : 1̊ to the select men to Capt. Capen : 2 2 in Country pay : which is 1 – 12 – 2 in Country pay : to left hall money 5̊.

these may Satisfie any whome it may Consarne that the present Selectmen of Dorchester att the Requeste of henry Straight of Greenwich in the Colony of Rhode Island who married with mary Long Daughter of mary Long Formerly widow But Since Called mary Litchfield Latly deceeced Doe giue Free Consent vnto the said Henry Straight and mary his wife that the Land that was Giuen to the widdow Long her mother as in 'page 267 may be sould by them to Ephraim Howard of Dorchester or anny other whom the Select men shall approue of 7 June 1703

By order of the Select men
ROBERTT SEARLE towne Clark

[376.] An account of the Rates that were Comitted to the Constabes to Colect in the yeare : 1684 : Ebenezar Williames and Bernard Capen :

	l – s – d
A Rate for the schoole	35 – 04 – 06
Bernard Capen his part	18 – 17 – 02
payed to Mr John Williames schoole master	16 – 00 – 00
to Thomas Barret	02 – 00 – 00
to John Brecke	00 – 03 – 00
to the select men	00 – 14 – 00
payed of the same Rate by Ebenezar Williams to Mr Danforth for Mr Williams board	10 – 10 – 00
to Thomas Barret for sanders	01 – 05 – 00
to Mr. Williams	04 – 00 – 00
abatements for that which can not be had widow Laurence	00 – 00 – 10
John Weekes	00 – 01 – 00
Obediah hawes being Rated twice in this Rate	00 – 04 – 05
to the select men	00 – 06 – 00
	35 – 04 – 04

A towne Rate Comitted to the same Constables to Collect	24 – 10 – 00
Coustable Capen payed to leiut. hall	00 – 06 – 01
to Nathan Bradley	04 – 00 – 00
to Timothy Tilstone for Entertainement	00 – 12 – 00
to Isaake Ryall for the barne	04 – 00 – 00
to John Brecke for the Raters	00 – 06 – 00
to samuel hix	00 – 15 – 00
to John Minot	00 – 07 – 04
to William Sumner	02 – 07 – 11
to William Sumner	00 – 07 – 10
	13 – 02 – 2

Constable Williams payed of the same Rate to Ensigne Clapp
for Entertainement . . . . 00 – 11 – 00
to Enoch Wiswell for the same . . . . 00 – 12 – 00
to William Trescote . . . . 00 – 06 – 06
to Isaake Joanes . . . . 00 – 04 – 00
to James Blake Senr . . . . . . 04 – 04 – 02
to James Bird . . . . 00 – 05 – 00
to William Sumner . . . . 04 – 08 – 04
to mathias puffer for an woulfes head . . . 00 – 04 – 06
to henery White . . . . 00 – 02 – 03
abated: Thomas Williams: 7^d: John Weekes: 7^d: 00 – 01 – 02
for a woulues head in part of what is due . . 00 – 08 – 02

11 – 07 – 1

the Constables haue payed of this towne Rate   24^{ls} – 09^s – 03^d
and they are discharged: by the Select men: 4: 10: 85:

[377.] At a generall Towne meeting the first day of the 10th: m̅o̅: 1684 it was put to the vote whether there should be a Rate made for to pay the Charge of tryeing our title to the land which is taken vp in farmes by seuerall men: within the towneshipe of Dorchester:
the vote was in the afirmatiue.

The same day it was passed by a vote that henery White (because of his Remote liueing from the meeting) should be free from payeing to the minestry by way of Rate for the yeare insueng and vntill the towne see Cause to allter it:

The same day Capt. Capen William Sumner Timothy Tilstone and John Brecke were Chosen a Comittee to setle the boundes betweene the minestry land and Thomas Vose his farme.

The same day towne officeres Chosen.
                 Ensigne Clap
                 Leiut Hall
Recorder Deacon Blake ⎫
                 Serg^t Wiswel ⎬ these Select men
                 William Sumner ⎭
the same day there was chosen for Raters
                 William Pond ⎫
                 Samuel Paul ⎬ these Raters
                 John Brecke ⎭

The same day Deacon Blake was Chosen Colecter for the yeare 1684:

The same day it was put to the vote whether purgatory swampe should be deuided to the ancient p'prietors and there sucsessors:
the vote was in the affimatiue

The same day an account was giuen by the Colector of the Rate that was made for Mr Danforths salery in the yeare 1682: and Mr Danforth is payed the Exact sum of 1̇00: 50: in money and 5̇0: in Country pay as doth apeare by his Receipt bearing date the 26: nouemb: 1684:

The Colector is discharged.

[**378.**] the :26 :11 : 84 : at the meeting of the ancient p'prietors and there successors

John Minott ⎫ were Chosen for a Committee to take a
Samuel Robinson ⎬ veiw of purgatory swamp and get an artice
and John Withington ⎭ to take
a plote of it in order to the diuiding of it ; the same day it was passed by a vote that all the p'prietors should pay theire p'portion for the layeng of it out ;

At a meeting of the select men : 10 : 12 : 84 : men appointed to Run the lines betweene the townes as followeth :

betweene milton and Dorchester from the outside ⎫
of the last six deuissions towards the blue hills : ⎬ Timothy Tilstō
and allso the line betweene brantre and Dorches- ⎪ Increase
ter from milton boundes to the sea . . ⎭ Sumner

⎫ John Brecke
for the line betweene Dorchester and Dedham ⎬ James Foster
⎭ Robert Spurr iun^r

for the line between brantree and Dorchester ⎫ Ezra Clap
from the top of the blue hills towards the pa- ⎬ John Tolman
tent line . . . . . . ⎭ Thomas Trott iun^r

⎫ Obediah hawes
for the line betweene Roxbury and Dorchester ⎬ John Capen iun^r
⎭ John Blakeman

the same day the select men agreed with John Minott to pay vnto him : 30 : for woulues heads which is to bee payed annualy in his towne Rates ;

payed of the abouesayed summe in the yeare : 84 : by Bernard Capen Constable ; 7 :^s 4 :^d

for the lines aboute the Indian plantation Ebenezar Withington Samuel hall.

At a meeting of the select men the : 9 : 1 : 85 : men appointed for to veiw fences

for Capt necke . . . . . ⎱ lift hall
⎰ John Brecke

for the feild behind Thomas Modsleys . ⎱ Thomas Modsley
⎰ John Capen iu^r

for the hill feild . . . . . ⎱ Isaack Joanes
⎰ hopestill humfrey

for the feild behinde John Birds . . ⎱ John Bird
⎰ John Blackman

for the feild behind Rich. Leeds . . ⎱ Joseph Leeds
⎰ John Baker

for the feild behind Mr Mathes . . ⎱ William Trescote
⎰ Joseph Math

for that part of the great lotes from Timothy ⎱ Timothy Tilstone
Tilstons to Thomas Tolman sen^r . . ⎰ John Tolman

[**379.**] from Thomas Tolmans to the Riuer ⎱ Thomas Tilstone
⎰ and Israell How :

And all fences to be made sufficient by the 25 day of march :

The same day there was appointed for tithing men : for the yeare 1685 :
Jacob huen
Joseph Weekes
William Trescot
John Wales
Joseph Leedes
Nathaneel Glouer
Timothy Tilstone
Rodger Billinge
Samuel Capen
Thomas Trot sen^r
Edward Pason
Clement Maxfeild
John Garnesey
James Blake iun^r

super visors for the necke way } Nathaneel Clap / James Bird

the men apointed to Cleare the necke } Thomas Modsley / John Blackeman

and the necke to be Cleared by the 16 day of Aprill :

The same day there was liberty granted to Daniel Ellen to get 1400 : of Clouebord in the Cedar swamps.

At a generall towne meeting the 10th : of the first moneth 1685 — William Sumner was Chosen Deputy for the yeare ensueng — for Constables hopstill humfrey and Ebenezar Withington the same day there was men Chosen to act by themselues or by an aturney in the behalfe of the towne to try our title to the land that is taken vp in farmes ; the men Chosen are { Capt Capen / henery Leadbetter / Timothy Tilstone / John Brecke / John Minott }

super visers for the highwayes { Joseph Leedes / charles Dauenport }

The same day there was men Chosen to take notice where there is or may be a nesessity of high wayes for the vse and benefite of the towne and to make report thereof to the towne —

the men Chosen : are the select men ; Capt Capen ; Timothy Tilstone ; Samuel Paul ; John Brecke ; accordingly they had a meeting on the : 6 : 2 : 85 : and haueing veiwed and taken notice of what they were betrusted with : doe make our Returne : that for the suply of high wayes wee think nessesary that the parelel line betweene the first and second Range be left open throughout and allso that the paralell line betweene the second and third [380.] Range be left open : Except those that haue fenced in any part therof Can satisfy the towne for it : Wee allso iudge it nessesary that there should be a high way layed out ; from the Country high way by Widow Wiets : to the twenty acre lotes : and a high way from Robert Searles his house ; by Elder humfrey his land vnto the Country high way that lyeth betweene Roxbury and Dorchester ;

William Sumner, lift. Hall, and James Blake being appointed a

Comittee to lay out a high way to the fresh marsh: Doe make their Returne as followeth: on the: 6: day of aprill: 1685: we layed out a way: we begane at the northeast Corner of Richard Withingtons marsh and there marked a white oake tree; and from thence marked seuerall trees; vntill we came to a stake in the parelell line; with a heape of stones aboute it; and from thence alonge by the old way through Isaak Joanes his lote vntill wee Come to a brooke; and so through Daniel Prestons lote in the old way vntill we Come to the corner of Richard Withingtons fence: by Robert searles the way is to be two Rods wide to ly on the west and north west side of those trees that are marked:

Anno: 1684 Deacon Blake Collector; Receiued of the Rate made for the vse of the ministry of Dorchester for the yeare one thousand six hundred eighty and foure the full summe of fourty nine pounds three shillinges and a penny in new English money or other wise to my content. As allso forty and nine pounds three shillings and a penny in Country pay or the value thereof to Content: as allso foure and thirty Shillings worth of Iron of Elder Withingtons gift to the ministry of Dorchester; which Came from Taunton in the yeare one thousand six hundred eighty and fiue: so that the Totall summe delliuered to me and Receiued by me is an hundred pounds

Receiued by mee John Danforth

Dated this 15th: of february: 1685.

Entered and Examined and Compared with the originall which is on file; by mee James Blake Recorder

[**381.**] 7: 10: 1685: At a generall towne meeting the towne oficers then Chosen were as foloweth:

Select men	Raters	
Ensigne Clap	William Pond	Capt Capen: Colector
James Blake	Samuel Paul	James Blake Recorder
Enoch Wiswel	Samuel Topliffe	
lift hall		
John Brecke		

11: 11: 1685: At a meeting of the select men at the house of samuel hix: Timothy Foster was apointed by the select men to get what is due to the towne vpon account of the Rates that were Committed to Nehemah Clap to collect;

the same day there was liberty granted John Trescote to take some Cedar trees in the Common swamps for his owne use p'uided he take none but what is all Ready fallen;

the same day John Brecke and Timothy Foster were apointed by the select men to ioyne ishues with hudsons farmer: in a Course of law; in the behalfe of the towne for the Recouery of Rates;

the same day henery Leadbetter samuel paul and samuel Topliffe were appointed (by the select men) a Comittee to lay out a high way of two Rods wide from the house of Joshua henshaw to the highway that leadeth from Naponset mill towards Dedham; And Obediah Hawes John Tolman and John Withington to lay out a high way from the Country Rode by Widow Wyets house and so from thence so far as the twenty acre lotes;

8: 1st: 1686: at a meeting of the select men it was then agreed that the order made aboute high wayes and super visers should be Recorded

the same day there were fence Veiwers appointed by the select men

for the feild behind Thomas Modsleyes { Isaak Joanes
Joseph Weekes

for the feild vpon the hill . . . { Ensigne Clap
hopstill humfrey

for the feild behind John Birds . . { James Bird
Thomas Andrewes

[382.] for the feild behind Richard Leedes { Ammiel Weekes
James Baker

for the feild behind Mr Mathers . . { William Pond
Ebenezar Williames

for that part of the greate lotes from Timothy { Samuel Paul
Tilstones to Thomas Tolmans . . Timothy Foster

from Thomas Tolmans to the Riuer . { Thomas Trott sen^r
Samuel Robenson

all fences to be made sufficient according to the towne order by by the : 25 : day of march ; and all Common feildes to be Cleared by the : 16th : day of aprill ;

the men apointed to Cleare the necke . { Isaake Joanes
Richard Mather

super visers for the necke way . . { hopestill Clap
James Foster

all swine are to be Ringed according to law, and to be yoked according to the towne order ; from the 15th : day of aprill vntill the 15th : day of october next Ensueng ;

the same day were men apointed to Run the line betweene dedham and Dorchester ; and betweene Wrentham and Dorchester ;

the men apointed for that worke is . { John Bird
their Returne is vpon file ; . . . Roger Billing
Standfast Foster

Whereas wee see by long Experience that those persones that doe at any tyme keepe sheepe on the Commons they haue Receiued great loss and damag by Reason of the Rames goeing at liberty amongest the flocke all the yeare ; for the preuenting whereof ;

[383.] At a generall towne meeting the 9th 1st : m̄o : 168⅝

Daniel Preston iu^r
Preserued Capen } were Chosen Constables

Clement Maxfeild
John Capen iu^r   } were Chosen supervisers of the highwayes
John Tolman

The same day it put to the vote whether they would apoint a Committee to lay out for Mr Stoughton 50 acres of land in some Conuenient place in the : 500 : acres vpon Condission Mr Stoughton giue and asure to the towne his Right in the : 400 : acres that was layed out for the minestry ; and allso all his Right in the fiue hundred acres ;
The vote was in the afermatiue :
the Committee Chosen to lay out this land

Lieut hall
Obediah hawes   }
John Withington

the same day William Sumner was chosen deputy for the year Ensueng.

the same day it was passed by a vote that all the Common land on this side punquepaug should be layed out in lotes by proportion to Each man according to what Right they have theire.

The same day : John Capen iu^r : John Bird and Joseph Weekes were Chosen a Committee to lay out a little land to Ebenezar Williams not Exeding two or three foote p'uided it be not preiudiciall to the towne.

the same day
Ebenezar Billing   } were Chosen a Committee to agree with an
Thomas Holman   } artist[1] to take a plot of the Common land in
Henery Leadbetter } order vnto the deuiding of it ;

12 : 2 : 86 : at a meeting of the select men their was liberty granted to henery leadbetter to get : 3 : or : 4 : hundred of Cedar cloueboards in the Common swampes : the same day liberty granted to Ammiel Weekes to get : 300 : railes : and : 2800 : of Cedar Cloueboard : the same day liberty granted to leit Hall to get : 400 : of Cedar Railes and : 100 of postes in the Common swampes

the same day a warrant given to the Constable to take by distress or otherwise the penalty due (to Nathan Bradley according to the towne order :) from those that haue been defectiue in yokeng and Ringeng there swine.

the same day there was liberty granted to Ezra Clap to get 4000 : of Cloueboards in the Common swamps.

[384.] the 13. 7 : 1686 : at a meeting of the selectt men, warrant was granted to the ratters, to make a ratte for the use of the schoole of 17[1] mony.

the same day it was also agreed, that obediah haws, John withington and John tolman, should go thorow, with the highway (to the cuntry rods leading to dedham, from twenty acore lots, by samuel Sumners

the 6 : 10 : 1686 chosen for selecttmen :

---

[1] survaior in margin.

Samuel Clap
Lift^n hall
William Sumner
Sarg^nt wiswall
John breck

for ratters { Sarg^nt pond
Sarg^t tilstone
Samuel topliff

for superuisers, it was then passed by a uote, that the selecttmen, for future time, should appoint men for that work: Sarg^t wiswall recorder: (but Sarg^t wiswall refusing to serf in othar place) their was chosen in his steed,

John withington: selecttman
and Samuel Clap: recorder:

18th of feburary: 168$\frac{7}{8}$: then a rate made by the selecttmen and committed to the constabls, daniel preston and preserued capin, of: 31^{li} – 2^s – 7^d: for the contrys use.

this 19th feburary 168$\frac{7}{8}$ then reseued forty nine shilings in full, of all my dues, for the ministry howse, bult by me in this towne, for which i was to Receue. 200. pounds I Say receued the full, the towne discharginge me of all other work to bee dun about sayd howse as witness my hand
  wittnes JOHN BRECK   ISAAC RIALL ✕ his mark
  NOAH BEEMAN
this is a true coppy of that which is in the day book undar his mark and wittnes:
  as attest   SAMUEL CLAP recorder

the: 13: 4: 87 Lift^nt Thomas vose of miltowne appeared, to agree with the select men of dorchester, on the account of land taken in by said uose and for timber that he fell, for to fence his medow; it was then agreed that said uose for the time past, shall paye flue shilings in mony, and for the time to come, the s^d uose, to paye to the selecttmen or their order flue shillings a year, yearly in money. so long as he continews his fence on dorchester land, and the year to end the 29 day of Septembar yearly, and in cause s^d. uose, shall make strip or wast, of wood or timber, more then of nessesity. to repair the fence wheir now it stands it shall be in the selectt mens liborty, to disposes him of it, or at any time, the selectt men giung timly notis, to said Vose
    THOMAS VOSE

this is a trew copy of the agreement in the daye book recorded, and compared by samuell clap
The day aboue written, Samuel Clap recorder reseued the first flue shillings of lift^t thomas uorse, for the use of the towne.
The 21: 12: 8$\frac{8}{9}$ receued of lift^t thomas uose 5^s for the rent of the year which ended the 29: September: 87: reseued by me Samuel Clap recorder for the use of the towne: the: 19: march: 8$\frac{8}{9}$ reseued of lift thomas vose flue shillings, for the rent of the year, 88 by samuel Clap, recorder.

the 6th of aprell: 1692: receiued of capt thomas vose, sixe shillings mony: toward the aboue sd. rent of land, by Samuel Clap, recorder, for the use of the towne:

The mony receiued by Samuel Clap of thomas vose before: aprell: 92: was recond for as appears: page 443 and the 6° receuid this 6th. aprell: 92: payd to the glasier Mr Coningham.

[**385.**] 1638 The Booke of acc°: for the Country and towne rates taken from the Constables and the treasurers appoynted for that purpose

Ip acc°. taken p. Nathaniell Duncan and Humphrey Atherton treasurers frō seūall Constables, and Colectors frō the 14th Nouember 1638 to the 16th of January 1642.

first wee audited 2 accoumpts of Country rates and one about the neck with John Eales for the tyme of his Constable shipp wherin hee hath Cleered all.

Christopher Gibson oweth for Rest
of all his acc° . . . . 4 – 1^d
Joseph Long was owing on his acc ⎫
10ˢ – 6^d which hee alloweth not ⎬
Good: Denslows Rate also not p^d ⎭

we whose Nams are underwritten being sent upon Daniell Elders request to uew the land formerly giuen him, and to setell his bonds, that it might be recorded, did attend it, according to order by the Select men, the 7th of iuly 87, which is as Followeth.

Wee began at a roke befor John triscots door unto which he hath sett his fenc the rock bearinge N. W. N and From thenc through the swamp to an ash tree, which was formerly markt and from thens as the Fenc stands to a small blake oke stump, with a stone upon it, on the brow of the hill, and so forward, the fence beinge the bounds to a white oke stump, with a stone on the top of it, and from this stump, as the fenc stands roundinge to the high way, which highway is leadinge to Dedham, which highway bounds him Southerly till his bounds runs to the rok wher wee began which bounds is bounded with a highway layd up into the woods betwixt Elders land and John triscotts, the pees of land on which his house stands is bounded with dedham highway on the north, the riuer on the South, on the est a hedge fence of robert stantons, on the west with a blacke oke tree by the riuer side, the pees linge triangll the quantyty on both sids Dedham highway wee Judge to be 6 ackers

This is a true coppy, of the origenall which remains on fille.

as attest, SAMUEL CLAP, recorder:

RICHARD HALL
ENOCH WISWELL

memorandom; this aboue bounded land is granted to Daniel Eldars and his heirs for euer, upon condisen that said Eldars or his heairs, shall not haue liberty to sell, or exchang or hire out the same, or any way alinat the same, without the consent of the selectmen of Dorchester from time to time first obtained.

thes terms agreed on by the Selectmen acording to what the

towne uote directs in pag: 247: recorded, and the termes agreed upon: this 14th: 9: 1687; by us the select men —

WILLIAM SUMNER
RICHARD HALL
JOHN BRECK
SAMUEL CLAP
JOHN WITHINGTON

[386.] Debitor: Williā Blake Constable was apoynted to Receiue 86 – 10 for the purchase for Mr Burre butt could Receiue only . . . . £73 – 1 –
more to Receiue p' a Country Rate . . . £93 – 13 – 7

166 – 14 – 7

19 March 168$\frac{7}{8}$

the select men met in order to settle the highways in parelel lines where need requiars: and where no need is to haue them layd open there where no need is of hauing them open, to alow them to proprietors for the liake ualue, or quantity of land; where it is nessesary to haue highways for the use of the towne & 1st we began at the parelell line betwene Ebinezer withingtons pasture, and James Robinsons; and there we found the lande betwene them to amount to the same quantity of the highway layd out throw James Robinsons land and that we alow him for that way, it being 2 rod wide and. 38. and. 2. quarters long: next we mesureed oner mr stoughtons: and we found his land at the parelel line to be 44: rod and 2 quarter 2 rod wid

the next samuel Jones hase fenst in 21rod and halfe 2 rods wide: next william Riall fenst in of coman land. 7 rod. 2 rod wid: then we mesured Joshuas henshas land that the highway taks towards Samuel somners and we find it to be: 24 rods and the highway at his hows .28. rods both 52 rods and the land that he is to haue at the parelel line betwene Mr glouer and his land being one rod wide extending from the highway by his hows to twenti acor lots only John Capins exsepted, which is one rod wide and 13 and the third pt of a rod long, the whole of Josheues on both sids of both ways is in lenth . 137. when the highways both alowed for there rest due to the towne .85. rods for which he tenders land next samuel sumners: Mr glouers land from the highway to Joshuas land. 6 rods 2 quarters long. one wide. and at the este end of 20 acre lots and of obadiah hawses in pt and Mr glouer is to haue one rod wide sixty 5 rods in lenth and in the swamp he is to haue two rod wide 20 rod long in full of the highway layd throw his land their being 80 rods long 2 rods wide: obadiah haws land at 20 acor lots hase 23 rods taken out for a highway.

Mr Bates is Debitor For so much gathered on a Rate for mending the way to the necke . . . . . £19 – 16 – 4

Samuel and barnerd capin is to haue the land at the parellell line, betweene the .1. and .2. deuision from a great swamp to goodman sumners medoe 2 rods wide and 44 in lenth, they lowing so much land mº conueniant for a highway or alowing the ualue of the land to som other person for land all redy taken up for the use of the towne for a highway

Richerd bakers land layd out for a highway next James robinsons fence is 42 long and 2 wide. this we designe to pay by exchange with m^r stoughton for land next his if m^r stoughton please; the higway cuts samuel maxfeels in lenth 20 rods. two wide.

the boue sayd lines may as we conceue, be shut up without reallpregidese to any person: and with aduantage to many in regard of there fencing: and to the whole towne, in there answering for lands taken up for the use of the towne in places more conuenient and absolutly nessasary

recorded, and compared, with the origenall which is on fille
by Samuel Clap recorder

the origenall was publickly read at a towne meeting and no obiection made against it

[387.]   Willm Blake is Creditor For so much payd m^r
  minot p' order . . . . £72 – –
more he payd to the treasurer . . . . 93 – 7 – 9
more for so much he Could not
Receiue frō Wm Barber, Jo: Betson, and Ralfe
  Cornish . . . . – 12 – –
Remayning yet p' m^r. Blake to ballance the acc^o £ –   – 14 – 10
                                                     ─────────────
                                                     165 – 19 – 9

Att a meeting of the proprietors of purgetory swamp: 15th feb^{ry}: 8⅝ m^r stoughton, Requested, that the proprietors would grant that his forty acors might ly next his medow, this was put to the uote Whether or no it be your minds, that m^r stoughton haue his 40 acors in a square, next to his owne medow, reserfing a high way throw sayd 40 acors; this was uoted on the affermitiue.

2^d. is it your minds, to begin at dedham line, to lay out purgetary, and so leaue it to the descretion of the suruayer, and Commity; this was uoted in the afermitiue.

John Withington, Samuel Robinson and John Minot are Continued a Comity to agree with the seruayer and to perfitt the work, of laying out the same

we whos nams are under written, haue this: 22: 1: 1686: been at work as folows: and acording to warant: we began at nathaniell wiats his feild and layd out a way too rod wid in m^{rs} fosters lane next his fence and so right along, betwen goodman bakor, his lot, and the next lott, on the north side. a rod on the one lot, and one rod on the other lot: 20 rod along then we went acrose, 3 lots southward, in the best place we could: then we went betwen goodman trott sen and lift^n hall there lotts, a rod of each lot, to the end of there land, then through^t goodman henshaws land, seuen or eight rod, where the twenty acor lots begin:

JOHN WITHINGTON.   OBADIAH HAWES.   JOHN TOLMAN

a true copy of the returne on file

M^r. Bates is Credit For moneys payd out about
  mending the way to the neck . . . . £17 – 17 – 11

the : 13 : 2 : 1687 : it was agreed upon betwen the selectt men and samuel Capin and barnerd capin : that s^d capins should haue the two rods by the paralell line betwene the . 1 and 2 deuision from the corner of there land next richerd backers lot unto goodman summers medow they paying to samuel maxfeeld : 1^1 – 10^s (which the towne was to pay to said maxfeeld for land taken from him for a highway) and also s^d capins to giue liberty to incrase sumner to pase ouer there land, to his medow to fech offe his haye, he pasing ouer wheire he may do them least dammag, and he shuting up the fence after him for there security, and s^d capins bringing a resaight from s^d maxfeeld, should be their discharge : which s^d capins haue done this : 15 : 2 : 87 : under samuel maxfeelds hand : which resaitt is on fille.

The : 13th : feb^{re} : 16$\frac{8 9}{9 0}$ there was deliuered to sarg^{nt} Samuel Topliff, the weights and mesurs, that weir the towns standerds, to trye weights and mesurs by

of waights of bell fashon	of flatt, brass waits	of mesurs
one : — 56 pound	one pound	one halfe bushell
one — 28 p^o	one halfe pound	one peck
one — 14 p^o	one quarter	one ell
one — 7 p^o	one halfe quarter	one yearden
one — 4	one ounce	one eale quart
one — 2 pounds	one half ounce	one wine pint
	one quarter of ounce	two sealling eiorns
	one 8th part of ounce	

[388.] William Blake and Nicholas Clap Constables owe for a towne Rate p' them Collected £40 – 9 –

The Rate for the Castle dated 30th : 5th 1646 is   li 30 – s 8 – d 11

wherof Bro. Humphries pt is   li 13 – ls 8 – d 2

Bro : kibbeys p^t is   15 – 0 – 9

[389.] William Blake and Nicholas Clap Constables are to haue for moneys p' them disbursed as foll :

Ip^{rs} payd to Mr Meinot . . . . . £6 – " – "
For surveying lands and Carying the Comp^o ōu the
   Ferry . . . . – 9 – 6
more payd m^r Holman for making p^t of the high }
   way aboue the mill . . . . . } 1 – 18 –
more payd Jo : Phillipes for his help in measur- }
   ing land . . . . } – 12 –
more payd Christoū Gibson for the same . . – 17 –
To Nathaniel Wales . . . . . . – 10 –
For work at Muddie Riū . . . . . – 19 –
more for worke there . . . . . . 1 – 4 –
more for Corne for Goo : Webb which the treas- }
   urer should pay to the County . . . } 1 – 5 –
more p^d for a Rugg for Steeven . . . . – 6 –
more payd Mr Stowghtons bill . . . . 3 – 14 – 6
more payd Mr Oliuer . . . . . . 3 – –

more payd Roger Clap for a lock and setting vp Rayles at the neck . . . . . . — 8 —
more payd Jo: Smith for worke at the bridge . 1 — 3 —
more payd him for a gate to the mill . . . — 5 —
To Alexander Miller and Peeter Aspinall for worke at the Bridge . . . . . . — 5 — 6
p^d Mr Atherton at seūall tymes . . . .4 — 3
p^d Goo: Grinway for Steeven . . . .1 —
more payd Mr Gloū^r bill . . . . .4 — 8 —
mord p^d Ed: Breck for mending the high way . — 12 —
more payd the Deacons for charges about the bell . 2 — 10 —
more p^d Jo: Smith for worke at the bridge . . — 4 — "
To Natha: Duncan for his Rate . . . . — 11 — "
To Nicholas Vpshall . . . . . . 16 — "
To Richard Collicot . . . . . . 1 — " — "
To Robert Deeble . . . . . . 1 — " — "
To Nicho: Clap for his teeme 2 dayes and other worke for a man . . . . . . — 15 —
To John Smith for a towne fence . . . — 6 — 8
To allow for nonpayment of w^m Reed and Thom: Starr . . . . — 3 — 6
Rests p' Williā Blake and Nicho: Clap to ball. this acc^o . . . . 3 — 4

[390.] 1641. Nathaniel Duncan treasurer for the towne oweth for m^o Rc^d frō Mr. Bates . 3 — — —
For so much allowed p' Wm Blake and Nicholas Clap on there acc^o for a Rate . . . 11 —
For Beaver Re^d frō deacon Clap . . . . 11 — 6
In his hands in lead Re^d frō Christoue Gibson . 1 — 1 — 8
For so much owing on a Rate . . . . — — 8
For a noate of the Rest of a Rate frō Joseph Watesworth and Natha. Wales which I will giue acc^o of when Re^d I Re^d in wheate and Indein 3 8 the wheate att 6 the 6 the Indean according when I Re^d the Corne that was but 4 the bushell so there was ⅓ pte losse. Rest I owe . . . . 2 — 11 — 4

£7 — 16 — 2

1641. Sargent Atherton treasurer for the towne oweth for money Re^d for the towne . . £12 — 16 —
For m^o Re^d Williā Blake, and Nich: Clap . . 4 — 3 —
For m^o Re^d frō Mr Bates . . . . . — 7 —

£17 — 6 —

DORCHESTER TOWN RECORDS.

[**391.**] Nathaniel Duncan treasurer for the
towne is to haue for my being at the Castle and
for 10 dayes at Court . . . . . £2 -- 7 – 6
For m⁰ payd Mʳ Oliuer for measuring . . . 1 – 5 –
p'te of the lead vnsould . . . . . 16 –

For powder spent p' souldiers at Mʳ Stoughtons }
going to the Pequoit warres . . . } 1 – 4 –

For 15½ li of powder to try the gunnes . . . 1 – 11 –
For so much pᵈ for a drummer 1 day . . . 1 – 6
Rest of this acc⁰ is . . . . . . 11 – 2

£7 – 16 – 2

Sargeant Atherton treasurer for the towne is to
haue for beeing at Castle and Generall Court
and fetching a bull for Mʳ Stoughtons farme . £2 – 1 – 6
more pᵈ mʳ Withington for mending the meeting }
howse . . . . } 8 – 8 – 2
For a bridge in the way to the mill . . . 2 – 1 – 4
For mending the way p' Richard Hawes . . – 5 –
For m⁰ pᵈ mʳ Joanes his beeing at Castᵉ and }
Court . . . . } 1 – " – "
more pᵈ the gunner of the Castle . . . " – 5 – "
For a holbert . . . . " – 11 – "
pᵈ Bartholemew . . . . . . " – 1 – "
For a post to the pound . . . . . " – 2 – "
For loss on Wampampeg . . . . . " – 2 –
to John Blake for sawing planks . . . " – 6
To Bro: Farnā for making the Cariedg . . – 3 – 8
To Tho: Wiswell for fetching mʳ Bishops . . – 11 –
For mending the pound . . . . . – 6 – 6
For Court busnesse about the meddow . . – 3
Rests p' Sariaant Atherton to ball. this acc⁰ . – 18 10

£16 – 7 – 2

[**392.**] Nathaniel Duncan oweth For Rest of
the accoumpt p' the other side . . . £ – 11 –
more for the powder spent p' the souldiers since
allowed to the Country . . . . . 1 – 4 –

19: March 168⅚

The Selectmen met, in order to settle the highways in parclel
lines where need requires and where no need is to haue them layd
open there where no need is of hauing them open to alow them to
proprietors for the like ualue or quantity of land: where it is nessasary to haue high ways for the use of the towne: and 1ˢᵗ we began
at the parelell line, betwene Ebinezer withingtons pasture and
James Robinsons; and there we found the land between them to
amount to the same quantity of the highway layd out through
James Robinsons land: and that we alow him for that way, it

being 2 rods wide : and 38 and 2 quarters longe : next we mesured ouer Mr Stoughtons and we found his land at the paralel line, to be 44^{rod} and 2 quarter, 2 rods wide : the next Samuel Jones, hase fenst in 21^{rod} and halfe 2 rods wide : next William Riall fenst in of coman land 7^{rod} 2 rods wide : then we mesured Joshua henshas land, that the highway taks towards Samuel Sumners and we find it to be .24. rods and the highway at his hows. 28 rods : both 52 rods : and the land that he is to haue at the parelel line betwene M^r glouer and his land, being one rode wide, extending from the highway, by his hows, to twenti acor lots only John capins exsepted, which is one rod wide and 13 and the third p^{t}e of a rod long, the whole of Joshuaes, on both sids, of both ways is in lenth 137 when the highways both alowed for, there rest due to the towne 85 rods, for which he tenders land next Samuel Sumners : M^r glouers land from the highway, to Joshuas land 60 rods, 2 quarters long, one wide and at the este end of 20 acre lots and of Obadiah hawses in p^t. M^r glouer is to haue one rod wide sixty 5 rods in lenth, and in the swamp he is to haue two rods wide 20 rod long in full of the highway layd throw his land there being 80 rods long 2 rods wide : obadiah haws land at 20 acre lots hase 23 rods taken out for a highway : Samuel and barnerd capin is to haue the land at the parellell line betweene the 1 and 2 : deuision from a great swamp to gooman sumners medoe 2 rods wide and 44 in lenth they lowing so much land, mor conuenient for a highway or alowing the ualue of the land, to sume other person for land all redy taken up for the use of the towne for a highway.

Richerd Bakers land layd out for a highway next James Robbinsons fence is 42 rods, and 2 wide, this we designe to pay by exchang with M^r stoughton for land next his if m^r Stoughton please : the highway cuts samuel maxfeels, in lenth, 20 rods. two rods wide.

the boue sayd lines may as we conceiue be shut up with without reall pregidess to any person, and with aduantage to many in regard of there fencing and to the whole towne, in the answaring for lands taken up for the use of the towne, in places more conuenient ; and absolutli nessasary.

At a genarall towne meetting : 2 : 10 : 89 : it was uotted that the selecttmen should haue powr to dispose of lands in the highways by the parelell lines, for to sattisfy for land taken out of mens lots for high ways.

a true record of what is on file, recorded and compared by Samuel Clap

record^r.

[393.] Nathaniel Duncan is to haue p' so much spent, and
layed out in goeing to Castle	£ – 16 – 1½
For so much p^d James Bourne	1 – 11 –
For 7^{li} of powder taken for the Townes vse . .	– 14 –
For so much p^d James p' my howse in p'te of his labour at the Castle	10 – 10 –
For a load of wood for the watchmen . .	– 3 –
For so much payd the gunner of the Castle . .	2 – "

Dorchester acounts for the yere 1649 how there Rattes ware disbursed :
for the Cuntery Rate thet was payed by the Trasurers order for the Rate for our elders that is payed to them.

[394.]   10 (7) 49
agreed to bye brō Clerke case with trot as towne Case

[395.]   24 10 mo 1645
Wee the pr^{e}sent inhabitants of Dorchester being p'voked and excited herevnto by the godly and Religious Request of some amonge vs that haue laid to hart the disorders that too often Fall out amonge vs and not the Least nor seldomest in o^r Towne meetinges and the sleightinge of the orders for the orderly Carringe on of our prudentiall Bussines and affaires in the Towne of Do^r afforesaid as also being hartily sorry For and ashaīmed of the p'misses and desireinge to manefest the same for the tyme to come and also accordinge to the Chardge that lyes vpō vs in many Respects to p'uide for peace and the Floreshinge in o^r owne tymes and in o^r childrens, haue thought good vpon mature and deliberate consideratiō to compose theise Few lines Followinge as a platforme or an abridgm̄t of such orders which by the blessinge of god both we and o^r Select men from yeare to yeare will Endeavor to walke in to the honno^r of god and Jesus christ whose name we p'ffese (Amen)

First of all we doe bind our selues that vpon the 1 second daye of the 10 mo. yearely about 9 or 10 of the clock we will come together warninge beinge giuen vpō some lecture daye (or other meetinge before) which shall be the chardge of the Select men for the tyme being to see it done, for these vses Following. viz, to Elect 7 or so many of o^r most graue moderate and prudent bretheren as shall then be thought meet for the managinge of the prudentiall affaires of the Towne for that yeare 2 and also all other officers as maie be vseffull for the Carringe on of the Towne affaires viz Baliffe sup'visors Raters &c: and that all our elections be by papers and not p'pounded by their p^{r}dicessors : 3 that daye to be a daye of liberty for orderly agitatiō for the Redressinge of any greauance that maie be discouerd 4 or for the addinge or detractinge to or From these Rules or any thinge concerninge the whole Towne Liberty and Power.

Secondly we doe giue vpō Confidence of their carefull and prudentiall imp'uem̄t Full power and liberty of orderinge all our prudentiall affaires withn the Towne of Dor. with theise limitations and Cautions : First that they shall not meddle with the giueinge or disposinge of any of the Towne land wthout the consent and good will of the Towne First obtained :

2 neither shall they take vpon them to alter any p'cell of land from the p^{r}sent improuem̄t wthout the consent of p'prietors (or the p'prietors shall doe it themselues by the maior vote beinge fairely p'ceeded in. in 2 or 3 peaceable agitations before the 7 men.

Neuertheles : we doe giue them all accustomed liberty concerninge comon Landes in Fence also our towne lotts that they shall haue power to iniovne the seuerall p'prietors to make and Repaire such

Fence as is due vnto them by p'portiō and vpō default therein to chardge such penalty vpō them as they see meet. Item that they order the Ringeinge and youkeinge of Hogges; the keepeinge of our Cowes in the pen stintinge the Cow walke baringe the woods in season and that they carefully p'uide for the saffty of our Comons: in the wood and Timber

Thirdly wee doe Require that the 7 men shall Faithfully and prudently ouersee all the bussines of the Towne or betweene p'ty and p'ty that are comitted to them and carefully and peaceably issue them seasonably as also that they shall take care of all inferiō officers that they dischardge there places Faithffully and take accompt From them and therof to make Faithffull and punctuall Record in ther Towne booke that soe satisfaction maie be giuen in any Doubt vpon Demand as also that all Delinquences and mistakes in Rates taxed upon the Tow̄: by the generall co't or other wise maie be Discouerd and Condignely dealt withall as also that the 7 men for the tyme beinge doe tenderly and prudently p'uide that all abuses hitherto haue beene greevious and iustly offenciue unto many [**396.**] in the disorderly Jarringe of our meetings and the intemperate Clashinges and hasty indigested and Rash votes maie be p'uented (viz) that votes of any concernment be First drawne vp in writinge and then deliberately published 2 or 3 tymes and Liberty giuen for any to Speake his mind moderately and meekly and then the signe to be Required, and thinges more orderly carried and dispatch[d] and also that care be Taken that such Remainders of Rates as are vnpaid and expose the Towne to blame or any ingaged for the towne For non payment be accordinge to their best Light they can get be acquired after and Reformed and we do giue them Full Liberty and power to impose vpō the offendors in this case or the Like such penallty as they Find cause p'uided they Exceed not 5[s] for the First offence to be Leuid p' distresse and Furthermore we doe by theise p'sents declare our intent to be that the 7 men From tyme to tyme shall haue power to Releiue any p'sō or p'sons that the Towne Doth Require to Transact any busines For or any waye to become ingaged For them and afterwards Failes them to their damage and discredit (p'uided they doe their vtmost to Find out the delinquents that the inocent suffer not:

Fourthly we require that our 7 men shalbe careffull to meet 8 tymes in the yeare viz the 2 mondaye of euery month in the yeare except the 2: 5: 6: 8 at some place which shal be Certainely Knowne vnto all the Tow̄ and there to be Resident from 9 aclocke in the affore noone vnto 3 aclocke in the afternoone: that so all such as haue any complaints or Requests to make or any informations to giue or anything whatsoeuer to doe with them maie Certainely Find all or 5 of them at the Least vpō paine 5[s] for the first deffault and also that displaceanse if good accompt be not Renderd vpō demand and Further that they Readily receaue all complaints Requests informations as shalbe and speedily and seasonably apply themselues to their best prudence and abillity to issue all such bussines in a faire peaceable and quiet maner and thereof to make a Faire and plaine Record in the Tow̄ booke that in case any p'ue Contentious and will not be satisfied there maie be a Testimony For the wronged p'ty and we alow them 12d. a peece for their dinners at the ordinarie or elswhere vpō the Towne chardge : also we doe giue them power to chardge the Towne with such summe or summes of mony From tyme to tyme as they shall haue need of for the prudent and orderly manuginge of such thinges as Fall out in their tymes p'uided that one Rate be not aboue 20^{li} and that they make Faithffull colectiō and also disbursement thereof to be Recorded before another Rate be made and we require that all their orders about Towne bussines be seasonably drawne vp in writing and published vpō some meetinge and also fixed vpō some obseruable place that soe the offendors maie haue no exscuse or p'tence.

Fifthly For asmuch as hitherto it hath beene vpō sad experience seene that what soeuer good orders haue beene made haue come to no thinge be Reason of want of executiō : we the Freemen of Dorchester desireinge the Reformatiō thereof for the tyme to come haue ordered as Followeth viz that vpō the daye of Electiō accordinge to the p'misses we submit ourselues vnto the Electiō by papers of the maior p't to be at the 7 mens : appointment in the point of executiō of all their orders and takinge Distrenes by comissiō from them For one yeare and Further we order that such a one so chosen shall not be blamed by any for [**397.**] his Faithffull executiō but for his incorugement shall haue all Due Respect and Freedome From all other Towne offices that yeare and also such Recompence as the 7 men shall iudge meet out of the distreynes or otherwise and euery one Refuseinge shall Forfeit for the First offence 13^s 4^d to be Leuied by distresse

Sixtly for our 7 mens incorrugem̄t with the Freemen of Do^{r}chester do agree that it shall not be Lawfull for any of Dorchester whosoeuer to sleight either the p'sons or orders of the 7 men For the tyme beinge but that all their orders for prudentiall order shall stand Ratified from the Liberty affore giuen and whosoeuer shall offend in the p'misses we will Require it of him as sume beside such Penalty as his offence shall deserue

Seauenthly we the Freemen of Dorchester doe vnto the p'misses assent and agree and hartily and Truely by the helpe of god will Endeavour the inviolable observatiō of the same and for the confirmatiō of the p'misses according to our vsuall maner we haue solemnly giuen our vote and also chosen and intreated our brō John Wiswall this 24 of the 10 mo. 1645 to Record the same to be a Rule for our selues and successors except god shall put into our or their harts some more p'fitable and prudent waye and we doe Further p'ffese that we intend no neglect or contempt of the generall Corte or the wholsome Lawes from thence Estableshd

The 7 men chosen this 24 10 mo. 45
were Humhprey Atherton
Rodger Clap
John Wiswall
Tho Joanes
Hopestill Foster
George Weekes
William Blake

Baliffe
Sergeant Sum̄ner

At a Ginerall meeting the 1 of the 10 M° it is Voated that vpon Consideration of a Court order which requireth the voate for the Election of Maiesterats it shall be made in the 9th M° it is therfore ordered that the day of o^r yearly meeting for the choys of towne officers which formerly was to be on the first 2^d day of the 10th M° it shalbe changed from hencforth vnto the last 2^d day of the 9th M°

[The above paragraph seems to be crossed out in the originall] —

The Court order for Election of Maiest [rates] being alterid the day for choseing towne officers is to be on the first 2^d day of the 10 month as in the directory.

The 12th of the 11th moneth 1645

It is ordered that whosoeuer are damaged by others makinge of wayes ouer there meadowes or any that doe want wayes Vnto there meadowes should repayre vnto Mr Atherton wthin fifteene dayes who is appoynted by the seaven men to receive there demaunds.

Uppon the informacōn of M^r. Howard that some goe ouer his meadow there is a way allowed them that goe that way of two rod broad fiftie rod longe frō the first entring into his marsh, staked out along by Ather . . . . ditch and allowance giuen him for it:

Alsoe George weekes informinge that a way is made oū his meadow he is consented to haue allowance for it the way is 1 rod and quarter broad and 36 rod longe

[398.] The 27 of the 11 mon : 1645.

An order for the orderinge of o^r Towne Meettinges.

Forasmuch as the intemperate Clashings in our Towne meettinges as also the vnorderlie dep'tings of sundry before other bretheren and Neyghbours, and the indigested and imp'tynent motyues by divers devulged haue bine not only greeveous but Justlie offensive vnto Divers as also great occation of mispence of p^{r}cious tyme and an hindrance that good orders and other bussines haue not soe succeeded as otherwise p'bably they myght haue done the p^{r}mises beinge taken into Consideration it hath pleased the freemen and bretheren of Dorchester to commend the Care of the Redresse vnto the seaven men for the tyme beinge. These are therfore to declare vnto all our lovinge Bretheren and Neyghboures of Dorchester that accordinge to the care Commended vnto vs and by the authority conferred one vs. It is Ordered first that Whensoeuer the seaven men shall haue occacōn of the assemblinge

of the Towne or fremen and therof shall give due notice and
Cognisance vnto them And we accompt this to be due notice viz:
that if it be one a lecture day that soe many as are p'sent shall take
it for notice or if it be by sendinge a speciall Messenger from house
to house that if notice be left at the house with wife or Child aboue
the age of twelue yeares the husband or father not beinge within
or not at home if he come home before the day appointed and not
repayre to the seauen men or some of them to give in his Excuse
or appeare vppon the day of meettinge soe many as shal haue such
notice and Cognisance and attend not nor give in some valuable
Excuse vnto the seauen men shall forfeite six pence for the first
offence.

Secondlie when the Company is asembled as aforesayd it is
ordered that all men shall attend vnto what is p'pounded by
the seauen men and thervnto afford ther best help as shalbe required in due order avoydinge all Janglings by two or three in
seuerall companyes as also to speake vnorderlie or vnseasonably
which neuertheles is this to be construed that we intend not the
least infrindgment of any brother or neybours libertie or any way
to suppresse the abilities of any nor to quench the smoakinge flax
but that all in due tyme and order may Communycate and contry-
bute such help as they may haue opp'tunitie to doe: but only that
Confusion may be avoyded and bussines more orderlie dispatched,
for the ends before mencōned we the seauen men haue appoynted
one of vs [**399.**] to be our moderator to p'pound and also to
order our meettinges: And that all the assembly shall addresse
and direct there speech vnto him and shalbe attentiue vnto the
bussines of the assembly

Thirdly that noe motions be divulged or p'pounded but such
as the seauen men shall haue seasonable knowledge offe and they
to p'pound the same which is thus to be vnderstood that in case
the seauen men shall refuse to p'pound any mans motion the p'tie
shall after some Competent tyme of patience and forbearance haue
libertie to p'pound his owne cause for hearinge at some meettinge
p'vided all disturbance and confusion be avoyded.

Fourthly that noe man shall dep'te the assembly without give-
ing due notice vnto the moderatoure and declareinge such occacōn
as shalbe approved by the seauen men vppon paine of twelue pence
for the first offence.

An order for Fence made 27th of the 11 mo: 45 It is ordered
that all the p'prietors of the seuerall corne fieilds in this twone of
Dorchester shall make vpp there fences suffitientlie by the Tenth
day of the first moneth next and whosoeuer within this towne that
is a p'prieter in any feild shalbe negligent to repayre or make vpp
his fence in the sayd feild of which he is a p'prietor by the sayd
day shall forfeit for Euerie rode he shalbe found defectiue three
shillings and foure pence And soe for a greater or lesser p'porcōn
accordinge to that forfiture. And we doe also order that some of
the sayd p'prietors shalbe appoynted for the veiwinge and ouersce
inge of that feild who shall Diligentlie attend there sayd worke
once euerie moneth at farthest and that as often as need shalbe or
they may be required thervnto. And if it soe fall out that there

be any p'porcōn of fence which none of the p'prietors will owne it shall then be in the power of the sayd veiwers and ouerseers speedilie to call the p'prietors togethers to agree about the same that euerie man may make fence accordinge to p'porcōn but if the p'prietors agree not amongst themselues the sayd veiwers shall lay it accordinge to p'porcoñ for his peace one euerie man that they cannot find wher it ought to be layd, but if they cann find where it ought to be layd they should lay it where it ought. And whosoeuer shall refuse the determynation of the sayd veiwers and oū seers shall forfeit for ther neglect therin three shillings and foure pence for euerie rode &c., as aboue sayd. And if the sayd veiwers and ouerseers shalbe negligent of there dutie heerin they shall forfeit for euerie neglect of thē two shillings And we further order that those veiwers and oū seers of euerie feild shall within six dayes returne what defects they find vnto the seaven men.

And also p^{s}entlie assone as they find any defect in fence give notis to the owners of the sayd fence

    the names of those which are to veiw the feilds

    of the feild betweene Mrs Stoughtons Mr Athertons Jo: kinsley: John Greenaway

    of the feild behind Mr Mathers Mr Bates and George Dyer

    of the feild behind Joseph Farnworths Mr Butler and Joseph Farnworth

    of the feild betweene Mr Jones and Brother Blakes Mr Hayward and Christopher Gibson

    of the feild behind bro: Hawes Robt Pond and Nycho Clapp

    of the twentie acr lotes Mr Patten and Richard Baker

    of the great lotes and captines neck Jo: Phillips John Smyth Henrie Way and John Pope senior

    of the six acker lotes John Smyth and Thomas Tilstone Jo: Phillips and Henrie [Way?]

[**400.**] the 27th of the 11 mo: 1645

It is Ordered that all kind of Cattle horses mares Colts and all swine be removed out of all Corne feilds by the tenth day of the first moneth next

12 (1st) 166$\frac{5}{6}$

It is ordered that all hoggs and swine in this Towne of Dorchester that shall goe abroade out of mens p'ticuler inclosure shalbe suffitiently yoked and suffitiently ringed at or before the tenth day of the first moneth next And whosoeuer hoggs or swine yonge or old that shalbe taken abroade either in the Commons or common feilds Corne or meadowes not sufficientlie yoked or ringged or vnyoked or vnringged the owner or Owners of the sayd hoggs or swine shall forfeit for euerye hogge or swine soe defectiue foure pence to be levied vppon there goods by distres if they shall refus to pay And it shalbe lawfull for any Inhabitant within this Towne of Dorchester to take vp such hogg or hogges or swine and drive them to the pound and they shall haue for there laboure hearin the sayd forfeiture And also it is yet further ordered that if any such swine be found in any manns Corne or meadow ether vnyoked or vnringged the owner of the sayd swine shall pay doobble damages but if they be yoked and ringged accordinge to this our order the

Owner of the fence where such hoggs or swine came in and did the trespas shall pay the damages And oʳ true intent in this our order is that all hoggs and swine yong and old shalbe kept yoked vntill after Indian harvest next and to be kept ringged in Contynuence all the yeare.

the same day of meettinge viz 27ᵗʰ of the 11ᵗʰ mo : 1645

The seaven men Chose out from amongst themselues four men viz John wiswell William Blake Roger Clap and Hopestill Foster to veiwe where may be thought the best and fittest place for the fencinge of the necke of land and the best manner of fencinge of it Either by Ditchinge or raylinge and also that they doe p'cure it to be done at or before the foure and Twentyeth of the fourth moneth next which Charges is agreed one to be defrayed and discharged by a rate one those that haue the benefitt of the land in tyladge.

It was voted this day viz 27 of 11 mo : 45 that if there should be any more that should haue land in lewe of Calfe pasture ther was a vote first for and after against but the Vote passed Cleare against the same.

[**401.**] The 28ᵗʰ of the 11ᵗʰ moneth A° : Dm. 1645.

It is ordered and also agreed by the p'prieters of the feild behind Mʳˢ Stoughtons that they shall make vpp all the fence belonginge to the sayd feild and not to alter the sayd fence by farther inlargment of the feild And that the p'prieters of that side the sayd feild next the high way against Mʳ Clarkes house shall fence that side and theire ends p'porcōnable to there antient fencinge accordinge to former agreement. And the other side and ends next vnto the meadows and Rockey hill shalbe fenced by the p'prietors of that side accordinge to former p'porcōn agreed vppon. And if by any p'vidence any of the sides of the fence be altered in future tyme to the benifitt or hindrance of any of the sayd sides each side shall haue the benifitt or hindrance of such alteration without respect one to the other.

It is further agreed that the fence of the sayd feild shalbe kept vp winter and summer for the better securinge English graine And two men to be Chosen yearelie to see that the fence be sufftient.

It is also agreed that the sayd feild shalbe stinted for the pasture of it according to p'porcōn of each mans land accomptinge and valueinge one acker of the meadow to two ackers of the stubble and for the stinte to be one acker and half to a Mare and two ackers to a mare and Colt and one acker for a Cowe or ox and to accounte for yonger three two yeare olds to two Cowes two yearlings to a Cowe and fower Calues to one Cowe the tyme when to put in Cattle and how long to be kept there to be left to the Discretion of the two men which are yearlie Chosen to looke to the feild. And the two Chosen men at the yeares end to warne a meettinge of all the p'prietors to make Eleccōn of two others to Efect the same worke.

And it is agreed by the p'prietors abouesayd that whosoeuer shall leaue oppen his gates dores or barres shalbe accounted letters downe of fence.

And whosoeuer shall pulle vp ther fence and lay the feild open shall forfeit for soe doinge fiue shillings p' the rode and soe p'porconable for a greater or lesser number of rods or measure

And whoseū shalbe found defectiue in there fence or in there stinte or shall transgresse against this order shalbe lyable for euerie rode of fence found insufftient three shillings and fower pence for this year accordinge to the towne order and after this yeare shalbe lyable for euerie rode of fence found insufftient Two shillings And for euerie beast put in aboue the stint twelue pence for euerie tyme to be levied by distresse by the sayd Chosen men to the vse of the othere p'prietors And the Chosen men to be carefull to see to those that shall pull vp there fence and to levie there fines.

The two men appoynted by the seaven men are to looke to these orders and agrements and to doe the duties of the same they are Chosen for this yeare viz John Greenaway and John Kinslie

These orders and agrements abouesayd to contynue and not to be altered but by the consent of two thirds of the p'prietors.

HUMFREY ATHARTON
HENRY WITHINGTON
THO: JONES
GEO: WEEKES
JOHN KINGSLEY

[Page 402 blank.]

[**403.**] The 10th day of the first moneth 1646.

The day abouesayd there was a vote published whether the litle wood should be app'priated for the keepinge of sheep if any should buy some sheep to incorage them therein soe as they doe make vse of the same within one yeare.

the vote passed and was graunted by the whole towne except but 3 or 4 and they say they are not against it but for some ends of ther owne did not vote for it it was graunted for seaven yeares onlie for that vse and noe other Catle to be putt therin

It is intended that all and eurie man may if they will put sheep there in the time of the seaven yeare, soe as he be a Commoner | nor is it hearby intended that any many man shall giue there right away which they haue therin if they doe not or are not able to purchase sheep but that those which doe enioy the same shall giue a valuable consideracon vnto them for the same yearlie.

[Page 404 blank.]

[**405.**] The 20th day of the 1st moneth: 46.

These p'sents witnesseth that Christopher Gibson of this Towne of dorchester hath sould vnto Martin Saunders of Brantree one p'cle of meadow lyinge one the yonder side of Naponset river Contayninge by estymation five ackers be it more or lesse beinge the sixtie sixth lote Bounden betweene the lotes of John kinslie and Augustin Clements which were the lotes of Thomas Holcombe and Thomas Duee the lot which John Kinslie hath and William Hulbert the lote that Augustin Clements hath To haue and to hold the same from the day of the date hearof for euer, without any disturbance or denyall of the sayd Christopher Gibson or the heires or assignes of George Phillips to whom it was first graunted or any other by his

meanes or p'curement   In witnes wherof I haue hervnto put my hand[t] he day and yeare aboue writen.
CHRISTOFER GIBSON
GEO: WEEKES test:

The 31° day of the 1st mo: 1646.
These p^{e}sents witnesseth that Nathaniell Wales of this Towne of Dorchester hath given graunted bargained and sould vnto John Holland of the same all that his lote lyinge and beinge one Captaines necke Contayninge by estymation three ackers be it more or lesse To haue and to hould the same lote vnto the sayd John Holland his Heires and assignes frome the day of the date hearof for euer without any let or trouble or denyall of the sayd nathaniell wales or his heires or any other by his meanes or p'curement In witnes I haue hervnto put my hand the day and the yeare abousaid
GEO: WEEKES test:
NATHANIEL WALES

The 9th of the 5th moneth 1646
These p^{e}sents are to testifie that Mr Nathaniell Duñcan of Boston Marchant hath sould vnto Henrie Kibbey of this Towne of Dorchester one p'cle of land lyinge in the feild west from the house M^r makepeace liues in the sayd p'cle of land lyinge betweene the lote belonginge to the Church one the south east sid which lote was Mr Tillies and the lot that Petter Aspinell latlie enioyed the sayd percle of land Containes by Estymacon 3 acr 3 quarters more or lesse which sayd lote was belonginge vnto Mr James marshall of Exeter in England to haue and to hold the sayd lote p'cle of land vnto the syd Henrie kibbey and his heires for euer as by an obligacon vnder the hand and seale of the sayd Mr Duncan more at large appereth which Bond is in the hands of the hands of the sayd Henrie Kebbey.
Witnes.   GEO: WEEKES.

The 7th of the 10th 1646
These p^{r}sents are to testifie that I John Phillips of dorchester haue given graunted bargained and sould vnto william Blake sen^r of the same all my great lote within pale being eight accers mor or lesse laying amongst the great lotes and betweene the lotes of William Clearke one the north sid and the great lote of Thomas makpeace one the south to have and hold the same from the date herof for euer.   In witnes I haue hervnto set my hand,
the enter lyning was befō
signing herof
JOHN PHILLIPES.
witnes GEO: WEEKES.

[**406.**]   The 7th of the 10th 1646.
These p^{r}sents do testifie that I william Blake sen^r of Dorchester haue given graunted Bargained and sould vnto John Phillips of the same all my Eight Acker lote leyinge amongst the eight acker lotes beinge 8 ackers be it mor or lesse and lyinge betweene the lotes of

Richard leeds one the East sid which was once the lote of Thomas Millet and the lot of Richard Leeds one the west the south end vppon the meadow of John Phillips and one the north the high way to haue and to hold the same lote to him and his heires for euer.

In witness wherof I haue hervnto set my hand
witnes hervnto   WILLIAM BLAKE
GEO: WEEKES

[407.]   Dorchester
The 7 men Elected and Chosen the 6th day of the 10th mo: 1647

    John Wiswall   Joseph Farnworth
    Thomas Jones   William Sumner
    William Blake   George Weekes
    William Clarke

The day abouesaid beinge a day appoynted for a Generall towne meettinge there was given and graunted vnto Edward Clappe a Certaine p'cle of meadow lyinge to the Eastward of Powwow poynt in the great necke beinge all the rest of the salt marsh there not in lote and adioyninge vnto two ackers of meadow of William Blake and p'tlie at the end of the lote of the sayd Edward Clappe Contayning by Estimation one acre be it more or lesse.

Sup'vissors of the highwayes Chosen the
samē day are   Raters then Chosen ar
    John Pearse and   Nycholas Clapp
    Richard Leeds   Richard Baker

sup'vissors for the necke of
land wayes
then Chosen Mr Howard and Geo: Procter

Memorand. that it is agreed by the towne at that meettinge that september shalbe put in for one of the tymes of the 7 mens sittinge in steed of October viz the 2d second day therof at the time   The Eleventh of the Eleventh month John Kinsley was Chosen bayleife of the Towne

the 11th of 12th mon: 1647. An order Concerninge fence.

It is Ordered that all and euerie p'prieter of the seūal Corne feilds in this Towne shall make vpp there fences suffitientley by the tenth day of the first moneth next and whosoeū within this towne that is a p'prieter to any of the sayd feilds shalbe negligent to make vp and repayre his fence in that feild or feilds whereof he is a p'prieter by the sayd day shall forfeit for his neglect therein two shillings for eurie rode that he shalbe found defectiue and soe for a greater or lesser p'porcōn accordinge to that forfiture, and we doe alsoe order and appoynt some of the p'prietors of each feild to veiwe and ōūsee the sayd fence of that feild vnto which he is appoynted to veiwe and ōūsee the same who shall diligentlie attend there sayd worke once everie moneth at farthest and oftener if they shalbe thervnto required and if it soe fall out that there be any p'portion of fence which none of the p'prietors will owne that then it shalbe in the powre of the sayd ōūseers to Call the p'prietors togethers speedily that they may agree together about the settlinge of the sayd fence one him or them that ought to maintaine the same but if it soe fall out that it Cannot be found who ought to maintaine and make vpp the same fence then we order that it shalbe in the powre of the sayd ōūseers to lay it p'portionablie one everie man for the p'vention of Damadge for this yeare And whosoeū shall refuse the determynacōn of the sayd Oūseers and shall neglect to make vpp that portion [408.] of fence that is soe layd vppon them shall forfeit for their neglect hearin two shillings p' rode and soe consequentlie for a greater or a lesser p'portion as aboue sayd, and if the sayd veiwers and Oū'seers shalbe negligent hearin they shall forfeit for eurie neglect of thers two shillings all which sayd forfeitures to be levied by distresse. And wee further order that the sayd veiwers and Ouerseers ouer Euerye feild shall within six dayes after there sayd tymes of veiwing there seūall feilds returne vnto the select men of this towne what defects they find that soe they may be made to pay there said forfeitures who doe neglect to maintaine there sayd fences.

The oūscers appoynted are these followinge Augustine Clements Jonas Humphrye and nycholas Clapp of the great lotes and the lands therevnto adioyninge

Mr Howard and Henrie Kibbey of the hill feild betweene M^r. Jones and Mr Blakes

Wm Lane and John Butler of the feild by Joseph Farworths Hopestill Foster and Goodman Dyer of the feild behind there houses.

Richard Leeds and Richard withington of the feild betweene them

Tho: Andrewes and Th^o: Bird of ther feilde Mr Patten and Richard Baker of Twentie Aker lotes

An Order for removinge of all Cattle out of all Corne feilds

It is ordered that all kind of Cattle horses mares Colts and all swine shalbe removed out of all Corne feilds in the sayd towne at or before the tenth day of the first moneth next.

The 21th of the 2^d moneth 1648

It is further ordered and accordinglie puplished that the penaltie of twelue pence p' head shalbe levied by distresse of all that shall suffer ther Cattle to goe in any Corne feilds from the sayd day vntill all Indian Corne be gathered and into house.

It is Ordered that noe p'son or p'sons shall at any tyme or tymes fill or make sale of any timber or wood vppon the Commons of Dorchester to make sale of or to Carrie out of the sayd towne vnto other places vppon forfeit of five shillings for euerie load soe filled and Carried out of this plantacōn

Neither shall any that is not a Commoñer in this towne fill or Carrie any from the Commons of the same to sell to any vppon the like penalties of five shillings for euerie load soe filled and Carried.

[409.] An order about swine.

It is Ordered that all hoggs or swine that shall goe abroad in any p't of this towne out of mens p'ticuler inclosure shalbe suffitientlie yoked with stronge yokes viz the sword of the sayd yokes to be for swine of a yeare old and vpwards at least two foot longe and to be good and stronge and the shuttles or bowes that doe goe through the same to stand vpright aboue it at least six ynches and all swine of aboue halfe a yeare old vnto a yeare old the swords of there yokes to be one foot and halfe longe at the least and there shuttles and bowes to be six ynches high as before and they are to Contynue there swine soe yoked as before vntill after Indian harvest next And wee also order that all vnder halfe a yeare old shall not be suffered to goe abroad because generally such litle piggs doe most spoyle in Corne. And we also doe order that all hogges swine and piggs shall not be suffered to goe abroad at any tyme not beinge suffitientlie ringged and we Judge it to be suffitient ringginge of hoggs &c when there ringes will not suffer them to turne and muzzell vpp the ground. And whosoeū shall suffer his her or there hoggs swine or litle piggs to goe abroad vnyoked or vnringged Contrarie to this our order shall forfeit for euerie such hogge or pigge soe found foure pence to be levied by distresse And we order that if any Inhabitant within this Towne shall see any such hogge swine or pigge goe abroad Contrarie to this our order it shalbe suffitient to goe and acquaint the owner of the sayd swine with it and the Owner of the sayd swine shall pay vnto him that soe acquaints him with it the sayd penaltie of foure pence p' swine which if he shall refuse to doe it shalbe lawfull to levie the same by distresse and sale of his goods to make payment of the same. And further we order if any such swine hoggs or pigges shalbe taken in any manes Corne or meadow or enclosuer and not being yoked or ringged accordinge to this order they that soe owne them shalbe lyable to pay damages but if the hoggs swine or pigs be yoked or ringged then the owners of the sayd hoggs shall inquire for the fence and whosoeū they be that ownes the same insuffitient fence where the hogges Came in shall pay the damage and we think it the safest and peacablest way when any trespasse is done that the trespasse be veiwed p'sently to avoyd future Evills.

the 13th of the 2d 1648: An order about stinttinge the Commons.

Whereas the inhabitants of this Twone of Dorchester at a generall meettinge of the twone haveinge voted that the Cowe walke within the three divissions should be stinted at Eight akers to a Cowe for this yeare.

It is ordered by the select men that all those that putt any Cowes or heaffers vnto the heard doe give in vnto some of the select men a uote in writtinge how many Cowes and heaffers they haue and also what land they put in for at or before the first day of the 3d moneth next vppon penaltie of Two shillinges a peece for there neglect and it is further ordered that if any Cowes be found vppon the Commons or in the heard Contrarie to this Stint they shalbe liable to such penaltie as the select men Judge meete:

[410.] The 11 of the 11th 1647 an order about dogs &c. wheras we find it by sad Experience that great disturbance and distractions and disturbance is often occationed by the frequentinge of doggs &c into the meettinge house from tyme to tyme Especially in the tyme of the publique worshep of god

It is therefore ordered by the seaven men of this towne that henceforth noe doggs Mastifes houndes Curres of any sex of them shalbe suffered to Come to the meettinge house vppon any day that is a day for publique worship of god and — Whatsoeuer p'son or p'sones that shall after the tenth day of the last moneth ensueinge suffer his or her or there sayd doggs &c. to Come to the meettinge house vppon any day of publike worship shall forfeit for the first offence or neglect of theres six pence and for the second offence twelue pence and soe consequentlie to forfeit twelue pence p' tyme for soe many tymes as they shall offend hearein the same to be demaunded of them and if vppon the demaund they shall refuse or neglect to pay then it shalbe lawfull to levie the same by distresse and sale of there goods rendringe to them the oū plusse and the same fines to be bestowed by the select men about the meettinge house at there discretion.

The 24th of the 3^{d} moneth 1648

It was voted by the towne at a generall meettinge of the Towne that the litle woods should be a place at the libertie of those that haue Oxen to rest there oxen there at nyght when they worke them p'uided they doe not putt them there before six a Clocke in the Eueninge and take them away by six next morninge and the Rockey hill by George Procters and rockes behind brother Clements is assigned in like manner for that vse Provided also those be carefull to p'vent damage thereby by Eateinge vp the Cowes feed.

It was also then voted that what worke was to be done about the makinge of the house for the oxkeep's should be ordered by the select men both for the doinge of it and payinge for it when it is done.

It was voted then also that Richard way should haue a little plote of land neare vnto his house to sett a Cow house one it and a stacke of hay of about five rod of ground Mr Glouer and Brother Brecke are desired and appoynted to lay out the same soe as it be not p'iudiciell to the way.

John kinsley also desired libertie to set out his fence of that lote he hath bought of the Decons that was Prices vppon the rockes one the sid next dead swampe for the savinge of fence his request was to be considered and veiwed by bro : Sumner and by brother Clarke and brother Clements they were to see the place make returne to the towne.

Vppon the 2^{d} day of the 4th moneth at a like meettinge of the Towne the sayd veiwers did make returne of the same who affirminge the demaund was soe smale and the Commoditie of it to him was so great it was then graunted vnto him by a generall vote [**411.**] vppon the same day George Procter havinge desired the like favoure and libertie vppon Rockey hill by his house and lote there and havinge bine also veiwed it was then graunted vnto him by the like vote.

one the same 2^{d} day of the 4th moneth at a generall meettinge of the p'prietors of the necke of land

It was voted by the maior p't of the p'prietors of the sayd necke that the sayd necke should be fenced.

It was then Ordered by the sayd p'prietors that the sayd fence of the necke of land shalbe ordered for the place and directinge and setlinge of the sayd fence by 3 or 5 men who haue powre graunted vnto them by the sayd p'prietors to Chuse the place p'porcōn the land by the acker one euerie man and to Charge the doinge of it one euerie man either by a rate or otherwise.

It was also desired that Elder Withington Captaine Atherton and Joseph Farnworth myght be the men who were willinge which was also voted who are to order it as abouesayd.

1 (3) 1648

theise p'sents do beare witnes that the daye aboue said I henry withington of dorchester haue sould vnto John Birchall of the same towne the House plot that Late was m^r Senssions with the Celler and the Land now Fenced Round by the afforesaid John Birchall estimated halfe an acre or there about be it more or Lesse to be by him and his heires enioyed Foreuer And further that the afforesaid John Birchall and his heires and successors shall From tyme to tyme at al tymes sufficiently maintaine and keepe vp the said Fence Round about the afforsaid Land to saue the Foresaid henry and his successors from damage through any p^t of that fence and it is moreouer agreed and consented vnto by the afforesaid John Birchall for himselfe and his heires and successors that neither he nor they shall sell or Lett the house and Land afforesaid vnto any p'son or p'sons but such as shall be aproued of by the Select men of Dorchester for the tyme beinge: witnes our hands the daye and yeare abouesaid

Witnessed and Recorded	HENRY WITHINGTON
by JOHN WISWALL	the marke C of JOHN
moderator p' tempore:	BIRCHALL

[**412.**] 4 of 10 1648:

The accompt of the select men of Dorchester for the yeare abouesaid giuen in vpō the daye and yeare abouesaid as Followes —

1 Imp^r for a 10^{li} Rate by them Receaued was thus disbursed.

2 for Certaine distresses taken vpon breach of order

3 for certaine other bussiness about grants of Land we declare what wee haue done as m. Robert Thornton case: we only gaue advise to set it vp with submission to the Townes censure and pleasure about it when they heard of it but no Leaue at all

for brō Harris buildinge we haue opposed it as not knowinge him to haue sufficient ground to set it vp without further Leaue from the Towne.

the daye abousaid a Complaint made by Rodger clap that Mr Butler hath incroached vpō the high waye betweene vs and Roxbury: that it maye be Looked into:

13 (4) 1648

The day aboue Captaine Atherton: vpon his Request had granted and giuen vnto him a corner of Land adioyneinge vnto a p'cell of Land he Lately purchased of Thō: Jones with all the priuilidges and advantages therevnto: belonginge (only) with this p'uiso: that henry Cunliffe and william Pilsbury maye fetch pott water which is to be vnderstood that they are to make vp the Fence after them from tyme to tyme soe that no damage come by their meanes

Jo: WISWELL

8 (11) 48 John Blake demand what might be set for him for damage cattell beinge there against order of 12^d head

[413.]   4 of 10 48
at a generall meetinge the Towne did vote that the number of their select men for the yeare ensuenge should be but 5 and accordingly did chuse the daye and year abousaid.

Captaine Atherton
John Wiswall
John Glover
Rodger Clapp
Thomas Joanes

Baliffe
John Smith

Raters
George Weekes
Hopestill Foster
John Kingsley

Sup'visors
Edward Brecke
Joseph Farnswoorth

3 of 11 mo. 48 the select men gaue order that Richard Baker haue his warminge pan taken vpō destresse for not mendinge the waye by M^{rs} stoughton house he promisinge to Redeliuer it at our Demand   witnes his hand
Richard Baker

8 (11) 48
the select men accompted with m^r Butler and by the witnes of George weekes and John smith it appeared that m^r Butler had acknowledged all paid but about 14^s but for peace sake and to take awaye all occasiō of complaint from m^r Butler though we saw no iust ground m^r mather and Edw. Clap patience considered: we Remitted 20^s on m^{rs} Stoughtō accompte and do acknowledge 1 : 19 = ii due the daye aboue said and at that tyme did tender vnto him if he could make any damage appeare due to him for non payemt we would satisfie him but we well p'ceaued not any due but his demand was 5^s: but we conceaued if any thinge was due it would be due to m^r mather and so concluded the 5^s should be tendered to m^r mather

[Page 414 blank.]

[415.] 12 (9) 49 the Returne of Edward Brecke and William Blake senior beinge Requested by the select men of dorchester to Laye out the waye for John Greennwaye from John Hill house in the great Lotts in Dorchester vnto pyne neck as Followeth

We declare that by Comissiō from you Raceaued we did appoint the high waye First from John Hill house to Rune vpon a straight Lyne on the north side of the great Lott that Late was John Phillips vntill you come to the east end of the great Lotts and soe it goes on a straight Line vpon the south side of the land that Late was Allexander Bradfords vntil it come to the Marsh and then it turnes vpon the said Land to the Marsh side vntill it come to the Meddow that was Allexand and so is Runne vpō a straight Lyne vnto the pyne necke : (and all alonge the path is to be a Rod and halfe broad) witnes our Hands the day and yeare abouesaid.

EDWARD BRECKE
WILLIAM BLAKE senior

At the Generall Towne meetinge the 2^d of the 10th 1650 the select men then Chosen are

Mr John Glouer
Leiftenant Clapp
Ensigne Foster
Sergeant Clarke
John Smyth

Bayleife then Chosen is James Humphry

Sup'visors are . . . . . . { John Mynot
Thomas Lake

Raters Chosen are . . . . . { M_r Joanes
John Capin
Richard Baker

[416.] At a towne meeting the 19 : 3 : 1651 It was uoted whether there should be a scoole In dorchester the major part present then did uote that they would haue a scoole and a scoolemaster forthwith prouided

The 4th of June 1651 It was uoted at a towne meeting that the select men together with Mr Jones and Deacon wiswall should forthwith treate and agree with M^r henery Butler for to teach scoole in dorchester which was accordingly agreed on as it is at the end of the booke showed the agreem^t :

The 4th : of 4 : (51) it was the request of Leiftenant Clap sergeant clarke goodman Munings for a way to ther eight aker lotts it was then uoted whether they should haue the land at the end of there lottes next to Rocksbery bounds which was there left For a hye way it was granted they should haue the breadth of there lotts home to Rocksbery bounds prouided they procure a way for themselues to there owne lotts :

The same day Thomas wiswall requested that he might haue liberty of passage to his owne lott throw his owne fence on the side next the hygh way betwixt the pound and nico : boltous it was granted him a rode breadth for passadg next to the 9 goad of the captaines.

14 (3) 49 : the select men of Dorchester veiwinge the house that Late was Mr Tilliyes doe thinke fit to haue it sufficiently ground seeled and the Cellar Righted vp and the walls of the house borded and the Rooffe shingled: and desire Leuetenant Clap and John Smith to p'cure it done and p'mise them to discharge the ingagments for the doeinge of it in the seaventh mo: if Towne do not in corne or Cattell.

JOHN WISWALL
in the name and with the consent of the Rest

Desayeres of sum p'tys to the towne. Rich. withinton for a litill land by his swampes

Jōh Barchalls for a litill land by it   Edmund Browne : for a house plot   gamaliell Baman for a litill land by his house
Jōh gill for sum medow :
brother Lawrance Smith being Cunstable for the yeare 51 brought a holbard and a bill for the vse of the towne or towne watch

9 : 12 mo : 51

It is agreed that Robt Stanton shall keep the oxe : heard on the further side of Norponsit River and aboue the Cow walke the tyme of goeing out to be on the 10 day of the 3 month vntill the [   ] of October next they at their first goeing ont to be deliu'red vnto him, and for his pay 2^s a head to be payd at 2 paymt the one halfe at or wth in one month after they be put to him and the other halfe at the end of the tyme.

8 of the 1 mo : 52.

It is agreed that Steven Hoping and Nicholas Gorge shall keepe the Cowes they ar to goe forth the 16 day of the 2^d month and continue keeping them vntill the 20 of the 9 mo : Steuen saitt it was 16 8 mo and for their pay to haue 30^{li} one third at the beging a second when the tyme is halfe expired and the residue at the end of the tearme.

1 day of meeting

Dorchester 8 of 10 mo : 51 :

Goodman Moninges desireth to haue the land about his howse recorded :

The men appointed to be the vewers of the fence about the Towne Fields in Dorchester for the year 51

{ for the great and little neck
{ Joseph Farnsworth and Edward Clap

for the great lotes Nicolas Clap and John Smith to vew the fence thereof from the beginning of the fence at that p^t. of th' great lotes called Captayne neck and so rownd by the rockey hill vntill you com at the west end of the Widdow Popes lote. And Abraham How and Robt Pearse to vew forth downe to the river.

for the field behind the captaynes neck
Richard Witherington and Richard Curtis

---

for the field behind M^r. Johnes
John Capin and Henry Cibby

---

for the field behind M^r. Mathers
Decon Wiswell and Ensigne Foster

---

for the field behind Tho: Wiswell
Tho: Wiswell and Isack Johnes

---

for the field behind Richard Hawes
Nicolas Clap and Tho: Andrues

---

for the 20 acre lotes
Thomas Burd and James Humferis

2 day of meetenge
12 day of the 11 mo: 51

To give notice vnto the Cunstables to pay Willm̄ Endian 20^s for cilling a wolfe within 1 mo:

to repairing of the defects of the meeting howse wall to be clapborded Edmund Browne desirerth 6 foot in bredth of ground behind his howse

John Minot desirerth a little land to set his stone wall vpon.

b^r. Johnes intreated to speake with brother Smith about powder

Brō Blake and Brō howard are deseyered to buy a Cow for Edmund Browne: a Cow is bought of R. Witheringtō for 4^{li}. 10^s. and deliūed to Edward Browne according to agremt.

Mr Butler desireth that the scole rate may be gathered with the towne rate.

b^r Clements desireth that the way to his howse might be recorded as his p'rietie and how far the extent shalbe.

It is agreed between the select men and b^r Tolman that hee shall take Henry lakes child to keepe it vntill it com to 21 yeares of age &c and therefore to haue 26^{li} and to give securitie to the towne and to teach it to read and wright and when it is capable if he lives the said b^r Tolman to teach it his trade

further agreed if it dies wthin 2 monthes b^r Tolman is to returne 21^{li}. if die at one yeares end b^r T. is to returne 18^{li} if within 2 yeares wide he is to returne 11^{li} if it die before 3 yeare be expired then he is to returne 5^{li}. This Covent̄ with the bond of b^r Tolman ar both mad and agreed vnto.

It is agreed among the select men that Captayne Artherton shall give out bills to such p'ties as the towne is indebted vnto.

9 of the 12 mo: 51

To be commended to the consideracion of the Towne who must beare 20^s that was layed vpon the Elders in the Cunterey rate.

b^r Woodward desireth a little ground to set his barne vpon in lew of som ground he left out at the 8 acre lottes for a high way

To know the mind of the plantation whether they will give a little land at Vncatie in consideration of makeing and mayntayning a way their by John Gills &c vnto such as will vndertake it and so free the towne of aney charge or damage their by for eū.

To advise with the towne about one to be chosen whom the towne shall thinke meete to record such thinges as are to be recorded in th' new Towne bood [book?] that a more p'fct record may [be] kept and continued vndefased for the good of the plantation.

To advise with the towne about Cow kepers

the 8 day of the 1 mo: 52:

bᵣ Blake to give the Cunstable notice to warne the Inhabitance for the choseing of Deputies.

The men agreed vpon to goe the boundes betwen Branterey and Dorchester according to the order made in that cause ar Richard Witherington Willm Robenson and Willm Trescot

The men agreed vpon to goe the boundes betwen Roxbury and Dorchester and Dedham and Dorchester according to the said order ar John Minot Willm Clarke and Willm Sumner.

Generall Cort Order about Swyne.

Memorand. that Captayne Artherton and Mᵣ Bates are to p'uid for the relefe of ould Bartholmu.

the 10 of 3 mo: 1652:

it is p'posed to the towne about deliūing goodman Johnson powder or giving him a note.

to p'sent the returnes of the p'rambulators to the towne

It'm remayneing in brother Humferis hand dve vnto the towne . . . . . } 0 : 12 : 0

Memorand. that bᵣ Clarke being set downe 2 p'sons vnto the Cuntrey rate and is but one p'son he must be abated the next yeare 3ˢ 9 for that mistake

[**417.**] An Account of the Rates gathered In the yeare 1651 For the Vse of the towne of dorchester

	li	s	d
It. scoole Rate	30	– 00	– 00
It. towne Rate	20	– 00	– 00
It. Rate for powder and the castle . . .	35	– 00	– 00
It. Rate for the garison debt	24	– 00	– 00
some Totall	109	– 00	– 00

Disbursed as followeth:

	li	s	d
To mʳˢ hallett as dew to her husband . .	19	– 10	– 00
It. to her 40ˢ allowed by the towne for spoile in his books . . . . }	02	– 00	– 00
It. to Alce pope for laks child 3ˡⁱ 14ˢ and for cloths 10ˢ . . . . . }	04	– 04	– 00
It. for glasse For the meeting house . .	01	– 12	– 00
It. to John Smith For wood for mʳ hallett . .	01	– 10	– 00
It. abated and of those removed out of towne uoted not to pay . . . . }	01	– 14	– 07

It. to m^r phillips of boston for chardges In sute for the Iland	03 – 07 – 05
It. to Nico: Georg for the yeare 1650	02 – 15 – 00
It. to Tho: burch for Iron work for the meeting house	00 – 04 – 00
It. to Wm Robinson for a wolfe killing	01 – 00 – 00
It. to bro Clark for bartholmew	00 – 06 – 00
It. to bro Dickerman For timber for the meetting house	00 – 07 – 00
It. bro clark for 4 men for town buissnes spent at Rosbery	00 – 03 – 04
It. loss in corne and peag 12^s and caring corn to boston 16^s	01 – 08 – 00
It. Timothy mather not paid	00 – 08 – 03
It. to goody georg In part of 1651	00 – 07 – 00
It. to captain danford for the garison and repayrations	34 – 08 – 00
It. for a barills of pouder 8^{ll} : 10^s and for lead 4 : 7 : 6	12 – 17 – 06
It. to deacon wiswall for towne debt as by bill appears	03 – 09 – 00
It. to Thomas wiswall 1 : 2 : 6 to m^r Jones 3 : 3 : 4	04 – 05 – 10
It. to elder minott for wood to m^r hallett	00 – 03 – 09
It. to bro. Conliff for cutting wood for bartlemen	00 – 01 – 06
It. to the ponds and blackman for work at meeting hous	00 – 14 – 04
It. to bro. clark For m^r hallett	01 – 03 – 04
It. for repairing the pound by brother Clarke	01 – 15 – 00
It more for laks child	00 – 16 – 00
It. to Ensigne Foster as by bill appears	04 – 09 – 00
It. to Rich baker 6 : 2 and bro. callicott for a holbert 5^s	00 – 11 – 02
It. to an Indian for a wolf of nico woods	01 – 00 – 00
Itm. to Peter Lyon for a wolfe	1 – 00 – 00
Itm. for worke which brother Clarke did at the Scole howse and tymber and Carting	00 – 9 – 00
Itm. vnto brother Dickerman for more boultes by brother Clarke	00 – 7 – 6

Total: 10 : 01 : 00

[**418.**] 1 of the 10 m° 51 At the meeting for the Choys of towne officers for the yeare insewing there is Chosen for Select men

              Captin Athertun
              William Blake Senr
              Mr James Bate
              Mr Joanes
              Mr Howard
Superuizers of highways
              Henery Cunlife
              Thomas Trote

Superuizers of the way to the neck
John Butler
Nicholas Clap
Raters
John Capen
Thomas Dickerman
William Sumner Senr
for a Baylife
Richard Haale
This 14 of the 4 mo : 52.
Memorand to take order that the bridge goeing to sea Conke may be made before the first of the 7 mo : or els we lye vnder a fine.

Steven Hoppinges note of layings out about the church howse and fence to be p'sented vnto the Decons for further Consideration.

To speak with the Captayne about some difference in the Cow order.

Conserning the goodes of Ould Bartholme we conceive that those goodes which he borrowed or otherwise made vse of ar first to be restored 2^{ly} that what hath been expended for kepers and tendance of him in the tyme of his sicknesse Coffen and grave makeing to be payd out of what he hath 3^{ly} what els remayneth may be to whomsoeū he hath bequeathed aney thing.

for the notes of them that ar behind and haue not payd their rate to the ministers we conceive such as ar members their neglect, rather concerne the Cognicance of the Church then the towne for non members it is conceived that a warrant be got from som of the ma^{tas} to dystrayne.

Memorand. that we call the towne together to chuse a Commissioner to ioyne with the select men to make a rate for the Cuntrey and to goe to Boston &c according to order.

Memorand that the towne be spoke to for Robt Stantons pay according to order.

The 13 : of the 7 mo : 42 :
It is ordered by the selectmen for the tyme being that the seūall owners of the Cowes in the Cow heard shall pay for the keepeing of each cow vnto the heardsmen and for bull money after the rate of three and nine pence a head and fower heffers 2^s 6^d a head.

[**419.**] The 8 day of the 6 mo :
It is agreed by and betweene the Select men for the towne of Dorchester for the tyme being and Roger Billinges and Henry Woodward of the same towne that the said Roger and Henry shall make a bridge over the river of Norponsit in the way leading from Dedham vnto Rehoboth sufficient and stronge the said bridge to be in bredth fower foote standing vpon three sufficient trussells being three foote high betwen the ioyntes or their abouts, and duble biased. the peeces that lye over to be very well pinned and fastned also a rayle on either side about twoe foot and a halfe high from the bridge. In Considerration whereof they ar to haue five poundes to be paid out of the next towne rate for the rayles of

each side the bridge they are to be paid for over and aboue — to which agrement we haue subscribed our handes:

      Rob[T] Howard with the consent and in the name of the rest of the select men

      Roger Billing
      Henry H Woodward
       his marke.

This 2[d] day of the 9 mo : 52 sister George being payd as appeareth by a uote given to th' Constable the some of 55ˢ there rest in her hand and Dve vnto th' towne the some of 15ˢ :

[420.] An account of the disbursmts of a rate of one hunderid poundes gathered in the year 52 for the vse of the Towne of Dorchester by Tho. Swift and A : How :

	li	s	d
Inprimis to Insigne Foster for the Cullers bought in England and som worke done at the Scoolehowse	—5	18	11
Itm paid to Richard Witherington as p'te of a Cow price which Edmund Browne had .	2	0	0
Itm paid to John Wiswall for som lyning ould Barthol had and some bordes for the meeting howse	—0	12	5
Itm paid to John Smith for worke done at the meeting howse and helping the Joyner and carring som tymber	—1	18	9
Itm paid to Willm Clarke for worke about the Buring place	8	5	
memorand of 1 : 5 of this 8 5 to b[r] Clark was desbursed by b[r] th Swift for nayles for th scolehowses and wood for Bartholmue . .			
Itm paid to Lawrence Smith for charges about Ales Lake childeren 4ˢ : 6[d] for warning the Inhabitants to meete when the Cuntery rate was to be made 3ˢ : 6[d] wrighting out a Coppie of a Cort order 2ˢ and for the Elders rate to the Cunterey 20ˢ	—1	10	0
Itm paid to Richard Evans for worke done about the Scoolehowse	—0	10	0
Itm paid to Captayne Davenport for pay for the Souldiers	—20	16	0
Itm paid to Sister George for p'te of the last yeare and this yeare with 15ˢ resting in her hands Dve to the towne the some of .	—6	15	0
Itm to John Popes wife about Ales Lakes childeren	—0	10	8
Itm to John Minot for a locke and hindges for the Scoole howse	—0	4	7
Itm Willm the Indian for killing a wolfe . .	—0	10	0
Itm paid to Richard Hall for clapbord for the Scoole howse	1	15	0

DORCHESTER TOWN RECORDS. 311

Itm paid to Willm Trescot for carrnge wood	0 : 3 : 6
Itm paid to Mr Peck for glasse for the Scoole howse	1 : 1 : 0
Itm to Willm Ierland for worke abought the Scoole howse	— 0 : 6 : 0
Itm to Edward Blake for a load of wood for ould Barthol.	— 0 : 3 : 0
Itm to John Smith for more worke done abought the meeting howse	— : 6 : 7
Itm to brother Capin for wrighting out a Court order	— 0 : 1 : 0
Itm to Wm Betts for Stoppills for the great Gunes	0 : 1 : 0
Itm to brother Smith for carring Captayne Davenports corne to the further end of the neck 1^s : 6^d, for carring corne to Boston 1^s : 3^d tot.	— 0 : 2 : 9
Itm to brother Wm Blake for tymber to mend the high way	— 0 : 1 : 4
Itm to brother Swift for a quier of paper to lap vp the nots for Ma^{ts} :	— 0 : 0 : 6
Itm for carring Captayne Davenports corne to Mill	— 0 : 1 : 0
Itm for a barrill of fine powder	8 : 0 : 0
Itm for a payer of bullet moulds	0 : 6 : 0
Itm killing of 5 wolves 3 to Indians and the 4^t, to Abraham How the younger	2 : 10 : 0
Itm paid to Mr Glouer 1^l that he laid out 'about H Lakes childeren also for trespas done in the Indians corne by the towne bull 3^s also to Richard Woodes for worke done on the pulpit in the meeting howse 3^l 4^s also in seu'all somes laid out abought the busines of Tompsons Island 1^l 10^s	— 5 : 17 : 0
Itm paid and to be paid to Tho : Tolman for the bring vp of Henry Lakes child according the covenant recorded th· some of	26 : 0 : 0
Itm p'mised to be paid for drawing and recording the covenant with brother Tolman 2^s and for the bond for p'formance thereof 1^s to Ro : Howard	— 0 : 3 : 0
Itm paid by Edward Brick vnto John Smith for Carridge of and for seu'all sortes of nayles about the meeting howse	— 0 : 6 : 7
Itm paid to Willm Weeks for wrighting out the three divisions. The lootes at the Neck of land and wayes layd out their contyning in the book of records 13 pages	— 0 : 14 : 0
Itm paid to Robt Howard for recording the same with a towne order for the way by John Gills and covenant with him for the mayntayning thereof	— 0 : 8 : 0
[421.] Itm paid to Mr Rawson for wrighting out of Court orders	— 0 : 10 : 0
Tot.	98^{li} : 8^s : 7^d

so their rest Dve in their handes
the some of 1ˡⁱ : 11ˢ : 5ᵈ
Their is allowed by the towne at a generall meeting this 28 of the 9 mo. 53 vnto Tho: Swift for corne that haue shrunke in his hands which he received for the townes vse as a free gift the sume of . . . . } 0ˡⁱ : 10ˢ : 0ᵈ
he not taking notice at the delivering out, (when called for by the towne,) what it had shurnke, now brought it into accompt vnto the select men as it is said before it is allowed him as a free gift . . . .
rest dve in their handes
the some of 1ˡⁱ : 1ˢ 5ᵈ

this 19ᵗʰ (9) 55 brō Swift gaue in an accompt vnto the Select men then beinge of the Remainder of the Rate being 1 – 1 – 5ᵈ hauenge by order paid it vnto brō Smith for the towne vse and the Summe afforsaid is to be put vpo brō Smith accompt and he to be aquite:
this 19ᵗʰ (9) 55 brō Foster accepts of 3ˡⁱ from bro Gurnel in Lether for So much Due to him from the Towne which the Towne was to paye him For Leiuetenant Hudson of Boston to whom so much was Due from the Towne for the Deputyes Dyet in the yeare 1654 . } 3 – 0 – 0

Theise pʳsents bynd me Thomas Tollman of Dorchester myne heires executors and admiñistrators to paye vnto the select men of Dorchester for the vse of the Towne in the yeare 1656 witnes my hand this 19ᵗʰ (9) 55 The summe of Fyue Poundes tenn shillinges   THOMAS TOLMAN

memorandum that the words (vpō demand) were put out in both before signinge:

These pʳsents bynd me Thomas Tollman myne heires executors and Administrators to paye vnto the select men of dorchester For the vse of the Towne in the yeare 1657 the summe of Fyue powndes tenn shillinges witness my hand this 19ᵗʰ (9) 55
THOMAS TOLMAN

Receiued of these bills aboue written of Thomas Tolman
Inpʳmis the towne forgaue him . . . . 4 – 0 – 0
It. payd vnto Nicolas George the 30: 1: 58 . 1 – 10 – 0
It. payd vnto Robert Stanton . . . . 1 – 10 – 0
soe then remaine Due of these bills aboue written vnto the towne . . . . . } 4 – 0 – 0
It. payd vnto nicholas George the 8: 9: 58: . 0 – 12 – 0
soe their remaines Due from Thomas Tolman but . 3 – 8 – 0

[422.] The 29 day of the 9 mo: 52

At a meeting for the choyse of towne officers for the yeare in-*suing* their is chosen for selectmen.
Captayne Humfery Atherton
Wm Sumner sen^r
Robt Howard
Thomas Johnes
Ensigne Foster
Surveyors for the high wayes
Richard Leeds
Willm Turner
for the Balife
brother Gurnel
Raters
Sergent Capen
Thomas Wiswell
Sergent Clarke.

The day and year aboue said being the 29 day of the 9 moneth 52 it is voted that Robt Howard shall haue a little spot of land at the Corner or his garden where their is a sawing pit and next the land which he bought of the towne being abought the quantie of three roods more or lesse.

The 15 day of the 10 mo : 52
Memorand to desier a stay of the Inhabitance to chose a man to receiue the voluntary collextion for mayntaying of scollers for such vses and mdes in a law of the Generall Court Oct. 9 : 52 page th 1.

Itm to p'pound to the towne what they will doe about a Scoole.

Also to advis with the towne about the choyse of a clarke of the writs vntill b^r Wiswell returne agayne.

The 21 day of the 10 mo : 52 at a Generall towne meeting it is voted that Elder Minot Elder Witherington and Ensigne Foster should take the volentary collection of the Inhabetance of the towne of Dorchester for the mayntenance of the President certayne Fellowes and poore Scollers in Harvard Colledge according to a Court order October 9 : 52.

the same day it was voted that the Select men should provide a Scoolemaster for the towne of Dorchester this p^{r}sent yeare.

the same day it is voted that Robt Howard shalbe Clarke of the writts for the towne of Dorchester vntill Deacon Wiswals returne from England

[423.] 25 of the tenth month 52.
It is agreed by and between the Select of the towne of Dorches- ter for the tyme beinge and M^r. Henrey Butler that the said Hen- rey Butler shall keepe scoole in the towne of Dorchester from the next second day being the 28 of this instant month vntill the first of may following and for the said tyme of Scooleing he is to haue tenn poundes.

The 10 day of the 11 mo : 52.
Memoran^d to p'pose to the towne about another sute in Cort for Tompsons Island. to p'pose to the towne the sale of Bartholmews house.

At a Generall towne meeting the 18 of the 11 mo: 52 it was voted (without aney Contra dissent appearing) that their should be an indeavoring to obtayne Tomsons Iland agayne by an other sute in Court.

The same day it was voted that Lefetenant Clap Ensigne Foster and brother Richard Collicot should mannage the businesse about the said sute in the behalfe of the towne of Dorchester.

Meeting of select men this last day of th 12 mo: 52.

A letter coming from Dedham about land in controversie in the runing of the lyne between the two townes to be proposed to the towne the next Generall meeting.

new officers to be chosen for waites and measures.

To brother W$\bar{m}$ Blakes the younger and brother Dauenports motion abought paying for the cowes in th heard &c (at p^{r}sent)

that for the tyme past we see nothing to the contrary but they must pay; for the tyme to com we intend the next towne meeting to p'pose it to the towne.

To p'pound to the towne abought a rate of 50^{li} for castle scoole bridges and other thinges.

The captayne and Ensiyne is desired to take som care abought watch for the townes vse.

To p'pose to the towne abought ould Bartolmis howse w^{r}ther brother mead may have graunt to by it or not, there was a vote agaynst the sale theirof on the 7 day of the 1 mo: 52.

We the select men for this p'sent yeare 52 &c. conseive it meet that the order for yoking and ringing swine made in the yeare 48 shall stand in forse for this yeare onely the word that by that order was to be aboue is now to be below.

To p'pose to the towne about foulding of the sheepe by the ox pen:

The men appointed to be the vewers of the fence for the seūall fieldes in Dorchester for this yeare 52 and p'te of 53. for the great lootes Nathaniell Glover and John Minot to vew from the begining of the fence at that p'te of the great lotes called Captaynes neck and so round about Rockey hill vntill you com to th west end of widdow Popes lote and Tho: Tilston and Tho: Trot to vew forth downe to the river.

[424.]   for the 20 acre lotts
         Richard Baker
         Willm Clarke

The field on the back of Mrs Stoughton
    Richard Leeds and Hugh Patten

The field behind Mr Joanes;
    William Weekes and Thomas Burch

The field behind Tho: Wiswalls
    Joseph Farnworth and Tho: **Wiswall**

The field behind M^r. Mathers
    Tymmothy Mather for his father
    George Dier

The field behind Richard Hawes
    Goodman williams

Richard Hawes and
Jasper Rush
For the necke of land
Lefetenant Clap and Nicolas Clap

To speake to the Constable to warne all the freemen to meete for the choyse of new Maiestrates and the planters inhabtance for other businesses that the select men haue to p'pose vnto them on the next second day being the 7 of this first month.

Dorchester the 7 day of the 1 mo: 52 or 53. It is voted that Austyn Clement shall haue a p'cill of land lyeing on the south side of his land that he bought of Mr Makepeace and on the north side of John Capen's lote in way of exchange for a p'cill of land at the heather end of the same bought of Mr Makpeace neere the gate Mr Joanes Wm̄ Blake sen̄ Wm̄ Clarke and John Capen is appointed to lay it out.

It is also voted the same day and at the same meeting that Richard Collicot Leftenent Clap Thomas Joanes and Wm Clarke shall confer with our bretheren of Dedham as in Answer to theire letter and make returne theriof to the towne

It is also voted the same day and at the same meeting that a rate shalbe made of fiftie poundes for the vse of the towne.

The 14 day of the 1 mo: 52 or 53

It is voted that whereas Walter Harris desireth a little p'cell of land, p'cill of the garden belonging to Pristes howse, and which he form'ly haue enioyed, to by the same, it is by vote left vnto the select men.

[**425.**] 19 day of the 1 mo: 52 or 53.

An order to be published abought cowes &c. goeing on th Commons without sufficient keepers.

a warrant to the raters &c

brother Moselyes note for worke and tendance abought ould Bartolmew to be considered it being 12^s, to be paid by th Counstable out of the towne rate.

Dorchester the 25 day of the 1 mo: 53.

That w^{r}as their was a conference with some of our bretheren of Dedham abought the land in difference between this towne and that, açcording to former order, and returne theriof made accordingly by these bretheren appointed for that service it is this day voted that Lefetenant Clap and Ensigne Foster shall wright a letter in the behalfe of this towne in answer to their letter as also their demandes at the said late conference,   and on the 28 following at a gen'all towne meeting the said letter or answer of this towne was red and voted to be sent in the townes name. without any contra dissent.

The 9 day of the 3: mo: 53.

Memoran^d that the balife haue notice to bring in an account of the towne rate what he hath gathered and what remayne on the Select means next meeting being the second day of the 4 moneth next.

The 13 of the 4 mo: 53:

The 22 of the 6 mo: 53:
It is ordered that Henry Cunlife and John Blake shall ioyne with Nicolas Clap to vew the fence at and abought the neck of land as also the high way according to order

The 14 day of the 9 mo: 53
Memoran^d that the balife haue notice to giue in his account to Eusigne Foster on the next second day abought 10 of the clocke in the forenoone at sister Georgis.

to acquaynt the towne abought the land which m^r. Hutchersons agents haue taken away from som p'ticuler men who had it by graunt from the towne.

brother Sumner is appointed by the Select men to p'hibit cutting of wood by non comonners at Squantoms neck by an order vnder their handes.

[**426.**] An account of the disbursm^{ts} of a rate of 51: 3: gathered in the yeare 53: for the towne of Dorchester by John Gurnit baylife,

	li s d
Inprimis paid vnto M^r_j Henry Butler for keeping Scoole	10: 1: 4
Itm paid to Henry Cunlife for the high way.	0: 3: 4
Itm paid to Roger Billing for a loade of wood and ould post for Mr Hallit	0 5: 0
Itm paid to Sergent Hall for the charge of the action agaynst Mrs Haukins for non paym't of the scoole rate 2^s 10^d sawing tymber and carting 9^s post makeing mending and setting of fence 4^s in tote.	0 15 10
Itm paid to Sergent Cappyn for Millitary Commissions.	0: 16: 6
Itm paid to Captayne Atherton for makeing and casting of bullets for the towne	0: 13: 10
Itm paid to Ensigne Foster for match and for 2 wolues.	3: 13: 2
Itm paid to Roger Billings and Henry Woodward for makeing the bridge oū norponsit abought Dedham	6: 0: 0
Itm paid to Richard Withington for two lods of wood for Ould Bartholmue	0: 7: 0
Itm to Sergent Capin for wrighting a Cuntery rate 2^s: 6^d: for a load of wood for the watchmen 3^s for allowance for as much as the afores'd 16^s: 6 is not to be paid in kind 1^s tot.	0: 6: 6
Itm paid to Captayne Davenport for the garrison at the Castle	20: 16: 0
Itm paid to Robt Howard for casting vp the seuall somes of maney p'ticuler mens estates when the Cuntery rate was made over and aboue that dayes worke when the Select men met together for that end 2^s: 6 for engrossing of the said Cuntery rate in the Cunstables hands	0: 6: 7

2ˢ : 6ᵈ for recording towne orders in the new Towne booke in page the 21 and 22 one shilling and for paper a good while since for the townes vse 7ᵈ in tot —		
Itm̄ paid vnto sister George the som of . .	3 : 10 : 0	
Itm̄ paid vnto Goodman Mosely for attendance vpon ould Bartholmy in the tyme of his sick- nesse the some of	0 : 12 : 0	
Suma	48 : 7 : 1	
rest dve in the balifes hand —	2 : 15 : 11	
19ᵗʰ (9) 55	51 : 03 : 00	
It paid by John gornett to John Smith toward meeting house reparaise	00 : 18 : 00	
It. paid by John Gurnell to mʳ butler 10ˢ which remaind due to mʳ butler when he taught scoole	00 : 10 : 00	

[**427.**] The 28 day of the 9 mo. Anno 53 at a meeting for the choyse of towne officers for the yeare insueing their is chosen for Select men.
        Captayne Humphrey Artherton
        Richard Baker
        Richard Leeds
        Mʳ Patten
        Leeftenant Clap

          Baylife
        John Wales

          Raters
        Sergent Capin
        John Minot
        John Smith
Survayers for the high wayes
    as also the neck of land
    Lawrence Smith and
    Richard Witherington

For as much as at the last Geñall meeting the day and yeare abouesaid their was offence taken that the Record of the disbursmᵗˢ of the towne rates for the yeare 52 and 53 was not so punctuall as was desired and conseived to be the neglect of the Select men then a being which som of vs confesse might haue ben more playne had it ben minded ; a greater falt would it haue ben if their had ben no record at all, as in the yeares 45 : 47 : 48 : their is none in the booke to be found.

If their wer in those yeares aney disbursmᵗˢ the directory made and agreed vpon the 24 of the 10 mo. 45 requier a faithfull discharge theirof vpon record.

For that their may be such a punctuall record as aforesaid ; I is conseived meete that bills of layinge out by aney, and brought in to the Select men to be allowed be a playne, and each p'ticuler thing to be distinctly set downe, with the disbursm^t for the same, els not to be received, that so the record of the same in the towne booke p'sentid vnto the towne at their Generall meeting for that end may be accordingly to the satisfaction of the Inhabitants of the same.

Severall votes past the day and yeare abouesaid which ar entered and recorded towards the beginning of the booke in page the 76 and 77.

[**428.**] Dorchester
The 4^t of the tenth moneth Anno 54 At a meeting for the Choyse of Towne officers for the yeare insueing their Chosen for Select men

Lefetenant Roger Clap
Mr Nathaniell Patten
Deacon John Wiswale
Ensigne Foster
Mr Tho. Joanes

Raters
Sergent Capen
John Minot
John Smith

Sup'visers of highwayes
Lawrance Smith and
Richard Witherington.

Baylife
Thomas Burd.

An acount of ratts comitted to the constabls for the year (86) Daniel Preston, preserued capin, for to colectt

	l.	s.	d
It. a county rate, mony amounting to the some of	16 –	7 –	0
of which ratte, payd by constabel preston in mony	09 –	10 –	0
and by preserued capin payd in mony	06 –	14 –	6
and by abattments	00 –	02 –	6
the wholl a mounting to	16 –	07 –	0

which mony was payd to John Usher, tresuarer, by John breck, as by the tresuarers resaitt, on fille may appear:

It. a schoole rate committed to the same constabels of	17 –	15 –	00
of which rate payd by constabel preston to m^r parpoint	07 –	00 –	00
and payd to m^{rs} flint 5^s. and to the selectt men £2 15^s. 0 : th wholl	03 –	00 –	00

and by abatment to constable preston of rats that cold not be got	0 – 1 – 6
and to m^rs flint	00 – 9 – 0
payd of this Schoole ratt by constable preserued capin to m^r parpoynt	03 – 10 – 00
and to the select men (which was by them payd m^r. parpoint	1 – 10 – 0
and by abatments of rats, that cold not be gott	0 – 3 – 6
and to m^rs flint, for m^r parpoynts diet	2 – 1 – 0
the wholl amounting to	£17 – 15 – 00
a Contry ratt committed to the same Constabls of which was payd into the tresurrer John usher as by his discharg, appears which is on fille	31 – 2 – 7
a towne ratte committed to the same Constabls to collectt, amounting to the some of	20 – 17 – 1
of which, payd by Constable Capin to william somner, due to s^d somner, as depety	2 – 5 – 0
to iohn bird for runing lines	1 – 2 – 0
to standfast foster for runing lines	0 – 12 – 0
to Samuel clap, for wood to the poore	0 – 13 – 0
to eldar blake towards recording	0 – 8 – 8
to James bird, for what was dou to him on account	2 – 5 – 5

An account of the rate made the yeare 1655 for the Vse of the towne.

and payd by constable preserued capen to will Deene for killing a wolfe	0 – 10 – 0
and for seuarell ratts that cold not be gotten, abated,	0 – 4 – 11
and to [ ]efferett, for a wolfe	0 – 10 – 0
payd of the towne rate, by Constable Daniel preston to nathan bradly, for work att the meeting howse	3 – 16 – 1
to m^rs foster, for Land taken out of her lott for a hyway	1 – 2 – 4
to franses ball towards his releef	1 – 10 – 0
to capt breck	1 – 2 – 6
to Roger billings for runing a line	0 – 12 – 0
to timothy tillstone	0 – 3 – 0
to william sumner	1 – 0 – 0
by abatments for rats that could not be gotton	0 – 3 – 1
to Samuel pelton for howse rent for frances ball.	2 – 0 – 0
to franses ball	0 – 6 – 4

[**429.**] This 10 of 7 55 agreed by the Select men of Dorchester wth bro william Pond for the ground seelinge of the meetinge house as Follow^th the Foresaid william p'miseth by the 24th of this month to Laye in place such timber as shall be needFul For the vse afforesaid and that at or beffore the 15th of the eight month next he will begine vpō the worke and finish it wthout delays if god giue Liffe and For his paynes to be Satisfied out of the Towne Rate in such as comes in at price Current which the select men p'mise to see him paid vpō accompt after 12d. the foote.

 witnes our hands enterchandgably this agreement Failed signinge because bro. smith had p'mis'd to paye in quantety what the paye did want in quallity.

Reconed with Decon Capin again this 4th of December And all the aboue mentioned parcells wheither of wood or mony, being roconed, as part of pay for the years eighty six; eighty seauen and eighty eight, yet not withstanding there is due to me for my sallary for those three years more then twenty pounds.

But Considering the frowns of prouidence upon his people here, I am willing to giue that in, and so doe acknowledge my self satisfyd, and aquitt the towne of Dorchester from all further Demands of my sallarys for those 3 years, eighty six, eighty seauen and eighty eight

 as witnesseth my hand this 4th 10m 91:

JOHN DANFORTH.

a true Record of the discharg giuen by mr Danforth, on file:
 examined and entred
 by Samuel Clap Recorder

[Here the miscellaneous entries which began with p. *385* (our page 282 *ante*) end. There are no pages numbered *430* to *437* inclusive, but the reverse of p. *429* is numbered *438*. Then begins the regular record of the town with a meeting March 14, 1686–7. The book continues to page *634* (pp. 635 and 636 being memoranda only, except the report on page 635 of a meeting held May 25, 1719), whereon is part of the record of a meeting on March 9, 1718–9. The remainder of the record is to be found in the second book, beginning on p. *194*. The previous pages of that volume contain miscellaneous deeds and other town matters of an earlier date. — W. H. W.]

DORCHESTER TOWN RECORDS. 321

GRANTEES OF MEADOW LANDS IN DORCHESTER.

The following list of grantees of meadow lands in Dorchester is copied by William B. Trask, of Boston, from the original, page 31, of which a reduced fac-simile is here given.

It is a rude map of localities, made probably not later than 1637. The names and quantities are given below.

The Map of the Meddows beyond the Naponset riuer and how y^t is allotted out.

1 Squantoms
2 mr. Hill 6 a.
3 Jo Phil [ips?] 6 a.
4 m^r Duncan 4 acres.
5 marshfeild 5 a.
[6] George way 8 acr.
[7]   Hall 4 a.
[8] J. Knill 2 a.
[9] R. Calicot · 8 a.
10 Mr Purchas 2 a.
11 m^r Richards 12 a.
12 J. Barber 2 a. ⎫ Mata-
13 Stev. ffrench 4 a. ⎬ chusets
14 m^r Hill 5 a.   ⎭ Rock.
15 m^r Johnson 6 a.
16 J: Eales 4 a.
17 Nich Vpshal 8 a.
   m^r Newbury v hows
18 Caping 6 a.
19 Swift 4 a.
20 J. Caping 2 a.
21 J. walcot [?] 1 a.
22 Jo: Pierce 4 a.
23 m^r marū 6 a.
24 m^r maverick
25 Jos: Holy 4 a.
26 Tho Jefrys 3 a
27 Roger Clap 3 a
28 m^r Smith 4 a.
29 G. Gibson 2 a.
30 Wa. ffller 6 a.
31 G. Gibbs 4 a.
32 J.
33 n. gillet 4 a.
34   Holland 3 a
35 m^r Hull 4 a.
36 T. J. more 4 a.
37 6 a.

[3]8 G. Dyer 4 a.
39 Eales,
40 w. Philps 6 a.
41 Hannā 2 a.
42 m^r Piney 10 a.
43 Denslow 3 a.
44 wilton 5 a.
45 meinot 4 a.
46 Pope 4 a.
47 m^r Hathorne
48 g. Picher
49 Rocket 4 a.
[50] rositer
51 lumbert 6 a.
52 m^r Egleston 4 a.
53 Hart 4 a.
54 m^r Branker
55 m^r [?] Hull 6 [a]
56 venner 6 [a]
57 Brinsme[ad]
58 H way
59 m^r Tery 12 [a]
   the next wilbe out of order.
   R a rock poynting to the place
   m^r Way had marsh on both
   sides of y^t
   m^r Tery.
60 J. wichfeild 4 a.
61 m^r Hosford 2 a.
62 m^r Sention 2 a.
63 J. Hull 6 a.
64 T. Dewis 4 a.
65 T. Holcom 3 a.
66 G. Phillips 5 a.
67 w^m Hulbert 6 a.
68 J. Heyden 3 a.
69 mathews 3 a.
70 Grenway 3 a.

71 m^r Holman
72 m^r Parker   4 a.
73 Ca[pt] Mason   6 a.
74 R. Elwel   3
75 w. Rockwel   4 a.
  + aboue Mr Rosciter ioyning
  to him m^r wolcot 14 a. next
  m^r wolcot
76 w. Gaylor   6 a.
77 T. Hach   2 a.
78 Henery Fooks   3 a.

79 T. Tileston   3 a.
80   Nuton   2 a.
81 ancien Stoughton   6 a.
  this runs vp between the high
  land & m^r Rosciter
82 John Hill   4 a.
83 m^r Tillie   4 a.
84 Elias Parkman   4 a.
85 El: Pomery   6 a.
  m^r Stowghton   16 a.

INDEX.

Aldis, 84, 94, 130.
Aldrich, Aldridge, 28, 70.
Allen, 7, 8.
Andrews, 8, 13, 31, 33, 67, 81, 85, 100, 102, 106, 107, 132, 158, 173, 175, 204, 212, 230, 241, 260, 263, 279, 299, 306.
Aspinwall, 61, 286, 297.
Atherton, 30, 33, 35, 38, 39, 40, 41, 44, 49, 50, 52, 53, 54, 57, 59, 60, 61, 63, 86, 93, 94, 98, 99, 102, 106, 110, 113, 115, 126, 127, 143, 159, 160, 163, 169, 197, 206, 237, 243, 244, 271, 282, 286, 287, 292, 296, 302, 303, 306, 307, 308, 313, 316, 317.
Avery, 80.

Bacon, 195, 196, 199, 201, 202, 203, 205, 207, 211, 212, 216.
Badcock, 94, 98, 103, 107, 111, 147, 214.
Baker, 48, 75, 88, 91, 99, 103, 106, 108, 109, 114, 115, 118, 121, 122, 142, 148, 150, 158, 162, 167, 170, 171, 175, 176, 192, 197, 198, 199, 200, 201, 203, 207, 212, 213, 215, 221, 222, 223, 230, 232, 234, 235, 238, 239, 244, 245, 246, 247, 248, 250, 252, 255, 257, 267, 269, 272, 276, 279, 284, 285, 288, 294, 298, 299, 303, 304, 308, 314, 317.
Ball, 119, 177, 220, 236, 237, 247, 261, 319.
Barber, 39, 250, 253, 284, 321.
Barchalls, 305.
Barge, 237.
Barnard, 243.
Barret, 274.
Bartholomew, 18, 214, 287, 307, 308, 309, 310, 311, 313, 314, 315, 316, 317.
Bascomb, 8.
Bass, 164.
Bates, 15, 17, 23, 24, 25, 26, 27, 28, 29, 32, 33, 35, 48, 50, 61, 62, 76, 78, 142, 283, 284, 286, 294, 307, 308.
Batle, 214.
Batten, 67, 91, 92, 97, 99, 115, 117, 149, 239, 253, 272.
Beale, 235.
Beaman, 90, 92, 238, 241, 242, 243, 245, 246, 247, 305.
Belcher, 70. 90.
Bellingham, 28, 31.
Benham, 1, 11, 15, 26, 28, 31, 33, 37.
Betson, 284.
Betts, 311.
Beverly, 185.
Biggs, 28, 30.
Billings, 104, 125, 128, 131, 140, 141, 145, 163, 166, 171, 185, 186, 191, 193, 199, 202, 204, 206, 208, 210, 225, 229, 230, 239, 240, 243, 246, 249, 250, 256, 259, 260, 263, 267, 270, 277, 279, 280, 309, 310, 316, 319.
Birch, 98, 125, 148, 149, 151, 153, 158, 159, 160, 168, 169, 173, 176, 182, 192, 193, 194, 214, 219, 229, 242, 308, 314.
Birchall, 302.
Bird, 67, 71, 72, 75, 81, 83, 85, 90, 91, 100, 103, 109, 112, 114, 117, 119, 121, 126, 127, 128, 132, 135, 136, 139, 149, 150, 152, 153, 155, 157, 158, 164, 167, 175, 183, 192, 197, 200, 201, 207, 208, 210, 211, 212, 214, 215, 216, 217, 219, 222, 224, 226, 227, 229, 230, 232, 235, 238, 242, 244, 245, 248, 250, 255, 256, 262, 263, 265, 267, 268, 269, 273, 275, 276, 277, 279, 280, 298, 306, 318, 319.
Bishops, 287.
Blackman, 67, 96, 102, 109, 112, 121, 145, 148, 150, 151, 156, 175, 183, 188, 191, 202, 207, 215, 222, 232, 245, 254, 255, 267, 276, 277, 308.
Blake, 26, 27, 28, 29, 31, 37, 41, 46, 52, 57, 58, 59, 67, 72, 75, 76, 78, 79, 81, 83, 84, 86, 88, 90, 92, 93, 94, 96, 97, 98, 99, 101, 106, 107, 109, 110, 111, 112, 114, 115, 117, 119, 122, 123, 128, 136, 140, 145, 148, 149, 152, 153, 154, 155, 159, 161, 162, 165, 168, 169, 170, 174, 176, 178, 180, 184, 187, 196, 204, 209, 210, 213, 215, 216, 218, 220, 221, 223, 224, 227, 228, 229, 234, 235, 236, 240, 244, 247, 250, 252, 256, 257, 258, 261, 262, 264, 266, 267, 268, 271, 272, 273, 275, 277, 278, 283, 284, 285, 286, 287, 292, 294, 297, 298, 299, 303, 304, 306, 307, 308, 311, 314, 315, 316, 319.
Boggerstow, 125.
Bolton, 87, 122, 139, 156, 160, 163, 164, 165, 166, 167, 170, 171, 172, 177, 179, 186, 194, 202, 211, 212, 219, 225, 227, 228, 234, 239, 241, 244, 247, 260, 262, 272, 304.
Boston, 6, 54, 83, 97, 98, 115, 118, 119, 130, 131, 147, 155, 156, 159, 160, 161, 163, 190, 192, 194, 198, 211, 216, 221, 233, 252, 254, 256, 297, 308, 309, 311, 312.
Bourne, 52, 288.
Bowker, 91, 96, 100, 115.
Bradford, 46, 58, 76, 804.
Bradish, 152, 159.
Bradley, 135, 148, 161, 182, 195, 196, 209, 212, 215, 230, 236, 237, 239, 240, 241, 242, 246, 247, 253, 254, 260, 261, 262, 270, 272, 273, 274, 280, 319.
Braintree, 49, 53, 70, 85, 90, 91, 102, 103, 107, 125, 140, 141, 163, 164, 166, 169, 187, 188, 191, 194, 205, 206, 230, 239, 264, 265, 276, 296, 307.
Branker, 10, 19, 23, 24, 25, 241, 321.
Bray, 151, 158.
Breck, 34, 35, 37, 49, 50, 53, 57, 58, 72, 74, 76, 78, 79, 83, 86, 91, 92, 96, 98, 101, 103, 183, 191, 197, 211, 214, 215, 220, 221, 225, 226, 227, 228, 230, 232, 235, 237, 246, 248, 249, 250, 251, 254, 255, 257, 258, 262, 263, 265, 266, 267, 268, 269, 270, 273, 274, 275, 276, 277, 278, 301, 303, 304, 311, 318, 319.
Bridgewater, 257.
Bridgman, 172.
Brinsmeade, 321.
Brook, the, 2, 8, 10, 18, 37.
Brown, 223, 224, 227, 237, 261, 272.
Browne, 81, 115, 200, 246, 260, 271, 272, 305, 306, 310.
Buck, 259.
Bullock, 30.
Burge, 217, 235, 245, 253.
Burges, 237.
Burr, 123.
Bursley, 7.
Butler, 25, 28, 30, 37, 40, 52, 53, 59, 61, 76, 79, 106, 120, 176, 294, 299, 302, 303, 304, 306, 309, 313, 316, 317.

324

INDEX.

Butt, 159, 181, 186.

Caine, 98.
Cambridge, 130, 196, 217.
Capen, Gapin, 2, 8, 14, 16, 17, 19, 25, 27, 28, 30, 31, 35, 50, 69, 83, 85, 89, 90, 91, 92, 93, 94, 97, 98, 101, 102, 106, 107, 110, 111, 112, 114, 116, 117, 118, 119, 122, 124, 126, 128, 129, 130, 131, 132, 134, 135, 136, 137, 138, 140, 141, 143, 144, 145, 147, 148, 149, 152, 153, 154, 155, 156, 157, 159, 160, 162, 164, 165, 166, 167, 168, 169, 170, 171, 172, 174, 176, 178, 179, 180, 182, 183, 184, 185, 186, 188, 189, 191, 192, 193, 194, 195, 196, 198, 200, 201, 202, 203, 204, 205, 206, 208, 210, 211, 212, 213, 214, 215, 216, 217, 218, 219, 220, 221, 222, 223, 225, 226, 227, 228, 229, 231, 232, 233, 234, 235, 236, 239, 240, 241, 243, 245, 246, 247, 248, 250, 251, 252, 253, 256, 257, 258, 259, 260, 261, 262, 264, 267, 268, 269, 270, 271, 272, 274, 275, 276, 277, 278, 279, 280, 281, 283, 285, 288, 304, 306, 309, 311, 313, 315, 316, 317, 318, 319, 320, 321.
Carribee Islands, 147.
Carter, 13, 160.
Cartwright, 137, 170, 171, 180, 181.
Castle Island, 52.
Chamberlen, 259.
Chandler, 151, 213, 233, 259.
Chaplin, 137, 138, 158, 199, 205, 209, 223, 235, 238, 253.
Charlestown, 226.
Cheney, 228, 236, 239, 261.
Chub, 185, 192, 199.
Clap, 14, 15, 21, 24, 25, 28, 29, 30, 31, 32, 33, 35, 37, 39, 44, 48, 57, 69, 70, 71, 72, 73, 75, 76, 78, 79, 80, 81, 87, 88, 89, 90, 91, 92, 93, 94, 95, 96, 98, 99, 103, 106, 107, 108, 111, 112, 113, 114, 115, 116, 118, 119, 124, 125, 126, 128, 129, 132, 134, 135, 136, 140, 145, 148, 149, 151, 152, 153, 154, 155, 157, 158, 161, 162, 164, 165, 166, 167, 168, 169, 170, 173, 174, 176, 178, 180, 181, 184, 186, 187, 188, 191, 192, 193, 195, 196, 197, 201, 202, 203, 204, 205, 207, 208, 209, 210, 211, 213, 214, 215, 216, 217, 218, 220, 221, 222, 223, 225, 227, 228, 229, 230, 232, 234, 235, 336, 239, 240, 241, 244, 246, 247, 248, 249, 250, 252, 253, 254, 256, 257, 258, 259, 260, 262, 263, 264, 266, 267, 268, 269, 270, 272, 273, 275, 276, 277, 278, 279, 280, 281, 282, 283, 284, 285, 286, 288, 295, 302, 303, 304, 305, 306, 309, 314, 315, 316, 317, 318, 319, 320, 321.
Clapp, 5, 9, 10, 57, 67, 85, 86, 87, 90, 96, 98, 101, 102, 103, 106, 110, 117, 157, 210, 244, 275, 292, 294, 298, 201, 303, 304.
Clark, 43, 80, 83, 170, 171, 174, 176, 308, 310.
Clarke, 7, 9, 31, 37, 43, 44, 48, 50, 53, 57, 67, 69, 70, 72, 73, 75, 76, 79, 80, 81, 85, 86, 87, 88, 90, 91, 92, 93, 94, 96, 97, 100, 106, 110, 116, 148, 170, 176, 221, 289, 295, 297, 298, 301, 304, 307, 308, 310, 313, 314, 315.
Clement, 15, 16, 17, 18, 26, 30, 60 62, 76, 78, 106, 147, 148, 155, 158, 162, 164, 167, 168, 170, 173, 174, 175, 180, 183, 184, 195, 203, 204, 315.
Clements, 296, 299, 303, 306.
Coddington, 9.
Cogan, 2.
Collacott, 7, 9, 15, 16, 17, 18, 19, 24, 25, 26, 31, 33, 40, 44, 45, 69, 76, 78, 106, 120, 141, 142, 307, 314, 315, 321.
Collins, 130, 131.
Concord, 178.
Coningham, 282.
Conliffe, 67, 98, 308.
Cooke, 7, 8, 14, 18, 26.
Cornish, 284.
Coundly, 69.
Crane, 70, 90.
Creek, 1, 8, 17, 20, 34, 52, 145, 147, 270.
" Hutchinson, 48.

Creek, Smelt Brooke, 57, 104.
" Way's, 100.
Crehore, 223.
Cunliffe, 63, 303, 308, 316.
Curtis, 67, 71, 89, 144, 306.

Danforth, 67, 139, 257, 264, 265, 274, 275, 320.
Daniel, 96, 103.
Daniels, 109.
Davenport, 59, 71, 85, 96, 109, 119, 121, 123, 124, 136, 137, 138, 139, 140, 149, 151, 153, 158, 159, 161, 164, 168, 169, 171, 172, 175, 178, 179, 186, 196, 197, 218, 219, 229, 234, 235, 242, 243, 259, 270, 277, 308, 310, 311, 314, 316.
Davis, 64, 83, 98, 264.
Deane, 260, 319.
Dedham, 51, 59, 68, 69, 80, 84, 86, 91, 103, 107, 108, 110, 117, 118, 120, 124, 125, 134, 140, 146, 152, 166, 168, 179, 185, 189, 191, 192, 193, 194, 200, 202, 203, 209, 214, 218, 221, 229, 232, 233, 253, 254, 264, 276, 278, 279, 280, 282, 284, 307, 309, 314, 315, 316.
Deeble, 13, 14, 31, 32, 83, 40, 42, 106, 286.
Dimmock, 12, 13, 14, 15, 16, 17, 18, 28, 31, 120.
Demonzaday, 232, 253.
Deneson, 262, 271, 272, 373.
Denslow, 2, 11, 16, 282, 321.
Dewey, Duee, 9, 11, 12, 206, 321.
Dickerman, 30, 42, 106, 308, 309.
Dorchester, 1, 12, 14, 23, 24, 26, 29, 34, 36, 37, 39, 40, 41, 43, 44, 45, 46, 47, 48, 50, 54, 57, 58, 59, 60, 61, 62, 63, 64, 65, 66, 67, 68, 70, 72, 73, 74, 75, 76, 79, 80, 84, 85, 87, 88, 89, 90, 91, 92, 94, 95, 96, 97, 99, 103, 104, 105, 107, 108, 109, 110, 112, 113, 115, 116, 117, 118, 119, 120, 122, 123, 124, 125, 126, 128, 129, 130, 131, 132, 133, 134, 136, 137, 138, 140, 141, 142, 143, 146, 152, 153, 155, 156, 157, 159, 160, 162, 164, 165, 166, 170, 171, 172, 177, 178, 181, 182, 184, 188, 191, 192, 193, 194, 200, 204, 205, 209, 213, 215, 219, 220, 224, 229, 230, 235, 239, 240, 249, 251, 252, 255, 256, 257, 258, 264, 265, 270, 271, 274, 275, 276, 277, 278, 279, 281, 282, 289, 291, 292, 293, 294, 296, 297, 298, 299, 301, 302, 304, 305, 307, 309, 310, 312, 313, 314, 315, 316, 318, 319, 320.
Dorchester house, 156.
Duncan, 2, 7, 12, 13, 15, 16, 17, 18, 19, 23, 24, 25, 29, 33, 34, 35, 38, 41, 44, 52, 53, 57, 58, 106, 199, 282, 286, 287, 288, 297, 321.
Dyer, 2, 15, 16, 17, 20, 21, 25, 27, 29, 30, 32, 50, 67, 79, 85, 96, 103, 106, 116, 121, 149, 150, 158, 294, 299, 314, 321.

Eales, 14, 16, 17, 18, 19, 30, 43, 282, 321.
Edwards, 113.
Egelstone, 2, 6, 10, 321.
Elder, 113, 140, 164, 187, 191, 206, 213, 220, 227, 231, 237, 244, 254, 268, 271, 274, 282.
Eliot, 86.
Ellen, 76, 121, 129, 148, 152, 177, 277.
Ellis, 70, 206, 218, 233, 250, 253.
Elwell, 7, 26, 28, 29, 31, 32, 42, 322.
England, 124, 197, 297, 310, 313.
England, New, 43, 57, 58.
England, Old, 53.
Evans, 71, 81, 90, 101, 103, 153, 161, 195, 203, 206, 220, 240, 253, 259, 310.
Evered, 202, 211, 227, 238, 244, 247, 250, 253.
Everington, 241, 247, 271.
Everett, 248, 319.
Exeter, 53, 297.

Fairbanks, 190, 200.
Fairweather, 210.
Farrington, 143, 184, 193, 194, 206, 218, 232, 233, 238, 253, 272.
Farnham, 106, 287.

INDEX. 325

Farnsworth, 21, 23, 31, 32, 38, 39, 48, 59, 67, 69, 75, 76, 79, 80, 81, 87, 88, 91, 92, 98, 106, 148, 176, 294, 298, 299, 302, 303, 305, 314.
Fawer, 15, 35, 45, 106.
Fenn, 31, 89, 108.
Fenno, 104, 113, 123, 147, 213.
Ferry, 226.
Field, East, 3, 6, 10.
North, 3, 6, 10.
South, 3, 10.
West, 3, 6, 10.
Filer, 4, 6, 8, 10, 11, 13, 15, 16, 321.
Fisher, 80, 82, 106, 107, 110, 113, 115, 116, 118, 124, 126, 128, 132, 135, 136, 138, 144, 148, 168, 169, 237.
Flint, 174, 175, 180, 182, 183, 184, 186, 188, 195, 196, 200, 201, 203, 208, 210, 213, 217, 221, 223, 227, 228, 233, 235, 236, 237, 238, 239, 240, 243, 245, 249, 250, 251, 263, 318, 319.
Flood, 15, 19, 25, 28, 30, 120.
Fookes, 14, 322.
Ford, 1, 3, 5, 6, 10, 11, 12, 14, 15, 16, 17, 22, 35.
Foster, 28, 30, 45, 52, 67, 70, 72, 76, 80, 82, 83, 86, 88, 90, 92, 95, 96, 98, 100, 101, 102, 106, 107, 108, 109, 111, 112, 113, 115, 117, 118, 119, 120, 124, 125, 126, 128, 132, 133, 135, 136, 139, 140, 141, 144, 145, 148, 149, 150, 151, 152, 153, 154, 155, 157, 158, 160, 161, 162, 163, 164, 165, 166, 168, 169, 170, 171, 172, 173, 174, 177, 178, 179, 180, 182, 183, 185, 186, 187, 188, 191, 192, 193, 194, 195, 196, 197, 198, 199, 200, 202, 204, 205, 206, 207, 208, 211, 212, 215, 216, 217, 222, 224, 225, 227, 228, 230, 232, 233, 234, 239, 240, 243, 244, 245, 247, 248, 249, 250, 254, 255, 258, 261, 262, 263, 264, 265, 266, 267, 269, 270, 271, 273, 274, 276, 278, 279, 284, 292, 295, 299, 303, 304, 306, 308, 310, 312, 313, 314, 315, 316, 318, 319.
Frances, 158.
French, 9, 70, 321.
Fry, 8.
Fuller, 214.
Funnell, 181, 212.

Gallop, 1.
Garnett, 82.
Garnsey, 73, 81, 82, 86, 132, 134, 135, 137, 138, 144, 145, 184, 185, 189, 195, 196, 199, 214, 235, 256, 263, 269, 270, 277.
Gaylard, 1, 2, 3, 4, 6, 7, 13, 15, 16, 19, 20.
Gaylor, 25, 26, 27, 29, 31, 322.
George, 59, 60, 61, 69, 70, 72, 76, 79, 81, 91, 97, 111, 116, 132, 133, 135, 140, 144, 151, 152, 157, 160, 164, 166, 170, 171, 172, 173, 176, 177, 179, 182, 186, 193, 194, 195, 199, 202, 209, 211, 212, 223, 225, 227, 236, 240, 241, 243, 245, 246, 247, 248, 252, 254, 261, 263, 265, 271, 272, 305, 308, 310, 312, 316.
Gibbs, 2, 4, 7, 9, 10, 11, 15, 26, 53, 321.
Gibson, 10, 15, 18, 19, 20, 21, 26, 28, 29, 30, 34, 35, 37, 48, 49, 50, 53, 76, 106, 208, 254, 282, 285, 286, 294, 296, 297, 321.
Gilbert, 15, 25, 26, 30, 120.
Gill, 70, 90, 93, 94, 96, 100, 102, 103, 104, 111, 123, 157, 235, 250, 305, 307, 311.
Gillett, Jellett, 11, 17, 18, 35, 321.
Gingine, 76, 79.
Ginjion, 58.
Glover, 19, 20, 22, 23, 24, 25, 26, 27, 29, 34, 35, 38, 39, 40, 41, 44, 50, 52, 53, 57, 67, 72, 75, 78, 80, 81, 83, 84, 85, 87, 89, 106, 108, 153, 161, 182, 201, 209, 218, 225, 239, 240, 243, 253, 262, 267, 271, 272, 273, 277, 283, 286, 288, 301, 303, 304, 311, 314.
Gond, 114, 120.
Goad, a Lincolnshire measure of ten feet, 3, 6, 9, 13, 14, 19, 26, 28, 33, 34, 42, 45, 59, 304.
Gookin, 132.
Gore, 94.

Gornell, 67, 70, 71, 82, 85, 98, 145, 146, 152, 153, 167, 168, 170, 174, 180, 201, 203, 205, 207, 219, 235, 312, 313, 316, 317.
Goyte, 1, 11.
Grant, 1, 6, 10, 12, 52, 96, 121, 139, 157, 158, 159, 173, 183, 189, 191, 207, 214.
Greene, 178.
Greenwich, 274.
Grenaway, 1, 3, 4, 6, 7, 11, 16, 17, 25, 26, 27, 30, 33, 58, 79, 106, 286, 294, 296, 304, 322.
Guile, 240, 262.
Gulliver, 53, 58, 67, 70, 73, 76, 78, 90, 102, 103, 107, 157, 229.
Gunn, 9.

Hale, 83, 136, 146, 148, 153, 156, 162, 165, 166, 167, 169, 170, 171, 173, 174, 179, 180, 182, 185, 186, 188, 191, 193, 196, 198, 199, 200, 203, 204, 206, 209, 211, 213, 214, 218, 219, 220, 222, 223, 225, 227, 235, 249, 250, 252, 254, 257, 258. See note, page 261.
Hall, 7, 69, 71, 72, 76, 79, 82, 87, 88, 92, 96, 102, 103, 104, 112, 113, 114, 117, 119, 122, 124, 128, 129, 130, 140, 145, 146, 155, 165, 178, 183, 261, 262, 263, 266, 268, 270, 273, 274, 275, 276, 277, 278, 280, 281, 282, 283, 284, 310, 316, 321.
Hallett, 307, 308, 316.
Hancock, 242, 246.
Hannum, 13, 14, 15, 24, 321.
Harker, 131.
Harris, 302, 315.
Hart, 1, 15, 321.
Hatch, 10, 31, 39, 48, 49, 322.
Hathorne, 6, 7, 8, 9, 13, 20, 28, 31, 321.
Hawes, 21, 24, 27, 31, 32, 48, 75, 76, 78, 96, 103, 105, 114, 132, 148, 150, 158, 164, 178, 183, 191, 193, 197, 200, 202, 212, 216, 222, 237, 238, 239, 255, 262, 264, 267, 269, 274, 276, 278, 280, 283, 284, 287, 288, 294, 306, 314, 315.
Hawkins, 26, 30, 33, 36, 38, 39, 41, 42, 43, 52, 87, 106, 316.
Hayden, 1, 9, 11, 15, 30, 322.
Heath, 75, 78, 79.
Hemmenway, 85.
Henshaw, 158, 164, 168, 207, 216, 223, 228, 230, 247, 248, 255, 259, 263, 264, 266, 278, 283, 284, 288.
Hewens, Huens, 98, 150, 160, 161, 171, 184, 213, 214, 227, 238, 241, 263, 264, 265, 267, 277.
Hicks, 180.
Hill, 2, 5, 13, 15, 16, 18, 19, 28, 30, 33, 34, 37, 43, 58, 76, 79, 106, 125, 147, 151, 155, 159, 206, 211, 229, 237, 253, 259, 304, 321, 322.
Hills, Blue, 34, 84, 85, 98, 99, 102, 103, 104, 113, 117, 118, 124, 129, 136, 147, 166, 169, 177, 184, 191, 195, 206, 229, 230, 236, 244, 250, 257, 264, 269, 270, 276.
Hill, Brush, 184, 219, 220.
Hill, great, 14.
Hill, Rocky, 17, 18, 29, 36, 53, 60, 61, 62, 64, 125, 127, 133, 168, 183, 187, 190, 213, 295, 301, 305, 314.
Hillys, 79.
Hims, 144.
Hingham, 53.
Hix, 129, 195, 196, 236, 256, 267, 274.
Holbrooke, 76, 133, 136, 137, 138, 140, 243, 247.
Holcombe, 9, 12, 206, 321.
Holland, 18, 21, 22, 25, 26, 27, 30, 37, 42, 44, 47, 50, 51, 57, 67, 75, 76, 78, 85, 91, 106, 207, 321.
Hollard, 9.
Hollaway, 82, 194, 196.
Hollet, 32.
Holly, 9, 321.
Holman, 7, 10, 15, 19, 20, 22, 23, 25, 26, 29, 31, 33, 39, 41, 45, 46, 47, 50, 51, 53, 76, 81, 106, 120, 205, 280, 285, 322.
Holmes, 103, 109, 132.
Homan, 24.

326   INDEX.

Homes, 114, 121, 133, 139, 140, 141, 142, 144, 150, 151, 152, 153, 154, 157, 158, 160, 164, 165, 166, 169, 175, 191, 200, 202, 207, 212, 225, 244.
Hoppin, 60, 61, 128, 140, 142, 158, 170, 171, 176, 177, 181, 186, 197, 208, 223, 224, 272, 273, 305, 309.
Horsly, 217, 221, 222, 229, 238, 239, 243, 244.
Hosford, 3, 4, 5, 7, 8, 10, 11, 321.
Hoskines, 2, 3, 4, 6.
Houghton, 243, 256.
How, 67, 91, 93, 95, 109, 144, 147, 152, 164, 197, 216, 243, 250, 255, 259, 263, 267, 276, 305, 310, 311.
Howe, 69.
Howard, 46, 52, 54, 56, 57, 61, 62, 63, 64, 68, 69, 79, 106, 130, 149, 258, 274, 292, 294, 298, 299, 306, 308, 309, 310, 311, 313, 316.
Howchin, 106.
Hoyt, 2, 3, 5, 6, 10, 11.
Hudson, 70, 111, 118, 129, 156, 190, 193, 195, 202, 212, 237, 272, 278, 312.
Hulbert, 1, 9, 15, 296, 322.
Hull, 1, 3, 4, 7, 9, 13, 15, 16, 17, 18, 29, 30, 32, 37, 39, 47, 321.
Humphrey, 24, 27, 30, 46, 57, 67, 76, 78, 83, 85, 91, 96, 100, 103, 106, 114, 118. 122, 129, 132, 145, 146, 164, 170, 171, 174, 176, 191, 195, 197, 198, 248, 249, 255, 256, 263, 265, 268, 269, 276, 277, 279, 285, 299, 304, 306, 307.
Hunting, 253.
Hutchinson, 22, 23, 31, 94, 95, 100, 120, 316.

Iles, 5.
Indian Field, 9.
Indian hill, 18.
Inghā [Hingham], 53.
Ipswich, 34.
Ireland, 59, 76, 79, 311.
Island, 36, 39, 40, 44, 69, 72.
Islands, Carribee, 147.
Island, Castle, 52.
Island, Rhode, 274.
Island, Tompson, 72, 311, 313.
Island, Tomson, 36, 39, 40, 69, 71, 96, 101, 104, 105, 112, 118, 181, 269, 314.
Island, Wheelbarrow, 141.

Jackson, 161, 236, 241.
James, 211.
Jefferys, 6, 10, 156, 321.
Jellet, 17.
Johnson, 1, 3, 4, 5, 6, 7, 16, 17, 18, 75, 78, 79, 235, 307, 321.
Jones, 12, 15, 19, 22, 24, 25, 27, 29, 30, 31, 35, 38, 39, 40, 41, 48, 49, 52, 53, 57, 59, 67, 71, 75, 80, 81, 82, 83, 85, 86, 87, 88, 91, 93, 94, 96, 97, 98, 99, 101, 102, 103, 104, 106, 107, 108, 111, 112, 114, 117, 119, 120, 121, 124, 126, 128, 132, 136, 139, 141, 145, 148, 149, 150, 151, 158, 161, 162, 164, 167, 173, 175, 184, 188, 192, 197, 204, 207, 208, 209, 211, 213, 215, 216, 219, 222, 224, 226, 227, 228, 230, 234, 236, 237, 239, 240, 243, 244, 246, 247, 248, 249, 250, 252, 253, 255, 260, 263, 266, 267, 268, 269, 270, 275, 276, 278, 279, 283, 287, 288, 292, 294, 296, 298, 299, 302, 303, 304, 306, 308, 313, 314, 315, 318.

Keane, 64, 81, 82.
Kellond, 178.
Kenion, 67.
Kibbey, 39, 40, 67, 85, 285, 297, 299, 306.
Kimberly, 15, 27.
Kingsley, 31, 67, 70, 76, 79, 90, 100, 119, 296, 303.
Kinsley, 26, 27, 31, 43, 63, 294, 296, 298, 301.
Knell, 21, 321.
Knight, 7, 8, 30, 120, 134, 135.

Lake, 67, 69, 70, 75, 83, 93, 99, 109, 121, 128, 134, 139, 148, 149, 151, 167, 198, 304, 306, 307, 308, 310, 311.

Lancaster, 192.
Lane, 28, 31, 50, 76, 79, 106, 236, 299.
Lawrence, 103, 143, 160, 168, 170, 179, 200, 237, 238, 240, 245, 274.
Leadbetter, 82, 100, 128, 131, 141, 173, 192, 201, 202, 203, 204, 212, 213, 214, 222, 223, 225, 229, 237, 239, 243, 251, 253, 262, 264, 269, 270, 271, 277, 278, 280.
Leavitt, 7, 8, 13, 26.
Leeds, 12, 40, 46, 67, 75, 76, 78, 79, 91, 96, 103, 104, 109, 111, 119, 121, 124, 127, 129, 132, 140, 145, 147, 148, 155, 158, 164, 167, 170, 171, 175, 180, 183, 191, 194, 196, 197, 201, 202, 207, 211, 213, 222, 225, 226, 228, 234, 240, 244, 248, 254, 255, 256, 267, 269, 271, 272, 273, 276, 277, 279, 298, 299, 313, 314, 317.
Leverett, 171.
Lewis, 24, 233, 237, 273.
Lippincot, 42.
Litchfield, 247, 258, 274.
Long, 101, 115, 148, 150, 153, 155, 167, 168, 169, 177, 179, 180, 187, 195, 197, 213, 216, 242, 245, 250, 258, 274, 282.
Looke, 28, 48, 50, 91.
Lovell, 2, 7.
Ludlow, 1, 2, 11, 16, 17, 18, 19, 114.
Lugg, a measure. See note, page 17.
Lumbert, 16, 28, 31, 321.
Lyon, 72, 141, 178, 181, 188, 214, 216, 224, 242, 263, 272, 308.

Makepence, 15, 19, 21, 26, 31, 32, 43, 46, 60, 62, 76, 78, 79, 106, 120, 190, 297, 315.
Marblehead, 134, 135.
Mare, 155, 235, 242, 245.
Marsh, Fresh, 17, 22, 43, 47, 51, 59, 117, 118, 119, 278.
Marsh, Great, 2, 16, 18.
Marsh, Salt, 17.
Marshall, 9, 34, 53, 297.
Marshfield, 14, 34, 321.
Martin, 24, 28, 30, 123, 150, 159, 245.
Mason, 9, 150, 217, 235, 237, 245, 252, 253, 322.
Massachusetts, 142.
Mather, 16, 25, 30, 42, 43, 63, 67, 69, 75, 79, 82, 85, 87, 89, 91, 93, 96, 98, 99, 100, 102, 103, 105, 108, 109, 112, 114, 116, 121, 123, 126, 127, 128, 132, 136, 140, 144, 145, 148, 150, 155, 158, 159, 161, 162, 163, 164, 167, 169, 170, 176, 177, 192, 197, 198, 212, 213, 214, 216, 219, 221, 226, 248, 255, 264, 265, 267, 268, 269, 270, 271, 272, 276, 279, 294, 303, 306, 308, 314.
Matthews, 9, 322.
Maudesley, 25, 38, 106.
Mavericke, 1, 2, 3, 4, 5, 6, 8, 19, 26, 32.
Maxfield, 93, 96, 100, 103, 108, 119, 124, 127, 132, 142, 151, 159, 166, 169, 173, 212, 215, 225, 230, 233, 240, 248, 253, 256, 267, 277, 280, 284, 285, 288.
Mayhew, 61.
Meade, 27, 69, 70, 101, 109, 114, 116, 123, 128, 135, 140, 144, 150, 152, 158, 161, 175, 197, 207, 314.
Mekens, 94, 95, 98, 100, 102, 103, 104.
Milton, 113, 116, 117, 123, 125, 136, 140, 144, 150, 152, 157, 163, 166, 168, 182, 184, 191, 192, 205, 209, 216, 229, 239, 240, 248, 255, 256, 257, 264, 265, 270, 276, 281.
Memory, 172, 190, 242, 245, 252.
Merrifield, 70, 90, 100, 112, 114, 115, 132, 146, 150, 158, 164, 165, 166, 167, 168, 169, 173, 174, 175, 179, 181, 193, 194, 195, 219, 234, 237, 238, 241, 243, 246, 247, 259, 261, 272.
Miller, 7, 10, 15, 30, 31, 37, 44, 79, 120, 286.
Millet, 28, 29, 31, 37, 46, 75, 79, 106, 298.
Minot, 7, 11, 13, 15, 16, 17, 18, 19, 20, 25, 29, 32, 33, 35, 38, 45, 53, 58, 59, 60, 61, 62, 67, 69, 71, 73, 76, 78, 79, 81, 83, 85, 92, 98, 100, 102, 103, 106, 107, 108, 109, 110, 112, 113, 114, 115, 116, 117, 118, 121, 123, 124, 125, 128, 133, 136, 137, 139, 140, 143, 144, 145, 146, 147, 148, 150, 151, 152, 153, 154,

155, 158, 159, 160, 162, 164, 166, 167, 169, 172, 174, 176, 183, 184, 189, 190, 191, 197, 210, 214, 215, 218, 219, 227, 228, 230, 233, 235, 239, 240, 242, 244, 246, 249, 251, 252, 253, 258, 262, 264, 270, 273, 274, 276, 277, 284, 285, 304, 306, 307, 308, 310, 313, 314, 317, 318, 321.
Modesly, 172, 227, 230, 232, 236, 240, 248, 254, 255, 256.
Modsley, 109, 132, 149, 158, 192, 197, 201, 205, 207, 215, 259, 263, 265, 267, 268, 269, 273, 276, 277, 279.
Molt, 226.
Moore, 6, 10, 15, 18, 20, 21, 25, 26, 30, 34.
More, 321.
Morgan, 159.
Morrell, 178.
Morse, 195, 212, 244.
Mosely, 207, 315, 317.
Mott, 246.
Munnings, 15, 20, 21, 25, 26, 28, 29, 32, 33, 80, 81, 82, 99, 106, 120, 148, 153, 304, 305.
Munnings Moone, 32.

Narraganset, 18.
Narrowmoore, 122.
Natick, 68.
Neck, 1, 3, 28, 32, 33, 40, 41, 48, 49, 86, 88, 91, 93, 96, 99, 100, 114, 140, 151, 158, 164, 184, 197, 204, 212, 215, 222, 230, 248, 254, 263, 268, 269, 279, 283, 301, 309, 311.
Neck, Captain's, 37, 39, 47, 58, 75, 76, 78, 91, 132, 139, 140, 149, 151, 164, 175, 176, 183, 190, 191, 197, 207, 211, 215, 222, 230, 231, 248, 253, 255, 263, 267, 293, 305, 306, 314.
Neck, Great, 37, 38, 41, 42, 43, 53, 80.
Neck, Hawkins, 50.
Neck, Hilly's, 79.
Neck, Ludlow's. 11, 13, 26, 28, 34, 35, 169.
Neck, Pine, 11, 26, 27, 28, 30, 49, 58, 59, 79, 304.
Neck, Squantum, 13, 15, 18, 25, 34, 43, 44, 57, 87, 104, 125, 131, 141, 316.
Neponset, 1, 2, 5, 6, 7, 8, 10, 12, 17, 18, 20, 22, 40, 89, 108, 110, 117, 137, 139, 143, 146, 149, 164, 175, 183, 188, 189, 218, 233, 256, 278, 316.
Newbery, 7, 8, 9, 10, 12, 13, 14, 20, 29, 87, 321, 322.
New Grant, 120.
Newman, 43.
Newton, 2, 8, 28, 32, 62, 147, 150, 173, 186.
Nile, 7, 8, 30.
Northampton, 93, 185.

Oliver, 27, 49, 144, 145, 155, 159, 285, 287.
Osburn, 238, 242, 247.

Paine, 70, 90, 186.
Painter, 144, 145, 249.
Park, 78, 79, 217.
Parker, 2, 9, 25, 30, 35, 40, 154, 178, 179, 185, 217, 229, 231, 247, 322.
Parkes, 72, 75.
Parkman, 2, 15, 17, 18, 322.
Parmiter, 144.
Patent line, 276.
Patten, 43, 52, 70, 71, 72, 79, 81, 83, 86, 87, 88, 89, 93, 94, 97, 98, 99, 102, 106, 108, 109, 110, 148, 151, 161, 176, 199, 230, 294, 299, 314, 317, 318.
Paul, 140, 148, 149, 151, 155, 167, 173, 175, 176, 178, 183, 190, 191, 194, 195, 204, 213, 221, 225, 230, 240, 243, 253, 261, 268, 275, 277, 278, 279.
Payson, 117, 118, 157, 167, 173, 189, 226, 236, 249, 251, 255, 257, 258, 260, 261, 262, 267, 277.
Pearse, 3, 7, 15, 58, 67, 76, 79, 81, 106, 139, 298, 305.
Peirce, 145, 147, 151, 157, 191, 198, 211, 237, 270.
Pierce, 19, 25, 26, 28, 29, 32, 33, 34, 38, 40, 44, 321.

Peck, 229, 311.
Peecke, 11.
Pecocke, 89,
Pelton, 91, 92, 148, 149, 168, 207, 215, 219, 230, 232, 237, 238, 243, 246, 259, 261, 273, 319.
Penny ferry, 110.
Pequoit, 287.
Phelps, 1, 3, 4, 7, 10, 12.
Phillips, 1, 3, 6, 7, 9, 10, 13, 15, 16, 17 18, 20, 21, 26, 27, 28, 30, 32, 35, 39, 41, 46, 49, 58, 79, 106, 115, 285, 294, 296, 297, 298, 304, 308, 321, 322.
Pierpoint, 318, 319.
Pitcher, 7, 8, 25, 30, 46, 67, 79, 106, 109, 194.
Pigg, 206, 232, 233.
Pike, 81.
Pilsbury, 303.
Pincheon, 7.
Pine Neck, 11, 26, 27, 28, 30, 49, 58, 59, 79, 304.
Pinney, 2, 14, 321.
Place, 156.
Plaster, Plastow, 18.
Plum, 125, 146, 181, 185, 189, 192, 193, 208, 214, 237, 259, 271.
Plumb, 82, 85, 98, 112, 114, 115, 133, 134, 181, 189, 199.
Plymouth, 34, 140, 152, 166, 169, 187.
Point, 2.
Point, Fox, 11, 28, 35.
Point, Powwow, 29, 298.
Point, Sandy, 11.
Pole, 101, 102, 107, 115, 119, 120, 121, 122, 123, 125, 127, 130, 131, 134, 135, 136, 145, 152, 169, 171.
Pole plain, 109.
Pommery, 2, 3, 4, 16, 322.
Pond, 71, 72, 75, 80, 81, 82, 83, 85, 96, 97, 100, 101, 109, 111, 112, 121, 128, 129, 130, 132, 145, 146, 148, 150, 53, 155, 158, 161, 166, 170, 176, 180, 191, 195, 196, 202, 204, 210, 218, 222, 225, 228, 229, 230, 235, 336, 244, 258, 265, 266, 268, 269, 275, 278, 279, 281, 294, 308, 319.
Ponkipog, 71, 136, 140, 153, 166, 173, 191, 202, 229, 236, 239, 251, 264, 280.
Poole, 108, 111, 114, 115, 116, 144, 145, 153, 267.
Pope, 8, 14, 21, 25, 26, 29, 30, 40, 46, 48, 49, 67, 75, 76, 79, 85, 91, 96, 100, 103, 106, 109, 120, 131, 158, 163, 164, 206, 207, 208, 209, 228, 237, 246, 247, 249, 259, 294, 305, 307, 310, 314, 321.
Prescot, 128.
Preston, 15, 31, 40, 96, 100, 103, 109, 114, 117, 122, 123, 132, 137, 138, 140, 141, 149, 153, 162, 166, 167, 170, 173, 180, 188, 202, 204, 205, 206, 210, 211, 213, 214, 216, 221, 225, 227, 228, 229, 239, 243, 251, 254, 261, 263, 269, 278, 279, 281, 318, 319.
Price, 15, 30, 86, 101, 102, 301.
Priest, 29, 32, 315.
Proctor, 9, 14, 15, 28, 29, 30, 48, 64, 85, 90, 92, 105, 106, 116, 123, 126, 127, 128, 132, 162, 199, 298, 301.
Puffer, 254, 270, 275.
Purchase, 2, 11, 14, 15, 24, 27, 31, 43, 321.

Rainsford, 1, 5, 6.
Randall, 2, 10.
Rawlins, 7, 8, 57.
Rawson, 311.
Read, 21, 31, 32, 43, 44, 54, 120.
Reed, 286.
Redman, 81, 100, 102, 103, 104, 111, 113, 116.
Rehoboth, 309.
Richards, 2, 3, 9, 10, 18, 20, 26, 27, 29, 321.
River, Muddy, 285.
River, Mother Brook, 21, 37, 124, 203, 209.
River, Neponset, 12, 13, 21, 24, 27, 29, 34, 40, 51, 60, 62, 74, 76, 89, 94, 96, 98, 117, 120, 296, 305, 309.
River, Smelt, 104.

River, Wading, 156, 179, 186, 194, 202.
Rigby, 31, 76, 79, 106, 114, 131, 138, 140, 141, 148, 158, 159, 163, 166, 170, 177, 186, 194, 220, 254, 256.
Rise, 261.
Robinson, 67, 85, 87, 93, 94, 95, 96, 97, 98, 99, 100, 101, 102, 103, 104, 108, 109, 112, 115, 117, 118, 119, 122, 129, 132, 136, 137, 139, 140, 146, 147, 148, 149, 150, 152, 153, 169, 173, 175, 184, 196, 198, 207, 209, 215, 218, 221, 225, 230, 234, 240, 243, 247, 250, 255, 260, 262, 264, 266, 267, 268, 270, 276, 279, 283, 284, 287, 307, 308.
Roberts, 158, 177, 218, 242, 263.
Rock, the, 5, 7, 8, 10.
Rock, Great, 64.
Rocket, 2, 4, 7, 10, 15, 32, 321.
Rockwell, 1, 2, 6, 7, 10, 13, 17, 18, 19, 26, 48, 322.
Rogers, 187, 233.
Rossiter, 1, 5, 6, 10, 17, 321, 322.
Roxbury, 2, 8, 9, 12, 14, 15, 24, 34, 58, 68, 70, 72, 75, 80, 90, 91, 99, 103, 117, 132, 140, 152, 157, 166, 177, 179, 191, 194, 222, 223, 235, 251, 261, 264, 265, 267, 276, 277, 302, 304, 307, 308, 321, 322.
Roxbury brook, 261.
Royall, 196, 227, 228, 232, 261, 263, 265, 272, 274, 281, 283, 288.
Rush, 75, 121, 315.
Russell, 2, 133, 152, 162, 271.
Rylands, 69.

Salsbury, 59, 62, 63, 234.
Sampford, 14, 15, 22, 29, 31, 42.
Sanders, 111, 133, 164, 175, 184, 221, 222, 226, 237, 238, 241, 242, 243, 244, 246, 247, 250, 259, 260, 261, 262, 271, 273, 274, 296.
Sandford, 8, 11.
Senconk, 143.
Searle, 110, 145, 146, 147, 148, 177, 258, 274, 277, 278.
Selleck, 43, 106.
Sension, 14, 22, 31, 33, 41, 205, 206, 302, 321.
Ship, the, 18, 20.
Silvister, 22, 243.
Simons, 98.
Skilton, 228.
Skriven, 97, 101.
Smead, 27, 30, 120.
Smith, 1, 3, 7, 9, 15, 29, 30, 32, 39, 46, 47, 53, 59, 61, 62, 63, 67, 69, 70, 73, 76, 79, 80, 82, 83, 88, 90, 91, 96, 97, 98, 100, 101, 102, 103, 104, 106, 107, 109, 117, 118, 119, 121, 122, 125, 127, 133, 135, 137, 138, 139. 140, 141, 142, 148, 150, 151, 152, 157, 158, 159, 160, 164, 167, 173, 174, 176, 180, 184, 213, 219, 223, 225, 227, 228, 250, 253, 258, 286, 303, 305, 306, 307, 310, 311, 312, 317, 318, 320.
Smyth, 294, 304.
Snelling, 221.
Southcott, 4.
Spurr, 70, 90, 104, 167, 173, 185, 193, 199, 215, 218, 238, 260, 276.
Squantum, 7, 13, 15, 18, 25, 34, 43, 44, 57, 59, 87, 104, 125, 131, 141, 316, 321.
Stanton, 60, 74, 75, 98, 99, 146, 149, 157, 182, 190, 191, 242, 243, 259, 261, 267, 272, 282, 305, 309, 312.
Starcy, 32, 34.
Starr, 286.
Stevens, 256.
Stiles, 100, 114, 122, 181, 183, 193, 194, 195, 197, 202, 208, 222, 228, 229, 237, 246, 251, 257, 258, 259, 260.
Stock, 160, 165, 166, 168, 173, 174.
Stoughton, 2, 4, 5, 7, 10, 11, 12, 13, 14, 16, 17, 19, 21, 22, 24, 25, 27, 29, 32, 33, 35, 36, 38, 41, 44, 47, 49, 54, 67, 75, 78, 82, 83, 85, 91, 96, 99, 103, 104, 105, 107, 109, 110, 111, 112, 113, 114, 115, 116, 118, 120, 121, 122, 124, 128, 132, 135, 140, 142, 145, 149, 150, 155, 158, 159, 162, 163, 164, 170, 171, 175, 180, 183, 184, 185, 188, 190, 191, 196, 197, 198,

200, 201, 204, 205, 207, 208, 209, 212, 215, 230, 239, 248, 249, 255, 257, 263, 267, 269, 280, 283, 284, 285, 287, 288, 292, 294, 295, 303, 314.
Straight, 274.
Strang, 8.
Suffolk, 133, 140.
Sumner, 1, 14, 15, 21, 24, 25, 27, 28, 31, 32, 35, 37, 38, 39, 41, 46, 52, 57, 67, 71, 76, 78, 80, 81, 85, 91, 93, 94, 98, 102, 106, 108, 110, 112, 113, 114, 115, 116, 117, 118, 119, 120, 122, 124, 125, 126, 128, 129, 132, 135, 136, 138, 139, 140, 141, 143, 144, 145, 146, 148, 150, 151, 152, 153, 154, 155, 157, 158, 160, 161, 163, 164, 166, 167, 168, 169, 170, 171, 172, 173, 174, 179, 180, 182, 183, 185, 186, 188, 191, 192, 193, 194, 196, 198, 199, 202, 203, 204, 206, 208, 209, 210, 211, 213, 218, 219, 223, 228, 229, 233, 235, 239, 240, 241, 246, 247, 248, 249, 250, 251, 252, 254, 256, 257, 258, 260, 261, 262, 263, 264, 267, 270, 272, 273, 274, 275, 276, 277, 280, 281, 283, 285, 288, 292, 298, 301, 307, 309, 313, 316, 319.
Swamp, Bear, 214.
Swamp, Cedar, 84, 163, 218.
Swamp, Cedar Common, 220.
Swamp, Common, 187, 209, 214, 216, 218, 219, 220, 222, 234, 248, 250, 256, 265, 278, 280.
Swamp, Dead, 7, 11, 18, 40.
Swamp, Purgatory, 94, 120, 135, 221, 275, 276, 284.
Sweet, 198.
Swift, 8, 14, 15, 16, 28, 31, 43, 75, 82, 93, 96, 99, 101, 103, 106, 107, 108, 109, 110, 111, 116, 121, 123, 128, 133, 135, 139, 142, 144, 148, 158, 160, 163, 180, 182, 183, 191, 194, 195, 201, 202, 203, 204, 205, 211, 213, 222, 225, 227, 232, 244, 256, 269, 310, 311, 312.

Tabor, 61.
Talbut, 226, 228, 239, 247, 250.
Taunton, 57, 179, 194, 232, 278.
Terry, 1, 10.
Thomas, 239.
Thornton, 3, 8, 11, 14, 15, 79, 302.
Tilestone, 7, 8, 18, 29, 31, 46, 71, 76, 85, 89, 100, 106, 108, 114, 122, 128, 141, 145, 147, 148, 155, 167, 169, 171, 172, 173, 174, 177, 178, 181, 186, 188, 190, 191, 194, 197, 202, 204, 206, 207, 210, 211, 213, 215, 220, 222, 223, 225, 226, 229, 230, 234, 235, 236, 239, 243, 248, 251, 253, 262, 263, 264, 266, 267, 268, 273, 274, 275, 276, 277, 279, 281, 314, 319.
Tilly, 2, 11, 18, 26, 27, 30, 297, 305, 322.
Tolman, 41, 69, 71, 75, 76, 79, 84, 88, 91, 96, 103, 110, 111, 114, 122, 124, 132, 139, 140, 147, 148, 149, 152, 153, 157, 164, 167, 172, 173, 174, 183, 191, 194, 198, 202, 204, 207, 210, 211, 216, 219, 220, 222, 223, 224, 226, 227, 228, 229, 230, 232, 238, 239, 241, 242, 243, 244, 245, 246, 247, 249, 250, 251, 253, 256, 262, 263, 264, 267, 276, 278, 279, 280, 284, 306, 311, 312.
Tomkins, 27, 30.
Tomson, 141.
Toplens, 69.
Topley, 31, 61, 62, 75, 114.
Topliff, 62, 76, 91, 99, 106, 167, 174, 176, 225, 233, 239, 240, 241, 246, 256, 259, 281, 285.
Tory, 117.
Treadwell, 31, 34.
Tree, 143, 150, 153, 160.
Trescot, 76, 81, 88, 89, 91, 94, 95, 96, 98, 100, 115, 125, 129, 135, 144, 148, 171, 176, 191, 197, 200, 201, 206, 215, 217, 218, 219, 220, 222, 223, 227, 228, 230, 234, 238, 239, 241, 244, 247, 251, 252, 255, 260, 262, 263, 267, 269, 270, 272, 273, 275, 276, 277, 278, 282, 307, 311.
Trott, 67, 69, 96, 97, 103, 104, 108, 122, 125, 131, 135, 139, 147, 151, 164, 167, 183, 197, 211, 219, 225, 247, 256, 257, 263, 269, 276, 277, 279, 284, 289, 308, 314.

INDEX. 329

Trowbridge, 27, 28, 30, 37, **41, 53.**
Tucker, 219, 224, 242.
Turner, 40, 76, 78, 103, 106, 108, 116, 171, 185, 237, 259, 313.
Tuchill, Tuchine, Twitchell, 7, 8, 15, 30, 35, 59, 76, 78, 79, 99, 101, 110, 112, 115.
Tyng, 82, 87, 123, 133, 169, 170.

Uncataquissett, Unquetie, 89, 97, 102, 103, 104, 108, 109, 110, 112, 307.
Upsall, 9, 19, 26, 31, 52, 106.
Upshall, 2, 8, 10, 16, 17, 18, 19, 26, 33, 35, 46, 48, 50, 52, 106, 286, 321.
Usher, 131, 318, 319.

Venner, 321.
Vose, 81, 84, 85, 88, 90, 94, 102, 181, 182, 261, 264, 275, 281, 282.

Wade, 14, 24, 27, 28, 31.
Wadsworth, 103, 257, 286.
Wainman, 202, 229.
Walcot, 321.
Wales, 31, 71, 83, 87, 106, 134, 142, 147, 158, 164, 168, 169, 174, 176, 181, 182, 191, 207, 222, 223, 237, 238, 240, 241, 245, 247, 248, 255, 260, 261, 263, 267, 270, 277, 285, 286, 297, 317.
Wampampeg, 287.
Warham, 1, 2, 3, 4, 5, 6, 9, 16, 106.
Warner, 122.
Waterhouse, 40.
Way, 2, 17, 27, 29, 30, 31, 32, 40, 46, 59, 76, 78, 79, 92, 100, 106, 294, 301, 321.
Webb, 285.
Weeks, 28, 30, 49, 53, 54, 58, 86, 87, 99, 106, 109, 114, 132, 139, 144, 148, 150, 157, 161, 164, 165, 166, 175, 184, 185, 187, 188, 189, 191, 192, 193, 196, 197, 198, 201, 202, 206, 208, 212, 213, 219, 221, 222, 225, 230, 235, 237, 241, 244, 247, 248, 249, 253, 255, 256, 263, 267, 268, 269, 272, 273, 274, 275, 277, 279, 280, 292, 296, 297, 298, 303, 311, 314.
Well, the, 2.
Welsteed, 271.
Westfield, 3, 6, 10.
Weymouth, 53, 216.
Whipple, 27, 76, 78.
Whitcomb, 18, 30, 40, 120.
White, 18, 27, 30, 48, 69, 71, 97, 100, 103, 114, 117, 139, 149, 158, 163, 169, 175, 180, 183, 194, 207, 209, 211, 222, 234, 239, 249, 250, 251, 265, 267, 275.
Whiting, 124, 209, 238, 240, 247.
Whitman, 21, 25, 29.
Wilkins, 19, 21, 29, 30, 32, 40, 46, 76, 78, 106.
Wilkinson, 131.
Willcocke, 103, 109, 113, 115, 121.
Williams, 2, 7, 11, 13, 15, 16, 17, 20, 57, 91, 149, 214, 222, 228, 238, 239, 243, 268, 269, 271, 274, 275, 279, 280, 314.
Willis, 76, 78, 215.
Wills, 106, 132, 133, 140, 141, 150, 151, 160.
Wilson, 32, 35.
Wilton, 3, 5.
Winchell, 14.

Wiswall, 28, 37, 88, 39, **41**, 45, 48, 52, 54, 57, 58, 59, 67, 69, 70, 71, 72, 73, 74, 75, 76, 79, 81, 82, 85, 86, 89, 91, 96, 99, 101, 102, 103, 106, 107, 109, 110, 111, 114, 119, 126, 128, 129, 132, 136, 140, 143, 148, 149, 150, 151, 152, 154, 157, 158, 164, 168, 169, 197, 207, 209, 211, 213, 222, 262, 263, 264, 266, 275, 278, 281, 291, 292, 298, 302, 303, 304, 305, 308, 310, 313, 314.
Wiswell, 31, 32, 99, 116, 134, 139, 172, 175, 184, 188, 191, 192, 198, 213, 214, 215, 220, 221, 225, 228, 229, 230, 232, 235, 236, 240, 242, 244, 248, 250, 255, 258, 268, 269, 275, 282, 287, 295, 303, 306, 313.
Witchfeild, 2, 6, 8, 11, 29, 31, 43, 321.
Withington, 19, 20, 21, 23, 25, 30, 33, 34, 41, 43, 67, 75, 76, 79, 85, 88, 90, 93, 96, 99, 103, 106, 109, 114, 119, 121, 132, 140, 147, 148, 150, 164, 166, 167, 169, 170, 171, 175, 180, 181, 183, 184, 192, 194, 196, 198, 200, 204, 205, 206, 207, 208, 209, 210, 211, 212, 213, 215, 217, 218, 221, 222, 223, 224, 225, 226, 227, 230, 232, 234, 236, 237, 239, 243, 247, 248, 249, 250, 251, 253, 257, 260, 262, 263, 264, 265, 270, 276, 277, 278, 280, 281, 283, 284, 287, 296, 299, 302, 305, 306, 307, 310, 313, 316, 317, 318.
Wolcott, 1, 4, 6, 7, 8, 10, 11, 26, 322.
Wolf Trap, 11.
Wolleston, Mount, 18.
Womsly, 195.
Wood, 38, 237, 241, 253, 254, 308.
Woods, 311.
Woodcock, 178, 185, 194.
Woodward, 67, 71, 75, 85, 86, 87, 88, 90, 91, 96, 97, 118, 194, 209, 221, 306, 309, 310, 316.
Wrentham, 268, 279.
Wright, 8, 14, 15, 16, 30, 42, 106, 150.
Wyatt, 83, 104, 185, 189, 199, 243, 277, 278, 284.

Surnames Omitted.

Augola, the Negar, 97.
Frances, 211, 216, 217, 225, 240, 241, 243, 244, 247.
Francis, 260, 261.
Frank, 226, 243, 244, 245, 247, 254, 262.
Isaac, 225.
Nathan, 240.
Richard, 45.

Indians.

Abda, the Indian, 87.
John Wanerite, 88.
Joseph, a Mashapag Indian, 137.
Josiah Sachem, 126.
Kitchamakin, 126, 142, 143.
Shocho, the Indian, 227.
Tom, the Indian, 179.
William, the Indian, 306, 310.
William Nahaton, 202, 262, 273.

www.ingramcontent.com/pod-product-compliance
Lightning Source LLC
Chambersburg PA
CBHW050836230426
43667CB00012B/2029